Everybody's

German Dictionary

GERMAN-ENGLISH · ENGLISH-GERMAN

Deutsches Wörterbuch

für Jedermann

DEUTSCH-ENGLISCH · ENGLISCH-DEUTSCH

DAVID McKAY COMPANY, INC.

New York

CONTENTS

PART I
GERMAN-ENGLISH DICTIONARY
Page 6

PART II
ENGLISH-GERMAN DICTIONARY
Page 92

MISCELLANEOUS
Page 183

PRINTED IN U. S. A.
COPYRIGHT: W. FOULSHAM & CO. LTD.

PART I
GERMAN-ENGLISH
(DEUTSCH-ENGLISCH)

ABBREVIATIONS (ABKÜRZUNGEN)

Nouns.—In the German-English section, nouns are indicated by the presence of their gender, thus *m., f.,* or *n.* In the English-German section, nouns are denoted by the letter *n*, and the gender is indicated in parentheses following the German word.

Verbs are in all cases followed by the letter *v.*

Adjectives are denoted by the letters *adj.* or *a.*

Adverbs are shown by the letters *ad.* or *adv.*

In many cases, it should be noted that the adverb corresponding to the adjective takes the same form and, therefore, there is no repetition.

Pronouns are denoted by the letters *pron.* or *pn.*

Prepositions are shown by the letters *prep.* or *pr.*

Conjunctions are shown by the letters *conj.* or *c.*

Interjections by the letters *interj.* or *i.*

GERMAN PRONUNCIATION

It is naturally impossible to reproduce exactly the sounds given to German letters and combinations of letters so that they will be available for English-speaking people. However, a very near approach is possible in all cases and the values of the letters of the German alphabet may be accepted as follows:

A=ah	N=enn
B=bay	O=oh
C=tsay	P=pay
D=day	Q=koo
E=ay	R=airr
F=eff	S=ess
G=gay	T=tay
H=hah	U=ooh
I=ee	V=fow
J=yot	W=vay
K=kah	X=ix (iks)
L=ell	Y=[ipsilon]
M=emm	Z=tsett

In the German-English section of this dictionary the sound of every German word is imitated in English and the reader is thus spared the trouble of having to learn the values of the German sounds.

It may be helpful to mention here that German nouns are always spelt with capital letters.

PART I
GERMAN-ENGLISH

A

Aal (ahrl) *m.* eel.
Aar (ahrr) *m.* eagle.
Ab (anp) *ad.* of: off: from.
Abänderlich (ahp'-en-der-lik) *a.* alterable.
Abändern (ahp'-en-dern) *v.* to alter: change.
Abänderung (ahp'-en-der-ong) *f.* alteration.
Abarbeiten, sich (ahp'-ahr-by-ten) *v.* to overwork: wear out.
Abäussern (ahp'-oys-sern) *v.* to evict: turn out.
Abäusserung (ahp'-oys-ser-ong) *f.* eviction.
Abbähen (ahp'-bahr-en) *v.* to make trouble.
Abbeissen (ahp'-by-sen) *v.* to bite off.
Abberufen (ahp'-b-roof-en) *v.* to summon: call away.
Abbilden (ahp'-billed-en) *v.* to portray.
Abbildung (ahp'-billed-ong) *f.* copy: representation.
Abbitten (ahp'-bit-en) *v.* to apologise.
Abbleichen (ahp'-bly-ken) *v.* to fade.
Abborgen (ahp'-bor-gen) *v.* to borrow from.
Abbrechen (ahp'-breck-en) *v.* to break off.
Abbrennen (ahp'-bren-en) *v.* to burn down.
Abbürsten (ahp'-boors-ten) *v.* to brush off.
Abdanken (ahp'-dan-ken) *v.* to resign.
Abdrucken (ahp'-droock-en) *v.* to print.
Abdunsten (ahp'-doons-ten) *v.* to evaporate.
Abdünstung (ahp'-deens-tong) *f.* evaporation.

Abflachen

Abend (ahp'-ent) *m.* evening.
Abendblatt (ahp'-ent-blaht-t) *n.* evening paper.
Abendessen (ahp'-ent-ess-en) *n.* supper.
Abendtisch (ahp'-ent-ish) *m.* supper.
Abenteuer (ahp'-ent-oy-er) *n.* attempt: enterprise: adventure.
Abenteurer (ahp'-ent-oyr-er) *m.* adventurer.
Aber (ah'-ber) *c.* however: but —*ad.* again.
Abermal, Abermals (ah'-ber-mahl) *ad.* again.
Abermalig (ah'-ber-mahl-ik) *a.* reiterated: repeated.
Aberwitzig (ah'-ber-vits-ik) *a.* foolish: crazy: absurd.
Abfahren (ahp'-fahr-ren) *v.* to depart: set off: start.
Abfahrt (ahp'-fahrt) *f.* departure.
Abfangen (ahp'-fahn-gen) *v.* to catch: snatch: stop.
Abfärben (ahp'-fair-ben) *v.* to stain.
Abfasern (ahp'-fass-ern) *v.* to unravel.
Abfassen (ahp'-fass-en) *v.* to compose: draft.
Abfassung (ahp'-fass-song) *f.* composition.
Abfaulen (ahp'-fowl-en) *v.* to putrefy.
Abfegen (ahp'-fay-gen) *v.* to scour: wipe: sweep.
Abfertigen (ahp'-fair-t-gen) *v.* to dispatch: finish: snub.
Abfinden (ahp'-finn-den) *v.* to satisfy.
Abfindung (ahp'-finn-dong) *f.* satisfaction.
Abflachen (ahp'-flahk-en) *v.* to level.

6

Abfliegen (ahp'-fleeg-en) *v.* to fly away.
Abflug (ahp'-flook) *m.* flight: departure.
Abfolgen (ahp'-folg-en) *v.* to deliver up.
Abfordern (ahp'-ford-ern) *v.* to demand.
Abfressen (ahp'-fress-en) *v.* to eat: consume: partake.
Abführen (ahp'-fear-en) *v.* to export: carry away.
Abgabe (ahp'-gah-be) *f.* delivery: tax: duty.
Abgang (ahp'-gang) *m.* departure: sale of goods.
Abgebrannt (ahp'-ge-brah-nt) *a.* ruined: penniless.
Abgebrochen (ahp'-ge-brok-en) *a.* abrupt: broken off.
Abgehen (ahp'-gay-n) *v.* to depart.
Abgelebt (ahp'-ge-lay-pt) *a.* decrepit: used up: worn out.
Abgelegen (ahp'-ge-lay-gen) *a.* remote.
Abgelegenheit (ahp'-ge-lay-gen-hite) *f.* distance.
Abgeneigt (ahp'-ge-ny-gt) *a.* averse: disinclined.
Abgesandte (ahp'-ge-zahn-te) *m.* delegate: emissary.
Abgeschieden (ahp'-ge-sheets-en) *a.* secluded: dead.
Abgeschmackt (ahp'-ge-shmahk-kt) *a.* tasteless.
Abgespannt (ahp'-ge-shp-an-nt) *a.* low-spirited.
Abgewinnen (ahp'-ge-vinn-en) *v.* to gain: win.
Abgewöhnen (ahp'-ge-vern-nen) *v.* to break off.
Abgiessen (ahp'-geesse-en) *v.* to pour off.
Abglätten (ahp'-glet-en) *v.* to smooth.
Abgleiten (ahp'-gly-ten) *v.* to slip.
Abgott (ahp'-gott) *m.* idol.
Abgrämen (ahp'-gray-men) *v.* to pine away.
Abgrasen (ahp'-grah-zen) *v.* to graze: browse.
Abgrund (ahp'-groo-nt) *m.* precipice.
Abgunst (ahp'-goon-st) *f.* envy: ill-will.
Abhalten (ahp'-hahl-ten) *v.* to restrain: detain.

Abhaltung (ahp'-hahl-tong) *f.* hindrance.
Abhang (ahp'-hahng) *m.* slope: declivity.
Abhängig (ahp'-heng-ick) *a.* sloping.
Abhärten (ahp'-hair-ten) *v.* to harden.
Abhauen (ahp'-how-en) *v.* to fell: chop off.
Abheften (ahp'-heft-en) *v.* to loosen: undo.
Abholen (ahp'-hohl-en) *v.* to fetch.
Abhoren (ahp'-hor-ren) *v.* to hear.
Abhülfe (ahp'-heel-fe) *f.* relief: redress.
Abhungera (ahp'-hoong-earn) *v.* to starve.
Abkaufen (ahp'-kow-fen) *v.* to purchase.
Abkehren (ahp'-kay-ren) *v.* to prevent: avert.
Abklang (ahp'-klah-ng) *m.* echo.
Abklauben (ahp'-klow-ben) *v.* to pluck off.
Abkneifen (ahp'-knee-i-fen) *v.* to pinch off.
Abknöpfen (ahp'-knerp-fen) *v* to unbutton.
Abkriegen (ahp'-kreeg-en) *v.* to seize: obtain: get.
Abkrümeln (ahp'-kreem-el-n) *v.* to crumble away.
Abkühlen (ahp'-keel-en) *v.* to cool: get cool.
Abkunft (ahp'-koon-ft) *f.* origin: descent.
Abladen (ahp'-lah-den) *v.* to unload.
Abladung (ahp'-lah-dong) *f.* unloading: discharging.
Ablass (ahp'-lahss) *m.* drain: sluice.
Ablassen (ahp'-lahss-n) *v.* to let go: leave off.
Ablauern (ahp'-low-ern) *v.* to watch for.
Ablaufen (ahp'-low-fen) *v.* to expire: become due.
Abläutern (ahp'-loy-ten) *v.* to filter.
Ablegen (ahp'-lay-gen) *v.* to lay aside: take off.
Ablehnen (ahp'-lain-en) *v.* to avert: refuse: decline.

Ableihen (ahp'-lye-n) *v.* to borrow from.
Ableugnen (ahp'-loy-gnen) *v.* to deny: disown.
Ablieferung (ahp'-leef-er-ong) *f.* delivery.
Ablöschen (ahp'-ler-shen) *v.* to extinguish.
Ablöslich (ahp'-ler-slik) *a.* redeemable.
Ablösung (ahp'-ler-zong) *f.* unloosening.
Abmachen (ahp'-mahk-en) *v.* to undo.
Abmachung (ahp'-mahk-ong) *f.* undoing.
Abmagern (ahp'-mahg-ern) *v.* to grow lean.
Abmattung (ahp'-maht-ong) *f.* fatigue.
Abmessen (ahp'-mess-en) *v.* to survey: measure.
Abnahme (ahp'-nah-me) *f.* decline: decrease.
Abnehmen (ahp'-nay-men) *v.* to take off: perceive: buy.
Abneigen (ahp'-nie-gen) *v.* to turn away.
Abneigung (ahp'-nie-gong) *f.* aversion.
Abonnent (ah-bonn-ent') *m.* subscriber.
Abonnieren (ah-bonn-eer'-en) *v.* to subscribe to.
Abort (ah-bought') *m.* closet: w.c.
Abpacken (ahp-pahk'-en) *v.* to unpack: unload.
Abplätten (ahp'-plet-ten) *v.* to flatten.
Abputzen (ahp'-poots-en) *v.* to clean.
Abquälen (ahp'-kvale-en) *v.* to torment: annoy.
Abraten (ahp'-rate-en) *v.* to dissuade.
Abräumen (ahp'-roy-men) *v.* to remove.
Abrede (ahp'-ray-der) *f.* contradiction.
Abreiben (ahp'-rye-ben) *v.* to rub off.
Abreise (ahp'-rye-ze) *f.* departure.
Abreisen (ahp'-rye-zen) *v.* to depart.
Abreissen (ahp'-rye-sen) *v.* to break off: tear off.

Abriss (ahp'-riss) *m.* sketch: design.
Abrufen (ahp'-roo-fen) *v.* to recall: proclaim.
Abrupfen (ahp'-roop-fen) *v.* to pluck off.
Abrutschen (ahp'-root-shen) *v.* to slip off.
Absagen (ahp'-zah-gen) *v.* to refuse: countermand.
Absatz (ahp'-zah-ts) *m.* pause: market: sale: heel.
Absätzig (ahp'-set-zig) *a.* interrupted.
Abschaffen (ahp'-shah-fen) *v.* to abolish: repeal.
Abschälen (ahp'-shay-len) *v.* to peel: pare: shell.
Abscharren (ahp'-shahr-en) *v.* to scrape off.
Abscheiden (ahp'-shi-den) *v.* to separate: die—*n.* death.
Abscheren (ahp'-shair-en) *v.* to shear.
Abscheulich (ahp'-shoy-lik) *a.* detestable.
Abschicken (ahp'-shic-ken) *v.* to dispatch.
Abschildern (ahp'-shild-ern) *v.* to depict.
Abschlag (ahp'-sh-lack) *m.* refusal: fall: decline in price.
Abschliessen (ahp'-shlee-sen) *v.* to close: conclude.
Abschluss (ahp'-shloos) *m.* settlement: conclusion.
Abschmelzen (ahp'-shmelt-sen) *v.* to melt down.
Abschmieren (ahp'-shmeer-en) *v.* to grease: stain.
Abschmutzen (ahp'-shmoot-sen) *v.* to soil.
Abschneiden (ahp'-shny-den) *v.* to cut off.
Abschrauben (ahp'-shrewb-en) *v.* to unscrew.
Abschrecken (ahp'-shreck-en) *v.* to scare away.
Abschreiben (ahp'-shry-ben) *v.* to copy.
Abschrift (ahp'-shrift) *f.* copy.
Abschütteln (ahp'-sheet-eln) *v.* to shake off.
Abschwören (ahp'-shver-en) *v.* to retract: abjure.
Absegeln (ahp'-say-geln) *v.* to sail away: leave.
Abseits (ahp'-zi-tes) *ad.* apart: aside.

Absenden (ahp'-zen-den) *v.* to send away.

Absetzen (ahp'-zet-sen) *v.* to sell: deposit.

Absetzung (ahp'-zet-soong) *f.* removal: deposition.

Absicht (ahp'-sickt) *f.* intention.

Absieden (ahp'-seed-en) *v.* to boil: seethe.

Absonderlich (ahp'-zon-derlik) *a.* particular: separate.

Absondern (ahp'-zon-dern) *v.* to separate.

Absonderung (ahp'-zon-der-ong) *f.* separation.

Absplittern (ahp'-shplit-tern) *v.* to splinter.

Absprechen (ahp'-shp-recken) *v.* to contradict: deny.

Abspülen (ahp'-shp-eel-en) *v.* to rinse.

Abstand (ahp'-sht-annt) *m.* distance.

Abstäuben (ahp'-sht-oy-ben) *v.* to dust.

Abstechen (ahp'-sht-ek-en) *v.* to stab: pierce.

Abstecher (ahp'-sht-ek-er) *m.* ramble: excursion.

Absteigen (ahp'-shty-gen) *v.* to descend: alight.

Absteigung (ahp'-shty-goong) *f.* descent: alighting.

Abstossen (ahp'-stobs-en) *v.* to repel.

Abstrafen (ahp'-strah-fen) *v.* to punish.

Absturz (ahp'-sht-ortz) *m.* precipice.

Abszess (ahp'-zess) *m.* abscess.

Abt (ahp'-t) *m.* abbot.

Abtauschen (ahp'-towe-ken) *v.* to exchange: barter.

Abtei (ahp'-ty) *f.* abbey.

Abteilen (ahp'-ty-len) *v.* to divide: share.

Abteilung (ahp'-ty-loong) *f.* division: separation.

Abtrag (ahp'-trahg) *m.* payment: compensation.

Abträglich (ahp'-trayg-lik) *a.* injurious.

Abtreiben (ahp'-try-ben) *v.* to repel: drive away.

Abtrennen (ahp'-tren-nen) *v.* to separate: unstitch.

Abtreten (ahp'-tray-ten) *v.* to resign: transfer.

Abtritt (ahp'-tritt) *m.* w.c.: stage-exit.

Abtrünnig (ahp'-tren-nik) *a.* rebellious: disloyal: faithless.

Abwarten (ahp'-vahr-ten) *v.* to await: expect.

Abwärts (ahp'-vearts) *ad.* downwards.

Abwaschen (ahp'-vash-en) *v.* to wash away.

Abwehr (ahp'-vair) *f.* defence: safeguard.

Abweichen (ahp'-vy-ken) *v.* to deviate: decline.

Abweichend (ahp'-vy-kend) *a.* varying: anomalous.

Abweichung (ahp'-vy-koong) *f.* variation.

Abweisen (ahp'-vy-zen) *v.* to reject: refuse.

Abwendbar (ahp'-vent-bar) *a.* preventable.

Abwenden (ahp'-vent-en) *v.* to avert.

Abwendig (ahp'-vent-ik) *a.* estranged.

Abwerfen (ahp'-vair-fen) *v.* to throw off: cast aside.

Abwesend (ahp'-vay-zend) *a.* absent.

Abwischen (ahp'-vish-en) *v.* to wipe.

Abzahlen (ahp'-t-sah-len) *v.* to discharge: pay off.

Abzählen (ahp'-t-say-len) *v.* to count: number.

Abzählung (ahp'-t-say-loong) *f.* payment.

Abzapfen (ahp'-t-sahp-fen) *v.* to tap: drain.

Abzeichnen (ahp'-tsyk-nen) *v.* to sketch: draw.

Abzielen (ahp'-tsee-len) *v.* to strive for: aim at.

Abzug (ahp'-tsook) *m.* retreat.

Abzwingen (ahp'-t-svin-gen) *v.* to extort.

Ach (ahk) *interj.* ah: alas.

Achsel (ahk'-zel) *f.* shoulder.

Acht (ahkt) *a.* eight—*f.* attention: care.

Achtbar (ahkt'-bar) *a.* respectable.

Achte (ahkt'-er) *m.* and *j.* eighth.

Achteck (ahkt'-ek) *n.* octagon.

Achten (ahk'-ten) *v.* to consider: mind: regard.

Achtlos (ahk'-t-lohs) *a.* careless.

Achtlosigkeit (ahk'-t-lohs-ik-kite) *f.* carelessness.
Achtsam (ahkt'-zahm) *a.* attentive.
Achtung (ahkt'-oong) *f.* notice: warning: beware.
Achtungsvoll (ahkt'-oongs-foll) *a.* respectful.
Achtzehn (ahkt'-tsayn) *a.* eighteen.
Achtzig (ahkt'-sik) *a.* eighty.
Ächzen (ehkt'-sen) *v.* to groan.
Acker (ahk'-er) *m.* acre: field.
Ackerbau (ahk'-er-bo) *m.* agriculture.
Ackern (ahk'-ern) *v.* to plough: till: cultivate.
Addieren (ah-deer'-n) *v.* to add up.
Ade (ah-day') *interj.* adieu: farewell: good-bye.
Adel (ah'-del) *m.* nobility: nobleness.
Adelig (ah'-del-ik) *a.* noble: title.
Adeln (ah'-deln) *v.* to ennoble.
Ader (ah'-der) *f.* vein: artery: grain of wood.
Adler (ah'-dler) *m.* eagle.
Affe (ahf'-ferh) *m.* ape: monkey.
Äffen (ef'-fen) *v.* to mimic: mock: imitate.
Affig (ahf'-fik) *a.* foolish: idiotic: silly.
Agentur (ah-ghen-toor') *f.* agency.
Agieren (ah-gheer'-n) *v.* to act as an agent.
Ahn (ahn) *m.* ancestor: grandfather.
Ahnden (ahn'-den) *v.* to resent: avenge: punish.
Ähneln (ayn'-eln) *v.* to resemble.
Ähnlich (ayn'-lik) *a.* like: resembling.
Akkomodieren (ahk'-kom-mohd-deer-en) *v.* to accommodate.
Akkordieren (ahk'-kord-deer-en) *v.* to agree: accord.
Aktionär (ahk'-tsee-ohn-air) *m.* shareholder.
Alaun (ah'-lowne) *m.* alum.
Albernheit (ahl'-bern-heit) *f.* foolishness.
Alge (ahl'g) *f.* seaweed.
All (ahll) *n.* universe.

All, Aller, Alle, Alles (ahll: er: e: es) *a.* all: every: whole.
Allein (ah'-lyne) *a.* alone: only —*c.* but.
Alleinig (ah'-lyne-ik) *a.* only.
Allemal (ahll'-e-marl) *ad.* always.
Allenfalls (ahll'-en-fahls) *ad.* perhaps: if needs be.
Allenthalben (ahll'-ent-hahl-ben) *ad.* everywhere.
Allerdings (ahll'-er-dings) *ad.* of course.
Allererst (ahll'-erst) *ad.* first of all.
Allezeit (ahll'-er-tsite) *ad.* always: at all times.
Allgemein (ahll'-gee-mine) *a.* common: general.
Allwo (ahll'-woh) *ad.* where.
Allzu (ahll'-tsoo) *ad.* too: too much.
Alzugleich (ahll'-tsoo-glyck) *ad.* altogether.
Almosen (ahll'-moh-zen) *n.* alms: charity.
Als (ahls) *c.* as: but: like: than: when.
Alsbald (ahls-bahlt) *ad.* directly: forthwith.
Also (ahlz'-o) *ad.* thus—*c.* therefore.
Alt (ahlt) *a.* old.
Altan (ahlt'-an) *m.* balcony.
Alter (ahlt'-er) *n.* age.
Altern (ahlt'-ern) *v.* to grow old.
Altmodisch (ahlt'-moh-dish) *a.* old-fashioned.
Am (ahm) *prep.* at the: on the: in the: by the.
Amboss (ahm'-bos) *m.* anvil.
Ameise (ah'-my-ze) *f.* ant.
Amortisieren (ah-mort-ee-zeer'-n) *v.* to cancel: liquidate debts.
Amsel (ahm'-zel) *f.* blackbird.
Amt (ahmt) *n.* office: employment: charge.
Amtlich (ahmt'-lik) *a.* official.
Amtmann (ahmt'-mahn) *m.* magistrate.
Amüsieren (ah-meer-zeer'-n) *v.* to amuse.
An (ahn) *prep.* about: at: against: by: near: of: on.
Anbauen (ahn'-bow-n) *v.* to cultivate.
Anbeginn (ahn'-b-ghin) *m.* commencement.

Anbei (ahn'-bye) *ad.* herewith.
Anbellen (ahn'-bel-n) *v.* to scold: bark at.
Anbeten (ahn'-bay-ten) *v* to adore.
Anbieten (ahn'-beat-n) *v.* to bid for: offer.
Anbinden (ahn'-bin-den) *v.* to fasten: tie up.
Anblick (ahn'-blik) *m.* look: appearance.
Anblicken (ahn'-blik-n) *v.* to look at.
Anbrennen (ahn'-bren-n) *v.* to set on fire.
Anbruch (ahn'-brook) *m.* beginning: dawn.
Andauern (ahn'-dow-urn) *v.* to last.
Andenken (ahn'-den-ken) *f.* souvenir: remembrance.
Ander (ahn'-der) *a.* other: next: different.
Ändern (n'-dern) *v.* to alter: change.
Andernfalls (ahn'-durn-fahls) *ad.* otherwise.
Anderswo (ahn'-durs-vo) *ad.* elsewhere.
Änderung (n'-der-ong) *f.* change: alteration.
Anderwärts (ahn'-der-vairts) *ad.* elsewhere: otherwise.
Andichten (ahn'-dik-ten) *v.* to attribute: impute.
Andrang (ahn'-drahng) *m.* crowd: throng.
Andringen (ahn'-dring-n) *v.* to urge: press forward.
Androhen (ahn'-dro-hen) *v.* to threaten: menace.
Aneignen (ahn'-y-gnen) *v.* to appropriate.
Aneinander (ahn'-ine-an-der) *ad.* together.
Anfachen (ahn'-fahk-n) *v.* to inflame: incite.
Anfahren (ahn'-fahr-n) *v.* to drive against: call at.
Anfall (ahn'-fahll) *m.* attack: fit: seizure.
Anfang (ahn'-fahng) *m.* commencement.
Anfangen (ahn'-fahng-n) *v.* to begin: commence.
Anfangs (ahn'-fahngs) *ad.* at first.
Anfassen (ahn'-fahs-sen) *v.* to seize: grab.

Anfechten (ahn'-fek-ten) *v.* to attack: tempt.
Anfeuern (ahn'-foy-ern) *v.* to set on fire: inflame.
Anflehen (ahn'-flay-n) *v.* to entreat: implore.
Anfordern (ahn'-ford-urn) *v.* to demand: claim.
Anfrage (ahn'-fray-ge) *f.* question: enquiry.
Anfragen (ahn'-fray-gen) *v.* to enquire.
Anfressen (ahn'-fress-n) *v.* to gnaw: corrode.
Anfrischen (ahn'-frish-n) *v.* to refresh: encourage.
Anfügen (ahn'-feeg-n) *v.* to add: annex: join to.
Anfühlen (ahn'-feel-n) to touch: feel.
Anführen (ahn'-feer-n) *v.* to guide, lead on.
Anfüllen (ahn'-feel-n) *v.* to replenish: fill up.
Angeben (ahn'-gay-ben) *v.* to declare: suggest.
Angeblich (ahn'-gay-plik) *a.* pretended.
Angehen (ahn'-gay-n) *v.* to solicit.
Angehend (ahn'-gay-ent) *pr.* concerning.
Angehören (ahn'-gee-her-ren) *v.* to belong to.
Angel (ahn'-gel) *f.* fish-hook: hinge.
Angelweit (ahng'-el-vyte) *a.* wide open.
Angemessen (ahn'-ge-mess-en) *a.* suitable: fit.
Angenehm (ahnge'-nay-me) *a.* pleasant: agreeable.
Angesichts (ahnge'-sikts) *ad.* in the sight of.
Angewöhnen (ahnge'-ver-nen) *v.* to accustom.
Angewohnheit (ahnge'-vohn-hyte) *f.* custom: habit.
Angezogen (ahn'-ge-tso-gen) *a.* dressed.
Angreifen (ahn'-grif-n) *v.* to touch: seize.
Angrenzend (ahn'-grent-sent) *a.* adjacent.
Angriff (ahn'-griff) *m.* assault.
Angst (ahn'-kst) *f.* anxiety: anguish.
Ängstigen (eng'-stee-gen) *v.* to worry.

Angstvoll (ahn'-gst-foll) *a.* painful: fearful.

Anhaben (ahn'-hab-ben) *v.* to wear.

Anhaften (ahn'-hahft-n) *v.* to adhere to.

Anhalten (ahn'-hahlt-n) *v.* to stop: hold: restrain.

Anhäufen (ahn'-hoy-fen) *v.* to heap up: accumulate.

Anheften (ahn'-heft-n) *v.* to fasten: fix: affix.

Anher (ahn'-her) *ad.* hither.

Anhöhe (ahn'-her-e) *f.* hill.

Anhören (ahn'-her-ren) *v.* to hear: listen to.

Animalisch (ahn'-e-mall-ik) *a.* animal: bestial: brutish.

Ankaufen (ahn'-kowf-en) *v.* to buy.

Ankern (ahng'-kern) *v.* to anchor.

Anklagen (ahn'-klah-gen) *v.* to accuse.

Ankleben (ahn'-klayb-n) *v.* to stick: paste.

Ankleiden (ahn'-kly-den) *v.* to dress.

Anklopfen (ahn'-kloop-fen) *v.* to knock at a door.

Ankommen (ahn'-komm-n) *v.* to arrive.

Ankunft (ahn'-koon-ft) *f.* arrival.

Anlage (ahn'-lahge) *f.* stock: tax.

Anlass (ahn'-lahss) *m.* cause: reason: motive.

Anlauf (ahn'-lowf) *m.* assault: onset.

Anlaufen (ahn'-low-fen) *v.* to swell.

Anlehnen (ahn'-lay-nen) *v.* to lean against.

Anliegen (ahn'-leeg-n) *n.* care: concern.

Anlocken (ahn'-lok-n) *v.* to entice: decoy: bait.

Anmachen (ahn'-mahk-n) *v.* to fasten.

Anmassen (ahn'-mahs-sen) *v.* to assume: arrogate.

Anmassend (ahn'-mahs-sent) *a.* arrogant.

Anmerken (ahn'-mairk-n) *v.* to remark: note.

Anmessen (ahn'-mess-n) *v.* to measure: fit.

Anmut (ahn'-mooht) *f.* charm: grace.

Anmuten (ahn'-moot-n) *v.* to require: demand.

Anmutig (ahn'-moot-ik) *a.* agreeable.

Annähen (ahn'-nay-n) *v.* to draw near: sew on.

Annektieren (ahn'-nek-teer-n) *v.* to annex.

Annonce (ahn'-nong-ser) *f.* advertisement.

Anordnen (ahn'-ord-nen) *v.* to bespeak: arrange.

Anpassen (ahn'-pahss-n) *v.* to accommodate: adapt.

Anpassend (ahn'-pahss-end) *a.* suitable: fit.

Anpochen (ahn'-pohck-n) *v.* to knock.

Anputzen (ahn'-pootz-n) *v.* to adorn: dress up.

Anraten (ahn'-raht-n) *v.* to advise: recommend.

Anrechnen (ahn'-rehk-nen) *v.* to charge: impute.

Anregen (ahn'-ray-gen) *v.* to incite.

Ansager (ahn'-zah-ger) *m.* radio announcer.

Ansammeln (ahn'-zahm-meln) *v.* to collect: accumulate.

Ansässig (ahn'-zess-ik) *a.* settled.

Anschaffen (ahn'-schaff-n) *v.* to furnish: provide.

Anschauen (ahn'-show-n) *v.* to look at.

Anschicken (ahn'-shick-n) *v* to prepare: behave.

Anschlagen (ahn'-shlag-n) *v.* to strike against.

Anschlägig (ahn'-shlayg-ik) *a.* ingenious.

Anschliessen (ahn'-shlees-n) *v.* to annex.

Anschluss (ahn'-shloos) *m.* junction: enclosure.

Anschmieren (ahn'-shmeer-n) *v.* to cheat: deceive: adulterate.

Anschuldigen (ahn'-shool-dig-n) *v.* to accuse.

Anschüren (ahn'-sheer-n) *v.* to stir-up: kindle.

Anschwellen (ahn'-shvel-n) *v.* to swell.

Ansehen (ahn'-zay-n) *n.* reputation: appearance.

Ansicht (ahn'-sickt) *f.* view: sight.
Ansiedeln (ahn'-seed-eln) *v.* to settle: colonize.
Ansiedelung (ahn'-zeed-e-long) *f.* colony.
Ansinnen (ahn'-sinn-n) *v.* to require: demand.
Anspannen (ahn'-spahn-nen) *v.* to stretch: exert.
Ansprache (ahn'-shprah-ke) *f.* speech: address.
Ansprechen (ahn'-shpreh-ken) *v.* to address.
Anspruch (ahn'-shprook) *m.* claim.
Anspruchslos (ahn'-shprooks-lohs) *a.* modest: unassuming.
Anspucken (ahn'-spook-en) *v.* to spit at.
Anstalt (ahn'-stahlt) *f.* establishment: institution.
Anständig (ahn'-shtend-ik) *a.* respectable: decent: reasonable.
Anstarren (ahn'-shtar-ren) *v.* to stare at.
Anstatt (ahn'-sht-att) *prep* instead of.
Anstechen (ahn'-sht-ecken) *v.* to prick.
Ansteckend (ahn'-sht-eckent) *a.* infectious: contagious.
Ansteigen (ahn'-shty-gen) *v.* to ascend: climb: mount.
Anstich (ahn'-shtik) *m.* puncture.
Anstiften (ahn'-shtif-ten) *v.* to contrive: look into.
Anstossen (ahn'-stohs-sen) *v.* to push or knock against.
Anstreichen (ahn'-shtry-ken) *v.* to paint.
Anstreicher (ahn'-shtry-ker) *m.* house-painter: decorator.
Anstrengen (ahn'-shtren-gen) *v.* to strain.
Antrag (ahn'-trahg) *m.* proposal: offer: suggestion.
Antrauen (ahn'-trow-n) *v.* to marry: wed.
Antreffen (ahn'-tref-fen) *v.* to find: meet with: run across.
Antritt (ahn'-tritt) *m.* entrance.
Antun (ahn'-toon) *v.* to inflict.
Antwort (ahnt'-vort) *f.* answer: reply.
Antworten (ahnt'-vort-n) *v.* to answer: reply.

Anwachs (ahn'-vahks) *m.* growth: increase.
Anweisen (ahn'-vy-zen) *v.* to advise.
Anwendbar (ahn'-vent-bar) *a.* practicable.
Anwenden (ahn'-vend-n) *v.* to employ.
Anwesend (ahn'-vayze-nt) *a.* present.
Anwuchs (ahn'-voox) *m.* growth: increase.
Anwurzeln (ahn'-vort-zeln) *v.* to take root.
Anzahl (ahn'-tsahl) *f.* number: quality: multitude.
Anzahlen (ahn'-tsahl-n) *v.* to reckon: pay on account.
Anzeigen (ahn'-tsyg-n) *v.* to advertise: proclaim.
Anzeiger (ahn'-tsyg-er) *m.* informer: gazette.
Anzug (ahn'-tsook) *m.* dress: clothes.
Anzüglich (ahn'-tseek-lik) *a.* offensive: suggestive: pointed.
Anzünden (ahn'-tseen-den) *v.* to light: set on fire.
Anzwängen (ahn'-tsveng-en) *v.* to squeeze.
Apfel (ahp'-fel) *m.* apple.
Apfelbaum (ahp'-fel-bowm) *m.* apple-tree.
Apfelwein (ahp'-fel-vyne) *m.* cider.
Apotheke (ah-poh-tay'-ke) *f.* chemist.
Apparat (ah-par-rate') *m.* apparatus.
Appetit (ah-pait-eat') *m.* appetite.
Applaudieren (ah-plow-deer'-n) *v.* to applaud.
Applizieren (ah-plee-zeer'-n) *v.* to apply.
Approbieren (ah-pro-beer'-n) *v.* to approve: agree with.
Aprikose (ah-pre-koh'-ze) *f.* apricot.
April (ah-preel') *m.* April.
Arbeit (ahr'-bite) *f.* work: labour.
Arbeiten (ahr'-bite-n) *v.* to work.
Arbeiter (ahr'-biter) *m.* workman: labourer.
Arbeitshaus (ahr'-bites-hows) *n.* workhouse.

Arbeitslohn (ahr'-bites-lohn) *m.* wages: pay.

Arg (ahrk) *a.* wicked: bad: severe.

Ärger (air'-ger) *m.* anger.

Ärgerlich (air'-ger-lik) *a.* vexations.

Ärgern (air'-gern) *v.* to vex: annoy.

Arglos (ahrk'-lohs) *a.* harmless.

Argwohn (ahrk'-vohn) *m.* suspicion.

Arm (ahrm) *a.* poor: needy: indigent—*n.* arm: branch.

Armbinde (ahrm'-binde) *f.* bandage: sling.

Ärmel (air'-mel) *m.* sleeve.

Armenhaus (ahrm'-en-hows) *n.* almshouse.

Armselig (ahrm'-zayl-ik) *a.* needy.

Armstuhl (arhm'-shtool) *m.* armchair.

Art (ahrt) *f.* kind: sort: manner.

Arten (ahrt'-n) *v.* to grow: resemble.

Artig (ahrt'-ik) *a.* polite: courteous.

Arzenei (ahrt-ze-ny') *f.* medicine.

Arzt (ahrtst) *m.* physician.

Asbest (ahss'-best) *m.* asbestos.

Assekurieren (ahss-ee-koor'-eer-n) *v.* to insure.

Ast (ahst) *m.* branch: twig: bough.

Atem (ah'-tem) *m.* breath: respiration.

Atemlos (ah'-tem-lohs) *a.* breathless.

Atlas (aht'-laz) *m.* satin: atlas.

Atmen (aht'-men) *v.* to breathe.

Attestieren (aht'-test-eer'-n) *v.* to attest: certify.

Ätzen (et'-zen) *v.* to corrode.

Ätzend (et'-zen-d) *a.* corrosive.

Auch (owk) *conj.* also: even: likewise.

Auf (owf) *prep.* in: at: to: up: on—*ad.* up: upwards.

Aufbauen (owf'-bo-n) *v.* to build: erect.

Aufbewahren (owf'-be-vahren) *v.* to store up.

Aufbieten (owf'-beet-n) *v.* to summon.

Aufblasen (owf'-blahr-zen) *v.* to inflate.

Aufbrauchen (owf'-brow-ken) *v.* to waste: consume.

Aufbruch (owf'-brook) *m.* departure.

Auferziehen (owf'-air-tsee-n) *v.* to nourish.

Auffahrend (owf'-fahr-end) *a.* irritable.

Auffordern (owf'-ford-ern) *v.* to challenge.

Auffrischen (owf'-frish-en) *v.* to revive: refresh.

Aufgeben (owf'-gayb-n) *v.* to relinquish: give up.

Aufgeblasen (owf'-gee-blahzen) *a.* arrogant.

Aufgehen (owf'-gay-n) *v.* to rise: open: come undone.

Aufgeschaut (owf'-ge-show-t) *interj.* look out: mind.

Aufgraben (owf'-grahb-n) *v.* to dig up.

Aufgreifen (owf'-gry-fen) *v.* to seize.

Aufhalten (owf'-hahlt-n) *v.* to stop: hold up.

Aufhaltung (owf'-hahl-toong) *f.* delay: hindrance.

Aufheitern (owf'-hite-ern) *v.* to cheer up.

Aufhetzen (owf'-het-sen) *v.* to stir up.

Aufhetzer (owf'-het-zer) *m.* instigator.

Aufhören (owf'-herr-ren) *v.* to cease: discontinue.

Aufklären (owf'-klay-ren) *v.* to clear: throw light upon.

Aufknöpfen (owf'-knerp-fen) *v.* to unbutton.

Aufkommen (owf'-komm-n) *v.* to grow up.

Aufkräuseln (owf'-kroyz-eln) *v.* to curl.

Aufkündigen (owf'-keen-dig-n) *v.* to warn.

Aufkünft (owf'-keenft) *f.* recovery.

Aufleben (owf'-lay-ben) *v.* to revive.

Auflesen (owf'-lay-zen) *v.* to gather.

Auflösen (owf'-ler-zen) *v.* to loosen.

Aufmachen (owf'-mahk-n) *v.* to open: unpack.

Aufmerken (owf'-maik-rn) *v.* to note: heed: attend to.

Aufmuntern (owf'-moon-tern) *v.* to awake: encourage.

Aufnahme (owf'-nahm-erh) *f.* admission: reception.

Aufpacken (owf'-phack-n) *v.* to pack up.

Aufpassen (owf'-phass-n) *v.* to attend to: look out.

Aufputz (owf'-pootz) *m.* dress: ornament.

Aufrecht (owf'-rekt) *a.* erect: upright.

Aufregen (owf'-ray-gen) *v.* to rouse: enliven.

Aufruhr (owf'-roor) *m.* uproar: riot: insurrection.

Aufrührer (owf'-reer-en) *m.* rebel.

Aufsagen (owf'-zahg-n) *v.* to recite.

Aufsätzig (owf'-seets-ik) *a.* hostile: opposed: adverse.

Aufschäumen (owf'-shoy-men) *v.* to foam: froth: seethe.

Aufscheuern (owf'-shoy-ern) *v.* to scour.

Aufschieben (owf'-shee-ben) *v.* to delay: retard.

Aufschneider (owf'-shny-der) *m.* boaster.

Aufschnitt (owf'-shnit) *m.* cut.

Aufschreien (owf'-shry-n) *v.* to scream: yell.

Aufschrift (owf'-shrift) *f.* inscription.

Aufschub (owf'-shoop) *m.* delay: respite.

Aufschütteln (owf'-sheet-eln) *v.* to stir or shake up.

Aufschwingen (owf'-shving-gen) *v.* to rise: raise.

Aufseher (owf'-say-er) *m.* overseer.

Aufsparen (owf'-shpar-n) *v.* to save.

Aufsteigen (owf'-shty-gen) *v.* to ascend: mount: rise.

Aufstellen (owf'-shtel-len) *v.* to set up.

Aufstören (owf'-shter-n) *v.* to rouse: stir up.

Aufsuchen (owf'-sook-n) *v.* to visit: look for.

Auftauen (owf'-tow-n) *v.* to thaw.

Auftreiben (owf'-try-ben) *v.* to chase.

Auftreten (owf'-tray-ten) *v.* to tread upon.

Auftritt (owf'-tritt) *m.* entrance: appearance.

Auftun (owf'-toon) *v.* to open: disclose.

Aufwachen (owf'-vak-n) *v.* to awake.

Aufwachsen (owf'-vak-sen) *v.* to grow up.

Aufwärts (owf'-vairtz) *ad.* upwards.

Aufweisen (owf'-vy-zen) *v.* to exhibit.

Aufweisung (owf'-vy-zong) *f.* exhibition.

Aufzählen (owf'-tsay-len) *v.* to reckon up.

Aufzeigen (owf'-tsy-gen) *v.* to show: display: exhibit.

Aufziehen (owf'-tsee-n) *v.* to draw up: wind up.

Aufzug (owf'-tsook) *m.* procession.

Augapfel (owk'-ahp-fel) *m.* eyeball.

Auge (ow'-ge) *n.* eye.

Augenarzt (ow'-ghen-ahrts-t) *m.* occulist.

Augenwimper (ow'-ghen-vimp-er) *f.* eyelash.

August (ow-goost') *m.* August.

Auktion (owk'-tse-ohn) *f.* auction.

Auktionator (owk'-tse-ohn-ah-tor) *m.* auctioneer.

Aus (owss) *prep.* out of: by: from: through: on: upon—*ad.* over: out: up.

Ausarten (owss'-ahrt-n) *v.* to degenerate.

Ausbildung (owss'-bill-dong) *f.* improvement.

Ausbrechen (owss'-breck-n) *v.* to break out: vomit.

Ausbreiten (owss'-bryt-n) *v.* to spread: extend.

Ausbrühen (owss'-bree-n) *v.* to scald.

Ausdenken (owss'-deng-ken) *v.* to imagine.

Ausdichten (owss'-dikt-n) *v.* to devise.

Ausdörren (owss'-der-n) *v.* to dry up: parch: season.

Auserwählen (owss'-ayr-vayl-n) *v.* to elect: choose.

Ausfahrt (owss'-fahrt) *f.* excursion.

Ausfallen (owss'-fahl-n) *v.* to sally forth: lunge.

Ausfegen — Aussaugen

Ausfegen (owss'-fay-gen) v. to cleanse: sweep out.
Ausfertigen (owss'-fairt-ik-en) v. to expedite: dispatch.
Ausfinden (owss'-find-n) v. to discover.
Ausfliegen (owss'-fleeg-n) v. to escape.
Ausfluss (owss'-floss) m. outlet.
Ausfordern (owss'-ford-ern) v. to challenge: defy.
Ausfragen (owss'-frahg-n) v. to question: examine.
Ausführbar (owss'-feer-bar) a. practicable.
Ausführung (owss'-feer-ong) f. exportation.
Ausgabe (owss'-gar-be) f. issue: edition.
Ausgang (owss'-ganhg) m. exit: result: event.
Ausgeber (owss'-gay-ber) m. manager.
Ausgeboten (owss'-ge-boht-n) a. offered.
Ausgelassen (owss'-ge-lahss-n) a. extravagant.
Ausgelernt (owss'-ge-lern-t) a. cunning.
Ausgemacht (owss'-ge-mahkt) a. decided.
Ausgraben (owss'-grahb-n) v. to dig out: unearth.
Aushalten (owss'-hahlt-n) v. to hold out: last out.
Aushändigen (owss'-hend-ig-n) v. to hand over.
Aushängen (owss'-heng-n) v. to suspend: unhinge.
Ausharren (owss'-hahr-n) v. to persevere.
Aushebung (owss'-hay-bong) f. conscription: levy of soldiers.
Aushecken (owss'-heck-n) v. to hatch: plan: scheme.
Aushilfe (owss'-hilf-e) f. aid: help.
Aushöhlung (owss'-herl-oong) f. excavation.
Aushusten (owss'-hoost-n) v. to expectorate.
Auskleiden (owss'-klyd-n) v. to undress.
Auskramen (owss'-krahm-n) v. to display: set out for sale.
Auskratzen (owss'-krahtz-n) v. to erase: scratch out.
Auskriechen (owss'-kreek-n) v. to creep forth.
Auskunft (owss'-koonft) f. information.
Auslachen (owss'-lak-n) v. to laugh at: poke fun at.
Ausladen (owss'-lah-den) v. to unload.
Ausland (owss'-lah-nt) n. foreign country: abroad.
Ausländer (owss'-lend-er) m. foreigner.
Ausläufer (owss'-loy-fer) m. errand-boy.
Auslecken (owss'-leck-n) v. to lick up.
Ausleeren (owss'-lay-ren) v. to evacuate.
Auslegen (owss'-lay-gen) v. to lay out: to display.
Ausleiden (owss'-ly-den) v. to end one's suffering.
Ausleihen (owss'-ly-n) v. to lend out.
Auslöschen (owss'-lersh-n) v. to quench, extinguish.
Ausmachen (owss'-mahk-n) v. to make.
Ausmessen (owss'-mess-n) v. to measure: survey.
Ausmitteln (owss'-mitt-ln) v. to find out: detect.
Ausnahme (owss'-nahm-e) f. exception.
Ausnehmen (owss'-naym-n) v. to except: exempt.
Auspacken (owss'-pahk-n) v. to unpack.
Ausplündern (owss'-pleen-dern) v. to pillage: loot: plunder.
Auspressen (owss'-pres-sen) v. to extort: squeeze out.
Ausrechnen (owss'-rek-nen) v. to calculate: reckon.
Ausreden (owss'-ray-den) v. to utter: speak.
Ausreisser (owss'-ry-ser) m. deserter: runaway.
Ausrenken (owss'-ren-ken) v. to wrench: dislocate.
Ausrinnen (owss'-rinn-n) v. to run out: leak.
Ausruhen (owss'-roo-n) v. to rest: repose.
Ausrüsten (owss'-reest-n) v. to equip: furnish.
Aussaugen (owss'-zah-gen) v. to exhaust.

Ausscheiden (owss'-shy-den) *v.* to separate.

Ausschiffen (owss'-shif-fen) *v.* to disembark.

Ausschnitzen (owss'-shnit-sen) *v.* to carve.

Ausschrauben (owss'-shrow-ben) *v.* to unscrew.

Ausschütten (owss'-sheet-ten) *v.* to pour out.

Ausschwitzen (owss'-shvit-sen) *v.* to perspire.

Aussendung (owss'-zend-oong) *f.* mission.

Aussenseite (owss'-sen-zyte) *f.* outside.

Ausser (owss'-ser) *prep.* out of: except: without: but: besides—*c.* unless.

Ausserdem (owss'-ser-dame) *ad.* moreover: besides.

Äussern (oys'-ser-n) *v.* to utter.

Äusserst (oys'-serst) *a.* utmost —*ad.* extremely.

Aussicht (owss'-sikt) *f.* view.

Ausspähen (owss'-spay-n) *v.* to spy out.

Ausspotten (owss'-shpot-n) *v.* to mock: make fun of.

Ausspruch (owss'-shproock) *m.* judgment: sentence.

Ausstehlich (owss'-shtay-lik) *a.* endurable.

Aussteuer (owss'-shtoy-er) *f.* dowry.

Ausstrecken (owss'-shtreck-n) *v.* to extend.

Austeilung (owss'-shty-loong) *f.* distribution.

Auster (owss'-ter) *f.* oyster.

Austräglich (owss'-trayg-lik) *a.* lucrative.

Ausübung (owss'-ee-bong) *f.* exercise: practice.

Auswägen (owss'-vay-gen) *v.* to retail: weigh.

Auswählen (owss'-vay-len) *v.* to select: choose.

Auswandern (owss'-vahn-dern) *v.* to emigrate.

Auswärts (owss'-vairts) *ad.* outward.

Ausweg (owss'-vayg) *m.* way out.

Ausweiten (owss'-vy-ten) *v.* to enlarge: widen.

Auszahlung (owss'-tsahl-oong) *f.* payment.

Auszehrung (owss'-tsayr-oong) *f.* consumption.

Ausziehen (owss'-tsee-n) *v.* to stretch: undress.

Auszug (owss'-tsook) *m.* departure: removal.

Automobil (ow-toh-moh'-beal) *a.* motor car.

Autor (ow'-tohr) *m.* author.

B

Bach (bahk) *m.* brook: stream: rivulet.

Backe (bahck'-erh) *f.* cheek.

Backen (bahck'-n) *v.* to bake

Bäcker (beck'-er) *m.* baker.

Backstein (bahck'-shtine) *m.* brick.

Backwerk (bahck'-vairk) *n.* pastry.

Bad (baht) *n.* bath.

Baden (bahd'-n) *v.* to bathe.

Bagage (bahg'-ah-gher) *f.* baggage: luggage.

Bahn (bahn) *f.* road: pathway.

Bahnen (bahn'-n) *v.* to facilitate: ease.

Bahnhof (bahn'-hohf) *m.* railway station.

Bald (bahlt) *ad.* almost: nearly: shortly: soon.

Balkon (bahlk'-on) *m.* balcony.

Ball (bahl) *m.* ball.

Ballen (bahll'-n) *m.* bale: bundle.

Ballon (bahll'-on) *m.* balloon: football.

Ballsaal (bahll'-zahl) *m.* dancing saloon.

Ballspiel (bahll'-shpeel) *n.* any game of ball.

Banal (bahn'-arl) *a.* trivial.

Banane (bahn'-ann-er) *f.* banana.

Band (bahnt) *n.* band: ribbon —*m.* volume.

Bandagieren (bahnt'-ah-gheer-n) *v.* to bandage.

Bänder (bend'-er) *n. pl.* bonds: fetters.

Bänglich (beng'-lik) *a.* anxious.

Bankanweisung (bahnk'-an-vy-zong) *f.* cheque: bank-note.

Bankerott (bahnk'-rott) *a.* bankrupt—*m.* bankruptcy.

Bankett (bahnk'-ett) *m.* banquet.

Bann (bahnn) *m.* ban: interdict.

Banquier (bahn'-key-eh) *m.* banker.
Bar (bahr) *a.* bare: naked.
Bär (bare) *m.* bear.
Barbarisch (bahr'-bar-ish) *a.* barbarous.
Barbier (bahr'-beer) *m.* barber.
Barfuss (bahr'-foos) *a.* barefoot.
Barschaft (bahr'-shahft) *f.* cash.
Base (bah'-ze) *f.* cousin.
Batist (bah'-tist) *m.* lawn: cambric.
Bau (bow) *m.* building.
Bauchgrimmen (bowk'-grimn) *n.* stomach ache.
Bauchweh (bowk'-veh) *n.* colic.
Bauen (bow'-n) *v.* to build.
Bauer (bow'er) *m.* pawn (chess).
Bauerhof (bow'-er-hohf) *m.* farmhouse.
Bäuerlich (bow'-er-lik) *a.* rural.
Baum (bowm) *m.* tree: beam: boom (navigation).
Baumeister (bow'-my-ster) *m.* architect.
Baumgarten (bowm'-gahrt-n) *m.* orchard: nursery.
Baumwolle (bowm'-vol-erh) *f.* cotton.
Beachten (be-ahkt'-toong) *v.* to consider: notice: observe.
Beantwortung (be-ant'-vor-toong) *f.* answer.
Bearbeiten (be-ar'-by-ten) *v.* to work.
Beben (bay'-ben) *v.* to shiver: quake: tremble.
Bedacht (be-dahn'-kt) *m.* prudence.
Bedächtig (be-dek'-tig) *a.* discreet.
Bedarf (be-dahrf') *m.* want: need.
Bedauern (be-dow'-ern) *v.* to regret: pity.
Bedecken (be-deck'-n) *v.* to cover: shelter.
Bedenklich (be-den'-klik) *a.* doubtful: hazardous.
Bedeutend (be-doy'-tend) *a.* important.
Bedienen (be-deen'-en) *v.* to serve.
Bediente (be-deen'-terh) *m.* servant.

Bedingen (be-ding'-n) *v.* to stipulate.
Bedrängt (be-dreng'-t) *a.* oppressed.
Bedrohen (be-droh'-n) *v.* to menace: threaten.
Bedürfen (be-deer'-fen) *v.* to want: need: require.
Bedürftig (be-deer'-f-tig) *a.* poor: needy.
Beehren (be-air'-n) *v.* to honour.
Beeilen (be-ile'-n) *v.* to hurry: hasten: be quick.
Beerdigen (be-ayrd'-ig-n) *v.* to bury.
Beere (bair'-erh) *f.* berry.
Beet (bait) *n.* bed (in garden, etc.).
Befahrbar (be-fahr'-bar) *a.* practicable.
Befehden (be-faid'-en) *v.* to declare war.
Befestigen (be-fest'-ig-n) *v.* to fasten.
Beflecken (be-fleck'-n) *v.* to stain: blot.
Befolgen (be-fol'-gen) *v.* to obey.
Befragen (be-frah'-gen) *v.* to interrogate.
Befreien (be-fry'-n) *v.* to exempt.
Befremden (be-fremm'-den) *n.* surprise—*v.* to surprise.
Befremdlich (be-fremm'-dlik) *a.* strange.
Befruchten (be-frook'-ten) *a.* to fertilize.
Befühlen (be-feel'-n) *v.* to feel: touch.
Befürchten (be-feerk'-ten) *a.* to fear.
Begaben (be-gah'-ben) *v.* to bestow: endow.
Begegnen (be-gaig'-n) *v.* to meet: encounter.
Begegnung (be-gaig'-noong) *f.* meeting: encounter.
Begehen (be-gay'-n) *v.* to visit.
Begehr (be-gay'r) *n.* desire: wish.
Beginn (be-gin') *m.* beginning: commencement.
Beginnen (be-gin'-n) *v.* to begin: commence: start.
Beglücken (be-gleek'-n) *v.* to bless, give happiness to.

Begnadigen (be-gnahd'-ig-n) v. to pardon.
Begraben (be-grahb'-n) v. to bury.
Begreifen (be-gra'-fen) v. to touch.
Begrüssen (be-grees'-sen) v. to salute: greet.
Begütert (be-geet'-ert) a. rich: wealthy.
Begütigen (be-geet'-ig-n) v. to appease: conciliate.
Behaglich (be-hank'-lik) a. comfortable.
Behalten (be-hahlt'-n) v. to keep.
Behandeln (be-hahn'-del-n) v. to handle: use.
Behändigen (be-henn'd-ig-n) v. to remit.
Beharren (be-hahr'-ren) v. to continue.
Behauen (be-how'-en) v. to cut: trim: prune.
Behaupten (be-howp'-ten) v. to maintain.
Behelf (be-help') m. excuse.
Behend (be-hent') a. quick.
Beherrschen (be-hayr'-shen) v. to govern.
Beherzt (be-hairts') a. bold: courageous.
Behüten (be-heet'-n) v. to guard: watch over.
Bei (by) prep. at: about: beside: by: in: near: with.
Beichten (byk'-ten) v. to confess.
Beide (by'-de) a. both.
Beil (bile) n. axe: chopper: hatchet.
Beileid (by'-lyte) n. condolence.
Beimessen (by'-mess-n) v. to attribute: impute.
Beimischen (by'-mish-n) v. to mix with.
Bein (bine) n. bone: leg.
Beinahe (by'-nah-erh) ad. nearly: almost.
Beiname (by'-nah-me) m. nickname.
Beisammen (by'-zahm-men) ad. together.
Beiseit (Beiseits) (by'-zyt) ad. apart: aside.
Beispiel (by'-shpeel) n. example.
Beissen (by'-sen) v. to bite: gnaw.
Beistand (by'-shtahnt) m. assistance.
Beitrag (by'-trahk) m. share: contribution.
Beitreten (by'-trayt-n) v. to assent to.
Bekehren (be-kayr'-n) v. to convert.
Beklagen (be-klahg'-n) v. to lament.
Beklatschen (be-klahts'-hen) v. to applaud: clap.
Bekleiden (be-kly'-den) v. to clothe: dress: attire.
Bekommen (be-kom'-men) v. to receive: get: obtain.
Bekritteln (be-krit'-teln) v. to criticize.
Bekümmern (be-keem'-ern) v. to be anxious about.
Beladen (be-lah'-den) v. to load.
Belagern (be-lah'-gern) v. to besiege.
Belang (be-lahng') m. importance.
Belangend (be-lahng'-ent) a. concerning.
Belästigen (be-leest'-ig-n) v. to molest.
Belauf (be-lowf') m. amount.
Belaufen (be-lowf'-n) v. to visit.
Belauschen (be-lowsh'-n) v. to listen.
Beleben (be-lay'-ben) v. to enliven: rouse.
Belebt (be-laypt') a. lively: rousing: animated.
Beleg (be-layk') m. voucher.
Belegen (be-lay'-gen) a. situated.
Belehren (be-lair'-n) v. to instruct: acquaint.
Belehrung (be-lair'-ong) f. instruction.
Belieben (be-leeb'-n) v. to please.
Beliebig (be-leeb'-ig) a. agreeable: pleasing.
Bellen (bel'-n) v. to bark: yelp.
Beloben (bel-loh'-ben) v. to praise: commend.
Belohnung (be-loh'-noong) f. reward: recompense.
Belustigend (be-loos'-tig-ent) a. amusing.
Bemächtigen (be-mekt'-ig-n) v. to take: seize.

Bemerken (be-mairk'-n) *v.* to remark.
Bemühung (be-mooh'-ong) *f.* trouble.
Benagen (be-nahg'-n) *v.* to gnaw.
Benähen (be-nay'-n) *v.* to patch.
Benehmen (be-nay'-men) *n.* behaviour.
Beneiden (be-nite'-n) *v.* to envy.
Benetzen (be-nets'-n) *v.* to moisten: wet.
Benutzung (be-nets'-ong) *f.* use: profit.
Benzin (bent-zeen') *n.* benzine.
Bequem (bek-vaim') *a.* fit: convenient.
Berauschen (be-ro'-shen) *v.* to intoxicate.
Berauschend (be-ro'-shent) *a.* intoxicating.
Bereden (be-rait'-n) *v.* to persuade.
Bereit (be-ryte') *a.* ready.
Bereits (be-rytes') *ad.* already.
Bereuen (be-roy'-n) *v.* to regret: repent.
Berg (bairk) *m.* mountain.
Bergab (bairk-ahp') *ad.* downhill.
Bergbau (bairk'-bo) *m.* mining.
Bergöl (bairk'-erl) *n.* petroleum.
Bergwerk (bairk'-vairk) *n.* mine.
Bersten (bairst'-n) *v.* to burst: split.
Beruf (be-roof') *m.* profession.
Berufen (be-roof'-n) *v.* to summon.
Berühmt (be-reemt') *a.* famous: celebrated.
Besänftigen (be-zenft'-ig-n) *v.* to soothe: calm.
Besaufen (be-zow'-fen) *v.* to become drunk.
Beschädigen (be-shay'-dig-n) *v.* to damage: injure: spoil.
Beschäftigen (be-shayf'-tig-n) *v.* to employ: occupy.
Beschäftigt (be-shayf'-tigt) *a.* busy.
Beschämen (be-shay'-men) *v.* to shame.
Beschattung (be-shaht'-ong) *f.* shadow.
Beschauen (be-show'-n) *v.* to contemplate.

Bescheiden (be-shy'-den) *a.* modesty.
Beschenkung (be-sheng'-kong) *f.* donation: gift.
Bescheren (be-shair'-n) *v.* to share.
Beschimpfen (be-shimf'-n) *v.* to insult.
Beschirmen (be-sheer'-men) *v.* to protect: shelter.
Beschlag (be-shlahk') *m.* arrest: seizure.
Beschmieren (be-shmeer'-n) *v.* to stain.
Beschmutzen (be-shmoots'-n) *v.* to soil: make dirty.
Beschränken (be-shrenk'-n) *v.* to restrict.
Beschränkt (be-shrenkt') *a.* narrow: limited.
Beschreibung (be-shryb'-ong) *f.* description.
Beschuldigen (be-shool'-dig-n) *v.* to accuse.
Beschummeln (be-shoom'-eln) *v.* to cheat.
Beschwerlich (be-shvair'-lik) *a.* troublesome: annoying.
Beschwichtigen (be-shvik'-tig-n) *v.* to calm: pacify.
Besehen (be-zay'-n) *v.* to examine: inspect.
Beseligen (be-sail'-ik-n) *v.* to bless.
Besessen (be-zes'-n) *a.* possessed.
Besetzen (be-zet'-sen) *v.* to occupy.
Besichtigen (be-zik'-tig-n) *v.* to inspect: view: survey.
Besiegen (be-zee'-gen) *v.* to vanquish.
Besitz (be-zits') *m.* property.
Besitzen (be-zits'-n) *v.* to own: possess.
Besoffen (be-zoff'-n) *a.* drunk: inebriated.
Besonder (be-zond'-er) *a.* special: peculiar.
Besonders (be-zond'-ers) *ad.* especially.
Besonnen (be-zon'-n) *a.* thoughtful: prudent.
Besorgen (be-zorg'-n) *v.* to look after: take care of.
Besorgnis (be-zork'-nis) *f.* care: worry: anxiety.
Besprechen (be-shprek'-n) *v.* to bespeak: talk to.

Besprengen (be-shpreng'-n) v. to sprinkle.
Besser (bess'-er) a. better.
Besserung (bess'-er-ong) f. improvement.
Bestallen (be-shtel'-len) v. to appoint.
Bestallung (be-shtel'-loong) f. appointment.
Bestand (be-shtannt') m. duration.
Beständig (be-shtend'-ik) a. constant: steadfast.
Bestandlos (be-shtannt'-loos) a. inconsistent.
Bestärken (be-shtayrk'-n) v. to strengthen.
Bestatten (be-shtaht'-n) v. to bury.
Bestechlich (be-shtek'-lik) a. corruptible.
Besteigen (be-shtay'-gen) v. to ascend: mount.
Besteuern (be-shtoy'-ern) v. to tax.
Besteuerung (be-shtoy'-er-ong) f. taxation.
Bestie (beste'-erh) f. beast: brute.
Bestimmen (be-shtim'-men) v. to decide.
Bestimmt (be-shtimt') a. appointed.
Bestrafung (be-shtrah'-foong) f. punishment.
Bestürzen (be-shteer'-tsen) v. to surprise: astonish.
Besuch (be-sook') m. visit.
Besuchen (be-sook'-n) v. to visit: frequent.
Besudeln (be-sood'-eln) v. to soil: dirty.
Betasten (be-tahst'-n) v. to touch: feel: handle.
Betäuben (be-toy'-ben) v. to stun: deafen.
Beten (bay'-ten) v. to pray.
Beteuern (be-toy'-ern) v. to protest.
Betonung (be-tohn'-ong) f. emphasis.
Betracht (be-trah'-kt) m. respect.
Betrachten (be-trah'-kt-n) v. to consider: contemplate.
Beträchtlich (be-trek'-tlik) a. considerable.
Beträchtlichkeit (be-trek'-tlik-kite) f. importance.

Betrag (be-trahk') m. amount.
Betragen (be-trah'-gen) n. behaviour: manner: conduct.
Betrauern (be-trow'-ern) v. to mourn for.
Betreffen (be-tref'-fen) v. to surprise.
Betreiben (be-try'-ben) v. to urge.
Betreten (be-tray'-ten) a. astounded: embarrassed: surprised.
Betrug (be-trook') m. deceit: fraud.
Betrügen (be-tree'-gen) v. to deceive: cheat.
Betrüglich (be-tree'-glik) a. false: deceptive: fraudulent.
Bett (bett) n. bed.
Bettdecke (bett'-decke) f. bedcover.
Betteln (bett'-eln) v. to beg.
Bettler (bett'-ler) m. beggar.
Bettstelle (bett'-shtel-e) f. bedstead.
Beule (boyle) f. boil: tumour.
Beutel (boyt'-el) m. bag: purse.
Beutelschneider (boyt'-el-shny-der) m. pickpocket.
Bevor (be-fohr') ad. before.
Bevorzugen (be-fohrt'-soo-gen) v. to favour.
Bewaffnen (be-vahff'-nen) v. to arm.
Bewahren (be-vahr'-n) v. to keep: guard.
Bewähren (be-vair'-n) v. to prove: verify.
Bewandert (be-vahn'-dert) a. skilled.
Bewegbar (be-vaig'-bar) a. movable.
Bewegen (be-vaig'-n) v. to stir: agitate: move.
Bewegt (be-veckt') a. moved: affected.
Beweibt (be-vipe'-te) f. married.
Beweisgrund (be-vice'-groont) m. proof: argument.
Bewilligen (be-vilig'-n) v. to grant: agree to.
Bewirten (be-veert'-n) v. to entertain friends.
Bewirtung (be-veert'-oong) f. entertainment.
Bewohnen (be-vohn'-n) v. to inhabit.

Bewunderung be-von'-der-oong) f. admiration.
Bezahlung (bett-zahl'-n) f. payment.
Bezeugen (bett-soyg'-n) v. to certify: attest.
Bezweifeln (bett-svyf'-eln) v. to doubt.
Bibliothek (beeb-le-o-take') f. library: study.
Bieder (bee'-der) a. upright: loyal—m. honest person.
Biegen (bee'-gen) v. to bend.
Biegsam (beek'-zam) a. pliant: flexible.
Biene (been'-e) f. bee.
Bienenkorb (been'-n-korp) m. beehive.
Bier (beer) n. beer.
Bierhaus (beer'-howss) n. alehouse: public house.
Bieten (beet'-n) v. to bid: offer.
Bijouterie (bee-shoo'-ter-e) f. jewellery.
Bilanz (bee-lahntz') f. balance.
Bild (bilt) n. picture: illustration.
Bilderbuch (bilt-er-book') n. picture book.
Bildhauer (bilt'-how-er) m. sculptor.
Bildsäule (bilt'-soyl-erh) f. statue.
Billard (bill'-yart) n. pl. billiards.
Billett (bill'-yet) n. ticket.
Billig (bill'-ik) a. cheap.
Binden (bin'-den) v. to bind: fasten: do up.
Binnen (bin'-n) ad. within.
Birke (beerk'-erh) f. birch tree.
Birne (beern'-erh) f. pear.
Bis (bis) prep. to: till: up to: as far as—c. till: until.
Bischof (bis-kof) m. bishop.
Bisher (bis'-hair) ad. hitherto.
Biss (biss) m. bite: sting.
Bitten (bit'n) v. to ask: beg: request.
Bitter (bit'-er) a. bitter: sharp: acrid.
Bittersalz (bit'-er-zalts) n. Epsom salts.
Blamieren (blahm'-eer-n) v. to make fun of (someone).
Blank (blahnk) a. bright: shining.
Blase (blahz'-erh) f. pimple.

Blasebalg (blah'-zee-bahlk) m. pl. bellows.
Blass (blahss) a. pale: pallid: wan: sallow.
Blatt (blahtt) n. page: leaf.
Blattern (blatt'-ern) f. pl. smallpox.
Blau (blow) a. blue.
Blei (bly) n. lead.
Bleiben (bly'-ben) v. to remain: stay.
Bleich (bly'-k) a. pale: pallid: wan.
Bleichen (bly'-ken) v. to bleach.
Bleirecht (bly'-rekt) a. perpendicular.
Bleistift (bly'-shtift) m. leadpencil.
Blenden (blen'-den) v. to blind: dazzle.
Blessieren (bless'-seer-n) v. to wound.
Blick (blick) m. glance.
Blind (blint) a. blind.
Blinzeln (blint'-sel-n) v. to blink: wink.
Block (block) m. prison.
Blöde (blerd'-erh) a. bashful.
Blödsinnig (blerd'-zin-ik) a. silly: idiotic.
Bloss (blohs) a. bare: naked.
Blühen (blee'-en) v. to bloom: blossom: flourish.
Blume (bloom'-erh) f. flower.
Blumenkohl (bloom'-n-kohl) m. cauliflower.
Blutbad (bloot'-baht) m. slaughter.
Blutend (bloot'-end) a. bleeding.
Bluthund (bloot'-hoont) m. blood-hound.
Blutrünstig (bloot'-reens-tik) a. bleeding: bloody.
Boden (boh'-den) m. ground: bottom: floor: soil.
Bogengang (boh'-gen-gahng) m. arch: arcade.
Bogenlicht (boh'-gen-likt) n. electric light.
Bogenzeichen (boh'-gen-tsy-ken) n. signature.
Bohne (bohn'-erh) f. bean.
Bohren (bohr'-n) v. to bore: drill: make a hole in.
Boot (boht) n. boat.
Borg (borg) m. credit.
Borgen (borg'-n) v. to borrow.

Börse (ber'-ze) *f.* purse: money exchange.
Borstig (bor'-shtik) *a.* bristly.
Böse (berz'-erh) *a.* wicked: bad.
Böslich (berz'-lik) *ad.* wickedly.
Bote (boht'-erh) *m.* messenger.
Botschaft (boht'-shaft) *f.* message: news.
Bouillon (boo'-llion) *f.* beef-tea: broth.
Box (boxe) *f.* boxing.
Brackgut (brahk'-goot) *n.* refuse.
Branntwein (brahnt'-vine) *m.* brandy.
Braten (braht'-n) *v.* to roast: fry: grill.
Bratpfanne (braht'-fahn-ne) *f.* frying-pan.
Bratwurst (braht'-voorst) *f.* sausage.
Brauchen (brow'-ken) *v.* to use: want: need: require.
Brauen (brow'-n) *v.* to brew.
Brauerei (brow'-er-y) *f.* brewery.
Braun (brown) *a.* brown.
Brausen (brow'-zen) *v.* to bluster: rush.
Brausend (brow'-zent) *a.* boisterous.
Braut (browt) *f.* bride.
Bräutigam (broy'-tig-ahm) *m.* bridegroom.
Brautjungfer (browt'-yoong-fer) *f.* bridesmaid.
Brautkleid (browt'-klite) *n.* wedding-dress.
Brav (brahf) *a.* brave: heroic.
Brechbar (breck'-bar) *a.* fragile.
Brechmittel (breck'-mit-l) *n.* emetic.
Breit (brite) *a.* broad: wide: large.
Breiten (bri'-ten) *v.* to spread.
Brennen (brenn'-n) *v.* to burn.
Brennend (brenn'-nt) *a.* burning.
Brennstoff (brenn'-shtoff) *m.* fuel.
Bridgespiel (bridge'-shpeel) *n.* bridge (game of cards).
Briefmarke (breef'-mark-erh) *f.* postage-stamp.
Briefpapier (breef'-pah-peer) *n.* notepaper.
Briefpost (breef'-post) *f.* letter-post.

Briefträger (breef'-tray-ger) *m.* postman.
Brille (brill'-erh) *f. pl.* spectacles: eye-glasses.
Bringen (brin'-gen) *v.* to bring.
Bröckeln (brer'-keln) *v.* to break up: crumble.
Brombeere (brom'-bair-erh) *f.* blackberry.
Brosche (brosh'-e) *f.* brooch.
Brot (broht) *n.* bread.
Brotbäcker (broht'-beck-er) *m.* baker.
Brotlos (broht'-lohs) *a.* hungry: penniless: starving.
Brücke (breeck'-erh) *f.* bridge.
Brudeln (brood'-eln) *v.* to bubble.
Bruder (brood'-er) *m.* brother.
Brühe (bree'-e) *f.* broth: soup: sauce.
Brühen (bree'-n) *v.* to scald.
Brüllen (breel'-n) *v.* to roar: bellow.
Brüllochs (breel'-okz) *m.* bull.
Brummen (broom'-n) *v.* to growl: grumble.
Brunnenkresse (broon'-en-kress-erh) *f. pl.* watercress.
Brünstig (breen'-stik) *a.* ardent: burning.
Brust (broost) *f.* breast: bosom.
Brüsten (breest'-n) *v.* to be proud.
Brut (broot) *f.* brood: breed: hatch.
Bübisch (boob'-ish) *a.* mischievous.
Buch (book) *n.* book.
Buche (book'-erh) *f.* beech tree.
Buchführer (book'-feer-er) *m.* book-keeper.
Buchhändler (book'-hend-ler) *a.* bookseller.
Büchse (beeck'-se) *f.* box.
Buchstabe (book'-shtab-erh) *m.* letter (of alphabet).
Buchstabieren (book-shtab-eer'-n) *v.* to spell.
Buckel (book'-l) *m.* hunchback.
Bücken (beeck'-n) *v.* to stoop.
Bude (bood'-erh) *f.* booth: stall.
Büffel (beef'-l) *m.* buffalo.
Buhler (booh'-ler) *m.* lover.
Buhlerei (booh'-ler-ei) *f.* coquetry: intercourse.
Bummeln (boom'-l-n) *v.* to be idle.
Bündel (beend'-l) *n.* bundle.

Bündig (been'-dik) *a.* binding: holding.
Bündigkeit (been'-dik-ite) *f.* validity.
Bündnis (beent'-niss) *n.* alliance.
Burg (boork) *f.* castle.
Bürger (beerg'-er) *m.* citizen.
Büro (Bureau) (beer'-o) *n.* office: bureau.
Bursche (boorshe) *m.* student: young fellow: lad.
Bürste (beers'-te) *f.* brush.
Bürsten (beers'-ten) *v.* to brush.
Bürzeln (beer'-sayl-n) *v.* to tumble.
Buschig (boosh'-ik) *a.* bushy.
Busen (boo'-zen) *m.* breast: bosom: bust.
Büssen (bee'-sen) *v.* to expiate: atone: compensate.
Bussfertig (boos'-fair-tik) *a.* penitent: repentant.
Büste (beeste) *f.* bust.
Butter (boot'-er) *f.* butter.
Butterbrot (boot'-er-broht) *n.* bread and butter.

C

(The tendency in German is to substitute K or Z for the initial letter C. In a less degree, Sch is also used. Therefore, many words that one would expect to find in this section are given under the letters K, Sch or Z.)

Café (kah'-fay) *n.* café: coffee house.
Canaille (kah-nahl'-ye) *f.* mob: rascal: rabble.
Censur (tsen'-soor) *f.* criticism: censure.
Chagrin (shag'-reen) *m.* sorrow: vexation.
Champignon (sham'-pin-yong) *m.* mushroom.
Charakter (kah-rhack'-ter) *m.* character.
Charakteristik (kah-rhack'-ter-istik) *f.* characteristic.
Chemiker (kehm'-ik-er) *m.* chemist.
Chemisch (kehm'-ish) *a.* chemical.
Chiffre (shiff'-er) *f.* cipher: figure.

Chinin (ke-neen') *n.* quinine.
Chirurg (kee-roork') *m.* surgeon.
Chirurgie (kee-roork'-e) *f.* surgery.
Chocolade (shok'-o-lard) *f.* chocolate.
Chok (kohk) *m.* shock.
Cholerisch (kohl-ayr'-ish) *a.* choleric.
Christabend (krist'-ar-bent) *m.* Christmas eve.
Christentum (krist'-en-toom) *n.* Christianity.
Christfest (krist'-fest) *n.* Christmas.
Christlich (krist'-lik) *a.* Christian.
Christtag (krist'-tahg) *m.* Christmas day.
Chronik (kron'-ik) *f.* chronicle.
Commis (komm'-ee) *m.* clerk.
Coupé (koo'-pay) *n.* compartment in a train.
Couplet (koo'-play) *m.* popular song.
Coupon (koo'-pong) *m.* coupon, warrant.

D

Da (dah) *ad.* there: then—*c.* when: because: as: since.
Dabei (dah-by') *ad.* thereby: near.
Dach (dahk) *n.* roof.
Dachen (dahk'-n) *v.* to roof over: cover over.
Dachstube (dahk'-shtoob-erh) *f.* garret.
Dadurch (dah'-doohk) *ad.* thereby: through there: through it.
Dafür (dah'-feer) *ad.* for that: in place of: in return for.
Dagegen (dah'-gay-gen) *ad.* in return: on the other hand.
Daheim (dah-hime') *ad.* at home.
Daher (dah-hair') *ad.* therefore: thence: hence.
Dahin (dah-hin') *ad.* thither, to that place.
Dahinaus (dah-hin'-owss) *ad.* this way: thither.
Dahingeben (dah'-hin-gay-ben) *v.* to abandon: give up.
Dahinten (dah'-hint'-en) *ad* behind.

Dahlen (dah'-len) *v.* to trifle.
Damalig (dah'-mahl-ik) *ad.* then.
Damenspiel (dahm'-n-shpeel) *n.* draughts (the game).
Dämisch (dem'-ish) *a.* dull: foolish: silly.
Damit (dah-mit') *ad.* and *c.* in order that: with that.
Damm (dahm) *m.* dam, embankment: bank.
Dämmerig (dem'-er-ik) *a.* twilight: dusk.
Damon (dem'-ohn) *m.* demon.
Dampf (dahmf) *m.* steam. vapour.
Dampfboot (dahmf'-boht) *n.* steamboat.
Dampfen (dahmf'-n) *v.* to smoke: steam: suffocate.
Dampfkraft (dahmf'-krahft) *f.* steam-power.
Danach (dan-nack') *ad.* accordingly: after that: thereafter.
Daneben (day-nay'-ben) *ad.* and *c.* besides: near it: close by
Danieden (dan-need'-n) *ad.* down there: there below.
Dank (dahnk) *m.* thanks: gratitude: vote of thanks.
Dankbar (dahnk'-bar) *a.* thankful: grateful: appreciative.
Danken (dahnk'-n) *v.* to thank.
Dann (dahn) *ad.* then.
 Dann und wann (dahn oont vahn) now and then.
Dannen (dahn'-n) *ad.* thence.
Daran (dah-rahn') *ad.* thereby: thereat: thereupon: by: of.
Darauf (dah-rowf') *ad.* thereon: thereupon: after that.
Darein (dah-ryne') *ad.* therein: into it: thereinto.
Darlegen (dah'-lay-gen) *v.* to explain: state: set down.
Darlehen (dah'-lay-n) *n.* loan.
Darstellen (dah'-shtel-n) *v.* to exhibit: represent.
Darüber (dah-reeb'-er) *ad.* about it: concerning it: over it.
Darum (dah-room') *ad.* around it: therefore: for that reason.
Das (duss) *art.* the—*pn.* that: what: which.
Dasein (dah'-zine) *v.* to exist: be present— *n.* existence: presence.

Daselbst (dah'-zelp'-st) *ad.* in that place: there.
Dass (duss) *c.* that.
Dattel (dah'-tel) *f.* date.
Dauer (dow'-er) *f.* continuance: duration.
Dauerhaft (dow'-er-hahft) *a.* lasting: durable.
Dauern (dow'-ern) *v.* to last: endure: abide: continue.
Davon (dah'-fon) *ad.* thereof: of that: therefrom.
Davor (dah'-fohr) *ad.* for that: before that.
Dazumal (dah'-tsoo-mahl) *ad.* then: at that time.
Dazwischen (dah'-tsvish-n) *ad.* between them: an.ong them.
Debarkieren (day-bark-eer'-n) *v.* to disembark.
Debitor (day-bit'-ohr) *m.* debtor.
Deckel (deck'-l) *m.* lid: cover: covering.
Decken (deck'-n) *v.* to cover.
Defekt (def'-ekt-er) *a.* defective —*m.* defect: deficiency.
Deformität (dee-for-mee'-tayt) *f.* deformity.
Degen (day'-gen) *m.* sword: warrior.
Dehnbar (dain'-bar) *a.* elastic.
Dehnen (dain'-n) *v.* to stretch: extend.
Dehnung (dain'-oong) *f.* stretching.
Deich (dyk) *m.* dam: dike.
Dein (dine) *pn.* your: thy: thine.
Deinig (dy'-nig) *pn.* yours: thine.
Dekoration (day-kor-ar'-shoon) *f.* decoration: scenery.
Delikat (day-le-kaht') *a.* delicate: delicious: dainty.
Delikatesse (day-le-kaht'-ess-erh) *f.* delicacy: dainties.
Demgemäss (daim'-ge-mase) *ad.* according to.
Demnach (daim'-nahk) *c.* consequently: therefore.
Demokratie (day-moo-kraht'-e) *f.* democracy.
Demütig (day'-meet-ik) *a.* and *ad.* humble: submissive.
Demütigung (day'-meet-ik-oong) *f.* humiliation: submission.

Denkbar (denk'-bar) *a.* imaginable: conceivable.
Denken (denk'-n) *v.* to think: reason: conceive.
Denkschrift (dengk'-shrift) *f.* inscription.
Denkspruch (dengk'-shprook) *m.* motto: maxim.
Dennoch (denn'-ock) *c.* nevertheless: yet.
Depesche (day-pesh'-erh) *f.* telegram: dispatch.
Deponieren (day-pone-eer'-n) *v.* to deposit.
Der, Die, Das (der, dee, duss) *art.* the.
Derartig (der'-ahr-tik) *a.* such.
Derb (dairp) *a.* strong: firm: compact.
Dereinst (dair-ine-st') *ad.* in future: sometime or other.
Dergleichen (dair-gly'-ken) *ad.* such: such like.
Derjenige, Diejenige, Dasjenige (der', dee', duss'-yane-ig-erh) *pn.* that: this: he: she: he who: she who: that which.
Dermassen (der-mahss'-n) *ad.* in such a manner.
Derselbe, Dieselbe, Dasselbe (der', dee', dus'-zel-bee) *pn.* the same: he: she: it: that.
Des (dess) *art.* of the.
Deshalb (dess'-halp) *c.* therefore.
Dessen (dess'-n) *art.* of him: of it: of that.
Desto (dess'-toh) *ad.* so much (as in **destobesser**, so much the better).
Deswegen (dess'-vay-gen) *ad.* and *c.* therefore.
Detaillist (day-tahll'-ist) *m.* retail dealer.
Deuten (doy'-ten) *v.* to interpret: explain.
Deutlich (doyt'-lik) *a.* clear: explicit: evident.
Deutsch (doytsh) *n.* German language.
Dezember (day-tsem'-ber) *m.* December.
Diamant (de-ar-mahnt') *m.* diamond.
Diarium (dee-ahr'-yoom) *n.* diary: note book.
Dicht (dikt) *a.* dense: compact: close.

Dichten (dikt'-n) *v.* to compose.
Dichter (dikt'-er) *m.* poet.
Dick (dick) *a.* thick: big.
Dicke (dick'-erh) *f.* thickness: largeness.
Dieb (deep) *m.* thief.
Diebstahl (deep'-shtahl) *m.* theft: robbery.
Diener (deen-er) *m.* servant.
Dienstag (deens'-tak) *m.* Tuesday.
Dienstbote (deenst'-boht-erh) *m.* domestic servant.
Diensttreue (deenst'-troy-erh) *f.* faithfulness.
Dieser, Diese, Dieses (deez'-er, deez'-erh, deez'-es) *pron.* this: that.
Diesmal (dees'-mahl) *adv.* this time: for once.
Diesseits (dees'-zytes) *adv.* and *prep.* on this side.
Diktat (dik-taht') *n.* dictation.
Diktieren (dik-teer'-n) *v.* to dictate: command.
Diner (dee-nay') *n.* dinner.
Ding (ding) *n.* thing: matter.
Dirigent (dee-ree-ghent') *m.* director: conductor.
Dirigieren (de-ree-geer'-n) *v.* to direct: manage.
Diskont (dis-kont') *m.* discount.
Diskret (dis-kret') *a.* discreet.
Diskutieren (dis-koot'-eer-n) *v.* to discuss.
Disparat (dis-par'-aht) *a.* unlike.
Disputieren (dis-poot-eer'-n) *v.* to dispute.
Distanz (dist'-anz) *f.* distance.
Distel (dist'-l) *f.* thistle.
Dividieren (de-ve-deer'-n) *v.* to divide: apportion.
Doch (dok) *c.* but: however: nevertheless: still: yet.
Doktrin (dok'-trin) *f.* knowledge: learning.
Dolch (dolk) *m.* dagger.
Dolmetschen (dol'-metsh-n) *v.* to interpret.
Dolmetscher (dol'-metsh-er) *m.* interpreter.
Dom (dohm) *m.* cathedral.
Domizil (dohm'-e-zil) *m.* domicile: abode.
Donner (don'-er) *m.* thunder.
Donnerstag (don'-ers-tahk) *m.* Thursday.

Donnerwetter (don'-er-vet-ter) *n.* thunderstorm.
Doppeln (dop'-pel-n) *v.* to double.
Doppelt (dop'-pelt) *a.* double: doubly.
Dorf (dorf) *n.* village.
Dorfschenke (dorf'-shengkerh) *f.* country inn.
Dorn (dorn) *m.* prickle: thorn.
Dorren (dor'-ren) *v.* to fade: wither.
Dörren (deer'-ren) *v.* to bake.
Dorthin (dort'-hin) *ad.* thither: that way.
Dotter (dot'-ter) *m.* egg yolk.
Dozieren (doht-zeer'-n) *v.* to teach.
Draht (draht) *m.* thread: wire.
Drahtlos (draht'-loos) *a.* wireless.
Drauf, Darauf (drowf, dahrowf') *ad.* thereupon.
Draussen (drows'-n) *ad.* out of doors.
Drei (dry) *a.* three.
Dreieck (dry'-eck) *n.* triangle.
Dreissig (dry'-sik) *a.* thirty.
Dreist (dryst) *a.* bold: courageous: heroic.
Dreizehn (dry'-tzain) *a.* thirteen.
Drieseln (dry'-zeln) *v.* to turn: twist.
Dringen (dring'-n) *v.* to crowd.
Dritte (dritt'-erh) *a.* third.
Drogist (drohg'-ist) *m.* druggist.
Drohen (dro'-hen) *v.* to threaten.
Drohung (dro'-hong) *f.* threat.
Drollig (dro'-lik) *a.* droll: funny.
Drossel (dros'-sel) *f.* thrush.
Drückend (dreek'-ent) *a.* vexatious.
Drucker (drook'-er) *m.* printer.
Du (doo) *pron.* thou.
Duftig (dooft'-ik) *a.* fragrant.
Duldbar (doold'-bar) *a.* tolerable: endurable.
Dulden (doold'-n) *v.* to bear: put up with: suffer.
Dumm (doom) *a.* dull: stupid.
Dumpf (doomf) *a.* dull: stuffy: close.
Dünger (deeng'-er) *m.* manure.

Dünkel (deeng'-kel) *m.* arrogance: conceit.
Dunkel (doong'-kel) *a.* dark: gloomy.
Dunne (doon'-ner) *f.* thinness.
Dunsen (doons'-en) *v.* to swell (with pride, etc.).
Dunst (doonst) *m.* steam: vapour.
Dünsten (deenst'-n) *v.* to stew.
Dunstig (doons'-tik) *a.* damp: misty.
Durch (doohrk) *prep.* through: owing to.
Durchaus (doohrk'-ows) *ad.* thoroughly: quite.
Durchbringer (doohrk'-bring-er) *m.* spendthrift.
Durchdringend (doohrk'-dring-n) *a.* sharp: piercing.
Durchdüften (doohrk'-dooft-n) *v.* to perfume.
Durchfall (doohrk'-fahl) *m.* diarrhœa.
Durchfeuchten (doohrk'-foykten) *v.* to soak.
Durchfressen (doohrk'-fress-n) *v.* to corrode.
Durchgang (doohrk'-gahng) *m.* gangway: passage.
Durchgiessen (doohrk'-gees-n) *v.* to filter.
Durchglühen (doohrk'-glee-n) *v.* to inflame: heat.
Durchhelfen (doohrk'-hel-fen) *v.* to support: maintain.
Durchläutern (doohrk'-loytern) *v.* to purify: strain.
Durchleuchten (doohrk'-loykten) *v.* to light up.
Durchmesser (doohrk'-messer) *m.* diameter.
Durchreisender (doohrk'-ryzend-er) *m.* traveller.
Durchscheinend (doohrk'-shine-end) *a.* transparent.
Durchsieben (doohrk'-seeben) *v.* to sift.
Durchspähen (doohrk'-shpayn) *v.* to explore: examine.
Durchstechen (doohrk'-shtek-n) *v.* to stab.
Dürfen (deer'-fen) *v.* to dare: need: want.
Dürftig (deerf'-tik) *a.* poor: needy.
Dürr (deer) *a.* arid: barren: dry: withered.
Durst (doohrst) *m.* thirst.

Duselig (doo′-sail-ik) *a.* dizzy.
Düster (dees′-ter) *a.* dark: dismal: gloomy: mournful.
Dutzend (doot′-sent) *n.* dozen.

E

Eben (Eb′-n) *a.* even: flat: level.
Ebenfalls (ay′-ben-fahls) *ad.* also: likewise: too.
Ebenholz (ay′-ben-holtz) *n.* ebony.
Ebenso (ay′-ben-zo) *ad.* as: even now.
Eber (ay′-ber) *m.* boar.
Ecke (eck′-erh) *f.* corner: angle: edge.
Edieren (ed′-ire-n) *v.* to edit: publish.
Efeu (ay′-foy) *m.* ivy.
Egel (ay′-gehl) *m.* leech.
Ehe (ay′-erh) *c.* before.
Ehebrechen (ay′-ehr-brek-n) *v.* to commit adultery.
Ehegatte (ay′-ehr-gaht-erh) *m.* husband.
Ehelos (ay′-ehr-loos) *a.* unmarried.
Eher (ay′-er) *ad.* sooner.
Ehrenhaft (ayr′-en-haft) *a.* honourable.
Ehrlich (ayr′-lik) *a.* honest.
Eichel (i′-kel) *f.* acorn: club (at cards).
Eichhörnchen (ike′-hern-ken) *n.* squirrel.
Eidechse (i′-deck-see) *f.* lizard.
Eiderdaunen (i′-dair-down-n) *f.* eiderdown.
Eierkäse (i′-er-kay-ze) *m.* custard.
Eierkuchen (i′er-kook-n) *m.* omelet.
Eiferig (i′-fer-ik) *a.* zealous: passionate: eager.
Eifern (i′-fer-n) *v.* to be angry: to inveigh against.
Eifersüchtig (i′-fer-seek-tik) *a.* jealous.
Eigenbob (i′-gen-bobe) *n.* self-praise.
Eigenname (i′-gen-nahm) *m.* proper name.
Eigennützig (i′-gen-neet-sik) *a.* selfish: thinking only of self.
Eigens (i′-gens) *ad.* especially: particularly.
Eigensinnig (i′-gen-zin-ik) *a.* obstinate: wilful.

Eigentlich (i′-gent-lik) *a.* and *ad.* real: true: proper.
Eigentümer (i′-gen-teem-er) *m.* proprietor: owner.
Eigenwillig (i′-gen-vil-lik) *a.* self-willed.
Eignen (i′-gnen) *a.* to be suitable for: to suit.
Eigner (i′-gner) *m.* owner.
Eiland (i′-lahnt) *n.* island.
Eile (i′-le) *f.* speed: haste: hurry.
Eilen (i′-len) *v.* to hasten: hurry: to make haste.
Eilf (elhf) *a.* eleven.
Eilfertig (ile′-fair-tik) *a.* speedy: hasty.
Eilzug (ile′-tsook) *m.* fast train: express.
Eimer (i′-mair) *m.* pail: bucket.
Ein, Eine, Ein (ine, inerh, ine) *art.* one: a: an.
Ein (i′-ne) *ad.* in: into.
Eingang (ine′-gahng) *m.* entrance: way in.
Eingeben (ine′-gayb-n) *v.* to give: deliver: administer.
Eingebildet (ine′-gebil-det) *a.* imaginary: conceited.
Eingebung (ine′-gay-bong) *f.* inspiration: suggestion.
Eingefroren (ine′-gay-fror-n) *a.* and *p.* frozen up.
Eingemacht (ine′-gee-mahkt) *a.* pickled: preserved.
Eingessen (ine′-gess-n) *a.* resident.
Eingestehen (ine′-gest-ay-n) *v.* to avow: confess: admit.
Eingeweide (ine′-ge-vy-derh) *n. pl.* bowels: intestines.
Eingewöhnen, sich (ine′-ge-verh-nen) *v.* to accustom oneself to.
Eingezogen (ine′-ge-tsorg-n) *a.* modest: quiet: retiring.
Eingreifen (ine′-gry-fen) *v.* to catch: seize.
Einhalt (ine′-hahlt) *m.* stop: check: prohibition.
Einhalten (ine′-hahlt-n) *v.* to stop: check: prohibit.
Einhandeln (ine′-hahn-del-n) *v.* to buy.
Einhändigen (ine′-hen-dig-n) *v.* to deliver: hand over.
Einhängen (ine′-heng-n) *v.* to hang up.

Einheimisch (ine'-hy-misch) *a.* home-bred, native.

Einigen (ine'-ig-n) *v.* to unite: agree with.

Einiger, Einige, Einiges (ine'-ig-er) *pn.* any: some.

Einimpfen (ine'-im-fen) *v.* to inoculate.

Einkauf (ine'-kowf) *m.* purchase.

Einkaufen (ine'-kowf-n) *v.* to buy.

Einkaufspreis (ine'-kowf-price) *m.* cost price.

Einkehren (ine'-kay-ren) *v.* to stop at an hotel.

Einladung (ine'-laid-oong) *f.* invitation.

Einlaufen (ine'-lowf-n) *v.* to arrive: enter.

Einleitung (ine'-lyte-oong) *f.* introduction.

Einleuchtend (ine'-loyk-tend) *a.* obvious.

Einlösen (ine'-ler-zen) *v.* to redeem.

Einmal (ine'-mahl) *ad.* at once: once upon a time.

Einmütig (ine'-meet-ik) *a.* unanimous.

Einnahme (ine'-nah-merh) *f.* receipt.

Einnehmend (ine'-nay-men) *a.* charming: engaging: taking.

Einölen (ine'-erl-n) *v.* to oil: grease.

Einpökeln (ine'-perk-eln) *v.* to pickle.

Einrahmen (ine'-rahm-n) *v.* to frame.

Einräumen (ine'-roy-men) *v.* to cede: grant: proffer.

Einreden (ine'-ray-den) *v.* to interrupt: persuade.

Einreibung (ine'-ry-boong) *f.* embrocation.

Einrückung (ine'-reek-oong) *f.* advertisement.

Eins (ines) *f.* one—*ad.* of one mind: similarly.

Einsagen (ine'-sahg-n) *v.* to suggest.

Einsalzen (ine'-sahlt-sen) *v.* to salt: pickle.

Einsam (ine'-zahm) *a.* single: unique: only.

Einsammlung (ine'-zahm-loong) *f.* gathering.

Einschärfen (ine'-shairf-n) *v.* to enjoin: impress.

Einschiffung (ine'-shif-foong) *f.* embarkation.

Einschlafen (ine'-shlaf-n) *v.* to fall asleep.

Einschleppen (ine'-shlep-n) *v.* to smuggle.

Einschliessen (ine'-shlees-sen) *v.* to lock up: shut up.

Einschluss (ine'-shloss) *m.* enclosure.

Einschmutzen (ine'-shmoot-zen) *v.* to dirty: soil.

Einschreibung (ine'-shry-boong) *f.* entry (in a book, etc.).

Einschrumpfen (ine'-shroom-fen) *v.* to shrivel: shrink.

Einsenden (ine'-send-n) *v.* to remit: send.

Einsetzung (ine'-set-zoong) *f.* installation.

Einstmals (ine'-st-mahls) *ad.* once: formerly: in the past.

Einsturz (ine'-shtorts) *m.* crash.

Eintauchen (ine'-towk-n) *v.* to immerse.

Einteilen (ine'-tie-len) *v.* to distribute: divide.

Eintönig (ine'-ter-nik) *a.* monotonous.

Eintreten (ine'-tray-ten) *v.* to appear: begin: enter.

Einverstehen (ine'-fair-shtay-n) *v.* to agree with.

Einwanderung (ine'-vahn-der-oong) *f.* immigration.

Einwärts (ine'-vairts) *ad.* inward: inwards.

Einwechseln (ine'-veck-sel-n) *v.* to change.

Einweichen (ine'-vy-ken) *v.* to soak.

Einwenden (ine'-vend-n) *v.* to reply.

Einwilligung (ine'-vill-ig-oong) *f.* assent: consent.

Einwohner (ine'-voh-ner) *m.* inhabitant.

Einwurf (ine'-voorf) *m.* exception: objection.

Einwurzeln (ine'-vort-sel-n) *v.* to take root.

Einzeichnen (ine'-tsy-knen) *v.* to inscribe: note.

Einziehen (ine'-tsee-n) *v.* to collect.

Einzig (ine'-tsik) *a.* alone: only.

Einzug (ine'-tsook) *m.* entrance: entry.
Eis (ize) *n.* ice.
Eisbahn (ize'-bahn) *f.* slide.
Eisbär (ize'-bear) *m.* polar-bear.
Eisberg (ize'-bairk) *m.* iceberg: glacier.
Eisen (ize'-n) *n.* iron.
Eisenbahn (ize'-n-bahn) *f.* railway.
Eisenhandel (ize'-n-hahn-del) *m.* ironmongery.
Eisern (ize'-ern) *a.* iron: unfeeling.
Eisig (ize'-ik) *a.* frozen: icy.
Eitel (ite'-l) *a.* vain.
Ekel (ake'-l) *m.* aversion: disgust—*a.* disgusting.
Ekeln (ake'-eln) *v.* to loathe.
Ekelname (ake'-l-nahm-erh) *m.* nickname.
Elastisch (ay'-lahst-ish) *a.* elastic.
Elefant (ay'-lay-fhante) *m.* elephant.
Eleganz (ay'-lay-gahnts) *f.* elegance.
Elektrisch (ay-leck'-trisch) *a.* electrical.
Elend (ail'-ent) *n.* misery: need: want.
Elf (elf) *a.* eleven.
Elfenbein (elf'-n-byne) *n.* ivory.
Ellbogen (el'-boh-gen) *m.* elbow.
Ellenwaren (el'-n-vahr-n) *pl.* drapery.
Eltern (el'-tern) *pl.* parents.
Elternlos (el'-tern-loos) *a.* orphan.
Email (ay-mahl'-yer) *m.* and *n.* enamel.
Empfang (emp-fahng') *m.* receipt.
Empfangen (emp-fahng'-n) *v.* to receive.
Empfehlen (emp-fayl'-n) *v.* to recommend.
Empfindbar (emp-find'-bar) *a.* sensible.
Empfinden (emp-find'-n) *v.* to feel.
Empören (emp-err'-n) *v.* to excite: stir up: revolt.
Empörend (emp-err'-end) *a.* revolting.
Emsig (em'-zik) *a.* industrious: hard working.

Ende (en'-de) *n.* end: conclusion.
Enden (en'-den) *v.* to finish: end: conclude.
Energie (en'-air-gee) *f.* energy: force: strength.
Eng (eng) *a.* close: narrow: tight.
Engel (eng'-el) *m.* angel.
Enkel (eng'-kel) *m.* ankle: grandchild.
Enorm (en-norm') *a.* enormous: huge.
Entbieten (ent-beet'-n) *v.* to offer: bid.
Enterben (ent-air'-ben) *v.* to disinherit.
Entfernen (ent-fair'-nen) *v.* to remove: retire.
Entfliehen (ent-flee'-n) *v.* to fly: escape: get away.
Entgegen (ent-gayg'-n) *prep.* against: contrary.
Entgegnen (ent-gayg'-nen) *v.* to return: reply.
Enthaltsam (ent-hahlt'-sam) *a.* abstemious.
Entkleiden (ent-kly'-den) *v.* to undress.
Entlassen (ent-lahs'-sen) *v.* to discharge: dismiss.
Entlassung (ent-lahs'-soong) *f.* dismissal.
Entlaufen (ent-low'-fen) *v.* to run away: escape.
Entlaufung (ent-low'-foong) *f.* escape: elopement.
Entlegen (ent-lay'-gen) *a.* distant: remote.
Entlehen (ent-lai'-n) *v.* to borrow.
Entmenscht (ent-mensch') *a.* barbarous: savage.
Entpropfen (ent-proh'-fen) *v.* to uncork.
Entsatz (ent-sahts') *m.* help: relief: succour.
Entscheiden (ent-shee'-den) *v.* to decide.
Entschlossen (ent-shloss'-sen) *a.* determined: resolute.
Entschwinden (ent-shvin'-den) *v.* to disappear: vanish.
Entsetzen (ent-set'-zen) *v.* to displace—*n.* horror.
Entstehen (ent-shta'-oong) *v.* to begin.
Entwaffnen (ent-vahf'-nen) *v.* to disarm.

Entweder (ent-vayd'-er) *a.* either.

Entwenden (ent-ven'-den) *v.* to steal.

Entwerfen (ent-vayr'-fen) *v.* to design.

Entwirren (ent-verr'-n) *v.* to extricate: unravel.

Entwürdigen (ent-veerd'-ig-n) *v.* to degrade.

Entwurf (ent-voorf') *m.* design: pattern: sketch.

Entziehen (ent-tsee'-n) *v.* to avoid: withdraw.

Entzückend (ent-tseek'-ent) *a.* charming: delightful.

Entzündlich (ent-tseend'-lik) *a.* inflammable.

Entzwei (ent-tsvy') *ad.* asunder.

Er (air) *pron.* he.

Erachten (ayr-ahk'-ten) *v.* to imagine: presume.

Erbärmlich (ayr-bairm'-lik) *a.* miserable.

Erbarmung (ayr-barm'-oong) *f.* pity.

Erbauen (ayr-bow'-n) *v.* to build: erect.

Erbauung (ayr-bow'-oong) *f.* building.

Erbe (ayr'-ber) *m.* heir—*n.* inheritance.

Erbeben (ayr-bay'-ben) *v.* to quake: shake: tremble.

Erbieten (ayr-beet'-n) *v.* to offer: volunteer.

Erbitten (ayr-bitt'-n) *v.* to beg: request: supplicate.

Erbleichen (ayr-bly'-ken) *v.* to grow pale: blanch: faint.

Erborgen (ayr-borg'-n) *v.* to borrow.

Erbosen (ayr-bohs'-n) *v.* to exasperate: madden.

Erbrechen (ayr-brek'-n) *n.* vomiting.

Erbse (ayr-pse) *f.* pea.

Erbstück (ayrb-shteek') *n.* heirloom.

Erdbeben (ayrt'-baib-n) *n.* earthquake.

Erdbeere (ayrt'-bair-erh) *f.* strawberry.

Erde (ayrd'-erb) *f.* the world: earth.

Erdenken (ayr-denk'-n) *v.* to imagine: contrive.

Erdichtet (ayr-dik'-tet) *a.* fictitious.

Erdig (ayrd'-ik) *a.* earthy.

Erdöl (ayrd'-erl) *n.* petroleum.

Erdolchen (ayr-dolk'-n) *v.* to stab.

Erdrücken (ayr-dreek'-n) *v.* to crush: stifle: overwhelm.

Erdschnecke (ayr-shneck'-erh) *f.* snail.

Erdulden (ayr-doold'-n) *v.* to endure: suffer: put up with.

Ereignen, sich (ayr-i'-gnen, sik) *v.* to come to pass: happen.

Ereilen (ayr-i'-len) *v.* to overtake.

Ererben (ayr-ayr'-ben) *v.* to inherit.

Erfassen (ayr-fahs'-n) *v.* to seize: lay hold on.

Erfindung (ayr-fin'-doong) *f.* invention.

Erfolgreich (ayr-folg'-ryk) *a.* successful.

Erforderlich (ayr-ford'-er-lih) *a.* requisite, necessary.

Erfordern (ayr-ford'-ern) *v.* to require: need: demand.

Erfordernis (ayr-ford'-ern-is) *n.* requirement: necessity.

Erforschung (ayr-forsh'-oong) *f.* exploration.

Erfrechen, sich (ayr-frek'-n, sik) *v.* to dare.

Erfreuen (ayr-froy'-n) *v.* to please: cheer: rejoice.

Erfreulich (ayr-froy'-lik) *a.* encouraging: gratifying.

Erfrischen (ayr-frish'-n) *v.* to refresh.

Erfrischung (ayr-frish'-oong) *f.* refreshment.

Ergänzen (ayr-ghents'-n) *v.* to supply: complete.

Ergeben (ayr-gayb'-n) *v.* to yield: surrender—*a.* obedient: devoted.

Ergebnis (ayr-gayp'-niss) *n.* result.

Ergiessen (ayr-gees'-n) *v.* to fall into.

Ergötzen (ayr-gert'-sen) *v.* to amuse: please: delight.

Ergötzung (ayr-gert'-soong) *f.* amusement: enjoyment.

Ergreifen (ayr-gry'-fen) *v.* to seize.

Ergrimmen (ayr-grimm'-n) *v.* to become furious.

Erhandeln (ayr-hahn'-deln) v. to buy: purchase.
Erhaschen (ayr-hahs'-n) v. to snatch: catch: seize.
Erheben (ayr-hay'-ben) v. to lift up: raise up.
Erheblich (ayr-haip'-lik) a. considerable.
Erheitern (ayr-hyte'-ern) v. to brighten: make cheerful.
Erhellen (ayr-hell'-n) v. to light up: enlighten.
Erholen, sich (ayr-hohl'-n, sik) v. to recover.
Erholung (ayr-hohl'-oong) f. recreation: recovery.
Erinnern (ayr-inn'-ern) v. to remind: recollect: remember.
Erkälten (ayr-kel'-ten) v. to catch cold.
Erkannt (ayr-kahn'-nt) a. known.
Erkaufen (ayr-kow'-fen) v. to bribe.
Erkennbar (ayr-kenn'-bar) a. distinguishable.
Erkennen (ayr-kenn'-n) v. to understand: appreciate.
Erkenntlichkeit (ayr-kent'-lik-kite) f. gratitude.
Erkranken (ayr-krank'-n) v. to become ill.
Erkühlen (ayr-keel'-n) v. to cool: refresh.
Erkunden (ayr-koond'-n) v. to find out.
Erkünstelt (ayr-keenst'-elt) a. artificial: superficial.
Erlangen (ayr-lahng'-n) v. to reach: obtain.
Erlass (ayr-lahss') m. pardon.
Erlassen (ayr-lahss'-n) v. to pardon: set free.
Erlauben (ayr-low'-ben) v. to allow: let.
Erlaubt (ayr-lowpt') a. allowed: permitted.
Erlaucht (ayr-lowk'-t) a. eminent: noted: illustrious.
Erle (ayrl'-erh) f. alder (tree).
Erledigt (ayr-layd'-igt) a. arranged: planned: settled.
Erleiden (ayr-ly'-den) v. to suffer: bear: put up with.
Erlesen (ayr-lay'-zen) a. choice: select—v. to choose: select.
Erleuchten (ayr-loyk'-ten) v. to enlighten.
Erliegen (ayr-leeg'-n) v. to succumb.
Erlogen (ayr-lohsn'-n) a. false: untrue: fraudulent.
Erlöschen (ayr-ler'-shen) v. to extinguish.
Ermahnen (ayr-mahn'-n) v. to exhort.
Ermässigen (ayr-mayce'-ig-n) v. to reduce: moderate.
Ermatten (ayr-maht'-n) v. to grow weary.
Ermattung (ayr-maht'-oong) f. weariness.
Ermessen (ayr-mess'-n) v. to estimate: measure.
Ermorden (ayr-mord'-n) v. to murder.
Ermüdung (ayr-meed'-oong) f. weariness: fatigue.
Ermutigung (ayr-moot'-ig-oong) f. encouragement.
Ernennen (ayr-nen'-n) v. to name: nominate.
Erneurung (ayr-noy'-er-oong) f. revival: renewal.
Erniedrigend (ayr-need'-rig-ent) a. degrading: humiliating.
Ernst (ayrnst) m—earnestness —a. earnest: serious.
Ernte (ayrnt'-erh) f. harvest.
Ernten (ayrnt'-n) v. to gather: harvest: reap.
Erobern (ayr-ohbe'-rn) v. to conquer.
Eröffnen (ayr-erf'-nen) v. to open (ceremonial).
Erquicken (ayr-kvic'-ken) v. to renew: revive.
Erraten (ayr-raht'-n) v. to divine: guess.
Erröten (ayr-rert'-n) v. to blush.
Ersatz (ayr-zahts') m. compensation.
Erschaffen (ayr-shahf'-fen) v. to create: originate.
Erschöpfung (ayr-sherp'-foong) f. exhaustion.
Erschrecklich (ayr-shreck'-lik) a. terrible: frightful.
Erschrocken (ayr-shrock'-n) a. frightened: terrified.
Ersehen (ayr-zay'-n) v. to distinguish: observe.
Ersetzen (ayr-zet'-sen) v. to restore.
Ersetzung (ayr-zet'-zoong) f. compensation.

Ersinnen — Falte

Ersinnen (ayr-sin'-n) *v.* to contrive: devise: invent.
Ersinnlich (ayr-sin'-lik) *a.* imaginable.
Ersparen (ayr-shpar'-n) *v.* to save: spare.
Erst (ayrst) *ad.* first: at first: not until.
Erstaunen (ayr-shto'-nen) *n.* astonishment — *v.* to be astonished.
Erstaunlich (ayr-shtone'-lik) *a.* astonishing.
Erste (ayrst'-erh) *a.* first.
Erstens (ayrst'-ens) *ad.* firstly.
Ertragen (ayr-trag'-n) *v.* to bear: endure: suffer.
Erträglich (ayr-traik'-lik) *a.* tolerable.
Ertragsam (ayr-trag'-zam) *a.* profitable.
Ertränken (ayr-treng'-ken) *v.* to drown.
Ertränkung (ayr-treng'-koong) *f.* drowning.
Erträumen (ayr-troy'-men) *v.* to dream.
Erwählen (ayr-vail'-n) *v.* to choose.
Erwähnen (ayr-vain'-n) *v.* to mention.
Erzürnt (ayr-tsern'-t) *a.* angry.
Es (ess) *pron.* it.
Esel (ay'-zel) *m.* ass.
Essen (ess'-n) *n.* food—*v.* to eat.
Essenszeit (ess'-n-tsite) *f.* meal-time.
Essig (ess'-ik) *m.* vinegar.
Esslust (ess'-loost) *f.* appetite.
Etwa (et'-vah) *ad.* about: nearly: perhaps.
Euch (oyke) *pron.* you.
Eule (oyl'-erh) *f.* owl.

F

Fabel (fah'-bel) *f.* fable: story: plot.
Fabelhaft (fah'-bel-haft) *a.* fabulous: amazing—*ad.* marvellously.
Fabeln (fah'-beln) *v.* to tell stories (tales not untruths).
Fabrik (fah-brik') *f.* factory: works.
Fabrikant (fah-brik'-ant) *m.* manufacturer.
Fabrikarbeiter (fah-brik'-ahr-bite-r) *f.* factory hand.

Fabrizieren (fah-bree-tseer'-n) *v.* to manufacture.
Fach (fahk) *n.* compartment: drawer: shelf: pigeon-hole.
Facher (fahk'-er) *m.* fan.
Fachmassig (fahk'-mahss-ik) *a.* and *ad.* professional.
Fackel (fahck'-l) *f.* torch.
Fackeln (fahck'-eln) *v.* to tell stories (untruths).
Fackelzug (fahck'-el-tsook) *m.* torch-light procession.
Fade (fahd'-erh) *a.* insipid: tasteless.
Faden (fahd'-n) *m.* thread.
Fadennackt (fahd'-en-nahkt) *a.* stark naked.
Fadennudeln (fahd'-en-noodeln) *f. pl.* vermicelli.
Fähig (fay'-ik) *a.* capable: qualified: able.
Fahl (fahl) *a.* drab.
Fahnden (fahn'-den) *v.* to seek for.
Fahne (fahn'-erh) *f.* standard: flag: colours.
Fahrbar (fahr'-bar) *a.* practicable.
Fahren (fahr'-n) *v.* to drive.
Fahrend (fahr'-ent) *a.* going.
Fahrer (fahr'-er) *m.* driver.
Fahrt (fahrt) *f.* drive: journey.
Faktisch (fahckt'-ish) *a.* real: actual.
Faktur (fahckt'-oor) *f.* invoice.
Fall (fahl) *m.* accident: fall: decline: ruin.
Fallbeil (fahl'-bile) *n.* guillotine.
Falls (fahls) *ad.* in case.
Fallschirm (fahl'-scherm) *m.* parachute.
Fallsucht (fahl'-sookt) *f.* epilepsy.
Falltür (fahl'-teer) *f.* trap door.
Falsch (fahlsh) *a.* wrong: false: forged: faithless.
Fälschen (fel'-shen) *v.* to falsify: adulterate.
Falschheit (fahlsh'-hite) *f.* falsehood.
Fälschlich (felsh'-lik) *a.* and *ad.* false.
Falschmünzer (fahlsh'-mentser) *m.* coiner.
Fälschung (felsh'-oong) *f.* adulteration: forgery.
Falte (fahlt'-erh) *f.* pleat: crease: fold: wrinkle.

Falten (fahlt'-n) v. to pleat.
Faltenwurf (fahlt'-n-vorf) n. drapery.
Falter (fahlt'-er) m. butterfly.
Falzen (fahl'-sen) v. to fold.
Familie (fahm'-eel-yee) f. family.
Famos (fahm'-oze) a. first rate: splendid: capital.
Fanatiker (fahn'-ahtik-er) m. fanatic.
Fang (fahng) m. capture: catch: stab.
Fangen (fahng'-n) v. to catch: capture: seize.
Farbe (fahrb'-erh) f. colour: paint: dye.
Färben (fair'-ben) v. to colour: paint: dye.
Farbenblind (fahr'-ben-blint) a. colour blind.
Farbenkasten (fahr'-ben-kahst-n) m. box of paints.
Farbig (fahr'-bik) a. coloured: tinted: variegated.
Farbstoff (fahrp'-shtoff) m. dye: colour: pigment.
Farn (fahrn) m. fern: bracken.
Fasan (fah-zahn') m. pleasant.
Fasching (fahsh'-ing) m. carnival.
Faselei (fah'-sel-eye) f. twaddle: tittle-tattle: silly talk.
Faser (fah'-zer) f. string.
Fass (fahss) n. cask: barrel: tub.
Fasslich (fahss'-lik) a. intelligible.
Fast (fahst) ad. nearly: almost.
Fasten (fahst'-n) v. to fast—pl. Lent.
Fastnacht (fahst'-nahkt) f. Shrove Tuesday.
Fatal (faht-ahl') a. unlucky: nasty: disagreeable.
Fatalität (faht-ahl'-e-tayt) f. misfortune: ill luck.
Fauchen (fowk'-n) v. to spit.
Faul (fowl) a. rotten: bad: lazy.
Faulheit (fowl'-hite) f. laziness.
Faustkampf (fowst'-kahmf) m. prize-fight: boxing contest.
Fazit (fah'-seet) n. result: amount.
Februar (feh'-broo-ahr) m. February.
Fechten (fek'-ten) v. to fight.
Feder (fay'-der) f. feather: pen.
Federharz (fay'-der-harts) n. india-rubber.

Federkraft (fay'-der-krahft) f. elasticity.
Federmesser (fay'-der-messer) n. pocket-knife.
Federvieh (fay'-der-fee) n. poultry.
Fee (fay) f. fairy.
Fegen (fay'-gen) v. to cleanse.
Fehl (fayl) m. error: fault—ad. in vain.
Fehlen (fayl'-n) v. to err: miss.
Fehler (fayl'-er) m. error: fault.
Fehlgeburt (fayl'-ge-bort) f. abortion: miscarriage.
Fehlgriff (fayl'-grif) m. mistake: error.
Feier (fy'-er) f. holiday.
Feierabend (fy'-er-ah-bent) m. holiday: leisure.
Feierlich (fy'-er-lik) a. festive.
Feig (fyg) a. cowardly.
Feige (fy'-ge) f. fig (fruit).
Feigling (fyke'-ling) m. coward.
Feil (file) a. mercenary: for sale.
Felbel (fel'-bel) m. velvet.
Feldbau (felt'-bow) m. agriculture.
Feldblume (felt'-bloom-erh) f. wild-flower.
Feldlager (felt'-lah-ger) n. camp.
Fenster (fens'-ter) n. window.
Fensterpfeiler (fens'-ter-pfyler) m. pier: jetty.
Ferne (fayrn'-erh) f. distance.
Ferner (fayrn'-er) a. farther: further.
Fernrohr (fayrn'-rohr) n. telescope.
Fernschreiber (fayrn'-shry-ber) m. telegraph.
Fernsprecher (fayrn'-shprek-er) m. telephone.
Fertig (fayr'-tik) a. ready.
Fertigen (fayr'-tik-n) v. to make: prepare.
Fertigkeit (fayr'-tik-ite) f. readiness.
Fest (fest) n. feast: festival.
Festlich (fest'-lik) a. festive.
Festung (fest'-oong) f. fortress.
Fett (fet) a. fat: greasy—n. fat. grease.
Feucht (foykt) a. damp: moist.
Feuchtigkeit (foykt'-ik-kite) f. moisture.
Feuer (foy'-err) n. ardour: fire: passion.

Feuerfangend (foy'-err-fahng-ent) *a.* inflammable.
Feuermal (foy'-err-mahl) *n.* scar.
Feuern (foy'-ern) *v.* to burn.
Feuerung (foy'-err-oong) *f.* fuel.
Feuerwerk (foy'-er-vairk) *n.* firework.
Feurig (foy'-rik) *a.* ardent: fiery.
Fieber (fee'-ber) *n.* fever.
Fieberfrost (fee'-ber-frost) *m.* chill.
Fieberhaft (fee'-ber-hahft) *a.* feverish.
Fiedel (feed'-l) *f.* violin: fiddle.
Fiktiv (feek'-tiff) *a.* fictitious.
Filtrieren (fil'-tree-ren) *v.* to filter: strain.
Finanzen (fin'-ahnt-sen) *f. pl.* finances.
Finden (fin'-den) *v.* to find: discover.
Finger (fin'-ger) *m.* finger.
Fingerhut (fin'-ger-hoot) *m.* thimble.
Finne (finn'-erh) *f.* fin.
Finster (finn'-ster) *a.* dark: gloomy: morose.
Finsternis (finn'-ster-niss) *f.* darkness.
Firnis (feer'-nis) *m.* varnish.
First (feerst) *m.* summit: top.
Fisch (fish) *m.* fish.
Fischerei (fish'-er-eye) *f.* fishery.
Fischgräte (fish'-grayt-erh) *f.* fish-bone.
Fixieren (fix'-eer-n) *v.* to fix: decide on: settle.
Fläche (flek'-erh) *f.* level surface: flatness.
Flachs (flax) *m.* flax.
Flachssamen (flax'-sahm-n) *m.* linseed.
Flackern (flahck'-ern) *v.* to flicker.
Flamme (flahm'-erh) *f.* flame.
Flammen (flahm'-n) *v.* to flare.
Flanell (flahn'-l) *m.* flannel.
Flasche (flash'-erh) *f.* flask: bottle.
Flattern (flat'-ern) *v.* to be fickle: flutter.
Flau (flow) *a.* dull: faint: feeble: languid.
Flaum (flowm) *m.* down: fluff.

Flechten (flek'-ten) *v.* to braid: plait.
Fleck (fleck) *m.* spot: place: freckle.
Fleckfieber (fleck'-fee-ber) *n.* measles.
Fledermaus (flayd'-er-mows) *f.* bat.
Flehen (flay'-n) *v.* to implore.
Fleisch (fly'-sch) *n.* meat: flesh.
Fleischen (fly'-scher) *m.* butcher.
Fleischkammer (fly'-sch kahm-er) *f.* larder.
Fleiss (flyce) *m.* diligence.
Fleissig (flyce'-ik) *a.* diligent: industrious.
Flektieren (flek'-teer-n) *v.* to bend.
Flicken (flick'-n) *v.* to patch: repair.
Fliege (fleeg'-erh) *f.* fly.
Fliegen (fleeg'-n) *v.* to fly.
Fliehen (flee'-n) *v.* to flee: run away.
Fliessen (flees'-sen) *v.* to flow.
Fliesspapier (flees'-pah-peer) *n.* blotting paper.
Flink (flink) *a.* agile: alert: nimble.
Flitter (flit'-ter) *m.* tinsel: spangle: frippery.
Flitterwochen (flit'-ter-vok-n) *f. pl.* honeymoon.
Floh (floh) *m.* flea.
Flor (flohr) *m.* blossom.
Flössen (fler'-sen) *v.* to float.
Flotte (flot'-erh) *f.* fleet: navy.
Fluchen (flook'-n) *v.* to curse.
Flucht (flookt) *f.* flight: escape.
Flugmaschine (flook'-mash-een) *f.* flying machine.
Flugs (flooks) *ad.* instantly: quickly: speedily.
Flüssig (flees'-ik) *a.* liquid: fluid.
Flüstern (flees'-tern) *v.* to whisper.
Folglich (folk'-lik) *ad.* therefore: consequently.
Folter (fol'-ter) *f.* torture.
Foltern (fol'-tern) *v.* to torture: torment.
Fördern (fer'-dern) *v.* to promote: further.
Fordern (for'-dern) *v.* to require: challenge.
Forelle (fohr'-el) *f.* trout.
Forke (fohr'-ker) *f.* pitch fork.

Formel (for'-mel) *f.* formula.
Förmlich (ferm'-lik) *a.* formal: regular.
Forsch (forsh) *a.* vigorous: lusty.
Forschen (for'-shen) *v.* to search: investigate.
Forst (forst) *m.* forest.
Fort (fort) *ad.* gone: off: away.
Fortban (fort'-bahn) *ad.* henceforth.
Fortbleiben (fort'-bly-ben) *v.* to stay away.
Fortdauern (fort'-dow-ern) *v.* to continue.
Forteilen (fort'-i-len) *v.* to hasten off.
Fortgang (fort'-gahng) *m.* departure: progress.
Fortlaufen (fort'-low-fen) *v.* to run away.
Forträumen (fort'-troy-men) *v.* to clear away.
Fortregnen (fort'-raig-n) *v.* to continue to rain.
Fortschritt (fort'-schrit) *m.* progress.
Fortsenden (fort'-zend-n) *v.* to send away.
Fracht (frahkt) *f.* freight, cargo, load.
Frackanzug (frahck'-ahn-tsook) *m.* dress clothes.
Fragen (frahg'-n) *v.* to ask.
Frankieren (frahnk'-eer-n) *v.* to pay postage.
Fransig (frahn'-zik) *a.* fringed.
Frass (frahss) *m.* food: eating: prey.
Fratz (frahts) *m.* a bad child.
Frau (frow) *f.* woman: wife: lady: Mrs.
Frauenglas (frow'-n-glahs) *n.* mica.
Frauenschneider (frow'-n-shny-der) *m.* ladies' tailor.
Fräulein (frow'-leen) *n.* young lady: Miss.
Frei (fry) *a.* free: disengaged: open: bold.
Freibeuter (fry'-boy-ter) *m.* pirate.
Freien (fry'-n) *v.* to court, make love: woo.
Freier (fry'-er) *m.* suitor: lover.
Freigeben (fry'-gay-ben) *v.* to release: set free.
Freiheit (fry'-hite) *f.* freedom.

Freikarte (fry'-kart) *f.* complimentary ticket.
Freimarke (fry'-mark) *f.* postage stamp.
Freimaurer (fry'-mow-rer) *m.* freemason.
Freimütig (fry'-meet-ik) *a.* frank: candid: open.
Freisass (fry'-sahss) *m.* freeholder.
Freisprechen (fry'-shprek-n) *v.* to acquit.
Freitag (fry'-tahk) *m.* Friday.
Freiwillig (fry' - vill - ik) *a.* voluntary.
Fremd (fremt) *a.* strange: foreign: unheard of.
Fremde (frem'-dehr) *f.* foreign country: abroad.
Fremdsprache (f r e m t'-shprah-kerh) *f.* foreign language.
Fressen (fress'-n) *v.* to eat: gobble: devour.
Fressend (fress'-ent) *a.* corrosive.
Fressgier (fress' - geer) *f.* voracity.
Frettchen (fret'-ken) *n.* ferret.
Freude (froyd'-erh) *f.* pleasure: joy: delight.
Freudig (froyd'-ik) *a.* joyful: cheerful: delightful.
Freund (froynt) *m.* friend.
Frevel (fray'-fell) *m.* crime: outrage: wickedness.
Friedfertig (freet'-fayr-tik) *a.* peaceable.
Friedhof (freet' - hohf) *m.* churchyard: cemetery.
Frieren (freer'-n) *v.* to freeze: feel cold.
Frisch (frish) *a.* new: fresh: vigorous: lively.
Friseur (free'-zur) *m.* hairdresser.
Frist (frist) *f.* time: respite: delay.
Frivol (free'-fol) *a.* flippant.
Froh (froh) *a.* glad: joyful.
Frohlocken (froh'-lock-n) *v.* to rejoice.
Fromm (fromm) *a.* religious: pious: God fearing.
Frömmigkeit (freerm'-ik-kite) *f.* godliness: piety.
Frosch (frosh) *m.* frog.
Frost (frost) *m.* frost: cold: chill.

Frostbeule (frost'-boy-le) *f.* chilblain.
Frösteln (freerst'-eln) *v.* to shiver.
Frostig (frost'-ik) *a.* chilly: cold: frosty.
Frottieren (frott'-eer-n) *v.* to rub.
Frucht (frookt) *f.* fruit.
Fruchtbar (frookt'-bar) *a.* fruitful: fertile.
Fruchtboden (frookt-boh-den) *m.* granary.
Fruchtlos (frookt'-loos) *a.* fruitless.
Früh (free) *a.* early.
Frühling (free'-ling) *m.* spring.
Frühstück (free'-shteeck) *n.* breakfast.
Fuchs (fooks) *m.* fox: red-hair.
Fuchsig (fook'-zik) *a.* reddish: sly.
Fügen (feeg'-n) *v.* to unite: join.
Füglich (feeg'-lik) *a.* easy: simple: convenient.
Fühlen (feel'-n) *v.* to feel: touch.
Fuhre (foor'-erh) *f.* conveyance.
Führen (feer'-n) *v.* to carry: guide: lead.
Führer (feer'-er) *m.* guide: leader.
Fuhrweg (foor'-vayg) *m.* road.
Fünf (feenft) *a.* five.
Fünfzehn (feenft'-tsain) *a.* fifteen.
Funfzig (feenft'-sik) *a.* fifty.
Funke (foonk'-erh) *m.* spark.
Für (feer) *prep.* for: instead of.
Furcht (foorkt) *f.* fear: fright.
Furchtbar (foorkt'-bar) *a.* fearful: frightful: dreadful.
Furchtlos (foorkt'-loos) *a.* fearless.
Fürsorge (feer'-zorg-erh) *f.* solicitude: care.
Fürst (feerst) *m.* prince.
Furt (foort) *f.* ford.
Fürwort (feer'-vort) *n.* pronoun.
Fuss (foos) *m.* foot: leg: base.
Fussbiege (foos'-beeg-erh) *f.* instep.
Fussboden (foos'-boh-den) *m.* floor.
Fusspfad (foos'-pfat) *m.* footpath.
Fusszehe (foos'-tsaye) *f.* toe.

G

Gabe (gahb'-erh) *f.* alms: dose: gift.
Gabelfrühstück (gahb'-el-free'-shteeck) *n.* luncheon.
Gackern (gahck'-ern) *v.* to giggle.
Gaffen (gahf'-fen) *v.* to gape: gaze at: stare at.
Gähnen (gay'-nen) *n.* yawn — *v.* to yawn: gape.
Galant (gah'-lahnt) *a.* gallant: polite.
Galanteriearbeit (gah'-lahnt-er-ee-ahr-bite) *f.* trinkets.
Galeere (gah'-lair-erh) *f.* galley.
Gallerte (gah'-ler-terh) *f.* jelly.
Gallig (gahll'-ik) *a.* bilious.
Gans (gahns) *f.* goose.
Gänseblume (ghen'-ze-bloom-erh) *f.* daisy.
Gauner (gow'-ner) *m.* cheat: swindler.
Gaunern (gow'-nern) *v.* to cheat: swindle.
Gebäck (ge-beck') *n.* pastry.
Gebären (ge-bair'-n) *v.* to bear: give birth.
Gebäude (ge-boyd'-erh) *n.* building.
Geben (gay'-ben) *v.* to give.
Gebet (ge-bayt') *n.* prayer.
Gebirgig (gee-beer'-gik) *a.* mountainous.
Gebiss (gee-biss') *n.* teeth: bridle.
Gebraten (gee-brah'-ten) *a.* roasted.
Gebrauch (gee-browk') *m.* use: rite: custom.
Gebrechen (gee-brek'-n) *n.* want — *v.* to want.
Gebrechlich (gee-brek'-lik) *a.* fragile.
Gebrüder (gee-breed'-er) *m. pl.* brothers.
Gebürtig (gee-beer'-tik) *a.* native: born.
Geburtstag (gee-boorts'-tahk) *m.* birthday.
Gebüsch (gee-beesch') *n.* bushes: copse: thicket.
Gedankenvoll (gee-dahn'-ken-foll) *a.* thoughtful.
Gedeck (gee-deck') *n.* cover: table-cloth.
Gedenken (gee-deng'-ken) *v.* to remember: think.

Gediegen (gee-deeg'-n) *a.* pure: solid: superior.
Gedrängt (gee-dreng'-terh) *a.* crowded.
Geduldig (gee-dool'-dik) *a.* patient.
Geeignet (gee-igg'-net) *a.* fit: suitable.
Gefährlich (gee-fayr'-lik) *a.* dangerous.
Gefahrlos (gee-farr'-loos) *a.* safe: secure.
Gefällig (gee-fell'-ik) *a.* courteous: pleasing: kind.
Gefälligst (gee-fell'-igst) *ad.* please.
Gefängnis (gee-feng'-niss) *n.* gaol: prison.
Gefasst (gee-fasst') *a.* calm: ready.
Gefecht (gee-fekt') *n.* battle: fight.
Geflügel (gee-fleeg'-l) *n.* poultry.
Geflüster (gee-flees'-ter) *n.* whisper.
Gefrieren (gee-freer'-n) *v.* to freeze.
Gefrierpunkt (gee-freer'-poonkt) *m.* freezing point.
Gefügig (gee-feeg'-ik) *a.* docile: pliable.
Gegen (gay'-gen) *prep.* against: towards.
Gegenantwort (gay'-gen-ahnt-vort) *f.* reply.
Gegend (gay'-gent) *f.* country: place: region.
Gegengift (gay'-gen-gift) *n.* antidote.
Gegenteilig (gay'-gen-tile-ik) *a.* opposite.
Gegenwärtig (gay'-gen-vair-tik) *ad.* at present.
Gegner (gay'-gner) *m.* adversary: opponent: rival.
Gehaltlos (gee-hahlt'-loos) *a.* valueless: worthless.
Gehässig (gee-hess'-ik) *a.* hateful.
Gehege (gee-hay'-ge) *n.* enclosure: hedge.
Geheim (gee-hime') *a.* private: secret.
Geheimnisvoll (gee-hime'-niss-foll) *a.* mysterious.
Gehen (gay'-n) *v.* to go: walk.
Geheul (gee-hoyl') *n.* howl: howling.

Gehirn (gee-heern') *n.* brain.
Gehör (gee-her') *n.* audience.
Gehorchen (gee-hork'-n) *v.* to belong to.
Gehörlos (gee-her'-loos) *a.* deaf.
Gehorsam (gee-horh'-zam) *a.* obedient: dutiful.
Geige (guy'-gee) *f.* violin.
Geiss (guys) *f.* goat.
Geissblatt (guys'-blaht) *n* honeysuckle.
Geissel (guys'-l) *f.* whip: lash.
Geistig (guys'-tik) *a.* intellectual.
Geiz (guyts) *m.* greed: avarice.
Geizhals (guyts'-haltz) *m.* miser.
Gekünstelt (gee-keenst'-elt) *a.* artificial: lofty: affected.
Gelächter (gee-leck'-ter) *n.* laughter.
Gelage (gee-lah'-gerh) *n.* banquet.
Gelass (gee-lahss') *n.* room: space.
Geld (gelt) *n.* money.
Gelehrig (gee-layr'-ik) *a.* docile: easy-going.
Gelehrt (gee-layrt') *a.* learned: scholarly.
Geleiten (gee-lyt'-n) *v.* to conduct: escort.
Geliebte (gee-leep'-terh) *m.* and *f.* lover: sweetheart: fiancé.
Gelingen (gee-ling'-n) *n.* success.
Gelispel (gee-liss'-phiel) *n.* whispering: lisping.
Gellen (ghell'-n) *v.* to yell.
Gelten (ghelt'-n) *v.* to cost.
Gelüst (gee-leest') *n.* appetite
Gemach (gee-mahk') *ad.* gently: slowly: comfortably.
Gemahlin (gee-mahl'-in) *f.* wife: spouse.
Gemälde (gee-mayl'-derh) *n.* painting: picture.
Gemäss (gee-mayss') *a.* and *ad.* comfortable.
Gemetzel (gee-met'-sel) *n.* carnage: massacre.
Gemisch (gee-misch') *n.* mixture.
Gemüse (gee-meez'-erh) *n.* greens: vegetables.
Gemüt (gee-meet') *n.* heart: mind: soul.

Gemütlich (gee-meet'-lik) *a.* genial: kindly.

Genau (gee-now') *a.* close: precise: strict.

Geneigt (gee-nyckt') *a.* disposed: inclined.

Genesen (gee-nay'-zen) *v.* to recover: get well again.

Genesung (gee-nay'-zoong) *f.* recovery.

Genie (shayn'-ee) *n.* genius.

Geniessbar (gee-nees'-bar) *a.* eatable: palatable.

Geniessen (gee-nees'-n) *v.* to enjoy: make use of.

Genoss (gee-noss') *m.* comrade: colleague.

Genug (gee-nook') *ad.* enough: sufficiently.

Genuss (gee-noos') *m.* enjoyment: pleasure.

Gepäck (gee-peck') *n.* baggage: luggage.

Gepäckausgabe (gee-peck'-owss-gah-be) *f.* cloak room.

Gepäckträger (gee-peck'-traih-ger) *m.* porter.

Gepäckwagen (gee-peck'-vahg-n) *m.* luggage-van.

Gerade (gerahd'-erh) *a.* direct: straight—*ad.* exactly.

Gerät (gee-rayt') *n.* implements: tools: utensils.

Geraten (gee-raht'-n) *v.* to prosper: succeed.

Gering (gee-ring') *a.* cheap: mean: small: trifling.

Geringfügig (gee-ring'-feeg-ik) *a.* insignificant: unimportant.

Gerippe (gee-ripp'-erh) *n.* framework: skeleton.

Gern (gairn) *ad.* readily: willingly: with pleasure.

Gerste (gayrst'-erh) *f.* barley.

Geruch (gee-rook') *m.* scent: smell.

Gerücht (gee-reekt') *n.* report: rumour.

Gerümpel (gee-reem'-pel) *n.* trash: rubbish: lumber.

Gesandtschaft (gee-zahnt'-shahft) *f.* embassy: legation.

Gesang (gee-zahng') *m.* melody: song.

Geschäftig (gee-sheff'-tik) *a.* active: busy.

Gescheit (gee-shyte') *a.* discreet: prudent.

Geschenk (gee-schenk') *n.* gift: present.

Geschicklichkeit (gee-schik'-lik-kite) *f.* adroitness: dexterity: skill.

Geschieden (gee-sheed'-n) *a.* divorced.

Geschliffen (gee-shlif'-n) *a.* refined: polite.

Geschmack (gee-shmack') *m.* flavour: taste.

Geschmeide (gee-shmy'-derh) *n.* jewellery: trinkets.

Geschrei (gee-shry') *n.* clamour: outcry.

Geschwätzig (gee-schvet'-sik) *a.* gossiping: talkative.

Geschwind (gee-shvint') *a.* swift: quick: prompt.

Geschwür (gee-shveer') *n.* abscess: boil: sore: ulcer.

Gesellig (gee-zehl'-ik) *a.* convivial: sociable.

Gesellschaft (gee-zehl'-shahft) *f.* company: association.

Gesetz (gee-zehts') *n.* law: rule: statute.

Gesetzlos (gee-zehts'-loos) *a.* illegal: lawless.

Gesetzmässig (gee-zehts'-mace-ik) *a.* legal: legitimate: lawful.

Gesetzt (gee-zehts'-ter) *a.* sedate.

Gesichtsfarbe (gee-zikts'-fahrb-erh) *f.* complexion.

Gesindel (gee-zind'-l) *n.* rabble: mob: unruly crowd.

Gespräch (gee-shprayk') *n.* conversation: talk.

Gestalt (gee-shtalt') *f.* form: figure: shape.

Gestatten (gee-shtat'-ten) *v.* to agree to: allow: permit.

Gestern (gest'-ern) *ad.* yesterday.

Gesundheit (gee-zoont'-hite) *f.* health.

Gewähr (gee-vair') *f.* bail: surety—*a.* aware of.

Gewalt (gee-vahlt') *f.* authority: force: power.

Gewand (gee-vahnt') *n.* dress: garment: raiment.

Gewandt (gee-vahnt') *a.* clever: quick: skilful.

Gewinn (gee-vin') *m.* gain: profit.

Gewitter (gee-vitt'-er) *n.* weather: storm: tempest.
Gewölbe (gee-verl'-b) *n.* emporium: store: shop.
Gewölk (gee-verlk') *n.* cloud.
Gezänk (gee-tsengk') *n.* dispute: quarrel.
Gierig (geer'-ik) *a.* eager.
Giftig (gift'ik) *a.* poisonous: venomous.
Glanz (glahnts) *m.* lustre: polish: gloss: glaze.
Glas (glahs) *n.* glass.
Glasur (glah'-zoor) *f.* varnish.
Glaube (glow'-be) *m.* belief: faith.
Gleich (glyk) *a.* straight: equal: even—*ad.* alike.
Gleichen (glyk'-n) *v.* to resemble: to be like.
Gleichfalls (glyk'-fahls) *ad.* also: likewise.
Gleichgefühl (glyk'-ge-feel) *n.* sympathy.
Gleichgültig (glyk'-geelt-ik) *a.* equivalent.
Gleichheit (glyk'-hite) *f.* equality.
Gleichlaufend (glyk'-low-fent) *a.* parallel.
Gleichsam (glyk'-sahm) *ad.* as if.
Gleichviel (glyk'-feel) *ad.* no matter.
Gleisner (glys'-ner) *m.* hypocrite: sneak.
Gleiten (gly'-ten) *v.* to slide: slip.
Gletscher (glet'-scher) *m.* glacier.
Gliederreissen (gleed'-er-ry-sen) *n.* rheumatism: gout.
Glimpflich (glim'-flik) *a.* lenient: gentle: kind.
Glitscherig (glit'-shair-ik) *a.* slippery.
Glorreich (glor'-ryk) *a.* glorious.
Glück (gleek) *n.* luck: good luck: good fortune.
Glühlicht (glee'-lik) *n.* incandescent lamp.
Glut (gloot) *f.* fire: heat: ardour.
Gnadenfrist (gnah'-den-frist) *f.* reprieve.
Gnadengehalt (gnah'-den-ge-hahlt) *m.* pension.
Gold (golt) *n.* gold.

Goldgrube (golt'-groob-erh) *f.* gold mine.
Goldhaar (golt'-hahr) *n.* golden-hair.
Goldlack (golt'-lahk) *m.* wallflower.
Goldschnitt (golt'-shnitt) *m.* gilt edge.
Goldwährung (golt'-vair-cong) *f.* gold standard.
Gosse (goss'-erh) *f.* drain: gutter.
Gott (got) *m.* God.
Götterdämmerung (gert'-ter-dem-er-oong) *f.* the twilight of the gods.
Gottlob (got'-tlop) *interj.* thank God.
Götze (gert'-tse) *m.* idol.
Graben (grahb'-n) *m.* trench: ditch—*v.* to dig.
Grämen (gray'-men) *v.* to grieve.
Grammatik (grahm-aht'-tik) *f.* grammar.
Granate (grahn-aht'-erh) *f.* shell: grenade.
Gras (grahs) *n.* grass: lawn.
Grasen (grah'-zen) *v.* to graze.
Grässlich (gress'-lik) *a.* awful: dreadful: terrible.
Gräte (grayt-erh) *f.* fish-bone.
Gratulieren (grah-too-leer'-n) *v.* to congratulate.
Grau (grow) *a.* grey.
Grauen (grow'-n) *n.* dread: fear: terror.
Grausam (grow'-zahm) *a.* cruel.
Graziös (grah-tsee-erse') *a.* graceful: polished.
Greifen (gry'-fen) *v.* to seize.
Grimm (grim) *m.* anger: rage: fury.
Grob (grop) *a.* coarse: rude.
Gross (grohs) *a.* great: big: large.
Grosshandel (grohs'-hahnd-l) *m.* wholesale business.
Grossmutter (grohs'-moot-er) *f.* grandmother.
Grosstuer (grohs'-too-er) *m.* boaster: prevaricator.
Grossvater (grohs'-fah-ter) *m.* grandfather.
Grübchen (greep'-ken) *n.* dimple.
Grube (groob'-erh) *f.* mine (coal, etc.): pit: hole.

Gruft — Hassen

Gruft (grooft) *f.* tomb.
Grün (gruen) *a.* green.
Gründen (gruen'-den) *v.* to establish.
Grüssen (grees'-n) *v.* to greet: salute.
Gucken (gook'-n) *v.* to look: peep: spy out.
Gültig (geel'-tik) *a.* legal.
Gummi (gommee) *n.* india-rubber: gum.
Gunst (goonst) *f.* kindness.
Gurgel (goor'-gel) *f.* throat.
Gurgeln (goor'-geln) *v.* to gargle.
Gurke (goork'-erh) *f.* cucumber.
Gürtel (geer'-tel) *m.* belt: girdle: sash.
Gut (goot) *a.* good: well.
Gutartig (goot'-ahr-tik) *a.* good-natured.
Gutdünken (goot'-deeng-ken) *n.* judgment: opinion.
Gutheissen (goot'-hyce-n) *v.* to approve: sanction.
Gutsbesitzer (goots'-be-sit-ser) *m.* landowner.
Gutwillig (goot'-vill-ik) *a.* obliging: willing.
Gymnasium (ghim-nah'-zee-īom) *n.* grammar school.

H

Haar (hahr) *m.* hair.
Haarbürste (hahr'-beers-terh) *f.* hairbrush.
Habe (hah'-ber) *f.* goods: possessions: fortune.
Haben (hah'-ben) *v.* to have: possess.
Habsucht (hahp'-sookt) *f.* avarice.
Hackbeil (hahk'-bile) *n.* chopper.
Hacke (hahk'-erh) *f.* hatchet: hoe.
Hacken (hank'-n) *v.* to chop.
Hafendamm (hahf'-n-dahm) *m.* pier: jetty.
Hafer (hahf'-er) *m.* oats.
Haff (hahff) *n.* bay: gulf.
Haften (hahf'-ten) *v.* to adhere to: cling to.
Hageln (hahg'-eln) *v.* to hail.
Haifisch (hy'-fish) *m.* shark.
Häkelnadel (hay'-keln-ahdl) *f.* crochet-needle.

Haken (hah'-ken) *m.* hook.
Halb (halph) *a.* half.
Hälfte (helf'-terh) *f.* half: middle.
Halle (hahl'-erh) *f.* hall: porch.
Hals (hahls) *m.* neck: throat.
Halsband (hahls'-bahnt) *n.* collar.
Halsbinde (hahls'-bind-erh) *f.* necktie.
Halsbräune (hahls'-broyne) sore throat.
Halten (hahlt'-n) *v.* to hold: keep: resist.
Hammel (hahm'-mel) *m.* mutton.
Hammer (hahm'-mer) *m.* hammer: knocker.
Hand (hahnt) *f.* hand: paw.
Handbecken (hahnt'-beck-n) *n.* washhand-basin.
Handelschaft (hahnt'-del-shahft) *f.* business.
Handgelenk (hahnt'-ge-lenk) *n.* wrist.
Handgemenge (hahnt'-ge-men-gerh) *n.* scuffle.
Handhabe (hahnt'-hahb-erh) *f.* handle.
Handhaben (hahnt'-hahb-n) *v.* to handle.
Handkauf (hahnt'-kowf) *m.* retail.
Händler (hen'dler) *m.* dealer: trader: merchant.
Handleuchter (hahnt'-loyk-ter) *m.* candlestick.
Handschrift (hahnt'-shrift) *f.* handwriting.
Handschuh (hahnt'-shoo) *m.* glove.
Handtuch (hahnt'-took) *n.* towel.
Handwerkerverein (hahnt'-vair-ker-fair-ine) *m.* trade-union.
Hangen (hahn'-gen) *v.* to hang.
Happen (hahp'-n) *m.* morsel: mouthful.
Harm (harm) *m.* grief.
Harn (harn) *m.* water: urine.
Hart (hart) *a.* hard: stern: severe.
Hartleibig (hart'-lipe-ik) *a.* constipated.
Haspe (hahs'-perh) *f.* hinge.
Hassen (hahs'-sen) *v.* to hate: loathe.

Hässlich (hess'-lik) *a.* hateful: detestable.
Hastig (hahs'-tik) *a.* hasty.
Hauchen (how'-ken) *v.* to breathe.
Häufig (hoy'-fik) *a.* abundant.
Haupt (howpt) *n.* head: chief.
Hauptbuch (howpt'-book) *n.* ledger.
Haus (hows) *n.* house: home.
Hausfrau (hows'-frow) *f.* housewife.
Haushältig (hows'-helt-ik) *a.* thrifty.
Hausierer (how'-zeer-erh) *m.* hawker: pedlar.
Häuslich (hoys'-lik) *a.* domestic.
Hausrath (hows'-raht) *m.* furniture.
Haut (howt) *f.* hide: skin.
Heften (hef'-ten) *v.* to fasten: stitch.
Hehr (hair) *a.* exalted: mighty: sacred.
Heil (hile) *n.* health: prosperity.
Heilen (hile'-n) *v.* to cure: heal.
Heilig (hile'-ik) *a.* holy: sacred.
Heilmittel (hile'-mitt-l) *n.* medicine: remedy.
Heilsam (hile'-sahm) *a.* wholesome.
Heilung (hile'-oong) *f.* cure.
Heim (hime) *ad.* home.
Heimlich (hime'-lik) *a.* secret.
Heimwärts (hime'-vairts) *ad.* homewards.
Heimweh (hime'-vaye) *n.* home sickness.
Heirat (hy'-raht) *f.* marriage.
Heiraten (hy'-raht-n) *v.* to marry.
Heischen (hy'-shen) *v.* to demand: request.
Heiserkeit (hy'-zer-keit) *f.* hoarseness.
Heiss (hice) *a.* boiling: hot.
Heissen (hice'-n) *v.* to call.
Heizen (hite'-zen) *v.* to heat.
Held (helt) *m.* hero.
Helfen (hel'-fen) *v.* to assist: help: aid.
Hell (hell) *a.* bright: clear.
Hemd (hemd) *n.* shirt.
Hemmen (hem'-n) *v.* to stop.
Henne (hen'-erh) *f.* hen.
Herab (hair'-aph) *ad.* down: downwards.

Herauf (hair'-owf) *ad.* up: upwards.
Herb (hairp) *a.* harsh: sharp: bitter.
Herbei (hair'-by) *ad.* here: hither.
Herberge (hair'-bayr-gerh) *f.* shelter: lodgings.
Herbst (hairpst) *m.* autumn: harvest-time.
Herd (hairt) *m.* fireplace: hearth.
Herde (hairt'-erh) *f.* herd: flock: troop: gang.
Herein (hair'-ine) *ad.* in this place.
Hereinlegen (hair'-ine-lay-gen) *v.* to swindle: to put in.
Herkommen (hair'-kom-men) *v.* to come here.
Herkunft (hair'-koonft) *f.* arrival.
Hernach (hair'-narhk) *ad.* after that: afterwards.
Herr (hair) *m.* Mr.: master: lord.
Herrisch (hair'-ish) *a.* lordly (in a domineering sense).
Herrlich (hair'-lik) *a.* magnificent.
Herrschen (hair'-shen) *v.* to rule: reign: direct.
Herstellen (hair'-shtel-n) *v.* to produce: make.
Herüber (hair'-eeb-er) *ad.* over here.
Herum (hair'-oom) *ad.* around.
Hervor (hair'-for) *ad.* forward.
Herz (hairtz) *n.* heart.
Herzensangst (hairtz'-n-sahngst) *f.* anguish: despair.
Herzhaft (hairtz'-hahft) *a.* hearty.
Herzig (hairtz'-ik) *a.* dear: sweet: charming.
Herzlich (hairtz'-lik) *a.* sincere: cordial.
Herzog (hairtz'-ohk) *m.* duke.
Hetze (het'-ze) *f.* hunt.
Heu (hoy) *n.* hay.
Heuchelei (hoy'-kel-ly) *f.* hypocrisy.
Heucheln (hoy'-kel-n) *v.* to sham: feign: pose as.
Heuschrecke (hoy'-shreck-erh) *f.* grasshopper.
Heute (hoyt'-erh) *ad.* to-day.
Heutzutage (hoyt'-soo-tahg-erh) *ad.* nowadays.
Hexe (hex'-erh) *f.* witch.

Hexenschuss (hex'-n-shoos) *m.* lumbago.
Hieb (heep) *m.* smack: hit: cuff: blow.
Hier (heer) *ad.* here: now.
Hierbei (heer'-by) *ad.* herewith.
Hilfe (hil'-fer) *f.* help: assistance: aid.
Hilfreich (hil'-fryk) *a.* helpful.
Hilfsmittel (hil'-fsmit'-l) *n.* remedy: help.
Himbeere (him'-bair-erh) *f.* raspberry.
Himmel (him'-l) *m.* heaven: sky.
Himmelfahrt (him'-l-fahrt) *f.* Ascension.
Himmelweit (him'-l-vyte) *a.* a long way off.
Hinab (hin'-ahp) *ad.* down: downwards.
Hinan (hin'-ahn) *ad.* up: upwards.
Hindern (hin'-dern) *v.* to hinder: prevent: stand in the way of.
Hinfahrt (hin'-fahrt) *f.* outward journey.
Hinfallen (hin'-fahl-n) *v.* to fall down.
Hinfällig (hin'-fell-ik) *a.* frail: decrepit: perishable.
Hinfort (hin'-fort) *ad.* henceforth.
Hinken (hing'-ken) *v.* to limp.
Hinlänglich (hin'-leng-lik) *ad.* sufficiently: enough.
Hinnehmen (hin'-nay-men) *v.* to take away.
Hinnen (hinn'-n) *ad.* hence.
Hinreichend (hin'-ry-kent) *a.* sufficient.
Hinschaffung (hin'-shahf-oong) *f.* conveyance: transport.
Hinschwinden (hin'-shvin-den) *v.* to disappear: vanish.
Hinsicht (hin'-sikt) *f.* respect: consideration.
Hinten (hin'-ten) *ad.* behind.
Hintere (hin'-ter-erh) *m.* posterior—*a.* back.
Hinterhalt (hin'-ter-hahlt) *m.* ambush.
Hinterlassen (hin'-ter-lahs-n) *v.* to bequeath: endow.
Hinterlist (hin'-ter-list) *f.* deceit: fraud: cheating.

Hinterrücks (hin'-ter-reeks) *ad.* backwards.
Hintritt (hin'-trit) *m.* death: decease.
Hinüber (hin'-ee-ber) *ad.* across: over.
Hirn (heern) *n.* brain.
Hirnlos (heern'-loos) *a.* brainless: daft: silly.
Hirsch (heersh) *m.* stag: hart.
Hirt (heert) *m.* shepherd.
Hitze (hit'-serh) *f.* heat: hot weather: warmth.
Hitzig (hit'-sik) *a.* ardent: hot.
Hoch (hohk) *a.* high: lofty: noble: exalted.
Hochblau (hohk'-blow) *a.* light blue.
Höchlich (herk'-lik) *ad.* greatly: highly.
Hochmütig (hohk'-meet-ik) *a.* haughty: proud: disdainful.
Hochrot (hohk'-roht) *a.* crimson.
Höchst (herkst) *a.* highest.
Hochzeit (hohk'-tsite) *f.* wedding.
Hof (hohf) *m.* court: yard: alley.
Hoffen (hohf'-n) *v.* to expect: hope: anticipate.
Höflich (herf'-lik) *a.* polite.
Höhle (herl'-erh) *f.* cavern.
Hohn (hohn) *m.* disdain: scorn.
Höhnen (hern'-n) *v.* to mock: make fun of: scoff at.
Holdseligkeit (holt'-sail-ik-keit) *f.* graciousness.
Holen (hohl'-n) *v.* to fetch: secure.
Holperig (hohl'-per-ik) *a.* rough: rugged: harsh.
Holz (holtz) *m.* timber: wood.
Holztaube (holtz'-towb-erh) *f.* wood-pigeon.
Honig (hohn'-ik) *m.* honey.
Horchen (hor'-ken) *v.* to listen.
Hören (her'-ren) *v.* to hear: listen.
Hörrohr (her'-rohr) *n.* ear-trumpet.
Hort (hort) *m.* hoard: treasure: valuables.
Hosenträger (hohs'-n-tray-ger) *m.* braces: suspenders.
Hübsch (heepsh) *a.* handsome: good-looking: pretty.
Hucke (hook'-ern) *f.* back.
Huf (hoof) *m.* hoof.

Hufeisen (hoof'-eye-zen) *n.* horseshoe.
Hügel (heeg'-l) *m.* hill.
Huhn (hoon) *n.* fowl: hen.
Hühnerauge (heen'-er-owg-erh) *n.* corn (on foot, etc.).
Huld (hoolt) *f.* grace: generous: kindness.
Hülflos (heelf'-loos) *a.* helpless.
Hülfsmittel (heelfs'-mitt-l) *n.* remedy: cure.
Hülse (heel'-ze) *f.* husk: pod: shell.
Hummer (hoom'-er) *m.* lobster.
Hund (hoont) *m.* hound: dog.
Hundert (hoond'-ert) *a.* hundred.
Hundertjährig (hoond'-ert-yair-ik) *a.* centennial.
Hüne (heen'-erh) *m.* giant.
Hungern (hoon'-gern) *v.* to feel hungry: to starve.
Hungersnot (hoon'-gers-noht) *f.* famine.
Hupe (hoop'-erh) *f.* motor-horn.
Hüpfen (heep'-fen) *v.* to hop: skip.
Hure (hoor'-erh) *f.* prostitute.
Hurtig (hoor'-tik) *a.* agile: swift: lively.
Husten (hoos'-ten) *m.* cough— *v.* to cough.
Hut (hoot) *m.* hat.
Hütsche (heet'-scherh) *f.* footstool.
Hütte (heet'-erh) *f.* hut: cottage: cabin.
Hyäne (hee-ayn'-erh) *f.* hyena.

I

Ich (ik) *pron.* I.
Idee (ee-day') *f.* idea.
Igel (ee-gel') *m.* hedgehog.
Ihm (eem) *pron.* to him: to it (dative).
Ihn (een) *pron.* him: it (accusative).
Ihnen (een'-n) *pron.* to you: to them (dative).
Ihr (eer) *pron.* to her: to you: her: hers: your: yours—possessive pron. your.
Im (im) *prep.* in the.
Immer (im-mer) *ad.* always: ever.
Immerdar (im-mer-dahr') *ad.* always: for ever.
Immerhin (im-mer-hin') *ad.* always: still.
Immerwährend (im-mer-vayr'-ent) *ad.* endless: ever, lasting: perpetual.
Impfen (im'-fen) *v.* to inoculate: vaccinate.
In (in) *prep.* at: in: into: within.
Indem (in-daym') *c.* and *ad.* because: when: while.
Indes, Indessen (in-des', in-dess'-n) *c.* meanwhile.
Indisponiert (in-dis-po-neart') *a.* indisposed.
Ingenieur (in-shay-near') *m.* engineer.
Ingwer (ing'-veer) *m.* ginger.
Inhalt (in-hahlt') *m.* contents.
Inländisch (in'-len-dish) *a.* home: native.
Inmitten (in-mitt'-n) *prep.* in the midst of.
Insekt (in'-sekt) *n.* insect.
Insel (in'-zel) *f.* island.
Inserant (in-zair-ahnt') *m.* advertiser.
Interesse (in-ter-ess'-erh) *n.* interest.
Intrigant (in-tree-gahnt') *m.* plotter.
Inwärts (in'-vayrts) *a.* and *ad.* inwards.
Inzwischen (int-svisch'-n) *ad.* meanwhile.
Irden (eerd'-n) *a.* earthen.
Irdisch (eerd'-ish) *a.* earthly: worldly.
Irgend (eerg'-ent) *ad.* any.
Irgendjemand (eerg'-end-yay-mahnt) *pr.* anybody.
Irre (eer'-e) *m.* madman.
Irremachen (eer'-e-mahk-n) *v.* to bewilder.
Irrenanstalt (eer'-n-shtahlt) *f.* lunatic asylum.
Irrig (eer'-ik) *a.* mistaken: false: wrong.
Irrtum (eer'-toom) *m.* mistake: fault: error.
Isolieren (ees-o-leer'-n) *v.* to insulate: isolate.

J

Ja (yah) *ad.* yes.
Jacht (yahkt) *f.* yacht.
Jacke (yahk'-erh) *f.* jacket.
Jagd (yahkt) *f.* hunt: chase.
Jäger (yaig'-er) *m.* hunter: sportsman.

Jäh (yay) *a.* sudden.
Jählings (yay'-lings) *ad.* suddenly.
Jahr (yahr) *n.* year.
Jahreswechsel (yahr'-es-vecksel) *m.* New year.
Jahreszeit (yahr'-es-tzite) *f.* season.
Jahrhundert (yahr'-hoondert) *n.* century.
Jährlich (yayr'-lik) *a.* annual: yearly.
Jahrmarkt (yahr'-markt) *m.* fair.
Jähzorn (yayr'-tzorn) *m.* irritability.
Jammer (yahm'-mer) *m.* misery: calamity.
Jämmerlich (yem'-mer-lik) *a.* wretched.
Jammern (yahm'-ern) *v.* to lament: pity.
Januar (yahn'-noo-ahr) *m.* January.
Jäten (yay'-ten) *v.* to weed.
Je (yay) *ad.* ever: each: always.
Jedenfalls (yayd'-n-fahls) *ad.* in any case: at all events.
Jeder (yayd'-er) *pr.* each: every: everyone.
Jedermann (yayd'-er-mahn) *pr.* everybody.
Jederzeit (yayd'-er-tsite) *ad.* at any time.
Jedoch (yayd'-och) *ad.* however: nevertheless: still.
Jeher (yay'-hair) *ad.* always.
Jemand (yay'-mahnt) *pr.* anybody: someone.
Jener (yay'-ner) *pr.* that: yonder.
Jetzt (yetzt) *ad.* now: at present: at the moment.
Johannisbeere (yoh-hahn-isbair-erh) *f.* red currant.
Jubel (yoo'-bel) *m.* jubilation.
Jubeln (yoo'-bel-n) *v.* to rejoice.
Jucken (yoo'-cken) *v.* to itch— *n.* itching.
Jude (yood'-erh) *m.* Jew.
Jugend (yoo'-gent) *f.* youth.
Jugendlich (yoo'-gent-lik) *a.* youthful.
Juli (yoo'-lee) *m.* July.
Jung (yoong) *a.* young: recent: new.
Junge (yoong'-erh) *m.* boy: lad.

Jünger (yeeng'-er) *m.* follower: adherent.
Jungfrau (yoong'-frow) *f.* maid: virgin.
Junggeselle (yoong'-ge-zellerh) *m.* bachelor.
Juni (yoon-erh) *m.* June.
Junker (yoonk'-er) *m.* young nobleman.
Juwel (yoo-vale') *m.* jewel.
Juwelier (yoo-vale-eer') *m.* jeweller.

K

Kabarett (kahb'-ah-ett) *f.* cabaret.
Kabel (kahb'-l) *n.* cable.
Kabine (kahb'-een) *f.* cabin: bathroom.
Kaduk (kah'-dook) *a.* decaying: rotting.
Käfer (kay'-fer) *m.* beetle.
Kaffee (kahff'-ay) *m.* coffee.
Käfig (kay'-fig) *m.* cage.
Kahl (kahl) *a.* bare: bald: barren: bleak.
Kahlheit (kahl'-hite) *f.* baldness.
Kahn (kahn) *m.* boat: punt: skiff.
Kahnfahren (kahn'-fahr-n) *v.* to go boating.
Kai (ky) *m.* quay: pier: wharf: jetty.
Kakao (kah'-kow) *m.* cocoa.
Kalb (kahlp) *n.* calf (cattle).
Kalbfleisch (kahlp'-flysh) *v.* veal.
Kalbsbraten (kahlps'-brahten) *m.* roast veal.
Kalender (kahl'-end-er) *m.* almanack: calendar.
Kalk (kahlk) *m.* chalk: lime.
Kalkul (kahl'-kool) *m.* calculation: reckoning.
Kalkulieren (kahl'-kool-eer-n) *v.* to calculate: reckon.
Kalmieren (kahl'-meer-n) *v.* to calm.
Kalt (kahlt) *a.* cold.
Kaltblütig (kahlt'-bleet-ik) *a.* cool.
Kälte (kelt'-erh) *f.* cold: coolness.
Kamerad (kahm'-er-aht') *m.* comrade.
Kamin (kahm'-een) *n.* chimney: fireside: hearth.
Kamm (kahm) *m.* comb.

Kammer (kahm'-er) *f.* chamber: room.
Kampf (kahmmf) *v.* to fight.
Kämpfer (kem'-fer) *m.* fighter: combatant.
Kanal (kahn'-ahl) *m.* canal.
Kanalisation (kahn'-ahl-e-zayts-yohn) *f.* drainage: sewage.
Kanapee (kahn'-ahp-ay) *n.* couch: sofa: settee.
Kanarienvoge (kahn-ahr'-yen-foh-gel) *m.* canary.
Kaninchen (kahn-een'-ken) *n.* rabbit: cony.
Kanne (kahn'-erh) *f.* can: jug: pot: tankard.
Kanone (kahn'-ohn-erh) *f.* cannon.
Kante (kahnt'-erh) *f.* border: edge.
Kanzel (kahnt'-sel) *f.* pulpit.
Kanzelrede (kahnt'-sel-rayd-erh) *f.* sermon.
Kanzler (kahnt'-sler) *m.* chancellor.
Kap (kahp) *n.* cape: headland: promontory.
Kapelle (kahp'-ell-erh) *f.* chapel.
Kapellmeister (kahp'-ell-my-ster) *m.* bandmaster.
Kapern (kahp'-ern) *v.* to capture.
Kapieren (kahp'-eer-n) *v.* to grasp: perceive: understand.
Kapitel (kahp-it'-ell) *n.* chapter.
Kappe (kahp'-erh) *f.* cap: hood.
Kapsel (kahp'-sel) *f.* capsule: case.
Karbatschen (kar'-baht-schen) *v.* to whip.
Karbonade (kar-bohn-ahd-erh) *f.* mutton cutlet: chop.
Karfreitag (kar-fry'-tahk) *m.* Good Friday.
Karg (kark) *a.* niggardly: parsimonious: stingy.
Kärglich (ker'-glyk) *a.* poor.
Karmesin (kar-mez-zeen') *n.* crimson.
Karneval (kar'-nee-vahl) *m.* carnival.
Karotte (kar'-otte) *f.* carrot.
Kartenspiel (kart'-en-shpeel) *n.* card game.
Kartoffel (kart-off'-l) *f.* potato.
Käse (kay'-ze) *m.* cheese.

Käsemilbe (kay'-ze-mil-berh) *f.* maggot.
Kaserne (kar-zern'-erh) *f.* barracks.
Kasse (kahs) *f.* till: cash register: cash box.
Kassier (kahs'-eer) *m.* cashier.
Kastanie (kahs-tahn'-ye) *f.* chestnut.
Kasten (kahs'-ten) *m.* trunk: case: box: chest.
Kastengeist (kahs'-ten-gyste) *m.* exclusiveness.
Kater (kaht'-er) *m.* tomcat: "hang-over."
Kattun (kaht'-oon) *m.* cotton: calico.
Katze (kaht'-se) *f.* cat.
Kauen (kow'-n) *v.* to chew.
Kauf (kowf) *m.* bargain: purchase.
Kaufen (kow'-fen) *v.* to buy.
Kaufherr (kowf'-hair) *m.* merchant: dealer.
Kaum (kowm) *a.* scarce: scarcely.
Kautschuk (kowts'-ook) *m.* and *n.* rubber.
Keck (keck) *a.* bold: fearless: hardy.
Kehricht (kay'-rikt) *m.* and *n.* dust.
Keichen (ky'-ken) *v.* to gasp: pant: be out of breath.
Keiler (ky'-ler) *m.* wild boar.
Keim (kime) *m.* bud: germ.
Keller (kel'-r) *m.* cellar.
Kellner (kel'-ner) *m.* waiter.
Kellnerin (kel'-ner-in) *f.* waitress.
Kelt (kelt) *m.* axe: chopper: hatchet.
Kennen (ken'-ner) *v.* to know.
Kenntnis (kent'-nis) *f.* information: knowledge.
Kerker (kair'-ker) *m.* gaol: prison.
Kerze (kair'-tse) *f.* candle.
Kessel (kess'-l) *m.* kettle.
Kette (kett'-erh) *f.* chain.
Keuschheit (koysh'-hite) *f.* chastity: purity.
Kicker (keek'-er) *m.* football player.
Kiefer (keef'-er) *m.* jaw: jawbone: *f.* pine-tree.
Kies (kees) *m.* gravel.
Kimm (keem) *m.* horizon.
Kind (kint) *n.* child.

Kinderei (kin-der-ry') *f.* tomfoolery: nonsense.
Kinderpocken (kin'-der-pock-n) *f. pl.* smallpox.
Kindheit (kint'-hite) *f.* childhood.
Kinn (kinn) *n.* chin.
Kirche (keerk'-erh) *f.* church.
Kirchhof (keerk'-hohf) *m.* churchyard.
Kirchspiel (keerk'-shpeel) *m.* parish.
Kirren (kerr'-n) *v.* to tame: induce.
Kirschbaum (keersh'-bowm) *m.* cherry tree.
Kirsche (keersh'-erh) *f.* cherry.
Kirschwasser (keersh'-vash-er) *n.* cherry brandy.
Kissen (kiss'-n) *n.* pillow: cushion.
Kitt (kitt) *m.* cement.
Kitzel (kitt'-sel) *m.* itching.
Kläffen (klef'-fen) *v.* to bark: yelp.
Klagen (klag'-n) *v.* to accuse: complain.
Klamm (klahm) *a.* compact: narrow: restricted.
Klang (klahng) *m.* clang: sound.
Klapp (klahpp) *m.* blow: slap: hit.
Klären (klayr'-n) *v.* to clarify: make clear: purify.
Klatschaft (klaht'-shahft) *a.* gossiping.
Klaue (klow'-erh) *f.* claw: paw.
Klavier (klah'-veer) *m.* piano.
Kleben (klay'-ben) *v.* to fasten: stick.
Klee (klay) *m.* clover: clubs (at cards).
Kleid (klite) *n.* dress: garment: gown.
Kleidung (kly'-doong) *f.* clothing: drapery.
Klein (kline) *a.* small.
Kleinhändler (kline'-hend-ler) *m.* retail merchant.
Kleister (kly'-ster) *m.* paste.
Klemmen (klem'-n) *v.* to pinch: squeeze.
Klettern (klet'-ern) *v.* to climb.
Klientel (klee'-n-tell) *f.* customers: clientele.
Klima (klee'-mar) *n.* climate.
Klinge (kling'-erh) *f.* blade.
Klinker (klink'-er) *m.* brick: tile.

Klopfechter (klop'-fekt-er) *m.* boxer: pugilist.
Klopfen (klop'-fen) *v.* to beat: knock: strike.
Klosett (klohs'-ett) *n.* lavatory.
Knabe (knah'-berh) *m.* boy: lad.
Knappe (knah'-pperh) *m.* workman.
Knasterbart (knahst'-er-bahrt) *m.* grumbler.
Knauserig (know'-zer-ik) *a.* stingy: mean.
Knebel (knay'-bel) *m.* cudgel: gag.
Knecht (knekt) *m.* labourer: servant: vassal.
Kneifer (kny'-fer) *m.* eye-glass.
Knie (knee) *n.* knee.
Knieband (knee'-bahnt) *n.* garter.
Knoblauch (knoh'-blowk) *m.* garlic.
Knochen (knoh'-ken) *m.* bone.
Knochenbruch (knoh'-ken-brook) *m.* fracture.
Knochengerippe (knoh'-ken-ge-rip-erh) *n.* skeleton.
Kober (koh'-ber) *m.* basket: hamper.
Kochen (kok'-en) *v.* to cook.
Kochsalz (kok'-en-sahlts) *n.* table-salt.
Kohl (kohl) *m.* cabbage.
Kohle (kohl'-erh) *f.* coal.
Koller (koll'-er) *m.* madness—*n.* collar.
Komiker (koh'-mik-er) *m.* comedian.
Kommen (kom'-men) *v.* to arrive: come.
Kommis (kom'-mee) *m.* clerk.
Königreich (kern'-ig-ryk) *n.* kingdom.
Konservieren (kon-zayr-veer'-n) *v.* to preserve: keep.
Kopf (kopf) *m.* head: top: summit.
Kopfkissen (kopf'-kiss-n) *n.* pillow.
Kopfweh (kopf'-vay) *n.* headache.
Korkzieher (kork'-tsee-er) *m.* corkscrew.
Kornblume (korn'-bloom-erh) *f.* cornflower.
Körper (kerp'-er) *m.* body: corpse.
Korrekt (kor'-rekt) *a.* correct: accurate: right.

Kosten (kost'-n) *n. pl.* costs: expenses—*v.* to cost.
Köstlich (kerst'-lik) *a.* delicious: dainty: nice.
Kot (koht) *m.* mud: filth: dung.
Kotelett (koht-lett') *n.* cutlet.
Kotflügel (koht'-fleeg-gel) *m.* mudguard.
Kotzen (kot'-zen) *v.* to vomit.
Krabbe (krahb'-berh) *f.* crab: shrimp: urchin.
Krabbeln (krahb'-beln) *v.* to crawl: wriggle.
Krach (krahk) *interj.* crash: smash: bang.
Krachen (krahk'-n) *v.* to crash: smash.
Kraft (krahft) *f.* power: force: strength.
Kräftig (kraft'-ik) *a.* powerful: forceful: strong.
Kraftwagen (krahft'-vahg-n) *m.* motorcar.
Kragen (krahg'-gen) *m.* collar.
Krähe (kray'-erh) *f.* crow.
Krallen (krahl'-len) *v.* to scratch.
Kram (krahm) *m.* retail shop: goods: merchandise.
Krampf (krahmpf) *m.* cramp: spasm.
Krank (krahnk) *a.* sick: ink.
Kränkeln (krenk'-eln) *v.* to ail: to be unwell.
Krankenhaus (krahnk'-n-hows) *n.* hospital.
Krankenwagen (krahnk'-n-vahg-n) *m.* ambulance.
Krankheit (krahnk'-hite) *f.* disease: illness: complaint.
Kranz (krahnts) *m.* wreath.
Kraus (krows) *a.* curly.
Kräuseln (kroy'-zeln) *v.* to curl.
Kraut (krowt) *n.* plant: vegetable.
Krawall (krah-vahl') *m.* riot.
Krawatte (krah-vaht'-terh) *f.* cravat: necktie.
Kreide (kry'-de) *f.* chalk.
Kreis (kryce) *m.* circle.
Kreischen (kry'-shenn) *v.* to scream.
Krempe (krem'-perh) *f.* edge: border.
Kremser (krem'-zer) *m.* charabanc.
Krepieren (kray-peer'-n) *v.* to die.
Kreuz (kroytz) *m.* cross.

Kreuzverhör (kroytz'-fayr-herr) *m.* cross-examine.
Kribbeln (krib'-beln) *v.* to prickle: tingle.
Krieg (kreek) *m.* war.
Kriegen (kree'-gen) *v.* to wage war.
Kriegsgericht (kreeks'-gee-rykt) *n.* court martial.
Krise (kree'-zerh) *f.* crisis.
Kristall (kree'-stall) *m.* crystal.
Kritik (krit'-eek) *f.* critique: review: criticism.
Kritzeln (krit'-zeln) *v.* to scribble.
Krönen (krer'-nen) *v.* to crown.
Kropf (kropf) *m.* gizzard: crop: goitre.
Kröte (krert'-erh) *f.* toad.
Krücke (kreeck'-erh) *f.* crutch.
Krug (krook) *m.* jug: pitcher: ewer.
Krume (kroom'-erh) *f.* crumb.
Krümmen (kreem'-men) *v.* to wind: curve: twist.
Krüppelig (kreep'-pel-ik) *a.* crippled.
Kruste (kroost'-erh) *f.* crust (food).
Küche (keek'-erh) *f.* kitchen.
Kuchen (kook'-n) *m.* cake: tart: pastry.
Kuchenbäcker (kook'-n-beck-erh) *m.* pastry-cook.
Küchenschrank (keek'-n-shrank) *m.* larder.
Küchlein (keek'-lyne) *n.* chicken.
Kuckuck (kook'-kook) *m.* cuckoo.
Kugel (koog'-l) *f.* ball: bullet: globe.
Kugeln (koog'-eln) *v.* to roll: make round.
Kuh (koo) *f.* cow.
Kühl (keel) *a.* cool: fresh: unfeeling.
Kühlen (keel'-n) *v.* to cool: to ice (foods, drinks).
Kühn (keen) *a.* bold: brave: hardy: rash.
Kukumer (koo-koo'-mayr) *f.* cucumber.
Kultivieren (koolt'-e-feer-n) *v.* to cultivate.
Kummer (koom'-mer) *m.* grief: sorrow: trouble.
Kümmerlich (keem'-er-lik) *a.* sorrowful: wretched.

Kundbarkeit (koont'-bahr-kite) *f.* notoriety.
Kundschaft (koont'-schaft) *f.* intelligence: information.
Künftig (keenf'-tik) *a.* future.
Kunst (koonst) *f.* art.
Künstlich (keenst'-lik) *a.* artificial: ingenious.
Kunstlos (koonst'-loos) *a.* simple: natural.
Kunstwolle (koonst'-voll-erh) *f.* shoddy.
Kunterbunt (koont'-er-boont) *a.* gaudy: variegated.
Kupfer (koop'-fer) *n.* copper.
Kuppeln (koop'-pel-n) *v.* to couple: join: unite.
Kur (koor) *f.* cure: healing.
Kuratel (koor-ah-tel') *f.* trusteeship.
Kurator (koor-ah-tor') *m.* curator: keeper.
Kurieren (koor-eer'-n) *v.* to cure: heal.
Kurios (koor'-ee-ohs) *a.* curious: unusual: wonderful.
Kurort (koor'-ort) *m.* health resort: seaside town: watering place.
Kurs (koors) *m.* currency.
Kürschner (keersh'-ner) *m.* furrier.
Kurz (koortz) *a.* short.
Kürzlich (keertz'-lik) *ad.* lately: shortly.
Kurzschrift (koortz'-shrift) *f.* shorthand.
Kurzsichtig (koortz'-zik-tig) *a.* short-sighted.
Kurzweilig (koortz'-vile-ik) *a.* merry.
Kuss (koos) *m.* kiss.
Kustos (koost'-ohs) *m.* custodian: guardian: keeper.

L

Labbern (lahb'-ern) *v.* to lap up.
Lache (lahk'-erh) *f.* laughter: pool: puddle.
Lächeln (lek'-eln) *v.* to smile.
Lachs (lahx) *m.* salmon.
Lackieren (lakk'-eer-n) *v.* to lacquer: varnish.
Lade (lahd'-erh) *f.* box: chest: trunk.
Laden (lahd'-en) *m.* shop: store —*v.* to summon.

Ladendieb (lahd'-en-deep) *n.* shoplifter.
Lagerbier (lahg'-er-beer) *n.* lager beer.
Lahm (lahm) *a.* crippled: lame.
Laib (lipe) *m.* loaf.
Lallen (lahl'-n) *v.* to lisp: stammer.
Lamentieren (lahm'-en-teer-n) *v.* to lament.
Lamm (lahm) *n.* lamb.
Landbau (lahnt'-bow) *m.* agriculture.
Landen (lahnd'-n) *v.* to land.
Landeskind (lahnd'-es-kint) *a.* native.
Landkarte (lahnt'-kart-erh) *f.* map.
Landläufer (lahnt'-loy-fer) *m.* loafer: vagrant.
Landwirt (lahnt'-veert) *m.* innkeeper.
Lang (lahng) *a.* long: tall: lengthy.
Langen (lahng'-n) *v.* to extend: fetch: reach.
Langrund (lahng'-roont) *a.* oval.
Langsam (lahng'-zahm) *a.* dull: late: slow: tardy.
Langweilen (lahng'-vile-n) *v.* to bore: weary.
Lappig (lahp'-pik) *a.* ragged: tattered.
Lärm (lairm) *m.* alarm: noise.
Lass (lahs) *a.* lazy: indolent: tired.
Lassen (lahs'-sen) *v.* to allow: grant: let.
Lässig (less'-ik) *a.* lazy: sluggish.
Laster (lahs'-ter) *n.* crime.
Lästerlich (lest'-er-lik) *a.* disgraceful: shocking.
Latschen (laht'-schen) *v.* to slouch.
Lattich (laht'-tik) *m.* lettuce.
Lau (low) *a.* lukewarm: tepid.
Lauch (lowk) *m.* garlic: leek.
Läufer (loy'-fer) *m.* bishop (at chess).
Laufjunge (lowf'-yoong-erh) *m.* errand-boy.
Laut (lowt) *m.* sound—*a.* loud.
Läuten (loy'-ten) *v.* to peal: ring.
Lauwarm (low'-varm) *a.* lukewarm.

D

Leben 50 **Löschpapier**

Leben (lay'-ben) *n.* life—*v.* to live.
Lebendig (lay'-bend-ik) *a.* alive: living.
Lebensart (lay'-bens-ahrt) *f.* profession: occupation: trade.
Lebensrente (lay'-bens-rent-erh) *f.* life annuity.
Leber (lay'-ber) *f.* liver.
Leberwurst (lay'-ber-voorst) *f.* liver sausage.
Lebhaft (laip'-hahft) *a.* lively: vivacious.
Leblos (laip'-loos) *a.* lifeless.
Lechzend (lekt'-sen) *a.* thirsty.
Lecken (lek'-n) *v.* to lick.
Leder (layd'-er) *n.* leather.
Ledigkeit (layd'-ik-kite) *f.* celibacy.
Leer (lair) *a.* empty: vacant: evacuated.
Legen (lay'-gen) *v.* to lay: place: retire to bed.
Lehm (laim) *m.* clay: loam.
Lehren (layr'-n) *v.* to inform: instruct: teach.
Leib (lipe) *m.* abdomen: body: womb.
Leicht (lykt) *a.* light: slight.
Leichtlich (lykt'-lik) *ad.* easily: simply.
Leichtsinnig (lykt'-zinn-ik) *a.* careless: frivolous.
Leid (lite) *n.* injury: pain: sorrow.
Leiden (ly'-den) *v.* to endure: suffer: put up with.
Leidenschaft (ly'-den-shahft) *f.* passion: ire: rage.
Leider (ly'-der) *ad.* unfortunately.
Leidig (ly'-dik) *a.* troublesome: annoying.
Leihen (ly'-n) *v.* to lend.
Leinen (ly'-nen) *n.* linen (goods)—*a.* linen.
Leingarn (ly'-nen-gahrn) *n.* thread.
Leinöl (ly'-nerl) *n.* linseed oil.
Leise (ly'-zee) *a.* slow: soft.
Leisten (ly'-sten) *v.* to perform: render: afford—*m.* last (shoe).
Leiten (ly'-ten) *v.* to guide: lead.
Leiter (ly'-ter) *f.* ladder: steps —*m.* guide.
Lenken (lenk'-n) *v.* to direct: govern.

Lenksam (lenk'-zahm) *a.* docile.
Lenz (lents) *m.* spring.
Lerche (layrk'-erh) *f.* lark (bird).
Lernen (layrn'-en) *v.* to learn —*n.* learning.
Lesen (lay'-zen) *v.* to read.
Letzt (letst) *a.* last: latest.
Letzthin (letst'-hin) *ad.* finally: lastly.
Leuchte (loyk'-terh) *f.* lamp: lantern.
Leuchten (loyk'-ter) *v.* to illumine: light.
Leuchtturm (loykt'-toorm) *m.* lighthouse.
Leute (loyt'-erh) *m. pl.* men: people.
Licht (likt) *n.* light—*a.* bright: light.
Lieb (leep) *a.* dear: beloved.
Liebchen (leep'-ken) *n.* darling: beloved: sweetheart.
Liebeln (leeb'-ee-ln) *v.* to flirt: fondle.
Lieber (leeb'-er) *ad.* rather. sooner: dearer.
Lied (leet) *n.* song: tune.
Limone (lim'-ohn-erh) *f.* lemon.
Linde (lin'-derh) *f.* lime-tree— *a.* mild: soft.
Lindern (lin'-dern) *v.* to alleviate: soften: ease.
Link (link) *a.* left: left-handed: port (navigation).
Lippe (lipp'-erh) *f.* lip.
List (list) *f.* artifice: cunning: craft.
Litze (lit'-zerh) *f.* lace: braid: edging.
Lob (lohp) *n.* praise: applause.
Lobgesang (lohb'-ge-zahng) *m.* hymn.
Loch (lok) *n.* aperture: gap: hole.
Lockern (lok'-ern) *v.* to loosen: slacken.
Lockig (lok'-ik) *a.* curly.
Löffel (lerf'-fel) *m.* spoon: ladle.
Lohn (lohn) *m.* reward: recompense.
Lokal (loh-kahl') *n.* premises: shop: rendez-vous.
Losbinden (lohs'-bin-den) *v.* to unbind: loosen.
Löschpapier (lersh'-pahp-eer) *n.* blotting-paper.

Lösegeld (lerz'-erh-gelt) *n.* ransom.
Losung (lerz'-oong) *f.* signal: sign.
Luftfahrer (looft'-fahr-er) *m.* aeronaut.
Luftfahrzeug (looft'-fahr-tsoyk) *n.* aeroplane: airship.
Luftig (looft'-ik) *a.* airy: lofty.
Lüge (leeg'-erh) *f.* lie: untruth: falsehood.
Lügen (leeg'-en) *v.* to lie.
Lügner (leeg'-ner) *m.* liar.
Lümmeln (leem'-meln) *v.* to slouch.
Lumpen (loom'-pen) *m.* rag: rubbish: tatter.
Lunge (loong'-erh) *f.* lung.
Lungern (loong'-ern) *v.* to loiter.
Lupe (loop'-erh) *f.* magnifying glass.
Lust (loost) *f.* desire: wish: inclination.
Lüstern (leest'-ern) *a.* longing for.
Lustig (loost'-ik) *a.* jovial: gay.
Lustspiel (loost'-spheel) *n.* comedy.
Lutschen (loot'-shen) *v.* to suck.
Luxus (loox'-oos) *m.* luxury.

M

Machen (mahk'-en) *v.* to make: do.
Macht (mahkt) *f.* might: power: authority.
Mächtig (mekt'-ik) *a.* mighty: powerful: vast.
Mädchen (mayt'-ken) *n.* girl: maiden.
Made (mahd'-erh) *f.* maggot: grub.
Magen (mahg'-n) *m.* stomach.
Mager (mahg'-er) *a.* thin: lean: skinny.
Mahagoni (mahah-gohn'-ee) *n.* mahogany.
Mähen (may'-n) *v.* to mow: reap: cut (crops).
Mahl (mahl) *n.* meal: feast.
Mahlen (mahl'-n) *v.* to grind: pulverize.
Mähne (may'-nerh) *f.* mane (hair).
Mahnen (mahn'-n) *v.* to remind.
Mai (my) *m.* May (month, etc.).
Maiglöckchen (my'-glerk-ken) *n.* lily of the valley.
Makel (mahk'-l) *m.* stain: blot.
Makler (mahk'-ler) *m.* broker: agent.
Makrele (mahk'-rale-erh) *f.* mackerel.
Makulatur (mahk'-oo-laht-oor) *f.* waste-paper.
Malen (mahl'-n) *v.* to paint.
Maler (mahl'-er) *m.* painter: artist.
Malerisch (mahl'-er-isch) *a.* picturesque.
Malz (mahltz) *n.* malt.
Man (mahn) *pr.* one: they: people.
Manch (mahnnk) *a.* many a (one).
Mancherlei (mahn-ker-ly') *a.* different: various.
Manchmal (mahnk'-mahl) *ad.* often: sometimes.
Mandel (mahnd'-l) *f.* almond: tonsil.
Mangel (mahng'-l) *f.* mangle —*m.* want: lack.
Mangelhaft (mahng'-l-hahft) *a.* lacking: defective.
Manierlich (mahn-eer'-lik) *a.* polite: civil.
Mann (mahn) *m.* man: husband.
Männlich (men'-lik) *a.* manly.
Markt (markt) *m.* market: fair.
Marktplatz (markt'-plahtz) *m.* market-place.
Marmel (marm-l) *m.* marble.
März (mairtz) *m.* March (month).
Maschine (mahsh'-in) *f.* machine.
Maser (mah'-zer) *f.* mark, spot.
Masern (mah'-zern) *pl.* measles.
Mass (mahss) *n.* measure.
Massieren (mahss'-ear-en) *v.* to massage.
Mässig (mace'-ik) *a.* moderate.
Mästen (mest'-en) *v.* to feed: nourish.
Matratze (maht'-raht-tze) *f.* mattress.
Matrose (maht'-roe-ze) *m.* sailor: mariner.
Matt (mahtt) *a.* faint: exhausted.
Maul (mowl) *n.* mouth: muzzle.
Maurer (mow'-rer) *m.* bricklayer.

Maus (mows) *f.* mouse.
Mauserei (mow'-zery) *f.* pilfering.
Meer (mair) *n.* sea: ocean.
Meerufer (mair'-roof-er) *n.* sea-shore.
Mehl (mayl) *n.* meal: flour.
Mehr (mair) *a. & ad.* more.
Mehren (mair'-en) *v.* to increase; augment.
Mehrere (mair' - er - re) *pl.* several.
Meiden (my'-den) *v.* to avoid; shun.
Mein, Meine, Mein (mine) *pn.* my: mine.
Meistens (my'-stens) *ad.* mostly.
Meister (my'-ster) *m.* master.
Melken (melk'-n) *v.* to milk.
Melone (mel'-own) *f.* melon.
Memme (mem'-ee) *f.* coward.
Menge (men'-gehr) *f.* multitude.
Mensch (mensh) *m.* man: human being: person.
Menschenscheu (men'-shen-shoye) *a.* shy.
Merkbar (mairk' - bar) *a.* noticeable.
Merken (mairk'-n) *v.* to mark: note.
Merkwürdig (mairk'-veer-dik) *a.* remarkable.
Messen (mess'-n) *v.* to measure: determine.
Messer (mess'-er) *n.* knife.
Messing (mess'-ing) *n.* brass.
Metallisch (mait'-ahl-lik) *a.* metallic.
Metzger (metz'-gher) *m.* butcher.
Meuchelmord (moyk' - ell - mort) *m.* assassination.
Mich (mik) *pr.* me: myself.
Miete (meet'-ee) *f.* rent: hire.
Milch (milk) *f.* milk.
Milchrahm (milk'-rahm) *m.* cream.
Mild (milld) *a.* mild: tender: gentle.
Militär (mil'-i-tair) *m.* soldier —*n.* the military.
Minder (min'-der) *a.* less: smaller.
Mindern (min'-dern) *v.* to diminish: lessen.
Mindest (min'-dest) *a.* least: smallest.

Minutenzeiger (meen-oot'-en-tsy-ger) *m.* minute hand.
Mischen (mish'-n) *v.* to interfere: mix.
Missbilligen (miss'-bil-ig-n) *v.* to disapprove.
Missbrauchen (miss-browk'-n) *v.* to abuse.
Missetat (miss'-ehr-taht) *f.* misdeed: offence.
Missfallen (miss-fahl'-n) *v.* to displease—*n.* displeasure.
Missgunst (miss'-goonst) *f.* envy: grudge: jealousy.
Misskennen (miss'-ken-n) *v.* to mistake.
Misslich (miss'-lik) *a.* doubtful: uncertain.
Mistel (mist'-l) *f.* mistletoe.
Mit (mit) *prep.* with: by—*ad.* also: likewise.
Miteinander (mit-ine-ahnd'-er) *ad.* together: with one another.
Mitgehen (mit'-gay-n) *v.* to accompany: go with.
Mithelfer (mit'-helf-erh) *m.* assistant: helper.
Mithin (mit-hin') *ad.* consequently: therefore: thus.
Mittag (mit'-tahg) *m.* midday.
Mitagsessen (mit'-tahg-gess-n) *n.* dinner.
Mitte (mit'-erh) *f.* middle: midst: centre.
Mitteilen (mit'-tyle-n) *v.* to communicate.
Mittel (mitt'-l) *n.* wealth: means: middle.
Mitten (mitt'-n) *ad.* midway.
Mitternacht (mitt'-er-nahkt) *f.* midnight.
Mittwoch (mit'-vok) *m.* Wednesday.
Mitunter (mit'-oon-ter) *ad.* occasionally: now and then.
Möbel (merb'-l) *n.* furniture.
Möbilieren (mer-bleer'-n) *v.* to furnish.
Mode (mohd'-erh) *f.* mode: fashion.
Modern (mohd' - ern) *a.* modern: fashionable.
Möglich (merk'-lik) *a.* possible: practicable.
Möglicherweise (merk'-lik-er-vyze) *ad.* possibly.
Mohn (mohn) *m.* poppy.

Mohr (mohr) *m.* Moor: negro: blackie.
Möhre (mer'-erh) *f.* carrot.
Mollig (moll'-ik) *a.* cosy: snug: comfortable.
Monat (mo'-naht) *m.* month.
Monatlich (mo'-naht-lik) *a.* monthly.
Mönch (mernk) *m.* monk.
Mond (mohnt) *m.* moon.
Mondsüchtig (mohnt'-seek-tik) *a.* lunatic.
Montag (mon'-tar-sche) *m.* Monday.
Morden (mord'-n) *v.* to murder.
Morgen (morg'-n) *m.* morning —*ad.* to-morrow.
Morsch (morsh) *a.* decayed: rotten.
Most (mosst) *m.* cider.
Motorrad (moh-tohr'-raht) *n.* motor-cycle.
Motte (mott'-erh) *f.* moth.
Mücke (meek'-erh) *f.* gnat: midge.
Müde (meed'-erh) *a.* tired: fatigued: weary.
Mühevoll (mee'-erh-foll) *a.* troublesome: annoying.
Mühsam (mee'-zahm) *a.* troublesome: wearisome.
Mühselig (mee'-zale-ik) *a.* laborious: wretched.
Mulde (moold'-erh) *f.* tray: trough.
Mumpitz (moom'-pitz) *m.* rubbish: nonsense.
Mund (moont) *m.* mouth (of beings).
Munden (moon'-den) *v.* to please.
Mundstück (moont'-shteek) *n.* mouth piece (of cigarette, etc.).
Mündung (meen'-doong) *f.* mouth (of rivers).
Münster (meen'-ster) *n.* cathedral.
Munter (moon'-ter) *a.* vigorous: forceful: lively.
Münze (meen'-tser) *f.* money: coin: mint.
Mürb (meerb) *a.* soft: tender.
Murksen (moork'-zen) *v.* to murder.
Murmeln (moor'-meln) *v.* to murmur.

Mürrisch (meer'-isch) *a.* sulky: sullen: morose.
Mus (moos) *n.* jam (preserve).
Muschel (moosh'-l) *f.* mussel.
Musikalisch (mooz-eek-ahl'-isch) *a.* musical.
Muskat (mooz-kaht') *m. & f.* nutmeg.
Muskel (mooz'-kel) *f.* muscle.
Muss (moos) *n.* necessity.
Musse (moos'-erh) *f.* leisure.
Mussig (mees'-ik) *a.* idle: unemployed: lazy.
Muster (moos'-ter) *n.* pattern.
Mutig (moot'-ik) *a.* courageous.
Mutter (moot'-er) *f.* mother.
Mutwillig (moot'-vil-ik) *a.* mischievous.

N

Na (nah) *interj.* now: now then.
Nabel (nah'-bel) *m.* navel.
Nach (nahk) *ad. & prep.* towards: after: to.
Nachäffen (nahk'-f-n) *v.* to copy: imitate.
Nachbar (nahk'-bar) *m.* neighbour.
Nachdem (nahk-daim') *ad. & conj.* afterwards: according.
Nachdenken (nahk'-deng-ken) *v.* to reflect: muse.
Nachdrücklich (nahk'-dreek-lik) *a.* emphatic.
Nachforschen (nahk'-for-schen) *v.* to investigate.
Nachgiebig (nahk'-gee-bik) *a.* indulgent: yielding.
Nachher (nahk'-hayr) *adv.* afterwards.
Nachhilfe (nahk'-hilf-erh) *f.* help: aid: assistance.
Nachlass (nahk'-lahss) *m.* relaxation.
Nachlassen (nahk'-lahss-n) *v.* to bequeath.
Nachlässig (nahk'-less-ik) *a.* careless: negligent.
Nachmachen (nahk'-mahk-n) *v.* to imitate: reproduce: counterfeit.
Nachricht (nahk'-rikt) *f.* information: news.
Nächst (naykst) *a.* nearest—*ad.* next.
Nächstens (nayk'-stens) *ad.* very soon: shortly.

Nacht — Nochmals

Nacht (nahkt) *f.* night: darkness.

Nachteil (nahk'-tyle) *m.* injury: damage.

Nachthemd (nahkt'-hemt) *n.* nightshirt.

Nachtigall (nahkt'-ee-gahl) *f.* nightingale.

Nachtisch (nahkt'-isch) *m.* dessert: sweets.

Nachts (nahkts) *ad.* at night: nightly.

Nachweisen (nahk'-vye-sen) *v.* to prove.

Nacken (nahk'-n) *m.* neck.

Nackend (nahk'-ent) *a.* naked: nude.

Nadel (nah'-del) *f.* needle: pin.

Nagel (nah'-gel) *m.* nail: pin.

Nagelneu (nah'-gel-noy) *a.* brand-new.

Nagen (nah'-gen) *v.* to gnaw: nibble.

Nahe (nah'-erh) *a.* near: close to: imminent.

Nähen (nay'-erh) *v.* to sew: stitch.

Nähgarn (nay'-garn) *n.* sewing cotton.

Nähren (nay'-ren) *v.* to nourish.

Nahrungsmittel (nah'-oongs-mitt-l) *n.* foodstuffs: provisions.

Namenlos (nah'-men-loos) *a.* unnamed: anonymous.

Narbe (nar'-berh) *f.* scar: mark: blemish.

Narr (nahr) *m.* fool: madman: idiot.

Narrisch (nahr'-isch) *a.* foolish: idiotic.

Nase (nahz'-erh) *f.* nose.

Nass (nahs) *a.* damp: humid: moist: wet: drunk.

Natter (naht'-er) *f.* adder: viper.

Natürlich (naht-eer'-lik) *a.* natural—*ad.* naturally: of course.

Nebelig (nay'-bel-ik) *a.* foggy: misty.

Neben (nay'-ben) *prep.* beside: by: close to: next.

Necken (neck'-n) *v.* to chaff: tease.

Neffe (neff'-erh) *m.* nephew.

Neger (nay'-ger) *m.* negro.

Nehmen (nay'-men) *v.* to accept: receive: seize: take.

Neid (nite) *m.* envy: grudge.

Neige (ny'-gher) *f.* end: slope: dregs: decay.

Nein (nine) *ad.* no: nay.

Nennen (nen'-n) *v.* to name: mention.

Nessel (nes'-l) *f.* nettle.

Nest (nest) *n.* nest: small village.

Nett (net) *a.* nice: neat: pretty: tidy.

Netz (nets) *a.* net: snare.

Netzen (nets'-n) *v.* to moisten: wet.

Neu (noy) *a.* new: novel: unusual.

Neulich (noy'-lik) *a.* recent—*ad.* lately: newly.

Neun (noyn) *a.* nine.

Neunzehn (noyn'-tsayn) *a.* nineteen.

Neunzig (noyn'-tsik) *a.* ninety.

Nicht (nikt) *ad.* not: no.

Nichte (nikt'-erh) *f.* niece.

Nichtig (nikt'-ik) *a.* vain: void: idle.

Nichts (nikts) *ad.* not at all—*pron.* nothing: nought.

Nichtsdestoweniger (nikts'-dest-oh-vayn-ig-er) *ad.* nevertheless.

Nichtsnutzig (nikts'-noots-ik) *a.* useless.

Nicken (nick'-n) *v.* to nod: wink.

Nieder (nee'-der) *a.* low: common—*ad.* down.

Niederlassen (nee'-der-lahs-sen) *v.* to sit down.

Niederschlagen (nee'-der-shlah-gen) *v.* to knock down.

Niederwärts (nee'-der-vayrts) *ad.* downwards.

Niedlich (neet'-lik) *a.* neat: nice.

Niedrig (need'-rik) *a.* cheap: vulgar.

Niemand (nee'-mahnt) *pron.* nobody: no one.

Niere (neer'-erh) *f.* kidney.

Niesen (nee'-sen) *n.* sneeze—*v.* to sneeze.

Nimmer (nim'-er) *ad.* never: at no time.

Nirgend (neer'-gent) *ad.* nowhere.

Nochmals (nok'-mahls) *ad.* again: once more.

Nord, Norden (nord, nord'-n) *m.* north.
Nordost (nord'-osst) *m.* north-east.
Nörgeln (nerg'-eln) *v.* to growl: grumble: complain.
Not (noht) *f.* need: necessity.
Notdringend (noht'-dring-ent) *a.* urgent.
Notieren (noht-eer'-n) *v.* to note.
Nötig (nert'-ik) *a.* necessary.
Notiz (noh'-teetz) *f.* notice.
Notwendig (noht'-vend-ik) *a.* necessary.
November (noh'-vemb-er) *m.* November.
Null (nool) *f.* void: nought: zero.
Numerieren (noom-er-eer'-n) *v.* to count: number.
Nun (noon) *ad. & conj.* at present: now.
Nur (noor) *ad.* only: solely—*conj.* but.
Nuss (noos) *f.* nut.
Nüster (neest'-er) *f.* nostril.
Nutzen (noot'-sen) *m.* benefit: profit: use.
Nutzlos (noots'-loos) *a.* useless.

O

Ob (op) *prep.* above—*conj.* if: whether.
Obacht (o'-bahkt) *f.* care: attention.
Obdach (op'-dahk) *n.* lodging: shelter.
Oben (o'-ben) *ad.* above: upstairs.
Obenan (o'-ben-ahn) *ad.* at the top of.
Ober (o'-ber) *a.* higher: over: upper.
Oberwärts (o'-ber-vayrts) *ad.* upwards.
Obmann (op'-mahn) *m.* chief: inspector: foreman.
Obwalten (ob-vahlt'-n) *v.* to prevail.
Obwohl (ob-vohl') *conj.* although: though.
Ochs (ocks) *m.* ox: bullock.
Öde (erd'-erh) *f.* desert: waste —*a.* deserted: dreary.
Ofen (o'-fen) *m.* oven: furnace: stove.

Offen (of'-fen) *a.* open: frank: candid.
Offenbar (of-fen-bahr') *a.* evident: clear: obvious.
Offerte (of-ayr'-terh) *f.* offer.
Öffnen (erf'-nen) *v.* to open: uncork.
Oft (oft) *ad.* frequently: oft: often.
Oheim (o'-hime) *m.* uncle.
Ohne (o'-ne) *ad. & prep.* except: without.
Ohr (ohr) *n.* ear: eye of needle: eyelet.
Ohrfeige (ohr'-fy-ge) *f.* box on the ears.
Oktober (ok-toh'-ber) *m.* October.
Öl (erl) *n.* oil.
Ölen (erl'-n) *v.* to lubricate: oil.
Onkel (ong'-kel) *m.* uncle.
Optiker (op'-tik-er) *m.* optician.
Orgelspieler (org'-el-shpeel-er) *m.* organist.
Ort (ort) *m.* place: locality.
Örtlich (ert'-lik) *a.* local.
Ost, Osten (osst) *m.* east: orient.
Osterfest (ohst'-er-fest) *m.* Easter.
Ostwärts (osst'-vairts) *ad.* eastward.
Oval (o'-vahl) *a.* oval.

P

Paar (pahr) *n.* pair: couple—*a.* like.
Pacht (pahkt) *m.* farm.
Pack (pah'-ck) *m. & n.* pack: package.
Packwagen (pah'-ck-vahg-en) *m.* luggage van.
Paket (pah-kaite') *n.* packet: parcel.
Paket-boot (pah-kait'-boht) *n.* packet-boat: mail-steamer.
Pakt (pahkt) *m.* compact.
Pantoffel (pahnn-tof'-ell) *m.* slipper.
Papagei (pah-pah-gy') *m.* parrot.
Papier (pah-peer') *n.* paper.
Papierhändler (pah-peer'-hend-ler) *m.* stationer.
Papierware (pah-peer'-vahre) *f.* stationery.
Pappel (pahp'-pel) *f.* poplar-tree.

Papst (pahpst) *m.* pope.
Parieren (pah-reer'-ren) *v.* to ward off: parry.
Paschen (pah'-schen) *v.* to smuggle.
Pass (pahss) *m.* passport.
Passagier (pahss'-ah-shair) *m.* passenger: traveller.
Passen (pahss'-n) *v.* to wait for: suit.
Passend (pahss'-ent) *a.* fit: convenient.
Passiva (phass'-ee-var) *pl.* debts.
Pastete (phass'-tayt-ee) *f.* pie: pastry.
Pastetenbäcker (phass'-tetenbeck-er) *m.* pastry-cook.
Patient (pah-tse-ent') *m.*
Patientin, *f.* patient.
Patriotisch (pah-tree-otisch') *a.* patriotic.
Patzig (pahtt'-sik) *a.* saucy: insolent.
Pausieren (pow'-seer-n) *v.* to pause.
Pein (pine) *f.* pain: torture.
Peinigen (py'-nee-ghen) *v.* to torment: torture: hurt.
Peitsche (pyte'-she) *f.* whip: lash.
Pelz (pelts) *m.* pelt: skin: fur.
Pelzhändler (pelts'-hend-ler) *m.* furrier.
Pendel (pen'-del) *m.* pendulum.
Per (payr) *pr.* per: by.
Periodisch (pair'-re-odd-isch) *a.* periodical.
Perle (pairl'-erh) *f.* pearl: bead.
Perlenmutter (pairl'-n-mooter) *f.* mother-of-pearl.
Person (pair'-zohn) *f.* person.
Pest (pest) *f.* plague: pestilence.
Petersilie (pait-er-zeel'-ie) *f.* parsley.
Petz (pets) *m.* bear: bruin.
Pfad (pfaht) *m.* path.
Pfand (pfahnt) *n.* pawn: pledge.
Pfändleiher (pfahnt'-ly-er) *m.* pawnbroker.
Pfau (pfow) *m.* peacock.
Pfauhenne (pfow-hen-ne) *f.* peahen.
Pfeffer (pfef'-er) *m.* pepper.
Pfefferdose (pfef'-er-doh-zerh) *f.* pepper-pot.
Pfefferkuchen (pfef'-er-kook-n) *m.* gingerbread.
Pfeife (pfy'-fee) *f.* pipe: whistle.
Pfeifen (pfy'-fen) *v.* to whistle.
Pfeil (pfyle) *m.* dart: arrow.
Pfeiler (pfy'-ler) *m.* post: pillar.
Pferd (pfayrt) *n.* horse.
Pferdearbeit (pfayrd'-er-ahr-bite) *f.* hard work (to work like a horse).
Pferdekraft (pfayrd'-er-krahft) *f.* horse-power (thus PS= HP).
Pfiff (pfyf) *m.* whistle.
Pfingsten (pfyng'-sten) *n. pl.* Whitsun.
Pfingstrose (pfyngst'-roh-ze) *f.* peony.
Pfirsich (pfeer'-sik) *f.* peachtree.
Pflanze (pflahn'-tse) *f.* plant.
Pflaster (pflah'-ster) *n.* plaster.
Pflaume (pflow'-merh) *f.* plum.
Pflaumenmus (pflow'-men-moos) *m.* plum jam.
Pflegen (pflaig'-n) *v.* to nurse.
Pflicht (pflikt) *f.* duty.
Pflücken (pfleek'-n) *v.* to pluck: pick.
Pflügen (pfleeg'-n) *v.* to plough.
Pforte (pfort'-erh) *f.* gate: doorway: porch.
Pförtner (pfert'-ner) *m.* porter: doorkeeper.
Pfote (pfoh'-terh) *f.* foot: paw.
Pfühl (pfeel) *m.* pool: puddle.
Photographieren (foh-toegrahf-eer'-n) *v.* to photograph.
Picke (pick'-ee) *f.* pickaxe: pick
Pickelhäring (pick'-el-hairing) *m.* pickled herring.
Picken (pick'-n) *v.* to peck: pick.
Pike (pike) *f.* pike: spade (cards).
Pille (pil'-e) *f.* pill.
Pilz (piltz) *m.* mushroom: fungus.
Pinsel (pin'-zel) *m.* paintbrush: pencil.
Pinseln (pin'-zeln) *v.* to paint.
Placken (plahck'-n) *v.* to patch.
Plagen (play'-hgen) *v.* to plague: annoy.
Plakat (plah'-kart) *n.* placard.
Plappern (plahp'-pern) *v.* to prattle: chatter.
Platt (plaht) *a.* flat: level.

Platzen (plaht'-tsen) *v.* to crash: explode.
Plauderei (plow'-der-ry) *f.* gossip: tittle-tattle: scandal.
Plötzlich (plurtz'-lik) *a. & ad.* sudden.
Plump (ploomp) *a.* coarse: awkward: rude.
Plündern (pleen'-dern) *v.* to pillage: plunder.
Pöbel (perb'-l) *m.* mob: rabble.
Pochen (pok'-n) *v.* to knock: beat.
Pocken (pock'-n) *f. pl.* small-pox.
Pökel (perk'-l) *m.* brine.
Pökeln (perk'-eln) *v.* to salt: pickle.
Polieren (poh'-leer-n) *v.* to polish.
Polizei (poh'-le-tsi) *f.* police.
Polster (pol'-ster) *n.* cushion: bolster.
Polstern (pol'-stern) *v.* to pad.
Poltern (pol'-tern) *v.* to bluster.
Porös (por'-ose) *a.* porous.
Porto (por'-toh) *n.* postage.
Porzellan (por'-tsel-lahn) *n.* china: porcelain.
Posse (pos'-erh) *f.* farce: jest.
Possierlich (pos-eer'-lik) *a.* droll: funny.
Post (poost) *f.* post: post-office: mail.
Posten (poost'-n) *m.* post: station.
Postgeld (poost'-gelt) *n.* postage.
Postschiff (poost'-schif) *n.* mail-boat.
Postzug (poost'-zug) *m.* mail-train.
Pracht (prahkt) *f.* splendour.
Prächtig (prek'-tik) *a.* magnificent.
Prägung (pray'-goong) *f.* coinage.
Prahlen (prahl'-len) *v.* to boast: brag.
Prahlerisch (prahl'-ler-ish) *a.* bragging: boastful.
Praktisch (prahck'-tish) *a.* practical.
Praktizieren (prahck'-tee-tseer-n) *v.* to practise.
Prangend (prahn'-gent) *a.* glittering.
Präsent (pra'-zent) *n.* present: gift: offering.

Präsentieren (pra-zent-eer'-n) *v.* to present.
Prasseln (prahss'-seln) *v.* to crack.
Predigen (pray'-d-ghen) *v.* to preach.
Preis (price) *m.* price: cost.
Preisen (pri'-zen) *v.* to praise: commend.
Prellen (prell'-len) *v.* to toss up: cheat.
Pressen (press'-sen) *v.* to press: squeeze.
Prickeln (prick'-eln) *v.* to sting: prickle.
Primel (preem'-l) *f.* primrose: cowslip.
Prinz (prints) *m.* prince.
Prinzessin (print-sess'-in) *f.* princess.
Pro (proh) *prep.* per: for.
Probe (proh'-berh) *f.* test: trial.
Proben (proh'-ben) *v.* to try: rehearse.
Produzent (proh-doot'-sent) *m.* producer.
Produzieren (proh-doot'-zeer-n) *v.* to produce.
Prolongieren (proh-long-eer'-n) *v.* to prolong.
Prophezeien (proh-fee-tsy'-n) *v.* to prophesy.
Protestieren (proh-test-eer'-n) *v.* to protest.
Protz (protz) *m.* boaster.
Protzig (protz'-ik) *a.* boastful.
Proviant (proh-vynts') *m.* provisions: food: victuals.
Provision (proh-vee-zee-ohn') *f.* commission.
Provisorisch (proh-vee-zohr'-isch) *a.* temporary.
Prozess (proht-sess') *m.* lawsuit.
Prüde (preed'-erh) *a.* prudish.
Prüfen (preef'-n) *v.* to obtain proof: examine: test.
Prügel (preeg'-l) *m. pl.* thrashing.
Prügelei (preeg-l-i') *f.* fight: rough and tumble.
Prügeln (preeg'-l-n) *v.* to thrash.
Prunk (proonk) *m.* pomp.
Prusten (proost'-n) *v.* to sneeze.
Pudel (pood'-l) *m.* poodle.
Puder (pood'-erh) *m.* powder.

Puderquaste (pood'-erh-kvahst-erh) *f.* powder-puff.
Puffen (poof'-n) *v.* to bang: thump.
Pulle (pool'-erh) *f.* bottle.
Puls (pools) *m.* pulse.
Pulsader (pools'-ah-der) *f.* artery.
Pumpe (poomp'-erh) *f.* pump.
Punkt (poonkt) *m.* full stop: point.
Pünktlich (peenkt'-lik) *a.* punctual.
Pupille (pooh'-pill-erh) *f.* pupil of the eye.
Puppe (poop'-erh) *f.* doll.
Pur (poor) *a.* pure.
Püree (peer'-ay) *f. & n.* mashed (food).
Purpur (poor'-poor) *m.* purple.
Purzeln (poort'-sel-n) *v.* to tumble: fall over.
Pute (poot'-erh) *f.* hen turkey.
Puter (poot'-er) *m.* cock turkey.
Putsch (pootsch) *m.* suppressed riot or rising.
Putzen (poot'-sen) *v.* to polish.

Q

Quabbeln (kvahb'-bel-n) *v.* to shake: shiver: quake.
Quacksalberei (kvahck'-zal-ber-i) *f.* quackery.
Quadrat (kvahd'-raht) *n.* square.
Quälen (kvayl'-n) *v.* to torture.
Qualität (kvahl'-ee-tayt) *f.* quality.
Qualle (kvahl'-lerh) *f.* jelly fish.
Qualm (kvahlm) *m.* smoke: steam.
Qualmen (kvahlm'-n) *v.* to emit fumes or smoke.
Qualvoll (kvahl'-foll) *a.* agonizing.
Quantität (kvahn-tee-tayt') *f.* quality.
Quappe (kvahpp'-erh) *f.* tadpole.
Quark (kvahrk) *m.* creamcheese: rubbish: trash.
Quasi (kvah'-zee) *ad.* so to speak.
Quasseln (kvah'-zell-n) *v.* to chatter.
Quatsch (kvahtsch) *m.* nonsense.

Quecksilber (kveck'-zil-ber) *n.* quicksilver: mercury.
Quelle (kvell'-erh) *f.* spring: fountain.
Quengelei (kven'-gel-li) *f.* bother: trouble: nagging.
Quengeln (kven'-gel-n) *v.* to grumble: nag.
Quer (kvayr) *ad.* across—*a.* slanting.
Quetschung (kvet'-schoong) *f.* bruise.
Quieken (kveek'-n) *v.* to squeal.
Quincaillerie (kvin'-kall-er-ee) *f.* hardware.
Quittung (kvit'-toong) *f.* receipt.

R

Rabatt (rah-baht') *m.* discount: rebate.
Rabe (rah'-berh) *m.* raven.
Rabenschwarz (rah'-ben-schvarts) *a.* intense black: jet black.
Rache (rahk'-erh) *f.* vengeance.
Rachen (rahk'-n) *m.* throat: jaw.
Rad (raht) *n.* wheel.
Radeber (raht'-eber) *f.* wheelbarrow.
Radfahrer (raht'-fah-rer) *m.* cyclist.
Radiergummi (rahr-deer'-gomm-ee) *m. & n.* india-rubber.
Radieschen (rahr-dees'-ken) *n.* radish.
Rahm (rahm) *m.* cream.
Rahmen (rahm'-n) *m.* frame.
Rakett (rah-kayt') *n.* racquet.
Rampenlichter (rahm'-pen-likt-er) *pl.* footlights.
Rand (rahnt) *m.* brink: edge: margin.
Rang (rahng) *m.* degree: rank.
Rank (rahngk) *m.* intrigue: trick.
Ranzen (rahnt'-zen) *m.* knapsack: wallet.
Rasen (rahz'-n) *v.* to bluster: rave—*m.* turf: sod: lawn.
Rasend (rahz'-end) *a.* raving: frantic.
Rasieren (rahz'-eer-n) *v.* to shave.
Rasiermesser (rahz'-eer-mess-er) *n.* razor.

Rassel (rahss'-el) *f.* rattle.
Ratlos (raht'-lohs) *a.* perplexed.
Ratsam (raht'-zahm) *a.* advisable.
Ratschluss (raht'-shlooss) *m.* resolution.
Ratte (rahtt'-erh) *f.* rat.
Rattenfalle (rahtt'-en-fahll-erh) *f.* rat-trap.
Raub (rowp) *m.* robbery.
Räuber (royb'-er) *m.* robber: brigand.
Räuberisch (royb'-er-ish) *a.* rapacious.
Rauch (rowk) *a.* shaggy; bristly—*m.* smoke.
Rauchen (row'-ken) *v.* to smoke.
Rauchfang (rowk'-fahng) *m.* chimney.
Rauchhändler (rowk'-hendler) *m.* furrier; fur dealer.
Rauchwerk (rowk'-vairk) *n.* furs.
Raufen (rowf'-n) *v.* to pluck: scuffle.
Rauh (row) *a.* rough: coarse.
Raum (rowm) *m.* chamber: room.
Raupe (rowp'-erh) *f.* caterpillar: worm.
Rausch (rowsh) *m.* intoxication.
Real (ray'-ahl) *a.* real: material.
Realistisch (ray'-ahl-ist-ish) *a.* realistic.
Rebhuhn (rep'-hoon) *n.* partridge.
Rebstock (rep'-sht-ock) *m.* vine.
Rechenkunst (rek'-en-koonst) *f.* arithmetic.
Rechentafel (rek'-en-tah-fel) *f.* multiplication-table.
Rechnen (rek'-n) *v.* to count: calculate.
Recht (rekt) *n.* right: claim.
Rechten (rekt'-n) *v.* to contest.
Rechtfertigen (rekt'-fair-tig-n) *v.* to justify.
Rechtlich (rekt'lik) *a.* just: upright.
Rechtlichkeit (rekt'-lik-kite) *f.* honesty.
Rechtlos (rekt'-lohs) *a.* unjust.
Rechtschaffen (rekt'-shaff-fen) *a.* honest.

Rechtshandel (rekt's-hahndel) *m.* lawsuit.
Rechtsspruch (rekts'-shprook) *m.* verdict.
Rechtswidrig (rekts'-veed-rig) *a.* illegal: unlawful.
Recken (reck'-n) *v.* to stretch.
Redakteur (ray'-dack-ter) *m.* editor.
Reden (ray'-den) *v.* to talk: converse.
Redlich (rayt'-lik) *a.* honest.
Redselig (rayd'-zayle-ik) *a.* chatty.
Reederei (rayd'-ee-ry) *f.* shipping.
Reell (ray'-l) *a.* real: honest.
Referent (ref'-er-rent) *m.* reporter.
Referenz (ref'-er-renz) *f.* reference.
Reflektant (ref'-leek-tahnt) *m.* buyer.
Reformieren (reform'-eer-n) *v.* to reform.
Regelmässig (ray'-ghel-mahs-ik) *a. & ad.* regular: regularly.
Regeln (ray'-ghel-n) *v.* to regulate.
Regen (ray'-ghen) *v.* to stir—*m.* rain.
Regenbogen (ray'-ghen-be-ghen) *m.* rainbow.
Regenmantel (ray'-ghen-mahn-tel) *m.* waterproof coat.
Regenschirm (ray'-ghen-sherm) *m.* umbrella.
Regentropfen (ray'-ghen-trop-fen) *m.* rain-drop.
Regieren (ray'-gheer-n) *v.* to rule: reign.
Regierung (ray'-gheer-ong) *f.* government.
Registrieren (ray'-shis-treee-ren) *v.* to register: record.
Regnen (raig'-nen) *v.* to rain.
Regung (rai'-goong) *f.* emotion.
Rehbock (ray'-bock) *m.* roebuck.
Reiben (ry'ben) *v.* to rub: grind: provoke.
Reich (ry'-k) *a.* rich: wealthy—*n.* empire: realm.
Reichlich (ryk'-lik) *a.* ample: plentiful.
Reichtum (ryk'-toom) *m.* wealth.
Reif (rife) *a.* ripe: mature—*m.* ring.

Reifen (ri'-fen) v. to ripen.
Reiher (ri'-er) m. heron.
Reimen (ri'-men) v. to rhyme.
Rein (rine) a. clean: pure.
Reinheit (rine'-hite) f. purity: clearness.
Reinigen (ri'-nig-n) v. to purify: clean.
Reinlich (rine'-lik) a. clean: neat: cleanly.
Reinlichkeit (rine'-lik-hite) f. cleanliness.
Reise (ri'-ze) f. journey: tour.
Reisebedarf (ri'-ze-b-dahf) m. travelling requisites.
Reisegepäck (ri'-ze-ge-peck) n. luggage: baggage.
Reisen (ri'-zen) v. to travel: journey.
Reisender (ri'-zen-der) m. traveller.
Reisepass (ri'-ze-pahs) m. passport.
Reissen (ri'-sen) v. to tear: rend: split.
Reiten (ri'-ten) v. to ride.
Reiz (rites) m. charm: attraction.
Reizbar (rites'-bar) a. susceptible.
Reizen (rites'-n) v. to charm: attract.
Reizlos (rites'-lohs) a. unattractive.
Reizung (rites'-oong) f. irritation: provocation.
Reklame (ray'-klahm) f. advertisement.
Rekommandiert (ray'-kommahnn-deer-t) a. registered (letters).
Remittenden (ray'-mit-n-den) pl. remainders.
Remittieren (ray'-mit-eer-n) v. to forward.
Rennbahn (ren'-bahn) f. racecourse.
Rennen (ren'-nen) v. to run — n. race.
Rennschlitten (ren'-shlit-n) m. sledge.
Renntier (ren'-tea-ay) n. reindeer.
Renommieren (ren-ohm-eer'-n) v. to boast.
Rentabel (ren-tahb'-l) a. remunerative: profitable.
Rente (ren'-terh) f. income: rent.

Reparieren (rep-ah-reer'-n) v. to repair.
Restlos (rest-lohs') a. unstinting: unsparing.
Retten (rett'-n) v. to rescue.
Rettich (rett'-ik) m. radish.
Rettung (rett'-oong) f. escape: rescue.
Reue (roy'-erh) f. repentance.
Reuen (roy'-n) v. to repent: regret.
Revidieren (ray-vee-deer'-n) v. to examine.
Revisor (ray-vee'-zohr) m. auditor.
Rezensent (ray-tsen-zent') m. critic: reviewer.
Rezept (ray-tzept') n. recipe: prescription.
Rhabarber (rah-barb'-er) m. rhubarb.
Richten (rikt-n) v. to adjust: arrange: plan.
Richter (rikt'-er) m. judge.
Richtig (rikt'-ik) a. right: correct: fair: proper.
Richtung (rikt'-oong) f. direction.
Riechen (reek'-n) v. to smell.
Riegel (reeg'-l) m. bolt: bar rail.
Riemen (reem'-n) m. strap.
Rieseln (reez'-eln) v. to drizzle.
Riesengross (reez'-n-grohss) a. gigantic.
Riesig (reez'-ik) a. enormous.
Rille (rill'-erh) f. furrow.
Rimesse (ree-mess'-erh) f. remittance.
Rinde (rinn'-de) f. crust: bark: rind.
Rinderbraten (rinn'-der-braht-n) m. roast beef.
Rindfleisch (rinnt'-fly-sch) n. beef.
Rindvieh (rinnt'-fee) n. cattle: any silly person.
Ringeln (ring'-eln) v. to curl.
Ringer (ring'-erh) m. wrestler.
Rings (rings) ad. in a circle: around.
Rinne (rinn'-erh) f. sewer: gutter: channel.
Rinnen (rinn'-n) v. to flow: trickle: leak.
Risiko (ree'-ze-koh) n. risk: peril.
Riss (riss) m. tear: gap: crack.

Rissig (riss'-ik) *a.* torn: gaping: cracked.
Rist (rist) *m.* instep.
Ritt (ritt) *m.* ride.
Ritterlich (ritt'-er-lik) *a.* chivalrous.
Rittlings (ritt'-lings) *ad.* astride.
Ritzen (ritt'-zen) *v.* to scratch: graze.
Rizinusöl (reet'-see-noos-erl) *n.* castor-oil.
Rock (rock) *m.* coat: gown skirt.
Roggen (rogg'-n) *m.* rye.
Roh (roh) *a.* rough: brutal: unkind.
Rohr (rohr) *n.* pipe: tube.
Rolle (roll'-erh) *f.* spool: reel: roll: roller.
Rollen (roll'-n) *v.* to roll.
Rollschuh (roll'-shoo) *m.* roller-skate.
Ronde (rohn'-der) *f.* round.
Rosine (roh'-zeen-erh) *f.* raisin.
Ross (ross) *n.* horse.
Rosskastanie (ross-kahss-tahn'-yee) *f.* horse chestnut.
Rösten (rers'-ten) *v.* to roast: toast.
Rostig (ross'-tik) *a.* rusty.
Rot (roht) *a.* red.
Röte (rer'-te) *f.* redness: blush: flush.
Röteln (rer'-tell-n) *pl.* measles.
Rotglühend (rot'-glee-end) *a.* red-hot.
Rotkehlchen (roth'-kayl-ken) *n.* robin redbreast.
Rotsucht (roth'-sookt) *f.* nettlerash.
Rotte (rott'-erh) *f.* gang: band.
Roulieren (rool'-eer-n) *v.* to roll.
Routiniert (root'-n-eert) *a.* experienced.
Rübe (reeb'-erh) *f.* turnip.
Ruchlos (rook'-loos) *a.* profligate: ne'er-do-well.
Rücken (reek'-n) to move: proceed.
Rückfahrt (reek'-fahrt) *f.* return.
Rückfällig (reek'-fahll-ik) *a.* relapsing.
Rückkehr (reek'-kayr) *f.* return.
Rücklings (reek'-lings) *ad.* backward: from behind.
Rückseite (reek'-zy-terh) *f.* back: reverse.
Rückwärts (reek'-vayrtz) *ad.* backwards.
Rückzahlung (reek'-tsah-loong) *f.* repayment.
Rückzug (reek'-tsook) *m.* return: retreat.
Ruder (rood'-er) *n.* rudder.
Rudern (rood'-ern) *v.* to row.
Rufen (roof'-n) *v.* to cry: call.
Ruhe (roo'-erh) *f.* calm: rest.
Ruhelos (roo'-erh-lohs) *a.* restless.
Ruhen (roo'-n) *v.* to rest: pause: stop awhile.
Ruhm (room) *m.* fame.
Rühmen (reem'-n) *v.* to praise.
Rühmlich (reem'-lik) *a.* glorious.
Ruhmwürdig (room'-veer-dik) *a.* praiseworthy.
Ruhr (roor) *f.* diarrhœa.
Rühren (reer'-n) *v.* to move: stir.
Rührig (reer'-ik) *a.* active: stirring.
Rührung (reer'-oong) *f.* emotion: sympathy.
Rummeln (room'-mel-n) *v.* to rumble.
Rümpfen (roomp'-fen) *v.* to pucker: wrinkle.
Rund (roont) *a.* round.
Runzel (roon'-tsel) *f.* fold: wrinkle.
Russ (roos) *m.* soot.
Rüstigkeit (reest'-ik-kite) *f.* vigour.
Rütteln (reet'-tel-n) *n.* jolt: shake—*v.* to jolt: shake.

S

Saal (sahl) *m.* room: hall: saloon.
Saat (saht) *f.* seed: sowing.
Säbel (say'-bel) *m.* sabre: sword.
Sachlich (sahk'-lik) *a.* essential: real.
Sacht (sahkt) *a.* soft: gentle.
Sack (sahck) *m.* bag: purse: pocket.
Säen (say'-n) *v.* to sow.
Saft (sahft) *m.* juice: gravy.
Saftig (sahf'-tik) *a.* juicy.
Sage (sah'-gerh) *f.* talk: rumour.
Säge (sah'-ge) *f.* saw.
Sägen (saig'-n) *v.* to saw.

Sagen (sahg'-n) *v.* to say: tell.
Sahne (sah'-nee) *f.* cream.
Salär (sal'-air) *n.* salary.
Salat (sal'-aht) *m.* salad.
Salbadern (sahlb'-bahd-ern) *v.* to gossip.
Salbe (sahl'-ber) *f.* ointment.
Salm (sahlm) *m.* salmon.
Salopp (sahl'-op) *a.* slovenly: untidy.
Salz (sahltz) *n.* salt: wit.
Salzbrühe (sahlz'-bree-ehr) *f.* pickle.
Salzig (sahlt'-zig) *a.* saline: briny.
Same (sahm'-ehr) *m.* seed: spawn.
Sämisch (sem'-ish) *a.* soft.
Sammeln (sahm'-meln) *v.* to collect: assemble.
Sammet (sahm'-et) **Samt**, *m.* velvet.
Samstag (sahms'-thag) *m.* Saturday.
Sand (sahnt) *m.* sand: gravel.
Sanft (sahnft) *a.* soft: smooth.
Sänfte (senfte) *f.* gentleness.
Sänftigen (senf'-tig-n) *v.* to soften: calm.
Sanftmütig (sahnft'-meet-ik) *a.* soft: gentle.
Sang (sahng) *m.* song.
Sarg (sark) *m.* coffin.
Sattel (saht'-tel) *m.* saddle.
Sau (sow) *f.* sow: swine.
Sauber (sow'-ber) *a.* pure: clean.
Sauer (sow'-er) *a.* sour: harsh.
Sauerkraut (sow'-er-kroot) *n.* pickled cabbage.
Sauerstoff (sow'-er-shtoff) *m.* oxygen.
Säufer (soy'-fer) *m.* drunkard.
Saugen (sow'-gen) *v.* to suck.
Säugen (soy'-gen) *v.* to suckle.
Säule (soy'-le) *f.* pillar: column.
Saum (sowm) *m.* seam: hem: edge.
Säumen (soym'-n) *v.* to hem: edge.
Schade (shahd'-erh) *m.* damage: hurt.
Schaden (shahd'-n) *v.* to damage: harm.
Schadhaft (shahd'-hahft) *a.* damaged.
Schädlich (shay'-tlik) *a.* hurtful.

Schadlos (shad'-loos) *a.* harmless.
Schaf (shahf) *n.* sheep.
Schaffen (shahf'-fen) *v.* to create: produce.
Schaffleisch (shahf'-fly-sch) *n.* mutton.
Schaffot (shahf'-fote) *n.* scaffold.
Schafpelz (shahf'-pelts) *m.* fleece.
Schafskopf (shahfs'-kop-pf) *m.* simpleton: dolt.
Schaft (shahfft) *m.* shaft: handle.
Schal (shahl) *a.* flat: insipid.
Schale (shahl'-erh) *f.* shell: peel: skin.
Schälen (shay'-len) *v.* to peel: shell.
Schalk (shahlk) *m.* rogue.
Schalkhaft (shahlk'-hahft) *a.* crafty: roguish.
Schallen (shahl'-len) *v.* to sound.
Schämen (shaym'-men) *v.* to be ashamed.
Schamhaft (shahm'-hahft) *a.* bashful: modest.
Schamrot (shahm'-roht) *a.* blushing.
Schändlich (shend'-lik) *a.* infamous.
Schanzen (shahn'-tsen) *v.* to fortify.
Scharen (shahr'-n) *v.* to assemble.
Scharf (shahrf) *a.* sharp: keen: acrid.
Schärfe (shair'-fen) *f.* edge: sharpness.
Scharfsinnig (shahrf'-zin-ik) *a.* sagacious.
Scharlach (shahrl'-ahk) *m.* scarlet.
Scharlachfieber (sharl'-ahk-feeb-erh) *n.* scarlet-fever.
Schärpe (shairp'-erh) *f.* scarf: sash.
Scharren (shah'-ren) *v.* to scrape: scratch.
Schartig (shahr'-tik) *a.* jagged.
Schatten (shaht'-ten) *m.* shade: shadow.
Schattig (shaht'-tik) *a.* shady: shadowy.
Schatz (shahts) *m.* treasure.
Schätzbar (shets'-bar) *a.* valuable.

Schatzen (shahts'-n) v. to tax.
Schätzen (shet'-sen) v. to value: esteem.
Schätzung (shets'-ong) f. tax: estimate.
Schauder (show'-der) m. shivering.
Schauderhaft (show'-der-hahft) a. horrible.
Schaudern (show'-der-n) v. to shudder.
Schauen (show'-n) v. to behold.
Schauerlich (show'-er-lik) a. awful: gruesome.
Schaufel (sho'-fel) f. shovel: scoop.
Schaufeln (sho'-fel-n) v. to dig.
Schaufenster (sho'-fenst-erh) n. shop-window.
Schaulustig (sho'-loost-ik) a. curious.
Schaum (showm) m. foam: froth: lather: surf.
Schäumen (shoy'-men) v. to skim.
Schauspielartig (sho'-shpeel-ar-tik) a. dramatic.
Schauspieler (sho'-shpeel-er) m. actor: performer.
Scheck (sheck) m. cheque.
Scheidbar (shyd'-bar) a. separable: divisible.
Scheide (shy'-der) f. sheath: vagina: boundary.
Scheideweg (shy'-de-vaik) m. cross-road.
Scheinen (shine'-n) v. to shine: appear.
Scheinwerfer (shine'-vair-fer) m. search-light.
Schellen (shell'-n) v. to ring.
Schelm (shelm) m. rogue: villain.
Schelmisch (shelm'-ish) a. roguish.
Schelsucht (shel'-sookt) f. jealousy.
Schelsüchtig (shel'-sook-tik) a. jealous.
Schenkel (sheng'-kel) m. thigh.
Schenken (sheng'-ken) v. to fill.
Schenkung (sheng'-koong) f. donation.
Schere (shair'-rerh) f. scissors: shears.
Scheren (shair'-ren) v. to shear: shave.
Scherz (shayrts) m. jest: joke.

Scherzhaft (shayrts'-haht) a. facetious.
Scheu (shoy) a. shy: timid—f. timidity.
Scheuchen (shoy'-ken) v. to frighten.
Scheuer (shoy'-erh) f. barn: shed.
Scheuern (shoy'-ern) v. to scrub.
Scheusslich (shoys'-lik) a. hideous.
Schicken (shick'-n) v. to send: suit.
Schicklich (shick'-lik) a. suitable: proper.
Schieben (sheeb'-n) v. to push.
Schiebkarren (sheeb'-kar-ren) m. wheelbarrow.
Schiedsrichter (sheets'-rik-ter) m. referee.
Schiefertafel (sheef'-er-tah-fel) f. slate.
Schielen (sheel'-n) v. to squint—n. squinting.
Schiessen (shee'-sen) v. to shoot.
Schiesspulver (shees'-pool-fer) n. gunpowder.
Schiff (shif) n. ship: vessel.
Schiffer (shif'-er) m. marines.
Schiffsvolk (shiffs'-folk) s. crew of ship.
Schild (shilt) m. shield.
Schildern (shilt'-ern) v. to paint: colour.
Schildpatt (shilt'-pay-ht) s. tortoiseshell.
Schilf (shilf) n. reed: rush.
Schimmelig (shim'-l-ik) a. musty: mouldy.
Schimmern (shim'-er-n) v. to glisten: sparkle.
Schimpf (shimpf) m. insult.
Schimpflich (shimpf'-lik) a. insulting.
Schimpfname (shimpf'-nahm-erh) m. nickname.
Schinken (shing'-ken) m. ham.
Schippe (ship'-erh) f. scoop: shovel.
Schirmen (sheer'-men) v. to screen: shelter: protect.
Schirmwand (sheerm'-vahnt) f. screen.
Schlacht (shlahkt) f. battle.
Schlächter (shlek'-ter) m. butcher.

Schlachthaus (shlakt'-hows) *n.* slaughter-house.
Schlafen (shlah'-fen) *v.* to sleep.
Schlafgemach (shlahf'-gee-mahk) *n.* bedroom.
Schläfrig (shlay'-frik) *a.* sleepy.
Schläfrigkeit (shlay'-frik-kyte) *f.* sleepiness.
Schlafwagen (shlahf'-vahg-n) *m.* sleeping car (railway).
Schlafzeit (shlahf'-tsyte) *f.* bed-time.
Schlag (shlahk) *m.* blow: hit: shock.
Schlagen (shlahg'-gen) *v.* to beat: kick: strike: kill.
Schlamm (shlahm) *m.* mud.
Schlammig (shlahm'-ik) *a.* muddy.
Schlange (shlahn'-gerh) *f.* snake: serpent.
Schlank (shlank) *a.* slim: slender.
Schlau (shlow) *a.* cunning.
Schlecht (shlekt) *a.* bad: mean.
Schleichhandel (shlyk'-hahn-del) *m.* smuggling.
Schleunig (shloyn'-ik) *a.* quick: alert: swift.
Schlicht (shlink) *a.* sleek: smooth.
Schliessen (shlees'-sen) *v.* to shut: close.
Schliessung (shlees'-soong) *f.* conclusion: end.
Schlinge (shling'-erh) *f.* noose: loop.
Schlingen (shling'-n) *v.* to weave: wind.
Schlitten (shlit'-n) *m.* sledge.
Schlittschuh (shlit'-shoo) *m.* skate.
Schloss (shloss) *n.* castle.
Schlummer (shloom'-mer) *m.* slumber.
Schlüpfen (shleep'-fen) *v.* to slide: slip.
Schlüssel (shlees'-l) *m.* key.
Schmachten (shmahk'-ten) *v.* to starve.
Schmähen (shmay'-n) *v.* to abuse.
Schmählich (shmay'-lik) *a.* insulting.
Schmälern (shmay'-lern) *v.* to diminish.
Schmalz (shmay'-ltz) *n.* lard.

Schmecken (shmeck'-n) *v.* to taste.
Schmeer (shmayr) *m.* fat: grease.
Schmeichler (shmy'-keln) *m.* flatterer.
Schmeissen (shmy'-sen) *v.* to throw.
Schmelz (shmelts) *m.* enamel.
Schmelzen (shmelts'-n) *v.* to melt.
Schmerz (shmayrts') *m.* ache: pain: sorrow.
Schmerzhaft (shmayrts'-hahft) *a.* painful: sorrowful.
Schmetterling (shmett'-er-ling) *m.* butterfly.
Schmettern (shmett'-ern) *v.* to shatter.
Schmiede (shmeed'-erh) *f.* smithy.
Schmieden (shmeed'-n) *v.* to forge.
Schmiegsam (shmeek'-zahm) *a.* flexible.
Schmiere (shmeer'-n) *f.* grease.
Schmierig (shmeer'-ik) *a.* greasy: dirty.
Schmollen (shmoll'-n) *v.* to sulk.
Schmoren (shmor'-n) *v.* to stew.
Schmücken (shmeek'-n) *v.* to adorn.
Schmucksachen (shmook'-sak-n) *f. pl.* jewels.
Schmuggeln (shmoog'-eln) *v.* to smuggle.
Schmutz (shmootz) *m.* dirt.
Schnabel (shnab'-l) *m.* beak (of bird).
Schnalle (shnahl'-erh) *f.* buckle: clasp.
Schnappen (shnap'-pen) *v.* to snap: catch: fasten.
Schnarchen (shnark'-n) *v.* to snore.
Schnaufen (shnow'-fen) *v.* to breathe loudly.
Schnauzbart (shnowts'-bart) *m.* moustache.
Schnauze (shnowts'-erh) *f.* snout.
Schnauzen (shnowts'-n) *v.* to scold.
Schnecke (shneck'-erh) *f.* slug: snail: worm of a screw.
Schnee (shnay) *m.* snow.

Schneeball — Schwermut

Schneeball (shnay'-bahl) *m.* snowball.
Schneegestöber (shnay'-gee-shterb-er) *n.* snowstorm.
Schneid (shnyte) *m.* smartness.
Schneiden (shny'-den) *v.* to cut.
Schneider (shny'-der) *m.* tailor.
Schnell (shnell) *a.* rapid: quick: express: fast.
Schnellzug (shnell'-tsuk) *m.* express train.
Schnitt (shnitt) *m.* cut: slash.
Schnitzen (shnit'-sen) *v.* to carve.
Schnüffeln (shneef'-eln) *v.* to sniff.
Schnupftuch (shnoopf'-took) *n.* pocket handkerchief.
Schnürband (shneer'-bahnt) *n.* lace for shoes, corsets, etc.
Schnüren (shneer'-n) to tie: lace.
Schon (shohn) *ad.* already: so far.
Schön (shern) *a.* beautiful: nice.
Schönheit (shern'-hite) *f.* beauty.
Schopf (shopf) *m.* tuft of hair.
Schornstein (shorn'-shtyne) *m.* chimney.
Schoss (shoss) *m.* bosom: lap.
Schosshund (shoss'-hoont) *m.* lap-dog.
Schote (shoht'-erh) *f.* pod—*pl.* green peas.
Schräg (shrayg) *a.* slanting.
Schrank (shrank) *m.* cupboard.
Schraube (shrow'-ber) *f.* screw.
Schrecklich (shrek'-lik) *a.* terrible.
Schrei (shry) *m.* shout: cry: shriek.
Schreiben (shry'-ben) *v.* to write.
Schreibfeder (shrype'-fay-der) *f.* pen (for writing).
Schrein (shryne) *m.* shrine: cupboard.
Schreiten (shryt'-n) *v.* to step.
Schriftführer (shryft'-feer-er) *m.* secretary.
Schrippe (shryp'-erh) *f.* roll of bread.
Schrubben (shrob'-ben) *v.* to scrub.
Schrubber (shrob'-ber) *m.* scrubbing-brush.

Schublade (shoo'-play-derh) *f.* drawer.
Schuh (shoo) *m.* shoe.
Schuhmacher (shoo'-mahk-er) *m.* shoemaker.
Schuhwichse (shoo'-vick-serh) *f.* shoe-blacking.
Schularbeiten (shoo'-lar-bite-n) *f.* homework.
Schuld (shoolt) *f.* fault: guilt.
Schulden (shool'-den) *v.* to owe.
Schüler (sheel'-er) *m.* scholar: pupil.
Schulterblatt (shool'-ter-blaht) *n.* shoulder-blade.
Schüreisen (sheer'-ry-zen) *n.* poker.
Schürze (sheer'-tsen) *f.* apron: pinafore.
Schüssel (shees'-l) *f.* dish.
Schütteln (sheet'-eln) *v.* to jolt: shake.
Schütten (sheet'-n) *v.* to spill: pour.
Schutzrede (shoots-ray'-der) *f.* apology.
Schwager (shvah'-ger) *m.* brother-in-law.
Schwägerin (shvay'-ger-in) *f.* sister-in-law.
Schwalbe (shvahl'-berh) *f.* swallow (bird).
Schwamm (shvahm) *m.* sponge.
Schwan (shvahn) *m.* swan.
Schwank (shvahnk) *m.* joke—*a.* flexible.
Schwarz (shvahtz) *a.* black: swarthy—*n.* black.
Schwärze (shvairtz) *f.* blackness.
Schwebe (shvayb'-erh) *f.* suspense.
Schwefel (shvay'-fel) *m.* sulphur.
Schwefelsäure (shvay'-fel-soyr-erh) *f.* sulphuric acid.
Schwein (shvyne) *n.* pig: swine.
Schweinfleisch (shvyne'-er-flysh) *n.* pork.
Schweiss (shvice) *m.* perspiration: sweat.
Schwellen (shvell'-n) *v.* to swell.
Schwer (shvayr) *a.* heavy.
Schwerlich (shvayr'-lik) *a.* hardly: scarcely.
Schwermut (shvayr'-moot) *f.* sadness.

E

Schwert (shvayrt) *n.* sword.
Schwesterkind (shvest'-er-kint) *n.* nephew: niece.
Schwiegermutter (shveeg'-er-moot'-er) *f.* mother-in-law.
Schwiegervater (shveeg'-er-faht'-er) *m.* father-in-law.
Schwimmen (shvym'-men) *v.* to swim:—*n.* swimming.
Schwindeln (shvyn'-del-n) *v.* to swindle.
Schwindsüchtig (shvynt'-seek-tik) *f.* tuberculosis.
Schwitzen (shvyt'-sen) *v.* to sweat: perspire.
Schwören (shver'-n) *v.* to swear.
Schwülstig (shveels'-tik) *a.* swollen.
Schwur (shvoor) *m.* oath: vow.
Sechs (sex) *a.* six.
Sechste (sext'-erh) *a.* sixth.
Sechzehn (sekt'-sayn) *a.* sixteen.
Sechzig (sekt'-sik) *a.* sixty.
See (say) *f.* sea—*m.* lake.
Seefahrt (say'-fahrt) *f.* voyage.
Seegras (say'-grahs) *n.* seaweed.
Seekrank (say'-krank) *a.* seasick.
Seekrebs (say'-krapes) *m.* lobster.
Seeküste (say'-keest-er) *f.* seacoast.
Seele (say'-lerh) *f.* soul: mind.
Seeleuchte (say'-loyk-ter) *f.* lighthouse.
Seeräuber (say'-royb-er) *m.* pirate.
Seereise (say'-ry-se) *f.* voyage.
Seestadt (say'-shtatt) *f.* seaport town.
Segelboot (say'-gel-boht) *n.* sailing boat.
Segeln (say'-gel-n) *v.* to sail.
Segnen (sayg'-nen) *v.* to bless.
Sehbar (say'-bahr) *a.* visible.
Sehen (say'-n) *v.* to see: look—*n.* sight.
Sehne (sayn'-erh) *f.* sinew.
Sehnen (sayn'-n) *v.* to yearn for: long for.
Sehr (sayr) *ad.* much: greatly: extremely.
Sehrohr (sayr'-rohr) *n.* telescope.
Seide (sy'-deh) *f.* silk.

Seidenartig (sy'-den-ahr-tik) *a.* silky.
Seidenpapier (sy'-den-pahp-eer) *n.* tissue paper.
Seidenwurm (sy'-den-voorm) *m.* silkworm.
Seife (sy'-fer) *f.* soap.
Seifen (sy'-fen) *v.* to wash.
Seil (syle) *n.* rope: cord.
Sein (sine) *v.* to be:—*n.* being—*pn.* his: its: of him: of it.
Seit (site) *pr. & c.* since.
Seither (site'-hayr) *ad.* since then: hitherto.
Seitwärts (site'-vayrts) *ad.* sideways.
Selbstbewusst (selpst'-b-voost) *a.* self-conscious.
Selbstmord (selpst'-mort) *m.* suicide.
Selbstsüchtig (selpst'-seek-tik) *a.* selfish.
Selig (sayl'-ik) *a.* blissful: happy.
Sellerie (sel'-er-ee) *m.* celery.
Selten (sel'-ten) *a.* rare: scarce.
Senden (send'-n) *v.* to send.
Sendung (send'-oong) *f.* sending: consignment.
Senf (senf) *m.* mustard.
Sengen (seng'-n) *v.* to singe: scorch.
Senkrecht (sen'-krekt) *a.* vertical: perpendicular.
September (sep-tem'-ber) *m.* September.
Sessel (sess'-l) *m.* armchair.
Setzen (sets'-n) *v.* to place: put.
Seufzen (soyft'-sen) *v.* to sigh—*n.* sighing.
Sich (sik) *pn.* oneself: himself: itself: themselves: each other.
Sicher (sik'-er) *a.* certain: sure.
Sicherlich (sik'-er-lik) *ad.* certainly: surely.
Sicht (sikt) *f.* sight.
Sichtbar (sikt'-bar) *a. & ad.* visible: conspicuous.
Sickern (sik'-ern) *v.* to trickle.
Sie (seep) *pn.* she: her: they: them: you.
Sieb (seep) *n.* sieve: strainer.
Sieben (see'-ben) *a.* seven.
Siebente (see'-ben-ter) *a.* seventh.
Siebzehn (seep'-tsayn) *a.* seventeen.
Siebzig (seep'-tsik) *a.* seventy.
Siech (seek) *a.* sickly: infirm.

Sieg (see'-ger) *m.* victory.
Siegel (seeg'-l) *n.* seal: impression.
Siegeln (seeg'-eln) *v.* to seal.
Siegelwachs (seeg'-eln-vahx) *n.* sealing-wax.
Siegen (seeg'-n) *v.* to triumph.
Sieger (seeg'-er) *m.* victor: conqueror.
Silber (sil'-ber) *n.* silver.
Silbern (sil'-bern) *a.* silver.
Singen (sing'-n) *v.* to sing—*n.* singing.
Sinken (sing'-ken) *v.* to sink.
Sinnig (sin'-nik) *a.* sensible.
Sinnlich (sin'-lik) *a.* sensual.
Sinnlos (sin'-loos) *n.* thoughtless.
Sinnreich (sin'-ryk) *a.* sensible.
Sitte (sitt'-erh) *f.* custom—*pl.* manners.
Sittenlos (sitt'-n-loos) *a.* immoral.
Sittenverfeinerung (sitt'-n-fair-fyne'-er-oong) *f.* civilization.
Sittig (sitt'-ik) *a.* well bred: modest.
Sittsam (sitt'-zahm) *a.* modest: chaste: respectable.
Sitz (sits) *m.* seat: chair.
Sitzen (sit'-sen) *v.* to sit: suit.
Skizze (skitt'-serh) *f.* sketch.
Sklave (sklah'-ferh) *m.* slave.
Sklaverei (sklah'-fery) *f.* slavery.
Smaragd (smar'-rahkt) *m.* emerald.
So (soh) *ad. & c.* so: thus: such.
Socke (sohck'-erh) *f.* sock.
Soda (soh'-dah) *f.* soda.
Sofern (soh'-fayrn) *ad. & c.* so far: as far as: in so far as.
Sofort (soh-fort') *ad.* forthwith.
Sogleich (soh-glyk') *ad.* immediately.
Sohle (soh'-ler) *f.* sole.
Sohn (sohn) *m.* son.
Solcher, Solche, Solches (sol-ker) *pn.* such.
Sold (solt) *m.* salary: pay.
Soldat (sol-dayht') *m.* soldier.
Solid (sol'-eed) *a.* solid: safe.
Sollen (soll'-n) *v.* to owe.
Somit (soh'-mitt) *ad.* therefore: consequently.
Sommer (somm'-er) *m.* summer.

Sommersprosse (somm'-er-sphross-erh) *f.* freckle.
Sondern (son'-dern) *v.* to sever, separate.
Sonnabend (sonn'-ah-bent) *m.* Saturday.
Sonne (sonn'-erh) *f.* sun.
Sonnenaufgang (sonn'-n-owf'-gahng) *m.* sunrise.
Sonnenblume (sonn'-n-bloom-erh) *f.* sunflower.
Sonnenlicht (sonn'-n-likt) *n.* sunlight.
Sonnenschein (sonn'-n-shyne) *m.* sunshine.
Sonnenstich (sonn'-n-shtik) *m.* sunstroke.
Sonnenuntergang (sonn'-n-oont-er-gahng) *m.* sunset.
Sonnig (sonn'-ik) *a.* sunny: bright.
Sonntage (sonn'-tahg) *m.* Sunday.
Sonst (sonst) *ad.* otherwise: besides.
Sorge (sor'-ge) *f.* sorrow: anxiety.
Sorgen (sor'-gen) *v.* to fear: be anxious.
Sorgenvoll (sor'-gen-foll) *a.* anxious.
Sorgfältig (sorg'-fell-tik) *a.* careful.
Sorglos (sorg'-loos) *a.* careless.
Sorgsam (sorg'-zahm) *a.* careful: cautious.
Sorte (sort'-erh) *f.* kind: sort.
Spähen (shpay'-n) *v.* to spy.
Spann (shpahn) *m.* instep.
Spannen (shpahn'-n) *v.* to stretch: strain.
Sparen (shpahr'-n) *v.* to save.
Spargel (shpahr'-gel) *m.* asparagus.
Sparkasse (shpahr'-kahss-erh) *f.* savings-bank.
Sparsam (shpahr'-zahm) *a.* thrifty.
Spass (shpahss) *m.* jest: joke.
Spassmacher (shpahss'-məhk-er) *m.* jester.
Spät (shpayt) *a. & ad.* late.
Spaten (shpaht'-n) *m.* spade.
Spatz (shpahts) *m.* sparrow.
Spazieren (shpaht-zeer-n) *v.* to walk.
Speck (shpeck) *m.* bacon: lard.
Spedieren (shpay-dee'-ren) *v* to expedite: forward.

Speer (shpayr) *m.* spear: lance.
Speichern (shpy'-kern) *v.* to hoard.
Speien (shpy'-n) *v.* to spit: vomit.
Speise (shpy'-zerh) *f.* food: fare.
Speisekammer (shpy'-zerh-kahm-er) *f.* larder.
Speisekarte (shpy'-zerh-kart-erh) *f.* bill of fare.
Speisesaal (shpy'-zerh-zahl) *m.* dining-room.
Speisezettel (shpy'-zerh-tset-tel) *m.* menu: bill of fare.
Spende (shpend'-erh) *f.* alms.
Sperling (shpayr'-ling) *m.* sparrow.
Sperren (shpayr'-n) *v.* to bar: obstruct.
Spesen (shpay'-sen) *f. pl.* expenses.
Spesenfrei (shpay'-sen-fry) *a.* exempt.
Spezerei (shpay'-tse-ry) *f.* grocery.
Spiegel (shpeeg'-l) *m.* mirror: looking glass.
Spiegelei (shpeeg'-l-i) *n.* fried egg.
Spiel (shpeel) *n.* game: sport.
Spielbrett (shpeel'-bret) *n.* draught-board.
Spielen (shpeel'-n) *v.* to play: perform.
Spieler (shpeel'-er) *m.* player.
Spielkränzchen (shpeel'-krents-ken) *n.* card party.
Spiessig (shpees'-ik) *a.* pointed.
Spinat (shpeen'-aht) *m.* spinach.
Spinne (shpin'-nerh) *f.* spider.
Spinnengewebe (shpin'-n-vaib-erh) *n.* cobweb.
Spion (shpee-ohnn') *m.* spy.
Spionieren (shpee-ohn-eer'-n) *v.* to spy—*n.* spying.
Spital (shpee-tahl') *n.* hospital.
Spottname (shpot'-nahm-erh) *m.* nickname.
Sprache (shprahk'-erh) *f.* language: speech.
Sprachlos (shprahk'-loos) *a.* speechless.
Sprechen (shprek'-n) *v.* to speak: pronounce: talk
Sprengen (shpreng'-n) *v.* to sprinkle: scatter.

Spriessen (shpress'-n) *v.* to germinate.
Springbrunnen (shpryng'-broon-n) *m.* fountain.
Springfeder (shpryng'-fay-der) *f.* spring.
Spritze (shpritz'-erh) *f.* syringe: squirt.
Spritzenleute (shpritz'-n-loyt-erh) *pl.* firemen.
Spröde (shprerd'-erh) *f.* prude.
Spruch (shprook) *m.* sentence.
Stachel (shtak'-l) *m.* thorn: sting: prickle.
Stachelbeere (shtak'-l-bayr-erh) *f.* gooseberry.
Stacheln (shtak'-eln) *v.* to goad.
Stachelschwein (shtak'-l-shvyne) *n.* porcupine.
Stadt (shtaht) *f.* town: city.
Stadthaus (shtaht'-howss) *n.* town hall.
Stählern (shtayl'-ern) *a.* steel: steely.
Stahlwaare (shtahl'-vahr-erh) *f.* hardware.
Stall (shtahl) *m.* stable: kennel.
Stammeln (shtahm'-eln) *v.* to stammer: stutter—*n.* stammering.
Stammvater (shtahm'-vat-er) *m.* ancestor.
Stand (stahnt) *m.* state: condition: rank.
Standhaftig (stahnt'-hahft-ik) *a.* steady: firm: stout.
Stange (shtahng'-erh) *f.* pole: perch.
Stänkern (shtenk'-ern) *v.* to wrangle: quarrel.
Stanniol (shtan'-yohle) *n.* tinfoil.
Star (shtar) *m.* starling.
Stark (shtark) *a.* robust: vigorous: healthy.
Stärke (shtayrk'-erh) *f.* vigour: energy.
Stärken (shtayrk'-n) *v.* to strengthen.
Starr (shtarr) *a.* stiff: rigid.
Starrsinnig (shtarr'-zin-ik) *a.* stubborn.
Stattlichkeit (shtaht'-lik-kite) *f.* magnificence.
Staub (shtowp) *m.* dust.
Staubig (shtowp'-ik) *a.* dusty
Stecken (shteck'-n) *v.* to put: place.

Steckenpferd (shteck'-n-pfayrt) *n.* hobby.
Stecknadel (shteck'-nahd-l) *f.* pin.
Steg (shtayk) *m.* bridge.
Stehlen (shtay'-len) *v.* to steal.
Stehler (shtay'-ler) *m.* thief.
Steif (shtiffe) *a.* stiff: rigid.
Steifen (shtiffe'-n) *v.* to stiffen.
Steig (shtyke) *m.* footpath.
Steigen (shty'-gen) *v.* to mount: ascend.
Steigern (shty'-gern) *v.* to raise.
Steigung (shty'-goong) *f.* ascent: incline.
Steil (shtyle) *a.* steep.
Steinbild (shtine'-bilt) *n.* statue.
Steinflachs (shtine'-flahx) *m.* asbestos.
Steinklippe (shtine'-klip-erh) *f.* cliff.
Steinnuss (shtine'-noos) *f.* brazil nut.
Steinöl (shtine'-erl) *n.* petroleum.
Stelle (shtel'-erh) *f.* place: situation: spot.
Stellen (shtel'-len) *v.* to put: place.
Stelze (shtel'-ser) *f.* stilt.
Stemmeisen (shtem'-mi-zen) *n.* chisel.
Stemmen (shtem'-n) *v.* to stem: dam.
Stempeln (shtem'-peln) *v.* to stamp.
Stengel (shten'-gel) *m.* stem: stalk.
Steppdecke (shtep'-deck-erh) *f.* quilt.
Sterben (shtayr'-ben) *v.* to die.
Sterbenskrank (shtayr'-benskrahnk) *a.* on the point of death.
Stern (shtayrn) *m.* star: asterisk.
Sternkunde (shtayrn'-koonder) *f.* astronomy.
Stetig (shtayt'-ik) *a.* steady: repeated.
Stets (shtayts) *ad.* ever: always.
Steuern (shtoy'-ern) *v.* to steer (vessel).
Stich (shtik) *m.* sting: bite: stitch (in one's side).
Sticheln (shtik'-eln) *v.* to sneer.
Sticken (shtic'-ken) *v.* to embroider.
Stickerei (shtic'-ker-ry) *f.* embroidery.
Stickig (shtick'-ik) *a.* choking.
Stickstoff (shtick'-shtoff) *m.* nitrogen.
Stiefel (shteef'-l) *m.* boot.
Stiefmütterchen (shteef'-meet-er-ken) *n.* pansy.
Stiege (steeg'-erh) *f.* stairs.
Stieglitz (shteeg'-litz) *m.* goldfinch.
Stier (shteer) *m.* steer: bull.
Stieren (shteer'-n) *v.* to stare.
Stift (shtift) *m.* pencil: peg: apprentice.
Stiften (shtift'-n) *v.* to create: found: originate.
Still (shtill) *a.* still: silent: quiet.
Stimme (shtim'-erh) *f.* voice.
Stinken (shtink'-n) *v.* to stink.
Stinkend (shtink'-ent) *a.* & *ad.* stinking.
Stint (shtint) *m.* smelt.
Stirn (shteern) *f.* brow: forehead.
Stoben (shtob'-n) *v.* to stew.
Stocher (shtok'-er) *m.* toothpick.
Stochern (shtok'-ern) *v.* to pick: poke.
Stockig (shtok'-ik) *a.* mouldy: fusty: musty.
Stockwerk (shtok'-vairk) *n.* flat: storey.
Stoff (shtof) *m.* stuff: material: cloth.
Stoffel (shtof'-fel) *m.* blockhead.
Stöhnen (shter'-nen) *v.* to groan.
Stolpern (shtol'-pern) *v.* to stumble.
Stolz (shtoltz) *m.* pride—*a.* proud: haughty.
Stopfen (shtop'-fen) *v.* to stuff: fill: cram: charge.
Stöpsel (shterp'-sel) *m.* stopper.
Stöpseln (shterp'-sel-n) *v.* to cork.
Stör (shter) *m.* sturgeon.
Stören (shter'-n) *v.* to disturb: stir: interrupt.
Störrig (shter'-ik) *a.* stubborn.
Stossen (shtoh'-sen) *v.* to push.
Stosszahn (shtohs'-tsahn) *m.* tusk.
Stottern (shtot'-ern) *v.* to stammer: stutter.
Strafe (shtrayf'-erh) *f.* punishment: penalty.

Strafen (shtrayf'-n) *v.* to punish: chastise.
Strafgeld (shtrayf'-gelt) *n.* fine: penalty.
Straflos (shtrayf'-loos) *a.* guiltless.
Strahl (shtrahl) *m.* beam: ray.
Strahlend (shtrahl'-ent) *a.* radiant.
Strähne (shtrayn'-erh) *f.* skein: hank.
Strampeln (shtramp'-eln) *v.* to trample.
Strand (shtrahnt) *m.* strand: beach.
Strang (shtrahng) *m.* rope: cord.
Strapaze (shtrah'-paht-ze) *f.* toil: drudgery: hardship.
Strasse (shtrahss'-erh) *f.* street.
Strassenfeger (shtrahss'-n-fayg-er) *m.* scavenger.
Strecken (shtreck'-n) *v.* to stretch: extend.
Streich (shtryk) *m.* stroke: blow.
Streicheln (shtry'-keln) *v.* to caress.
Streichriemen (shtryk'-ry-men) *m.* razor-strop.
Streifig (shtrife'-ik) *a.* streaky: striped: lined.
Streit (shtrite) *m.* dispute.
Streiten (shtrite'-n) *v.* to fight: dispute: quarrel.
Streitlustig (shtrite'-loost-ik) *a.* quarrelsome.
Strenge (shtreng'-erh) *a. & ad.* severe: strong—*f.* sternness.
Strick (shtrick) *m.* rope: cord.
Stricken (shtrick'-n) *v.* to knit: ensnare.
Strickerei (shtrick'-ery) *f.* knitting.
Stroh (shtroh) *n.* straw: thatch.
Strom (shtrohm) *m.* stream: current.
Stromfall (shtrohm'-fahl) *m.* cataract.
Strumpf (shtroompf) *m.* stocking.
Strumpfband (shtroompf'-bahnt) *n.* garter.
Strumpfwaren (shtroompf'-vahr-n) *pl.* hosiery.
Struppig (shtroop'-ik) *a.* rugged: rough.
Stube (shtoob'-erh) *f.* room: chamber.
Stubenmädchen (shtoob'-en-mate-ken) *n.* chamber-maid.
Stubenofen (shtoob'-en-oh-fen) *m.* stove.
Studieren (shtood'-eer-n) *v.* to study—*n.* study.
Stufenweise (shtoof'-n-vy-ze) *ad.* gradually.
Stuhl (shtool) *m.* chair: seat: stool.
Stumm (shtoom) *a.* dumb.
Stummheit (shtoom'-hite) *f.* dumbness.
Stumpf (shtoompf) *a.* blunt: obtuse.
Stumpfsinnig (shtoompf'-zin-ik) *a.* stupid.
Sturm (shtoorm) *m.* storm: fury: tumult.
Stürmend (shteerm'-ent) *a.* impetuous.
Sturmwetter (shtoorm'-vet-er) *n.* stormy weather.
Stürze (shteert'-se) *f.* cover: lid: top.
Stute (shtoot'-erh) *f.* mare.
Stutzig (shtoots'-ik) *a.* startled: surprised.
Subtrahieren (soop'-trah-heer'-n) *v.* to subtract.
Suche (sook'-erh) *f.* search: quest.
Suchen (sook'-n) *v.* to seek: search.
Süd (seet) *m.* south.
Sudeln (sood'-eln) *v.* to soil: foul.
Südlich (seet'-lik) *a.* southern.
Südwärts (seet'-vair-ts) *a.* southward.
Summe (som'-merh) *f.* sum: total.
Summen (som'-men) *v.* to hum—*n.* humming.
Sumpf (sompf) *m.* swamp: bog: marsh.
Sund (soont) *m.* strait: sound.
Sünde (seen'-derh) *f.* sin: offence.
Sünder (seen'-der) *m.* sinner.
Sündigen (seen'-dig-n) *v.* to sin.
Superfein (soop'-er-fyne) *a.* superfine.
Suppe (soop'-erh) *f.* soup.
Suppenlöffel (soop'-n-lerff-l) *m.* tablespoon.
Süss (sees) *a.* sweet.
Süssen (sees'-n) *v.* to sweeten.

Tabak 71 Tiergarten

T

Tabak (tah'-bahk) *m.* tobacco.
Tabaksbeutel (tah'-bahks-boy'-tel) *m.* tobacco-pouch.
Tabakshändler (tah'-bahks-hend'-ler) *m.* tobacconist.
Tabakspfeife (tah'-bahks-pfy'-ferh) *f.* tobacco-pipe.
Tadel (tah'-del) *m.* blame: fault.
Tadelfrei (tah'-del-fry) *a.* blameless.
Tadellos (tah'-del-lohs) *a.* blameless.
Tadeln (tah'-del-n) *v.* to blame.
Tafel (tah'-fel) *f.* table.
Tafeltuch (tah'-fel-took) *n.* table-cloth.
Tag (tahg) *m.* day: daylight.
Tageblatt (tahg'-eh-blaht) *n.* daily paper.
Tagebuch (tahg'-erh-book) *n.* diary.
Tagen (tahg'-n) *v.* to dawn.
Tagesanbruch (tahg'-es-ahn'-brook) *m.* daybreak.
Täglich (tayg'-lik) *a.* daily: every day.
Takt (tahkt) *m.* time: measure.
Taktvoll (tahkt'-foll) *a.* discreet.
Talg (tahlk) *m.* tallow: grease.
Tante (tahnt'-erh) *f.* aunt.
Tanz (tahnts) *m.* dance: ball.
Tanzboden (tahnts'-boh-den) *m.* ballroom.
Tanzen (tahnt'-sen) *v.* to dance.
Tapet (tahp'-ayte) *n.* carpet.
Tapfer (tahp'-fer) *a.* brave: courageous.
Tappe (tahp'-erh) *f.* paw: claw.
Tasche (tahsh'-erh) *f.* pocket: purse: wallet: handbag.
Taschendieb (tahsh'-n-deep) *m.* pickpocket.
Taschenspieler (tahsh'-n-shpeel-er) *m.* conjurer.
Taschenwörterbuch (tahsh'-n-vert'-er-book) *n.* pocket dictionary.
Tasse (tahss'-erh) *f.* cup.
Tasten (tahst'-n) *v.* to feel: fumble.
Tätig (tayt'-ik) *a.* active: busy.
Tätlich (tayt'-lik) *a.* violent.
Tätlichkeit (tayt'-lik-kite) *f.* violence.
Tatze (taht'-se) *f.* paw: claw.
Tau (tow) *n.* cable: rope.
Taub (towp) *a.* deaf.

Taube (towb'-erh) *f.* pigeon: dove.
Taubstumm (towp'-shtoom) *a.* deaf and dumb.
Tauchen (towk'-n) *v.* to dive.
Taucher (towk'-er) *m.* diver.
Taufen (tow'-fen) *v.* to baptize.
Taufname (towf'-nahm-erh) *m.* Christian-name.
Taufpate (towf'-paht-erh) *m.* god-father.
Taumelig (towm'-el-ik) *a.* reeling: staggering.
Taumeln (towm'-eln) *v.* to stagger.
Tauschen (towsh'-n) *v.* to exchange.
Täuschen (toysh'-n) *v.* to deceive: cheat.
Tausend (towz'-ent) *a.* thousand—*n.* thousand.
Tausendmal (towz'-ent-mahl) *ad.* thousand times.
Tauwerk (tow'-vayrk) *n.* rigging.
Taxe (tahx'-erh) *f.* tax: impost.
Taxieren (tahx'-eer-n) *v.* to tax: value.
Tee (tay) *m.* tea.
Teekanne (tay'-kahn-erh) *f.* tea-pot.
Teer (tayr) *m.* tar.
Teich (tyke) *m.* pond: pool: tarn.
Teller (tel'-er) *m.* plate: tray: platter.
Temperatur (temp'-er-ahtoor) *f.* temperature.
Tempo (temp'-o) *n.* time: measure.
Terminweise (tairm'-een-vyze) *ad.* by instalments.
Terpentin (tair'-pen-teen') *m.* turpentine.
Teuer (toy'-er) *a.* dear: costly.
Teufel (toy'-fel) *m.* devil.
Teufelisch (toy'-fel-ish) *a.* devilish: fiendish.
Theater (tay-ah'-ter) *n.* theatre.
Thron (trohn) *m.* throne.
Tief (teef) *a.* deep: profound.
Tiefsinnig (teef'-zin-ik) *a.* thoughtful.
Tier (teer) *n.* animal: beast.
Tierarzt (teer'-artst) *m.* veterinary surgeon.
Tiergarten (teer'-gart-n) *m.* Zoo: zoological gardens.

Tiger — Trommel

Tiger (teeg'-er) *m.* tiger.
Tilgen (til'-gen) *v.* to extinguish.
Tinte (tin'-te) *f.* ink: tint.
Tintenfass (tint'-n-fahss) *n.* inkstand.
Tintenfleck (tint'-n-fleck) *m.* blot.
Tisch (tish) *m.* table: dinner.
Tischdecke (tish'-deck-erh) *f.* table-cloth.
Tischen (tish'-n) *v.* to dine: sit at table: lay the table.
Tischtuch (tish'-took) *n.* table-cloth.
Titelblatt (teet'-l-blaht) *n.* title-page.
Toben (toh'-ben) *v.* to fume: rage.
Tochter (tohk'-ter) *f.* daughter.
Tochtermann (tohk'-ter-mahn) *m.* son-in-law.
Tod (toht) *m.* death.
Todesstrafe (tohd'-es-shtrayh-ferh) *f.* capital punishment.
Tödlich (tert'-lik) *a. & ad.* deadly: fatal: mortal.
Toll (tol) *a.* absurd: mad.
Tollhaus (tol'-hows) *n.* lunatic asylum.
Tollheit (tol'-hite) *f.* frenzy: rage.
Tönen (ter'-nen) *v.* to tune.
Tonfolge (tohn'-fol-gerh) *f.* melody.
Tonkunst (tohn'-koonst) *f.* music.
Topf (topf) *m.* pot: jar: jug.
Töpfer (terp'-fer) *f.* pottery.
Tor (tohr) *m.* fool—*n.* gate.
Torf (torf) *m.* turf.
Torheit (tohr'-hite) *f.* folly: foolishness.
Torte (tort'-erh) *f.* tart.
Tracht (trahkt) *f.* dress: fashion.
Trachten (trahkt'-n) *v.* to endeavour: attempt.
Träge (tray'-gerh) *a.* lazy: indolent.
Tragen (trahg'-n) *v.* to bear: sustain: endure.
Träger (trayg'-er) *m.* porter.
Trägheit (trayk'-hite) *f.* indolence.
Trampeln (trahm'-peln) *v.* to trample.
Träne (trayn'-erh) *f.* tear.

Tränenvoll (trayn'-en-foll) *a.* tearful.
Trank (trahnk) *m.* drink: beverage.
Transportieren (trahn'-sport-yehr-n) *v.* to transport: carry.
Trappe (trahp'-erh) *f.* footstep.
Traube (trow'-berh) *f.* grape.
Trauen (trow'-n) *v.* to marry: trust: venture.
Trauer (trow'-er) *f.* grief.
Trauern (trow'-ern) *v.* to mourn.
Trauerspiel (trow'-er-shpeel) *n.* tragedy.
Traum (trowm) *m.* dream.
Träumen (troy'-men) *v.* to dream.
Traurig (trow'-rik) *a.* mournful: melancholy.
Traurigkeit (trow'-rik-kite) *f.* grief: sadness.
Traut (trowt) *a.* dear: beloved.
Treffen (tree'-fen) *v.* to strike— *n.* fight.
Trefflich (tref'-lik) *a. & ad.* admirable.
Treiben (try'-ben) *v.* to drive: propel.
Trennen (tren'-n) *v.* to separate: part.
Treppe (trep'-erh) *f.* staircase: stairs.
Tresse (tress'-erh) *f.* lace.
Treten (trayt'-n) *v.* to tread: walk.
Treu (troy) *a.* faithful: true.
Treuherzig (troy'-hayrt-sik) *a.* sincere.
Treulich (troy'-lik) *ad.* truly: faithfully.
Trinker (trink'-er) *m.* drinker: drunkard.
Trinkgeld (trink'-gelt) *n.* gratuity: tip.
Trippeln (trip'-eln) *v.* to trip.
Trocken (trok'-n) *a.* dry: barren.
Trockenheit (trok'-n-hite) *f.* dryness.
Trockenplatte (trok'-n-plaht-erh) *f.* dry plate for photography.
Trocknen (trok'-nen) *v.* to dry up.
Trödel (trer'-del) *m.* second-hand goods.
Trog (trohk) *m.* trough.
Trommel (trom'-mel) *f.* drum.

Trompete (trom'-payt-erh) *f.* trumpet.
Tropf (tropf) *m.* lunatic: simpleton.
Tropfen (trop'-fen) *v.* to drop: trickle.
Tropisch (trop'-ish) *a.* tropical.
Trost (trohst) *m.* comfort.
Trösten (trerst'-n) *v.* to comfort: console.
Tröstung (trerst'-oong) *f.* consolation.
Trotten (trot'-ten) *v.* to trot.
Trotz (trots) *m.* boldness: defiance.
Trotzig (trots'-ik) *a.* insolent: daring.
Trübe (treeb'-erh) *a.* muddy: thick.
Trüben (treeb'-n) *v.* to trouble: sadden.
Trübseligkeit (treep'-zay-lik-hite) *f.* sadness: grief.
Trunken (troonk'-n) *a.* intoxicated.
Tuch (took) *n.* cloth: fabric.
Tuchhändler (took'-hahnd-ler) *m.* draper.
Tüchtig (teekt'-ik) *a.* able: capable: fit.
Tückisch (teek'-ish) *a.* malicious: spiteful.
Tugend (toog'-ent) *f.* virtue.
Tulpe (toolp'-erh) *f.* tulip.
Tunke (toong'-kerh) *f.* sauce.
Tunken (toong'-ken) *v.* to soak.
Tunlich (toon'-lik) *a.* practicable.
Tür (teer) *f.* door.
Türhüter (teer'-heet-er) *m.* doorkeeper: porter.
Turm (toorm) *m.* tower: spire.
Tüte (teet'-erh) *f.* paper bag.

U

Übel (eeb'-l) *n.* evil: misfortune: malady—*a.* evil: wrong.
Übelkeit (eeb'-l-kite) *f.* sickness: illness.
Übelstand (eeb'-l-shtahnt) *m.* indecency.
Übeltat (eeb'-l-taht) *f.* misdeed.
Übeltäter (eeb'-l-tayt-er) *m.* evil-doer.
Übelwollen (eeb'-l-voll-n) *a.* malevolent.

Üben (eeb'-n) *v.* to exercise. train.
Über (eeb'-er) *pr.* across: about: above: beyond: by: on: over: upon: during: more than —*ad.* over: remaining.
Überall (eeb'-er-ahl) *ad.* everywhere: all over.
Überaus (eeb'-er-ows) *ad.* exceedingly.
Überblicken (eeb'-er-blik-n) *v.* to overlook.
Überbringen (eeb'-er-bring-n) *v.* to deliver.
Überdecke (eeb'-er-deck-erh) *f.* coverlet.
Überdem (eeb'-er-daym) *ad.* besides: moreover.
Überdenken (eeb'-er-deng-ken) *v.* to reflect: consider: ponder over.
Überdruss (eeb'-er-dross) *m.* tediousness: disgust.
Überdrüssig (eeb'-er-dress-ik) *a.* tedious.
Übereilen (eeb'-er-ile-n) *v.* to overtake.
Übereinstimmung (eeb'-er-ine-shtim-moong) *f.* agreement: accord.
Überfahren (eeb'-er-fahr-n) *v.* to cross.
Überfahrt (eeb'-er-fahrt) *f.* passage: ferry.
Überfall (eeb'-er-fahl) *m.* surprise.
Überfallen (eeb'-er-fahl-n) *v.* to surprise: attack.
Überfällig (eeb'-er-fell-ik) *a.* overdue: unpaid.
Überfliessen (eeb'-er-flee-sen) *v.* to overflow.
Überfluss (eeb'-er-floss) *m.* abundance.
Überfordern (eeb-er-for'-dern) *v.* to overcharge.
Überführung (eeb-er-feer'-oong) *f.* conviction.
Übergabe (eeb'-er-gah-berh) *f.* surrender.
Übergang (eeb'-er-gahng) *m.* passage.
Übergeben (eeb'-er-gay'-ben) *v.* to deliver up: vomit.
Überhäufen (eeb-er-hoy'-fen) *v.* to overload: overwhelm.
Überhaupt (eeb'-er-howpt) *ad.* generally: altogether.

Überheben (eeb'-er-hay'-ben) *v.* to exempt.
Überholen (eeb-er-hoh'-len) *v.* to overtake.
Überhören (eeb-er-herr'-n) *v.* to overhear.
Überkleid (eeb-er-klite') *n.* overcoat.
Überklug (eeb-er-klook') *a.* overwise.
Überkochen (eeb'-er-kohk-n) *v.* to boil over.
Überkommen (eeb'-er-komm-n) *v.* to receive: come over.
Überlästig (eeb'-er-lest-ik) *a.* troublesome.
Überläufer (eeb-er-loyf'-er) *m.* deserter.
Überlegen (eeb-er-lay'-gen) *v.* to reflect: consider — *a.* superior.
Überlegenheit (eeb-er-lay'-gen-hite) *f.* superiority.
Überlegsam (eeb-er-layge'-sahm) *a. & ad.* considerate.
Überliefern (eeb-er-leef'-ern) *v.* to surrender.
Überlieferung (eeb-er-leef'-er-oong) *f.* delivery.
Übermachen (eeb-er-mahk'-n) *v.* to transmit: remit.
Übermächtig (eeb-er-mek'-tik) *a.* overpowering.
Übermachung (eeb-er-maht'-oong) *f.* remittance.
Übermässig (eeb-er-mace'-ik) *a.* excessive: exorbitant.
Übermorgen (eeb-er-mor'-gen) *ad.* the day after tomorrow.
Übermut (eeb'-er-mooht) *m.* insolence.
Übermütig (eeb'-er-meet-ik) *a.* haughty.
Überragen (eeb'-er-rah-gen) *v.* to surpass.
Überraschen (eeb-er-rah'-shen) *v.* to surprise.
Überrechnen (eeb'-er-rek-n) *v.* to calculate.
Überreden (eeb'-er-ray-den) *v.* to persuade.
Überreif (eeb'-er-rife) *a.* overripe.
Überrest (eeb'-er-rest) *m.* remainder: remnant.
Überrock (eeb'-er-rok) *m.* overcoat.
Überrumpeln (eeb-er-romp'-eln) *v.* to seize unawares.
Überschätzen (eeb-er-shet'-sen) *v.* to overrate: overestimate.
Überschrift (eeb-er-shryft') *f.* heading: address: inscription.
Überschuss (eeb'-er-shoss) *m.* surplus.
Überschütten (eeb'-er-sheet-n) *v.* to spill: overwhelm.
Überschwemmung (eeb-er-schvem'-oong) *f.* inundation: flood.
Übersehen (eeb-er-say'-n) *v.* to overlook: review.
Übersenden (eeb-er-send'-n) *v.* to send: forward: transmit.
Übersetzen (eeb-er-set'-sen) *v.* to translate: cross over.
Übersetzung (eeb-er-set'-soong) *f.* translation.
Übersicht (eeb'-er-zikt) *f.* survey: review.
Überspannen (eeb-er-shpan'-n) *v.* to exaggerate.
Überspringen (eeb-er-shpring'-n) *v.* to jump over.
Überstehen (eeb-er-shtay'-n) *v.* to endure: surmount: overcome.
Übertragen (eeb-er-trahg'-n) *v.* to transfer: carry forward.
Übertragung (eeb-er-trah'-goong) *f.* transfer.
Übertreffen (eeb-er-treff'-n) *v.* to surpass: excel.
Übertreiben (eeb-er-try'-ben) *v.* to exaggerate.
Übertreten (eeb-er-tray'-ten) *v.* to transgress: violate.
Übertreter (eeb-er-tray'-terh) *m.* offender.
Übertrieben (eeb-er-try'-ben) *a. & ad.* excessive: excessively.
Überwachsen (eeb-er-vahk'-zen) *v.* to outgrow.
Überwältigen (eeb-er-vel'-tig-n) *v.* to overpower: overcome.
Überweisung (eeb-er-vy'-soong) *f.* conviction: assignment.
Überwiegen (eeb-er-veeg'-n) *v.* to outweigh: prevail.
Überwinden (eeb-er-vin'-den) *v.* to vanquish: overcome.

Überwindung (eeb-er-vin'-doong) *f.* victory: triumph.
Überwintern (eeb-er-vin'-tern) *v.* to pass the winter: hibernate.
Überzählig (eeb-er-tsay'-lik) *a.* surplus.
Überzeugen (eeb-er-tsoy'-gen) *v.* to convince: prove.
Überzeugung (eeb-er-tsoy'-goong) *f.* conviction: persuasion.
Überzieher (eeb-er-tsee'-er) *m.* overcoat.
Üblich (eeb'-lik) *a. & ad.* usual: customarily: ordinary.
Übrig (eeb'-rik) *a.* remaining: superfluous: left over.
Übrigens (eeb'-rigg-ens) *ad.* moreover: besides.
Übung (eeb'-oong) *f.* exercise.
Ufer (oof'-er) *n.* shore: beach.
Uhr (oohr) *f.* clock: watch.
Uhrkette (oohr'-ket-erh) *f.* watch-chain.
Uhrmacher (oohr'-mahk-er) *m.* watchmaker.
Ulme (oolm'-erh) *f.* elm.
Um (oom) *pr. & ad.* about: round: at: for—*c.* in order to.
Umändern (oom'-end-ern) *v.* to change.
Umarmen (oom-arm'-n) *v.* to embrace.
Umbinden (oom'-bind-n) *v.* to bind: tie round: put on.
Umbringen (oom'-bring-n) *v.* to kill.
Umdrehen (oom'-dray-n) *v.* to turn.
Umfallen (oom'-fahl-n) *v.* to fall over.
Umfang (oom'-fahng) *m.* circumference.
Umfassend (oom'-fahss-ent) *a.* comprehensive.
Umfliegen (oom'-fleeg-n) *v.* to fly round.
Umgebung (oom-gay'-boong) *f.* neighbourhood.
Umgehen (oom-gay'-n) *v.* to evade: avoid.
Umgekehrt (oom'-ge-kayrt) *a.* contrary.
Umhalsen (oom-hahl'-zen) *v.* to embrace.
Umklammern (oom-klahm'-ern) *v.* to clasp.

Umkommen (oom'-komm-n) *v.* to perish.
Umringen (oom-ring'-n) *v.* to surround.
Umschlag (oom'-shlahk) *m.* envelope.
Umschliessen (oom-shlees'-n) *v.* to enclose.
Umschütten (oom-sheet'-n) *v.* to spill.
Umsetzen (oom'-set-sen) *v.* to sell.
Umsomehr (oom-zohm'-ayr) *ad.* all the more.
Umsonst (oom-zonst') *ad.* gratis: free.
Umständlich (oom'-shtentlik) *a.* fussy: troublesome.
Umstossen (oom'-shtohs-sen) *v.* to knock over: overthrow.
Umziehen (oom-tsee'-n) *v.* to move (from a house).
Umzug (oom'-tsook) *m.* procession.
Unangenehm (oon'-ahn-ge-nahm) *a.* unpleasant.
Unanständig (oon' - ahn - shtend-ik) *a.* indecent.
Unartig (oon'-art-ik) *a.* bad-mannered: badly behaved.
Unbeholfen (oon'-bee-holf-n) *a.* clumsy.
Unbesonnen (oon'-be-zonn-n) *a.* careless.
Unbewusst (oon'-be-voost) *a.* unaware.
Unbrauchbar (oon' - browk - bar) *a.* unfit.
Und (oont) *conj.* and.
Unduldsam (oon'-doolt-zahm) *a.* intolerant.
Unecht (oon'-ekt) *a.* faked: sham: counterfeit.
Unehelich (oon'-aye-e-lik) *a.* illegitimate.
Unehrlich (oon'-ayr-lik) *a.* dishonest.
Unentgeltlich (oon'-ent-gelt'-lik) *a.* gratuitous.
Unermüdlich (oon'-ayr-meet-lik) *a.* untiring.
Unfall (oon'-fahl) *m.* accident.
Unfrankiert (oon' - frahng - keart') *a.* unstamped: unpaid (postage).
Unfreundlich (oon'-froynt-lik) *a.* unkind.
Unfug (oon'-fook) *m.* mischief: offence.

Ungebildet (oon'-ge-bil-det) *a.* uneducated.
Ungebührlich (oon'-ge-beer-lik) *a.* improper.
Ungeduldig (oon'-ge-doold-ik) *a.* impatient.
Ungefähr (oon'-ge-fayr) *ad.* about.
Ungeheuer (oon'-ge-hoy-er) *a.* immense: monstrous — *n.* monster.
Ungemein (oon'-ge-mine) *a.* uncommon: rare.
Ungemütlich (oon'-ge-meet-lik) *a.* uncomfortable.
Ungeniessbar (oon'-ge-nees-bar) *a.* uneatable.
Ungerade (oon'-gerahd-erh) *a.* uneven: odd.
Ungerecht (oon'-ge-rekt) *a.* unjust.
Ungeziefer (oon'-ge-tsee-fer) *n.* vermin.
Ungläubig (oon'-gloy-bik) *a.* unbelieving.
Unglück (oon'-gleek) *n.* ill-luck: misfortune.
Unglücklich (oon'-gleek-lik) *a.* unhappy: miserable.
Unglücksfall (oon'-gleeks-fahl) *m.* misfortune.
Unheil (oon'-hile) *n.* evil.
Unheilbar (oon'-hile-bar) *a.* incurable.
Unkenntniss (oon'-kent-niss) *f.* ignorance.
Unkosten (oon'-kost-n) *pl.* expenses.
Unkraut (oon'-krowt) *n.* weed.
Unlängst (oon'-lengst) *ad.* recently: lately.
Unlauter (oon'-low-ter) *a.* impure: unclean.
Unlust (oon'-loost) *f.* disgust.
Unmännlich (oon'-men-lik) *a.* unmanly.
Unmassig (oon'-mace-ik) *a.* immoderate.
Unmenschlichkeit (oon'-mensh-lik-hite) *f.* barbarity.
Unmöglich (oon'-merk-lik) *a.* impossible.
Unmutig (oon'-moot-ik) *a.* peevish: cross.
Unnötig (oon'-nert-ik) *a.* unnecessary.
Unnütz (oon'-neetz) *a.* useless.
Unordentlich (oon'-or-dent-lik) *a.* disorderly.

Unpassend (oon'-pahss'-ent) *a.* unsuitable: improper.
Unpässlich (oon'-pess-lik) *a.* unwell: ill.
Unratsam (oon'-raht-sahm) *a.* unadvisable.
Unrecht (oon'-rekt) *a. & ad.* wrong: improper — *n.* wrong.
Unredlich (oon'-rayt-lik) *a.* dishonest.
Unreif (oon'-rife) *a.* unripe.
Unrein (oon'-ryne) *a.* impure: unclean.
Unrichtig (oon'-rik-tig) *a.* incorrect: false.
Uns (oons) *pn.* us: to us: ourselves.
Unschadhaft (oon'-shaht-haft) *a.* undamaged: sound.
Unschädlich (oon'-shay-tlik) *a.* harmless.
Unschuldig (oon'-shool-dik) *a.* innocent.
Unselig (oon'-sayl-ik) *a.* unhappy.
Unser (oon'-ser) *pn.* our: of us.
Unsicher (oon'-sik-ker) *a.* uncertain.
Unsichtbar (oon'-sikt-bar) *a.* invisible.
Unsinn (oon'-zin) *m.* nonsense.
Unsolid (oon'-sol-eed) *a.* unsafe: untrustworthy.
Untätig (oon'-tayt'-ik) *a.* idle.
Untauglich (oon'-towk-lik) *a.* unfit: unsuitable.
Unten (oon'-ten) *ad.* below: beneath.
Unter (oon'-ter) *pr.* under: below: between.
Unterbrechen (oon'-ter-breck-n) *v.* to interrupt.
Unterdessen (oon'-ter-dess-n) *ad. & c.* meanwhile.
Untergang (oon'-ter-gahng) *m.* fall: ruin.
Unterkunft (oon'-ter-keenft) *f.* shelter: lodging.
Unterlassen (oon'-ter-lahs-sen) *v.* to leave off.
Unterliegen (oon'-ter-leeg-n) *v.* to succumb.
Unternehmen (oon'-ter-nay-men) *v.* to venture.
Unternehmer (oon'-ter-nay-mer) *m.* undertaker.
Unterpfand (oon'-ter-pfahnt) *n.* pledge: mortgage.

Unterreden (oon'-ter-ray-den) *v.* to converse.
Unterrichten (oon'-ter-rikt-n) *v.* to teach: inform.
Untersagen (oon'-ter-saig-n) *v.* to forbid: prohibit.
Unterscheiden (oon'-ter-shy-den) *v.* to distinguish: discern.
Unterschieden (oon'-ter-sheet-n) *p. & a.* different.
Unterschrift (oon'-ter-shrift) *f.* signature.
Unterseeboot (oon'-ter-zay-boht) *n.* submarine.
Unterst (oon'-terst) *a.* lowest.
Unterstehen (oon'-ter-shtay-n) *v.* to dare: be bold.
Untersuchen (oon'-ter-zook-n) *v.* to examine.
Untersuchung (oon'-ter-zook-oong) *f.* examination.
Unterwegs (oon'-ter-vayx) *ad.* on the way.
Untreu (oon'-troy) *a.* faithless.
Unüberlegt (oon'-eeb-er-laygt) *a.* thoughtless: inconsiderate.
Unveränderlich (oon'-fayr-end-er-lik) *a.* unchangeable.
Unverantwortlich (oon'-fayr-ahnt-vort-lik) *a.* inexcusable.
Unverdächtig (oon'-fayr-deck-tik) *a.* unsuspected.
Unverdaulich (oon'-fayr-dow-lik) *a.* indigestible.
Unverdient (oon'-fayr-deent) *a.* undeserved: unmerited.
Unverfälscht (oon'-fayr-felsht) *a.* unadulterated.
Unvergleichlich (oon'-fayr-glyk-lik) *a.* unique.
Unverhoff (oon'-fayr-hoft) *a.* unexpected—*ad.* unawares.
Unverletzt (oon'-fayr-letst) *a.* unhurt.
Unvermutet (oon'-fayr-moot-et) *a.* unexpected.
Unverpackt (oon'-fayr-pahckt) *a.* unpacked: loose.
Unverschämt (oon'-fayr-shaymt) *a.* shameless: impudent.
Unverzüglich (oon'-fayr-tseek-lik) *a & ad.* immediate.
Unvollständig (oon'-foll-shten-dik) *a.* incomplete.
Unwandelbar (oon'-vahn-del-bahr) *a.* unchangeable.
Unweit (oon'-vyte) *ad.* not far off.
Unwert (oon'-vayrt) *a.* worthless—*n.* worthlessness.
Unwesen (oon'-vay-zen) *n.* disorder.
Unwichtig (oon'-vik-tik) *a.* unimportant.
Unwillig (oon'-vill-ik) *a.* indignant: unwilling.
Unwillkommen (oon'-villkomm-n) *a.* unwelcome.
Unwissend (oon'-viss-ent) *a.* ignorant.
Unwissenheit (oon'-viss-n-hite) *f.* ignorance.
Unwohl (oon'-vohl) *a. & ad.* indisposed: unwell.
Unzüchtig (oon'-tseek-tik) *a.* lewd: unchaste.
Unzufrieden (oon'-tsoo-freed-n) *a.* discontented.
Unzuverlässig (oon'-tsoo-fayr-less-ik) *a.* untrustworthy.
Urbild (oor'-bilt) *n.* original.
Urheber (oor'-hay-ber) *m.* author.
Urkunden (oor'-koond-n) *v.* to testify: witness.
Urne (oorn'-erh) *f.* urn.
Urplötzlich (oor'-plerts-lik) *a. & ad.* sudden: suddenly.
Ursprünglich (oor'-shpreeng-lik) *a.* original.
Urteil (oor'-tyle) *n.* judgment.
Urteilen (oor'-tyle-n) *v.* to judge.

V

Vater (fah'-ter) *m.* father.
Vaterland (fah'-ter-lahnt) *n.* native country.
Väterlich (fay'-ter-lik) *a.* fatherly: paternal.
Vaterlos (fah'-ter-loos) *a.* fatherless.
Vaterunser (fah'-ter-oon-zer) *n.* Lord's Prayer.
Veilchen (fyle'-ken) *n.* violet.
Ventil (vent'-eel) *n.* valve.
Verabfolgen (fayr'-ahp-fol-gen) *v.* to deliver.
Verabscheuen (fayr'-ahp-shoy-n) *v.* to abominate: detest: loathe.
Verabschieden (fayr'-ahp-sheed-n) *v.* to dismiss.
Verachten (fayr'-ahk-ten) *v.* to scorn.
Verändern (fayr-end'-ern) *v.* to alter: change.

Veranstalten (fayr-ahn'-shtahl-ten) *v.* to prepare.
Verarbeiten (fayr-ar'-by-ten) *v.* to use.
Verarbeitung (fayr-ar'-by-toong) *f.* manufacturing.
Verarmen (fayr-arm'-n) *v.* to impoverish.
Verausgaben (fayr-ows'-gahb-n) *v.* to spend.
Verbannen (fayr-bahn'-n) *v.* to banish: exile.
Verbergen (fayr-bayrg'-n) *v.* to conceal.
Verbessern (fayr-bess'-ern) *v.* to correct: amend.
Verbeugen (fayr-boyg'-n) *v.* to bow.
Verbieten (fayr-beet'-n) *v.* to forbid: prohibit.
Verbindung (fayr-bin'-doong) *f.* connection: relation.
Verbittern (fayr-bit'-ern) *v.* to embitter.
Verbleichen (fayr-bly'-ken) *v.* to fade.
Verblendung (fayr-blend'-oong) *f.* blindness.
Verbrechen (fayr-brek'-n) *n.* crime.
Verbrecherisch (fayr-brek'-er-ish) *a.* criminal.
Verbrennen (fayr-bren'-n) *v.* to burn.
Verbringen (fayr-bring'-n) *v.* to spend: waste: squander.
Verbrühen (fayr-bree'-n) *v.* to scald.
Verbürgen (fayr-beerg'-n) *v.* to guarantee.
Verdacht (fayr-dakt') *m.* suspicion.
Verdächtigen (fayr-dekt'-ig-n) *v.* to suspect.
Verdammen (fayr-dahm'-n) *v.* to condemn.
Verdampfen (fayr-dahmp'-fen) *v.* to evaporate.
Verdauen (fayr-dow'-n) *v.* to digest.
Verdaulich (fayr-dow'-lik) *a.* digestible.
Verdecken (fayr-deck'-n) *v.* to cover: conceal.
Verderb (fayr-dayrp') *m.* ruin: decay.
Verderblich (fayr-dayrp'-lik) *a.* perishable.

Verdicken (fayr-dick'-n) *v.* **to** thicken.
Verdienen (fayr-deen'-n) *v.* to gain: merit: earn.
Verdorben (fayr-dorb'-n) *a.* spoiled: damaged: tainted.
Verdriessen (fayr-drees'-n) *v.* to grieve: offend.
Verdrossen (fayr-dross'-n) *a.* cross: peevish.
Vereinfachen (fayr-ine'-fahk-n) *v.* to simplify.
Vereiteln (fayr-ite'-eln) *v.* to disappoint.
Verfall (fayr-fahll') *m.* decay: decline.
Verfallen (fayr-fahll'-n) *v.* decay: expire.
Verfälschen (fayr-felsh'-n) *v.* to adulterate: counterfeit.
Verfassen (fayr-fahss'-n) *v.* to bind: tie.
Verfaulen (fayr-fowl'-n) *v.* to rot: go bad.
Verfechter (fayr-fek'-ter) *m.* champion.
Verfehlen (fayr-fayl'-n) *v.* to fail: miss.
Verfertigen (fayr-fayrt'-ig-n) *v.* to manufacture: fabricate.
Verfinstern (fayr-fins'-tern) *v.* to darken: obscure.
Verfliegen (fayr-flee'-gen) *v.* to fly away.
Verfluchen (fayr-flook'-n) *v.* to curse: detest.
Verfolg (fayr-follk') *m.* progress.
Verfrieren (fayr-free'-ern) *v.* to freeze.
Verführen (fayr-feer'-n) *v.* to tempt.
Vergällen (fayr-ghel'-n) to embitter.
Vergangen (fayr-gahng'-n) *a.* past: gone: bygone.
Vergeben (fayr-gay'-ben) *v.* to forgive.
Vergeblich (fayr-gayp'-lik) *a.* futile: fruitless.
Vergebung (fayr-gay'-boong) *f.* forgiveness.
Vergehen (fayr-gay'-n) *n.* trespass.
Vergelten (fayr-ghelt'-n) *v.* to repay.
Vergessen (fayr-ghess'-n) *v.* to forget.

Vergeuden (fayr-goy'-den) *v.* to squander: waste.
Vergiessen (fayr-gees'-n) *v.* to spill: shed (blood).
Vergiften (fayr-gift'-n) *v.* to poison.
Vergissmeinnicht (fayr-giss'-mine-nikt) *n.* forget-me-not.
Vergleichen (fayr-gly'-ken) *v.* to compare.
Verglühen (fayr-glee'-n) to be burnt up.
Vergnügen (fayr-gneeg'-n) *v.* to amuse—*n.* amusement.
Vergnüglich (fayr-gneeg'-lik) *a.* delightful.
Vergnügt (fayr-gneegt') *a.* delighted.
Vergolden (fayr-gol'-den) *v.* to gild.
Vergraben (fayr-grahb'-n) *v.* to bury.
Vergrösserung (fayr-grers'-er-oong) *f.* enlargement.
Verhaft (fayr-hahft') *m.* arrest.
Verhaftung (fayr-hahft'-oong) *f.* imprisonment.
Verharren (fayr-har'-ren) *v.* to persist.
Verhärten (fayr-hayrt'-n) *v.* to harden.
Verhehlen (fayr-hayl'-n) *v.* to hide: conceal.
Verheiraten (fayr-hy'-raht-n) *v.* to marry.
Verhindern (fayr-hin'-dern) *v.* to obstruct: hinder.
Verhungern (fayr'-hoong-ern) *v.* to starve.
Verirren (fayr-eer'-ren) *v.* to err: lose the way.
Verkauf (fayr-kowf') *m.* sale.
Verkaufen (fayr-kowf'-n) *v.* to sell.
Verknüpfen (fayr-kneep'-fen) *v.* to tie: knot: connect.
Verkommen (fayr-komm'-n) *v.* to perish.
Verlachen (fayr-lahk'-ten) *v.* to mock: ridicule.
Verlangen (fayr-lahng'-n) *v.* ask—*n.* wish: desire.
Verleger (fayr-lay'-ger) *m.* publisher.
Verleihen (fayr-lye'-n) *v.* to lend.
Verleihung (fayr-lye'-hoong) *f.* loan: grant.

Verleiten (fayr-lye'-ten) *v.* to mislead: cheat.
Verletzen (fayr-letz'-n) *v.* to injure: wound.
Verlieben (fayr-leeb'-n) *v.* to fall in love.
Verloren (fayr-lor'-n) *a.* lost.
Verlust (fayr-loost') *m.* loss.
Vermeiden (fayr-my'-den) *v.* to avoid: shun.
Vermessen (fayr-mess'-oong) *v.* to measure.
Vermischen (fayr-mish'-n) *v.* to mix.
Vermögen (fayr-merg'-n) *v.* to be able to do.
Vermutlich (fayr-moot'-lik) *a.* likely.
Verpachten (fayr-pahkt'-n) *v.* to lease.
Verpacken (fayr-pahk'-n) *v.* to pack up.
Verpesten (fayr-pest'-n) *v.* to infect: poison.
Verpfänden (fayr-pfend'-n) *v.* to pawn.
Verpfuschen (fayr-pfoosh'-n) to spoil: mar: ruin.
Verrat (fayr-raht') *m.* treason: treachery.
Verraten (fayr-raht'-n) *v.* to betray.
Verräterisch (fayr-rayte'-er-ish) *a.* treacherous.
Verrauchen (fayr-rowk'-n) *v.* to smoke.
Verrechnen (fayr-reck'-nen) *v.* miscalculate.
Verrenken (fayr-reng'-ken) *v.* to dislocate: sprain.
Verrichten (fayr-rik'-ten) *v.* to do: perform.
Verringern (fayr-ring'-ern) *v.* to diminish: reduce.
Verrosten (fayr-rost'-n) *v.* to rust.
Versagen (fayr-zahg'-n) *v.* to deny: refuse.
Versagung (fayr-zahg'-oong) *f.* denial: refusal.
Versammlung (fayr-zahm'-loong) *f.* meeting: assembly.
Versauern (fayr-sow'-ern) *v.* to turn sour.
Versäumen (fayr-zoy'-men) *v.* to neglect: slight.
Verschämt (fayr-shaymt') *a.* bashful.

Verschanzen (fayr-shants'-n) v. to fortify.
Verscharren (fayr-shar'-n) v. to bury.
Verscheiden (fayr-shy'-den) v. to die: expire—*n.* death.
Verscherzen (fayr-shayrts'-n) v. to neglect.
Verschieden (fayr-shee'-den) *a.* different.
Verschlafen (fayr-shlahf'-n) v. to oversleep.
Verschleissen (fayr-shly'-sen) v. to wear out.
Verschleudern (fayr-shloyd'-ern) v. to squander.
Verschliessen (fayr-shlees'-n) v. to lock up.
Verschlossen (fayr-shloss'-n) *p. & a.* reserved: taciturn.
Verschmachten (fayr-shmak'-ten) v. to faint: fade away.
Verschmitzt (fayr-shmitst') *a.* crafty.
Verschnauben (fayr-shnow'-ben) v. to breathe.
Verschneiden (fayr-shny'-den) v. to prune.
Verschonen (fayr-shohn'-n) v. to spare.
Verschönern (fayr-shern'-ern) v. to beautify.
Verschuldet (fayr-shool'-det) *a.* indebted.
Verschweigung (fayr-shvy'-goong) *f.* reticence.
Verschwenden (fayr-shveng'-den) v. to squander.
Verschwinden (fayr-shvind'-n) v. to vanish: disappear.
Verschwörung (fayr-shver'-oong) *f.* conspiracy.
Versetzen (fayr-set'-sen) v. to misplace; remove: obstruct.
Versichern (fayr-sik'-ern) v. to insure.
Verwelken (fayr-velk'-n) v. to fade: decay.
Verwerfen (fayr-vairf'-n) v. to refuse.
Verwerflich (fayr-vairf'-lik) *a.* objectionable.
Verwertung (fayr-vairt'-oong) *f.* sale.
Verwesen (fayr-vayz'-n) v. to perish: decay.
Verwickeln (fayr-vick'-eln) v. to complicate: entangle.

Verwickelung (fayr-vick'-el-oong) *f.* entanglement.
Verwildern (fayr-vild'-ern) v. to neglect: grow wild.
Verwilligen (fayr-vill'-ik-n) v. to grant: permit.
Verwirklichen (fayr-veerk'-lik-n) v. to realize.
Verwirren (fayr-veer'-n) v. to entangle: embroil.
Verwirrung (fayr-veer'-oong) *f.* confusion: complication.
Verwischen (fayr-vish'-n) v. to efface: blurr.
Verworfen (fayr-vorf'-n) *a.* abandoned.
Verwunden (fayr-vonn'-den) v. to wound: hurt.
Verwundern (fayr-vonn'-dern) v. to astonish: wonder.
Verwünschen (fayr-veen'-shen) v. to curse.
Verwüsten (fayr-veest'-n) v. to waste.
Verwüstung (fayr-veest'-oong) *f.* devastation: ruin.
Verzagen (fayr-tsag'-n) v. to despair.
Verzaubern (fayr-tsow'-bern) v. to bewitch.
Verzauberung (fayr-tsow'-ber-oong) *f.* enchantment.
Verzieren (fayr-tsee'-ren) v. to decorate.
Verzögern (fayr-tserg'-ern) v. to delay: protract.
Verzuckung (fayr-tsook'-oong) *f.* convulsion.
Verzug (fayr-tsook') *m.* delay: postponement.
Vetter (fet'-ter) *m.* cousin: relation.
Vetterschaft (fet'-ter-shahft) *f.* relationship.
Vieh (fee) *n.* beast: cattle: live stock.
Viehisch (fee'-ish) *a.* brutal.
Viehweide (fee'-vy-de) *f.* pasturage.
Vielerlei (feel'-er-lie) *a.* many: various.
Vielmal (feel'-mahl) *ad.* frequently.
Vielmehr (feel'-mair) *ad.* rather.
Vier (feer) *a.* four.
Viereck (feer'-eck) *n.* square.
Viereckig (feer'-eck-ik) *a.* square.

Vierte (feer'-terh) *a.* fourth.
Viertel (feer'-tel) *n.* quarter.
Vierzehn (feer'-tzain) *a.* fourteen.
Vierzig (feer'-tsig) *a.* forty.
Viole (vee-oh'-ler) *f.* viol: violet.
Violine (vee-oh-leen') *f.* violin.
Visite (vee-zeet') *f.* visit.
Visitenkarte (vee-zeet'-n-karterh) *f.* visiting card.
Vogel (foh'-gel) *m.* bird: fowl.
Vogelbauer (foh'-gel-bow-er) *n.* bird-cage.
Vogelscheuche (foh'-gel-shoyk-erh) *f.* scare-crow.
Volk (folk) *n.* people: nation.
Volkreich (folk'-ryk) *a.* populous.
Volkslied (folks'-leet) *n.* song: ballad.
Volksmenge (folks'-meng-erh) *f.* population.
Voll (foll) *a.* whole: entire.
Vollauf (foll'-owf) *ad.* abundantly.
Vollstrecken (foll-shtreck'-n) *v.* to execute.
Vollstrecker (foll-shtreck'-er) *m.* executor.
Vollzählig (foll-tsay'-lik) *a.* complete: fully.
Vollziehen (foll-tsee'-n) *v.* to accomplish: execute.
Volontär (voll-ong-tare') *m.* volunteer.
Vom (von dem) (fom) *pr.* of the: by the: from the.
Von (fon) *pr.* of: by: from.
Vonnöten (fon-nert'-n) *a.* necessary.
Vor (for) *pr.* before—*ad.* formerly.
Vorabend (for'-ah-bent) *m.* eve.
Voran (for-ahn') *ad.* before: in front.
Voraus (for'-ows) *ad.* before.
Vorausnehmen (for'-ows-naymen) *v.* to anticipate.
Voraussagen (for'-ows-sahgn) *v.* to prophesy.
Voraussetzen (for'-ows'-zetzen) *v.* to presume.
Voraussicht (for'-ows'-zikt) *f.* prudence.
Vorbauen (for'-bow-n) *v.* to prevent: obviate.

F

Vorbedächtig (for-be-dek'-tig) *a.* cautious: prudent.
Vorbehalten (for'-be-hahlt-n) *v.* to reserve.
Vorbei (for-by') *ad.* by: past: over.
Vorbereiten (for'-be-ryt-n) *v.* to prepare.
Vorbild (for'-bilt) *n.* pattern: model.
Vorbilden (for'-bild-n) *v.* to represent.
Vorbildlich (for'-bilt-lik) *a.* typical.
Vorbringen (for'-bring-n) *v.* to allege.
Vordem (for'-daim) *ad.* formerly.
Vorderhand (for'-der-hahnt) *f.* wrist.
Voreiligkeit (for'-ile-ik-kite) *f.* rashness: hastiness.
Vorenthalten (for'-ent-hahlten) *v.* to withhold.
Vorenthaltung (for'-ent-hahltoong) *f.* detention.
Vorerst (for'-ayrst) *ad.* firstly.
Vorfall (for'-fahl) *m.* accident.
Vorfordern (for'-ford-ern) *v.* to summon.
Vorgeben (for'-gay-ben) *v.* to assert: pretend.
Vorgemach (for'-ge-mahk) *n.* ante-room.
Vorgesetzt (for'-ge-zetst) *a.* proposed.
Vorgestern (for'-ghest-ern) *ad.* day before yesterday.
Vorgreifen (for'-gry-fen) *v.* to anticipate.
Vorhand (for'-hahnd) *f.* wrist.
Vorhang (for'-hahng) *m.* curtain.
Vorhaus (for'-hows) *n.* vestibule.
Vorher (for'-hayr) *ad.* beforehand.
Vornersagen (for'-hayr-sahgn) *v.* to predict: foretell: forecast.
Vorhersagung (for'-hayr-sahg-oong) *f.* prophecy.
Vorlängst (for'-lengst) *ad.* long ago.
Vorlassung (for'-lahss-oong) *f.* admittance.
Vorlegen (for'-lay-gen) *v.* to exhibit.

Vormals (for'-mahls) *ad.* formerly.
Vormund (for'-moont) *m.* tutor.
Vormundschaft (for'-moont-shahft) *f.* guardianship.
Vorname (for'-nahm-erh) *m.* Christian name.
Vorrichten (for'-rik-ten) *v.* to prepare.
Vorrücken (for'-reek-n) *v.* to advance.
Vorsaal (for'-sahl) *m.* entrance-hall.
Vorsagen (for'-sahg-n) *v.* to rehearse: recite.
Vorschein (for'-shine) *m.* appearance.
Vorsicht (for'-sikt) *f.* foresight: prudence.
Vorsichtigkeit (for'-sikt-ik-hite) *f.* caution.
Vorsitzen (for'-sits-n) *v.* to preside.
Vorspiegelung (for'-shpeeg-el-oong) *f.* deceit.
Vorsprung (for'-shproong) *m.* advantage: lead.
Vorstadt (for' - shtaht) *f.* suburb.
Vortragen (for'-trah-gen) *v.* to carry forward.
Vortreten (for'-tray-ten) *v.* to advance.
Vortuch (for'-took) *n.* apron.
Vorüber (for-eeb'-er) *ad.* over: past: beyond.
Vorvater (for'-faht-er) *m.* ancestor: forefather.
Vorwärts (for'-vayrts) *ad.* forwards.
Vorweg (for'-vayg) *ad.* before.
Vorwenden (for'-vend-n) *v.* to pretend.
Vorwitzig (for'-vits-ik) *a.* inquisitive.
Vorwort (for'-vort) *n.* preface.
Vorwurf (for'-voorf) *m.* reproach.

W

Wach (vahk) *a. & ad.* awake: alert: alive.
Wache (vahk'-erh) *f.* guard: sentry.
Wachen (vahk'-n) *v.* to be awake: guard.
Wachs (vahx) *n.* wax.
Wachsam (vahk'-zahm) *a.* watchful: vigilant.
Wachsen (vahx'-n) *v.* to increase: thrive.
Wachslicht (vahx'-likt) *n.* wax-candle.
Wachstuch (vahx'-took) *n.* oilcloth.
Wachstum (vahx'-toom) *m. & n.* growth: increase.
Wächter (vekt'-er) *m.* watchman.
Wackelig (vahck'-l-ik) *a.* tottering: shaky.
Wackeln (vahck'-eln) *v.* to shake.
Wacker (vahck'-er) *a. & ad.* brave: bravely.
Waffe (vahff'-erh) *f.* weapon: arm.
Waffel (vahff'-el) *f.* wafer.
Waffenbruder (vahff'-n-brood-er) *m.* comrade.
Waffenhaus (vahff'-n-howss) *n.* arsenal.
Waffnen (vahff'-nen) *v.* to arm.
Wage (vahg'-erh) *f.* pair of scales: balance.
Wagen (vahg'-n) *v.* to risk: dare.
Wägen (vayg'-n) *v.* to weigh.
Wagenrad (vahg'-n-raht) *n.* carriage wheel.
Wagerecht (vahg'-erh-rekt) *a.* horizontal: level.
Wahl (vahl) *f.* choice.
Wählbar (vayl'-bar) *a.* eligible.
Wahlstimme (vahl'-shtimm-erh) *f.* vote.
Wähnen (vayn'-n) *v.* to presume.
Wahnsinn (vahn'-zin) *m.* madness.
Wahr (vahr) *a.* true: real.
Wahren (vahr'-n) *v.* to preserve: take care of.
Währen (vayr'-n) *v.* to last: endure.
Während (vayr'-ent) *pr. & ad.* during: lasting.
Wahrhaftig (vahr-haft'-ik) *ad.* truly: really.
Wahrheit (vahr'-hyte) *f.* truth.
Wahrlich (vahr'-lik) *ad.* truly.
Wahrsagen (vahr'-zarg-n) *v.* to tell fortunes.
Wahrscheinlich (vahr-shine'-lik) *a. & ad.* probable: likely.
Waise (vye'-ze) *f.* orphan.

Waisenhaus (vye'-zen-howss) *n.* orphan-asylum.
Wald (vahlt) *m.* wood: forest.
Waldung (vahlt'-oong) *f.* wood.
Wallen (vahl'-n) *v.* to bubble: boil.
Wallfahrt (vahl'-fahrt) *f.* pilgrimage.
Wallfisch (vahl'-fish) *m.* whale.
Walten (vahl'-ten) *v.* to govern: rule.
Walze (vahl'-tserh) *f.* roller.
Walzen (vahl'-tsen) *v.* to roll: waltz.
Walzer (vahl'-tser) *m.* waltz.
Wand (vahnt) *f.* wall.
Wandelbar (vahnn'-del-bar) *a.* perishable.
Wanderer (vahnn'-der-er) *m.* traveller.
Wandern (vahnn'-der-n) *v.* to wander—*n.* travelling.
Wandschrank (vahnns'-shrank) *m.* cupboard.
Wange (vahng'-erh) *f.* cheek.
Wanken (vahng'-ken) *v.* to stagger: vacillate: flinch.
Wann (vahnn) *ad.* when.
Wannen (vahnn'-n) *ad.* whence —*v.* to fan.
Wanze (vahnt'-ze) *f.* bug.
Wappnen (vahpp'-nen) *v.* to arm.
Warenlager (vahr'-en-lahg-er) *n.* warehouse.
Warenprobe (vahr'-en-prohberh) *f.* sample: pattern.
Warenrechnung (vahr'-en-rek-noong) *f.* invoice.
Warm (varm) *a.* warm: hot.
Wärme (vairm'-erh) *f.* warmth: heat.
Wärmemesser (vairm'-erh-mess-er) *m.* thermometer.
Wärmen (vairm'-n) *v.* to warm—*n.* heating.
Warnen (varn'-n) *v.* to warn.
Warnung (varn'-oong) *f.* warning.
Warten (vart'-n) *v.* to wait.
Warum (vahr'-oom) *ad.* why: wherefore.
Warze (vart'-se) *f.* wart: nipple.
Was (vahss) *pn.* what: whatever: that: something.
Waschbar (vahsh'-bahr) *a.* washable.
Waschbecken (vahsh'-beck-n) *n.* wash-hand basin.

Wäsche (vesh'-er) *f.* washing linen.
Waschen (vahsh'-n) *v.* to wash.
Wasser (vahss'-er) *n.* water.
Wasserbehälter (vahss'-er-behahlt-er) *m.* cistern: boiler.
Wasserblase (vahss'-er-blahzerh) *f.* blister.
Wasserdicht (vahss'-er-dikt) *a.* waterproof.
Wasserfall (vahss'-er-fahl) *m.* waterfall: cascade.
Wasserflasche (vahss'-er-flahsh-erh) *f.* water-bottle.
Wässerig (vess'-er-ik) *a.* watery.
Wasserkrug (vahss'-er-krook) *m.* water-jug.
Wasserkunst (vahss'-er-koonst) *f.* fountain.
Wasserleitung (vahss'-er-liteoong) *f.* canal.
Wasserstoff (vahss'-er-shtoff) *m.* hydrogen.
Wassersucht (vahss'-er-zookt) *f.* dropsy.
Wasservogel (vahss'-er-fohgel) *m.* water-fowl.
Waten (vaht'-n) *v.* to ford.
Watte (vaht'-terh) *f.* wadding.
Weben (vay'-ben) *v.* to weave: plot.
Weber (vay'-ber) *m.* weaver.
Wechsler (vex'-sler) *m.* money-changer: banker.
Wecken (veck'-n) *v.* to wake: awaken.
Weckuhr (veck'-oor) *f.* alarum clock.
Wedel (vay'-del) *m.* tail: fan.
Weder (vayd'-er) *c.* neither.
Weg (veck) *ad.* away: gone— *m.* way: road.
Wegbegeben (veck'-be-gayben) *v.* to go away.
Weggehen (veck'-gay-n) *v.* to depart.
Weglassen (veck'-lahs-sen) *v.* to omit.
Weglaufen (veck'-lowf-n) *v.* to run away: desert.
Wegsein (veck'-sine) *v.* to be absent.
Wegstellen (veck'-shtell-n) *v.* to put aside.
Wegstreichen (veck'-shtry-ken) *v.* to erase.
Wegtragen (veck'-trah-gen) *v.* to carry away.

Wegweiser (veck'-vy-zer) *m.* guide: finger-post.
Wegwenden (veck'-vend-n) *v.* to turn away.
Wegzug (veck'-tsook) *m.* removing: departure.
Weh (vay) *a.* painful: aching— *n.* pain.
Wehen (vay'-n) *v.* to blow: wave.
Wehklagen (vay'-klah-gen) *v.* to lament.
Wehmut (vay'-moot) *f.* sadness.
Wehmütig (vay'-meet-ik) *a.* melancholy.
Wehmutter (vay'-moot-er) *f.* midwife.
Wehr (vayr) *f.* weapon: fortification—*n.* dam.
Wehrlos (vayr'-lohs) *a.* weak.
Weib (vipe) *n.* woman: wife.
Weiberhaft (vipe'-er-hahft) *a.* effeminate.
Weiberhaus (vipe'-er-hows) *n.* harem.
Weiblich (vipe'-lik) *a.* female: feminine.
Weibsvolk (vipes'-folk) *n.* females: womenkind.
Weich (vyk) *a.* soft: tender.
Weichen (vyk'-n) *v.* to soften.
Weide (vyd'-erh) *f.* pasture. pasturage.
Weidenbaum (vyd'-n-bowm) *m.* willow-tree.
Weidenkorb (vyd'-n-korp) *m.* wicker basket.
Weidlich (vyd'-lik) *a. & ad.* brave: valiant.
Weidmann (vite'-mahn) *m.* huntsman.
Weigern (vy'-gern) *v.* to refuse: deny.
Weihnachten (vy'-nahkt-n) *pl.* Christmas.
Weihnachtsbaum (vy'-nahkts-bowm) *m.* Christmas tree.
Weihnachtsmann (vy'-nahkts-mahn) *m.* Santa Claus.
Weil (vyle) *c.* because: since: as.
Weilchen (vyle'-ken) *n.* moment.
Weilen (vyle'-n) *v.* to stay: linger.
Wein (vyne) *m.* wine: vine.
Weinbeere (vyne'-bair-erh) *f.* grape.

Weinberg (vyne'-bayrk) *m.* vineyard.
Weinen (vyne'-n) *v.* to weep.
Weinessig (vyne'-ess-ik) *m.* vinegar.
Weinflasche (vyne'-flahsh-erh) *f.* wine-bottle.
Weinglas (vyne'-glahs) *n.* wine-glass.
Weinhändler (vyne'-hend-ler) *m.* wine merchant.
Weinhaus (vyne'-hows) *n.* tavern.
Weinsauer (vyne'-sow-er) *a.* acid.
Weinschenke (vyne'-sheng-kerh) *f.* tavern: wine shop.
Weintraube (vyne'-trow-berh) *f.* bunch of grapes.
Weise (vy'-zerh) *a.* wise.
Weisen (vy'-zen) *v.* to show: teach.
Weisheit (vyce'-hite) *f.* wisdom: discretion.
Weiss (vyce) *a.* white: clean: blank.
Weissagen (vyce'-zahg-n) *v.* to prophesy—*n.* prophecy.
Weissbier (vyce'-beer) *n.* pale ale.
Weisse (vyce'-erh) *f.* whiteness: white.
Weissen (vyce'-n) *v.* to whiten: whitewash.
Weit (vyte) *a. & ad.* far: far off: distant.
Weite (vyte'-erh) *f.* width: extent.
Weiten (vyte'-en) *v.* to widen: enlarge.
Weiter (vyt'-er) *ad.* farther: larger.
Weitsichtig (vyte'-zik-tik) *a.* far-sighted.
Weizen (vyte'-sen) *m.* wheat.
Welcher, Welche, Welches, (velk'-er, -e, es) *pn.* who: which: some: any: that.
Welt (velt) *f.* world: universe: the earth.
Weltkugel (velt'-koog-l) *f.* globe.
Weltlich (velt'-lik) *a.* worldly.
Weltmarkt (velt'-markt) *m.* emporium.
Weltmeer (velt'-mair) *n.* ocean.
Weltweise (velt'-vy-ze) *m.* philosopher.
Wem (vaym) *pn.* to whom.

Wen (vayn) *pn.* whom.
Wenden (vend'-n) *v.* to turn.
Wendung (vend'-oong) *f.* turn: turning.
Wenig (vayn'-ik) *a. & ad.* little: few.
Weniger (vayn'-ik-er) *a.* less: fewer.
Wenigkeit (vayn'-ik-ite) *f.* smallness: trifle.
Wenn (ven) *c.* when: if.
Wer (vayr) *pn.* who: he who: whoever.
Werber (vayr'-ber) *m.* recruiting officer.
Werden (vayr'-den) *v.* to become: grow.
Werfen (vayr'-fen) *v.* to throw: cast.
Werft (vayrft) *n.* wharf.
Werk (vayrk) *n.* work: workmanship.
Werkleute (vayrk'-loyt-erh) *pl.* workmen.
Werkstatt (vayrk'-shtat) *f.* workshop.
Werkzeug (vayrk'-tsoyk) *n.* tool.
Wert (vayrt) *a.* worth: dear— *m.* value: price.
Wertlos (vayrt'-loos) *a.* worthless.
Wertvoll (vayrt'-fol) *a.* precious.
Wesenlos (vayz'-n-loos) *a.* unreal.
Wesentlich (vayz'-ent-lik) *a. & ad.* essential: real.
Wespe (vesp'-erh) *f.* wasp.
Wessen (vess'-n) *pn.* whose.
Weste (vest'-erh) *f.* vest: waistcoat.
Westen (vest'-n) *m.* west.
Westlich (vest'-lik) *a. & ad.* west: westerly.
Wettbewerb (vett'-b-vairp) *m.* competition.
Wette (vett'-erh) *f.* bet: wager.
Wetteiferer (vett'-ife-er-erh) *m.* competitor: rival.
Wetten (vett'-n) *v.* to bet: wager.
Wetter (vett'-er) *n.* weather: storm.
Wetterdicht (vett'-er-dikt) *a.* weather-proof.
Wetterfahne (vett'-er-fahn-erh) *f.* weather-cock.

Wetterglas (vett'-er-glahs) *n.* barometer.
Wettlauf (vett'-lowf) *m.* race.
Wettrennen (vett'-ren-n) *v.* to run a race—*n.* racing.
Wetzen (vett'-sen) *v.* to sharpen.
Wicht (vykt) *m.* person.
Wichtig (vykt'-ik) *a.* weighty: important.
Wider (veed'-er) *pr.* against.
Widerfahren (veed'-er-fahr-n) *v.* to happen.
Widerhallen (veed'-er-hahl-n) *v.* to echo.
Widerlegen (veed'-er-layg-n) *v.* to disprove.
Widerlich (veed'-er-lych) *a.* offensive.
Widern (veed'-ern) *v.* to loathe.
Widerrede (veed'-er-ray-derh) *f.* contradiction.
Widersacher (veed'-er-sahk-er) *m.* enemy.
Widersetzen (veed'-er-zets-n) *v.* to oppose: resist.
Widersprechen (veed'-er-shprek-n) *v.* to contradict.
Widerspruch (veed'-er-shprook) *m.* contradiction.
Widerstehen (veed'-er-shtay-n) *v.* to resist.
Widerwille (veed'-er-vill-erh) *m.* ill-will: aversion.
Widrig (veed'-rik) *a.* contrary: adverse.
Wie (vee) *ad.* how—*c.* as: like.
Wiede (veed'-erh) *f.* twig.
Wieder (veed'-er) *ad.* again.
Wiederbringen (veed'-er-bring-n) *v.* to restore: bring back.
Wiedereinbringen (veed'-er-ine-bring-n) *v.* to repair.
Wiederkehren (veed'-er-kay-ren) *v.* to return.
Wiedertun (veed'-er-toon) *v.* to repeat.
Wiege (veeg'-erh) *f.* cradle.
Wiese (veez'-erh) *f.* meadow.
Wieviel (vee'-feel) *ad.* how much.
Wiewohl (vee'-vohl) *c.* although: though.
Wild (vilt) *a.* wild: fierce: savage—*n.* game.
Wilddieb (vilt'-deep) *m.* poacher.

Wildpret (vilt'-pret) *n.* game: venison.

Willenlos (vill'-n-loos) *a.* weak.

Willfährig (vill'-fahr-ik) *a.* obliging: kind.

Willig (vill'-ik) *a.* willing: ready.

Windbeuteln (vinnt'-boyt-eln) *v.* to boast.

Windhund (vinnt'-hoont) *m.* greyhound.

Windpocken (vinnt'-pock-n) *pl.* chickenpox.

Wink (vink) *m.* wink: nod: sign.

Winkel (ving'-kel) *m.* corner: angle.

Winter (vinnt'-er) *m.* winter.

Wirbeln (veer'-bel-n) *v.* to whirl.

Wirken (veer'-ken) *v.* to work.

Wirksam (veerk'-zahm) *a.* powerful.

Wissen (viss'-n) *v.* to know— *n.* knowledge.

Witwe (vit'-vay) *f.* widow.

Wo (woh) *ad.* where: somewhere.

Wobei (woh'-by) *ad.* whereby.

Woche (vok'-erh) *f.* week.

Wöchentlich (verk'-ent-lik) *a.* & *ad.* weekly: every week.

Wodurch (voh-doohrk') *ad.* whereby.

Woge (voh'-gerh) *f.* wave.

Woher (voh-hayr') *ad.* whence.

Wohin (voh-hin') *ad.* whither.

Wohl (vohl) *ad.* well: indeed.

Wohlbehalten (vohl'-b-hahl-ten) *a.* safe.

Wohlerfahren (vohl'-erh-fahr-n) *a.* experienced.

Wohlfeil (vohl'-file) *a.* cheap.

Wohlgefallen (vohl'-ge-fahl-n) *n.* pleasure: satisfaction.

Wohlgemüt (vohl'-ge-meet) *a.* joyous: gay.

Wohltun (vohl'-toon) *v.* to benefit: do good.

Wohlwollend (vohl'-voll-ent) *a.* benevolent.

Wohnen (voh'-nen) *v.* to live: lodge.

Wohnlich (vohn'-lik) *a.* comfortable.

Wohnsitz (vohn'-sits) *m.* residence.

Wohnstube (vohn'-shtoob-erh) *f.* sitting-room.

Wohnzins (vohn'-tsins) *m.* rent.

Wolkenlos (volk'-n-loos) *a.* cloudless.

Wolkig (volk'-ik) *a.* cloudy.

Wolle (voll'-erh) *f.* wool.

Wollen (voll'-n) *v.* to be willing: wish: desire.

Wollenwaren (voll'-n'-vahr-n) *pl.* woollen goods.

Wollig (voll'-ik) *a.* woolly.

Wollust (vol'-loost) *f.* voluptuousness.

Wortbrüchig (vort'-breek-ik) *a.* faithless.

Wörterbuch (vert'-er-book) *n.* dictionary.

Wortspiel (vort'-shpeel) *n.* pun: quibble.

Worüber (voh'-reeb-er) *ad.* whereupon: whereat.

Woselbst (voh'-selpst) *ad.* where: wherever.

Wovor (voh-for') *ad.* before: of which: of what.

Wrack (vrack) *m.* & *n.* wreck.

Wucher (vook'-er) *m.* interest.

Wund (voont) *a.* sore: wounded.

Wundarzt (voont'-ahrtst) *m.* surgeon.

Wunde (voond'-erh) *f.* wound: bruise.

Wunder (voon'-der) *n.* wonder: marvel.

Wunderbar (voon'-der-bahr) *a.* wonderful.

Wunderlich (voon'-der-lik) *a.* odd: strange.

Wundersam (voon'-der-sahm) *a.* wonderful: miraculous.

Wunsch (voonsh) *m.* wish: desire.

Würde (veer'-derh) *f.* dignity: honour.

Würdigkeit (veer'-dig-kite) *f.* merit.

Würfel (veer'-fel) *m.* die—*pl.* dice.

Würgen (veer'-gen) *v.* to choke: strangle.

Wurm (voorm) *m.* worm: reptile.

Wurmen (voorm'-n) *v.* to vex: fret.

Wurst (voorst) *f.* sausage.

Wurzel (voort'-sel) *f.* root.

Wurzeln (voort'-seln) *v.* to root.

Wust (voost) *m.* trash: filth: chaos.
Wüten (veet'-n) *v.* to rage: fume.
Wütend (veet'-ent) *a.* furious: raging.

Z

Zacke (tsahck'-erh) *f.* prong: tooth (of comb): scallop.
Zagen (tsahg'-n) *v.* to be afraid—*n.* timidity.
Zaghaft (tsahg'-hahft) *a.* timid.
Zäh (tsay) *a.* tough: tenacious.
Zahl (tsayl) *f.* number: figure.
Zählbrett (tsayl'-bret) *n.* counter.
Zahlbruch (tsayl'-brook) *m.* fraction.
Zahlen (tsay'-len) *v.* to pay.
Zahlfigur (tsayl'-fig-oor) *f.* figure: cipher.
Zahlreich (tsayl'-ryk) *a.* numerous.
Zahlung (tsayl'-oong) *f.* payment.
Zahlungsanweisung (tsayl'-oong-sahn-vy-zoong) *f.* cheque.
Zahlwort (tsayl'-vort) *n.* numeral.
Zahm (tsahm) *a.* domestic.
Zähmen (tsay'-men) *v.* to tame: restrain.
Zähmung (tsay'-moong) *f.* taming.
Zahn (tsahn) *m.* tooth: cog (of wheel): prong (of fork).
Zahnbürste (tsahn'-beerst-erh) *f.* tooth-brush.
Zahnfleisch (tsahn'-flysh) *n.* gum: jaw.
Zahnpulver (tsahn'-pool-fer) *n.* tooth-powder.
Zahnrad (tsahn'-raht) *n.* cog-wheel.
Zahnweh (tsahn'-vay) *n.* tooth-ache.
Zange (tsahn'-gerh) *f.* pincers: tweezers: tongs.
Zank (tsahnk) *m.* quarrel.
Zanken (tsahnk'-n) *v.* to quarrel.
Zart (tsart) *a.* tender: fragile.
Zartheit (tsart'-hite) *f.* tenderness.
Zartsinn (tsart'-sin) *m.* delicacy.
Zauber (tsow'-ber) *m.* charm.

Zauberei (tsow'-bery) *f.* sorcery.
Zauberer (tsow'-ber-er) *m.* magician.
Zaubermittel (tsow'-ber-mitt-l) *n.* charm.
Zaudern (tsow'-dern) *v.* to hesitate.
Zaun (tsown) *m.* hedge: fence.
Zaunkönig (tsown'-kern-ik) *m.* wren.
Zehe (tsay'-erh) *f.* toe.
Zehn (tsayn) *a.* ten.
Zehren (tsay'-ren) *v.* to consume: waste.
Zeichen (tsy'-ken) *n.* mark: trade-mark.
Zeichnen (tsyk'-nen) *v.* to draw: sketch.
Zeichnung (tsyk'-noong) *f.* sketch.
Zeigen (tsy'-gen) *v.* to exhibit.
Zeit (tsyte) *f.* time.
Zeitgenoss (tsyte'-gen-oss) *m* contemporary.
Zeitig (tsyte'-ik) *a. & ad.* early.
Zeitigen (tsyte'-ik-n) *v.* to ripen.
Zeitschrift (tsyte'-shrift) *f.* journal.
Zeitung (tsyte'-oong) *f.* news: newspaper.
Zeitvertreib (tsyte'-fayr-tripe) *m.* pastime.
Zeitweilig (tsyte'-vill-ik) *a.* temporary.
Zelle (tsell'-erh) *f.* cell.
Zentral (tsent-rahl') *a.* central.
Zerbrechlich (tsayr-brek'-lik) *a.* fragile: brittle.
Zerbröckeln (tsayr-brerk'-eln) *v.* to crumble.
Zerdrücken (tsayr-dreek'-n) *v.* to crush.
Zerfliessen (tsayr-flees'-n) *v.* to melt: dissolve.
Zergliedern (tsayr-gleed'-ern) *v.* to dissect.
Zerhacken (tsayr-hahk'-n) *v.* to mince.
Zerknirschen (tsayr-kneersh'-n) *v.* to crush: bruise.
Zerknirscht (tsayr-kneer'sht) *a.* crushed.
Zerkratzen (tsayr-kraht'-sen) *v.* to scratch.
Zernagen (tsayr-nahg'-n) *v.* to gnaw.

Zernichten (tsayr-nik'-ten) v. to undo.
Zerreiben (tsayr-ry'-ben) v. to pulverize: grind.
Zerren (tsay'-ren) v. to worry.
Zerrinnen (tsayr-rinn'-n) v. to melt.
Zerschellen (tsayr-shell'-n) v. to dash to pieces.
Zerschneiden (tsayr-shny'-den) v. to cut: carve.
Zerstäuben (tsayr-shtoy'-ben) v. to scatter.
Zerstören (tsayr-shter'-n) v. to destroy.
Zerstörung (tsayr-shter'-oong) f. ruin.
Zerteilen (tsayr-ty'-len) v. to divide.
Zerteilung (tsayr-ty'-loong) f. division.
Zertrümmern (tsayr-treem'ern) v. to wreck.
Zertrümmerung (tsayr-treem'-eroong) f. ruin.
Zetteln (tset'-eln) v. to scatter.
Zichorie (tsee-kohr'-yee) f. chicory.
Ziege (tsee'-gerh) f. goat.
Ziegel (tsee'-gel) m. brick: tile.
Ziehen (tsee'-n) v. to draw: extract: derive: train: move (chess).
Ziemen (tsee'-men) v. to be suitable.
Ziemlich (tseem'-lik) a. moderate: tolerable: passable.
Zierat (tseer'-aht) m. embellishment.
Zierde (tseer'-de) f. ornament.
Zieren (tseer'-n) v. to decorate.
Zierlich (tseer'-lik) a. elegant.
Zigarette (tsee-gahr-ret'-erh) f. cigarette.
Zimmer (tsim'-mer) n. room: chamber.
Zimmermann (tsim'-mer-mahn) m. carpenter.
Zink (tsink) m. & n. zinc.
Zinn (tsinn) n. tin: tinware.
Zins (tsins) m. rent: interest.
Zirka (tseer'-kar) adv. nearly: about.
Zirkel (tseer'-kel) m. circle.
Zischeln (tsish'-eln) v. to whisper.
Zischen (tsish'-n) v. to hiss.
Zither tsit'-er) f. zither.

Zitrone (tsee-troh'-ner) f. lemon: lime: citron.
Zittern (tsit'-ern) v. to tremble: quiver: shiver.
Zobel (tso'-bel) m. sable.
Zögern (tser'-gen) v. to tarry: hesitate.
Zögerung (tser'-ger-oong) f. delay.
Zoll (tsoll) m. toll: duty: tax.
Zollamt (tsoll'-ahmt) n. custom-house.
Zollbeamte (tsoll'-be-ahmt-erh) m. custom-house officer.
Zollen (tsoll'-n) v. to pay duty.
Zollfrei (tsoll'-fry) a. duty free.
Zorn (tsorn) m. anger.
Zornig (tsorn'-ik) a. angry.
Zotig (tsoht'-ik) a. obscene.
Zu (tsoo) pr. to: at: by: in: for: on—ad. too.
Zubereiten (tsoo'-ber-ry-ten) v. to prepare.
Zucht (tsookt) f. education: race.
Züchtigen (tseek'-tig-n) v. to punish: chastise.
Züchtigung (tseek'-tig-oong) f. chastisement.
Zucker (tsook'-er) m. sugar.
Zuckern (tsook'-ern) v. to sweeten.
Zuckerwerk (tsook'-er-vairk) n. confectionery.
Zudecken (tsoo'-deck-n) v. to cover.
Zudem (tsoo-dayme') ad. besides: moreover.
Zuführen (tsoo'-feer-n) v. to convey: conduct: import.
Zug (tsook) m. train: passage: move (at chess): removal.
Zugabe (tsoo'-gah-berh) f. supplement.
Zugänglich (tsoo'-geng-lik) a. approachable: accessible.
Zugetan (tsoo'-ge-tahn) a. fond of: devoted.
Zugleich (tsoo'-glyk) ad. at the same time: together
Zuheilen (tsoo'-hile-n) v. to heal up.
Zuhören (tsoo'-her-n) v. to listen to.
Zuknöpfen (tsoo'-knerp-fen) v. to button up.
Zukunft (tsoo'-koonft) f. future.
Zulage (tsoo'-lah-gerh) f. addition: increase.

Zulassung (tsoo'-lahss-oong) *f.* admission: permission.
Zulauf (tsoo'-lowf) *m.* crowd.
Zuletzt (tsoo'-letst) *ad.* at last: finally.
Zumal (tsoo-mahl') *ad.* especially.
Zumeist (tsoo-myest') *ad.* mostly.
Zumuten (tsoo'-moot-n) *v.* to desire: expect.
Zumutung (tsoo'-moot-oong) *f.* demand: expectation.
Zuname (tsoo'-nahm-erh) *m.* surname: nickname.
Zünder (tseen'-der) *m.* match.
Zunehmen (tsoo'-nay-men) *v.* to increase: augment.
Zuneigung (tsoo'-ny-goong) *f.* affection.
Zunge (tsoong'-erh) *f.* tongue: language.
Zupfen (tsoop'-fen) *v.* to pluck.
Zureden (tsoo'-ray-den) *v.* to persuade.
Zurück (tsoo'-reek) *ad.* back: backwards.
Zurückbehalten (tsoo'-reek-b-hahl-ten) *v.* to retain.
Zurückhalten (tsoo'-reek-hahl-ten) *v.* to detain.
Zurückkehren (tsoo'-reek-kay-ren) *v.* to return.
Zurücklassen (tsoo'-reek-lahss-n) *v.* to leave behind.
Zurückreise (tsoo'-reek-ry-serh) *f.* return-journey.
Zurücksetzen (tsoo'-reek-zet-sen) *v.* to disregard: neglect.
Zusamt (tsoo'-sahmt) *pr.* together with.
Zusatz (tsoo'-sahts) *m.* supplement.
Zuschauer (tsoo'-show-er) *m.* spectator.
Zuschliessen (tsoo'-shlees-n) *v.* to close.
Zuschreiben (tsoo'-shry-ben) *v.* to write to.
Zuschrift (tsoo'-shrift) *f.* letter.
Zusprechen (tsoo'-shprek-n) *v.* to encourage: cheer up.
Zuspruch (tsoo'-shprook) *m.* encouragement.

Zutat (tsoo'-taht) *f.* addition.
Zuteilen (tsoo'-tyle-n) *v.* to allot.
Zutragen (tsoo'-trahg-n) *v.* to report: happen.
Zuträglich (tsoo'-tray-klik) *a.* beneficial: advantageous.
Zutrauen (tsoo'-trow-n) *v.* to trust—*n.* confidence.
Zuverlässig (tsoo'-fayr-less-ik) *a.* reliable.
Zuvor (tsoo-fohr') *ad.* before: previously.
Zuvorkommen (tsoo-fohr'-komm-n) *v.* to prevent.
Zuvorkommenheit (tsoo-fohr'-komm-hite) *f.* politeness.
Zwanzig (tsvahnt'-sik) *a.* twenty.
Zwar (tsvar) *ad.* certainly: indeed.
Zweck (tsveck) *m.* aim: purpose.
Zwei (tsvy) *a.* two.
Zweideutig (tsvy'-doyt-ik) *a.* ambiguous.
Zweifel (tsvy'-fel) *m.* doubt.
Zweifelhaft (tsvy'-fel-hahft) *a.* doubtful.
Zweifeln (tsvy'-fell-n) *v.* to doubt.
Zweig (tsvyke) *m.* branch: twig.
Zweikampf (tsvy'-kahmpf) *m.* duel.
Zweimal (tsvy'-mahl) *ad.* twice.
Zweite (tsvyt'-erh) *a.* second.
Zwerg (tsvayrk) *m.* dwarf.
Zwergig (tsvayrk'-ik) *a.* dwarf: stunted.
Zwetsche (tsvayrk'-ik) *f.* plum: damson.
Zwicken (tsvyk'-n) *v.* to pinch.
Zwieback (tsvee'-bahk) *m.* biscuit.
Zwiebel (tsveeb'-l) *f.* onion: bulb.
Zwilling (tsvil'-linge) *m.* twin.
Zwirn (tsveern) *m.* thread.
Zwischen (tsvish'-n) *pr.* between: betwixt.
Zwölf (tsverlf) *a.* twelve: dozen.
Zylinder (tsee-lyn'-der) *m.* cylinder.

PART II
ENGLISH-GERMAN
(ENGLISCH-DEUTSCH)

PART II
ENGLISH-GERMAN

A — According

A
A, an, *article,* Ein, eine, ein.
Aback, *adv.* Rückwärts.
Abandon, *v.* Verlassen.
Abandonment, *n.* Verlassenheit (*f*).
Abate, *v.* Vermindern, herabsetzen.
Abbey, *n.* Abtei (*f*).
Abbot, *n.* Abt (*m*).
Abbreviate, *v.* Abkürzen.
Abbreviation, *n.* Abkürzung (*f*).
Abdicate, *v.* Abdanken.
Abdomen, *n.* Unterleib (*m*).
Abdominal, *adj.* Unterleibs.
Abduct, *v.* Abziehen.
Abeyance, *n.* Unentschiedenheit (*f*).
Abhor, *v.* Verabscheuen.
Abide, *v.* Bleiben.
Abide by, *v.* Beharren.
Ability, *n.* Fähigkeit (*f*).
Abject, *adj.* Verworfen.
Abjure, *v.* Abschwören.
Ablaze, *adj.* & *adv.* Brennend, flammend.
Able, *adj.* Fähig, tüchtig, imstande.
Able-bodied, *adj.* Dienstfähig.
Aboard, *adv.* An bord.
Abode, *n.* Wohnsitz (*m*) a dwelling: Aufenthalt (*m*) a stay.
Abolish, *v.* Abschaffen.
Abominable, *adj.* Abscheulich.
Abominate, *v.* Verabscheuen.
Abound, *v.* Vorhanden sein.
About, *adv.* & *prep.* Um, etwa, ungefähr.
Above, *adv.* Oben, darüber, *prep.* Uber.
Abreast, *adv.* Nebeneinander.
Abridge, *v.* Abkürzen.
Abroad, *adv.* Auswärts, im Ausland.

Abrupt, *adj.* Schroff.
Abscess, *n.* Geschwür (*n*).
Abscond, *v.* Sich verbergen.
Absence, *n.* Abwesenheit (*f*).
Absent, *adj.* Abwesend: *v.* Ausbleiben.
Absentee, *n.* Abwesende (*m.* or *f.*).
Abstain, *v.* Sich enthalten.
Abstract, *v.* Abziehen: *adj.* Abgezogen: *n.* Abstrakt.
Absurd, *adj.* Albern.
Abundance, *n.* Überfluss (*m*).
Abundant, *adj.* Reichlich.
Abuse, *n.* Missbrauch (*m*): *v.* Missbrauchen.
Abusive, *adj.* Missbrauchlich.
Abutting, *adj.* & *prep.* Angrenzend.
Abyss, *n.* Abgrund (*m*).
Acacia, *n.* Akazie (*f*).
Accede, *v.* Einwilligen.
Accelerate, *v.* Beschleunigen.
Accent, *n.* Betonung (*f*), Akzent (*m*).
Accept, *v.* Annehmen, akzeptieren.
Acceptance, *n.* Annahme (*f*).
Access, *n.* Zutritt (*m*).
Accessible, *adj.* Zugänglich.
Accident, *n.* Zufall (*m*).
Accidental, *adj.* Zufällig.
Acclaim, *v.* Beifall.
Accommodate, *v.* Anpassen, unterbringen.
Accompaniment, *n.* Begleitung.
Accompany, *v.* Begleiten.
Accomplish, *v.* Vollenden, vollführen.
Accomplishment, *n.* Ausführung (*f*), Talente (*n. pl.*).
Accord, *n.* Übereinstimmung (*f*): *v.*, Übereinstimmen.
Accordingly, *adv.* Demgemass.
According to, *prep.* Gemäss.

Accordion — Advert

Accordion, *n.* Ziehharmonika (*f*).
Accost, *v.* Anneden.
Account, *n.* Rechnung (*f*).
Accoutre, *v.* Ausschmücken.
Accredit, *v.* Bevollmächtigen.
Accrue, *v.* Erwachsen.
Accumulate, *v.* Aufhäufen, anhäufen.
Accuracy, *v.* Genauigkeit (*f*).
Accurate, *adj.* Genau.
Accursed, *adj.* Verflucht.
Accuse, *v.* Anklagen.
Accuser, *n.* Kläger (*m*).
Accustom, *v.* Gewöhnen
Accustomed, *adj.* Gewohnt.
Ace, *n.* As (*n*).
Acerbity, *n.* Herbigkeit (*f*).
Acetic, *adj.* Essigsäure.
Ache, *n.* Schmerz (*m*): *v.* Schmerzen.
Achieve, *v.* Vollenden, vollbringen.
Achievement, *n.* Vollführung (*f*).
Acid, *n.* Säure (*f*).
Acidity, *n.* Säure (*f*).
Acidulated, *adj.* Säuerlich.
Acknowledge, *v.* Anerkennen.
Acknowledgment, *n.* Anerkennung (*f*).
Acme, *n.* Gipfel, Höchstepunkt (*m*).
Acorn, *n.* Eichel (*f*).
Acquaint, *v.* Bekannt machen.
Acquaintance, *n.* Bekanntschaft (*f*).
Acquiesce, *v.* Einwilligen.
Acquiescence, *n.* Einwilligung (*f*).
Acquire, *v.* Erwerben.
Acquirement, *n.* Fertigkeit (*f*).
Acquisition, *n.* Erwerbung (*f*).
Acquit, *v.* Freisprechen, quittieren.
Acquittal, *n.* Freisprechung (*f*).
Acquittance, *n.* Quittung (*f*).
Acre, *n.* Acker (*m*).
Acrid, *adj.* Beissend, scharf.
Across, *adv.* Hinüber, breit: *prep.* Über, durch.
Act, *n.* Tat (*f*), Akt (*m*): *v.* Spielen, handeln.
Acting, *n.* Spiel (*n*).
Action, *n.* Handlung (*f*).
Active, *adj.* Tätig, wirkend, belebt.
Activity, *n.* Tätigkeit (*f*).
Actor, *n.* Schauspieler (*m*).

Actress, *n.* Schauspielerin (*f*).
Actual, *adj.* Wirklich, tatsächlich.
Actuate, *v.* Antreiben.
Acute, *adj.* Scharf, spitz.
Adapt, *v.* Anpassen.
Add, *v.* Hinzufügen, addieren.
Adder (snake), *n.* Natter (*f*).
Addition, *n.* Addition (*f*).
Address, *n.* Anschrift (*f*). Adresse (*f*); *v.* Adressieren.
Adduce, *v.* Beibringen, anführen.
Adhere, *v.* Anhangen, anhaften.
Adhesive, *adj.* Anhangend, anklebend.
Adjacent, *adj.* Angrenzend, anliegend.
Adjective, *n.* Beiwort (*n*).
Adjoin, *v.* Angrenzen, anfügen.
Adjudge, *v.* Zuerkennen, verurteilen.
Adjunct, *n.* Zusatz (*m*).
Adjust, *v.* Ordnen, einstellen.
Administer, *v.* Verwalten, darreichen.
Admirable, *adj.* Bewunderungswürdig.
Admire, *v.* Bewundern.
Admirer, *n.* Bewunderer (*m*).
Admission, *n.* Zutritt (*m*).
Admit, *v.* Einlassen, zugeben, zulassen.
Admittance, *n.* Zutritt (*m*), Zulassung.
Admonish, *v.* Ermahnen, warnen.
Adopt, *v.* Adoptieren, annehmen.
Adore, *v.* Anbeten.
Adorn, *v.* Schmücken.
Adrift, *adv.* Treibend.
Adult, *n.* Erwachsene (*m*)· *adj.* Erwachsen.
Adulterate, *v.* Verfälschen.
Advance, *n.* Vorschuss (*m*), Steigen (*n*): *v.* Vorangehen vorrücken.
Advantage, *n.* Vorteil.
Advantageous, *adj.* Vorteilhaft.
Advent, *n.* Ankunft (*f*).
Adventure, *n.* Übenteuer (*n*), Abenteuer (*n*).
Adversary, *n.* Gegner (*m*).
Adverse, *adj.* Widrig.
Advert, *v.* Hinweisen auf, erwähnen.

Advertise, *v.* Anzeigen, annoncieren.
Advertisement, *n.* Anzeige (*f*).
Advertiser, *n.* Anzeiger (*m*), Inserent (*m*).
Advice, *n.* Nachricht (*f*), rat (*m*).
Advisable, *adj.* Ratsam.
Advise, *v.* Benachrichtigen, raten.
Adviser, *n.* Ratgeber (*m*).
Aerial, *n.* Antenne (*f*).
Aerodrome, *n.* Flugplatz (*m*).
Aeroplane, *n.* Flugzeug (*n*).
Afar, *adv.* Fern, weit.
Affable, *adj.* Freundlich.
Affair, *n.* Geschäft (*n*).
Affect, *v.* Angehen, affektieren.
Affectionate, *adj.* Liebevoll, liebend zugetan.
Afflict, *v.* Betrüben.
Affliction, *n.* Betrübnis (*f*).
Afford, *v.* Sich leisten.
Affray, *n.* Schlägerei (*f*).
Affront, *n.* Beleidigung (*f*).
Afraid, *adj.* Beforgt, bange.
Aft, *adj. & adv.* Hinten.
After, *adv.* Nachter: *prep.* Nacht.
Afternoon, *n.* Nachmittag (*m*).
Afterwards, *adv.* Nachher.
Again, *adv.* Wieder, entgegen.
Against, *prep.* Gegen.
Age, *n.* Zeitalter (*n*).
Age, to be of, *v.* Mündig sein.
Agency, *n.* Agentur (*f*), Wirkung (*f*).
Agent, *n.* Vertreter (*m*).
Aggravate, *v.* Verschlimmern, ärgern.
Aggregate, *n.* Häufen (*m*): *v.* Zusammenhaufen.
Aggression, *n.* Angriff (*m*), Unfall (*m*).
Aggressor, *n.* Angreifer (*m*).
Aggrieve, *v.* Betrüben.
Agile, *adj.* Behend, flink, gelenkig.
Agility, *n.* Behendigkeit (*f*).
Agitate, *v.* Schütteln, aufregen, bewegen.
Agitation, *n.* Erregung (*f*), Bewegung (*f*).
Agonize, *v.* Martern.
Agony, *n.* Todeskampf (*m*).
Agree, *v.* Übereinstimmen.
Agreeable, *adj.* Angenehm.

Agreement, *n.* Übereinstimmung (*f*).
Agricultural, *adj.* Landwirtschaftlich.
Agriculture, *n.* Landwirtschaft (*f*).
Aground, *adv.* Gestrandet.
Ahead, *adv.* Voran, vorwärts.
Aid, *n.* Hilfe (*f*).
Aid, *v.* Helfen.
Ailing, *adj.* Kränklich.
Ailment, *n.* Leiden (*n*), Krankheit (*f*).
Aim, *n.* Ziel (*n.*), Richtung (*f.*).
Aim, *v.* Zielen.
Aimless, *adj.* Ziellos.
Air, *n.* Luft (*f*), **Music —** Melodie (*f*).
Airship, *n.* Luftschiff (*n*).
Ajar, *adj.* Halb offen.
Akin, *adj.* Verwandt.
Alacrity, *n.* Bereitwilligkeit (*f*).
Alarm, *n.* Aufruhr (*m*).
Alarm, *v.* Beunruhigen.
Alarming, *adj. & adv.* Beunruhigend.
Alertness, *n.* Wachsamkeit (*f*).
Alias, *adv.* Alias.
Alien, *n.* Fremde (*m*), Ausländer (*m*).
Alight, *v.* Absteigen.
Alight, *adj.* Brennend.
Alignment, *n.* Einrichten (*n*).
Alike, *adj. & adv.* Ähnlich, gleich.
Aliment, *n.* Nahrung (*f*).
Alimentation, *n.* Unterhalt (*m*).
Alive, *adj. or adv.* Lebendig.
Alkali, *n.* Laugensalz (*n*).
All, *adj.* Aller, alle, alles, ganz: *adv.* gänzlich: *n.*, All (*n*).
After all, am ende.
All at, durchaus.
All at once, auf einmal.
All but, fast.
All right, schon gut.
All the better, desto besser.
All the more, umso mehr.
Not at all, gar nicht
Allay, *v.* Beschwichtigen.
Allege, *v.* Anführen.
Allegiance, *n.* Lehnspflicht (*f*), Treue (*f*).
Alleviate, *v.* Erleichtern.
Alleviation, *n.* Erleichterung (*f*).
Alley, *n.* Gasse (*f*).
Alliance, *n.* Bündnis (*n*).

Allied 95 **Apologize**

Allied, *adj.* Verbünden.
Alligator, *n.* Alligator (*m*).
Alliteration, *n.* Stabreim (*m*).
Allocation, Anweisung (*f*).
Allot, *v.* Zuerkennen.
Allow, *v.* Erlauben.
Allowance, *n.* Erlaubnis (*f*).
Alloy, *n.* Legierung (*f*).
Allude, *v.* Anspielen.
Allure, *v.* Anlocken.
Allusion, *n.* Anspielung.
Ally, *n.* Bundesgenoss (*m*): *v.* Verbünden.
Almanack, *n.* Almanach (*m*).
Almighty, *n.* Allmächtige (*m*).
Almond, *n.* Mandel (*f*).
Almost, *adv.* Beinahe, fast.
Alms, *n.* Almosen (*n*).
Almshouse, *n.* Armenhaus (*n*).
Aloft, *adv.* Erhaben, hoch.
Alone, *adj. & adv.* Allein.
  All alone, ganz allein.
  To let alone, in Ruhe lassen.
Along, *adv.* Entlang: *prep.* Längs.
Aloof, *adv.* Fern.
Aloud, *adv.* Laut.
Already, *adv.* Bereits.
Also, *adv.* Auch, ebenfalls.
Altar, *n.* Altar, *m*.
Alter, *v.* Ändern.
Alteration, *n.* Änderung (*f*).
Although, *conj.* Obgleich.
Altitude, *n.* Höhe (*f*).
Altogether, *adv.* Zusammen, gänzlich.
Alum, *n.* Alaun (*m*).
Aluminium, *n.* Aluminium (*n*).
Always, *adv.* Immer.
Amass, *v.* Anhäufen.
Amaze, *v.* Erstaunen.
Amazement, *n.* Erstaunen (*n*).
Ambassador, *n.* Gesandte (*m*).
Amber, *n.* Bernstein (*m*).
Ambiguous, *adj.* Zweideutig.
Amble, *v.* Pass gehen: *n.* Passgang.
American, *adj.* Amerikanisch.
Amiable, *adj.* Liebenswürdig.
Amid, amidst, *prep.* Inmitten, mitten in.
Amongst, *prep.* Unter, zwischen.
Amount, *n.* Betrag.
Ample, *adj.* Reichlich.

Amuse, *v.* Unterhalten, ergötzen.
Amusement, *n.* Belustigung (*f*).
An, article, Ein, eine, ein.
Analysis, *n.* Analyse (*f*).
Analyst, *n.* Wissenschaftliche Chemiker (*m*).
Anarchy, *n.* Anarchie (*f*).
Ancestor, *n.* Vorfahr (*m*). Ahnherr (*m*).
Anchor, *n.* Anker (*m*).
Anchovy, *n.* Sardelle (*f*).
Ancient, *adj.* Alt.
And, *conj.* Und.
Angel, *n.* Engel (*m*).
Anger, *n.* Zorn (*m*), Ärger (*m*).
Angry, *adj.* Ärgerlich, zornig.
Animal, *adj.* Tier (*n*).
Ankle, *n.* Fussknöchel (*m*).
Annex, *v.* Annektieren.
Anniversary, *n.* Jahresfeier (*f*).
Announce, *v.* Ankündigen.
Announcement, *n.* Anzeige (*f*).
Announcer, *n.* Ansager (*m*).
Annoy, *v.* Ärgern, belastigen.
Annoyance, *n.* Verdruss (*m*).
Annual, *adj.* Jährlich.
Another, *adj.* Ein anderer.
  One another, einander.
Answer, *n.* Antwort (*f*): *v.* Antworten.
Ant, *n.* Ameise (*f*).
Anthem, *n.* Hymne (*f*).
Anthracite, *n.* Anthrazit (*m*).
Anticipate, *v.* Vorwegnehmen, vorhersehen.
Anticipation, *n.* Voraussicht (*f*).
Antidote, *n.* Gegengift (*n*).
Antiseptic, *n.* Antiseptikum (*n*).
Anxiety, *n.* Besorgnis (*f*), Angst (*f*).
Anxious, *adj.* Unruhig, ängstlich.
Any, *adj.* Irgend ein (or eine)
Anybody, irgend jemand.
Anyhow, auf jedenfalls.
Anyone, as anybody.
Anything, etwas.
Anyway, immerhin.
Anywhere, irgendwo.
Apart, *adv.* Beiseite.
Apartment, *n.* Zimmer (*n*).
Apologize, *v.* Sich entschuldigen.

Apology   96   **Asleep**

Apology, *n.* Entschuldigung (*f*).
Appalling, *adj.* Schauderhaft.
Apparatus, *n.* Apparat (*m*).
Apparent, *adj.* Scheinbar.
Appeal, *n.* Appellieren (*f*): *v.* Appellieren.
Appear, *v.* Erscheinen.
Appearance, *n.* Erscheinung (*f*).
Appetite, *n.* Esslust (*f*).
Applaud, *v.* Beifall spenden.
Applause, *n.* Beifall (*m*).
Apple, *n.* Apfel (*m*).
Apply, *v.* Anwenden, auflegen.
Appoint, *v.* Ernennen, festsetzen.
Appointment, *n.* Festsetzung (*f*).
Appreciate, *v.* Schätzen, anerkennen.
Apprentice, *n.* Lehrling (*m*).
Approach, *n.* Annäherung (*f*): *v.* Nähern.
Appropriate, *v.* Sich aneignen: *adj.* Angemessen.
Approval, *n.* Billigung (*f*).
Approve, *v.* Billigen.
Apricot, *n.* Aprikose (*f*).
Apron, *n.* Schürze (*f*).
Apt, *adv.* Geschickt, geneigt, fähig.
Aqueduct, *n.* Wasserleitung (*f*).
Arbitrate, *v.* Entscheiden.
Arbitration, *n.* Schiedsspruch (*m.*); Entscheidung (*f*). Arbitrage (*f*).
Arbour, *n.* Laube (*f*).
Arc, *n.* Bogen (*m*).
Arcade, *n.* Bogengang (*m*).
Arch, *n.* Bogen (*m*), Gewölbe (*n*).
Archbishop, *n.* Erzbischof (*m*).
Archduke, *n.* Erzherzog (*m*).
Architect, *n.* Baumeister (*m*).
Architecture, *n.* Baukunst (*f*).
Archway, *n.* Bogengang (*m*).
Arc-lamp, *n.* Bogenlampe (*f*).
Ardent, *adj.* Feurig.
Area, *n.* Fläche (*f*).
Arena, *n.* Kampfplatz (*m*): Arena (*f*).
Argue, *v.* Disputieren, schliessen.
Argument, *n.* Beweisgrund.
Arithmetic, *n.* Rechenkunst (*f*), Rechen (*n*).

Ark (Biblical), *n.* Bundeslade (*f*).
Arm, *n.* Arm (*m*), Ast (*m*): *v.* Sich bewaffnen.
Armchair, *n.* Lehnsessel (*m*).
Armour, *n.* Rüstung (*f*).
Army, *n.* Heer (*m*), Menge (*f*).
Around, *adv.* Ringsherum: *prep.* Um . . . herum.
Arouse, *v.* Aufwecken.
Arrange, *v.* Ordnen, einrichten.
Arrangement, *n.* Anordnung (*f*).
Arrear, *n.* Rückstand (*m*).
In Arrears, rückständig.
Arrest, *n.* Hemmung (*f*), Verhaftung (*f*): *v.* Hemmen, verhaften.
Arrival, *n.* Ankunft (*f*), Ankömmling (*m*).
Arrive, *v.* Ankommen.
Arrow, *n.* Pfeil (*m*).
Arsenal, *n.* Zeughaus (*n*).
Arsenic, *n.* Arsenik (*n*).
Art, *n.* Kunst (*f*).
Artful, *adj.* Schlau.
Artfully, *adv.* Künstlich.
Article, *n.* Artikel (*m*), Punkt (*m*).
Artificial, *adj.* Künstlich.
Artisan, *n.* Handwerker (*m*).
Artist, *n.* Künstler (*m*).
Artistic, *adj.* Künstlerisch.
As, *conj.* Als, so, so wie, wenn, wie.
As for, was betrifft.
As if, als ob.
As soon as, sobald wie.
As though, als ob.
As to, in Bezug auf.
As well, auch.
As yet, bis jetzt.
Asbestos, *n.* Asbest (*m*).
Ascend, *v.* Besteigen, hinaufsteigen.
Ascent, *n.* Besteigung (*f*).
Ascertain, *v.* Feststellen, ermitteln.
Ascribe, *v.* Zuschreiben.
Ash, *n.* Asche (*f*).
Ash tree, *n.* Esche (*f*).
Ash Wednesday, *n.* Aschermittwoch (*m*).
Ashamed, *adj.* Beschämt.
Ashore, *adv.* Am Ufer, ans Land.
Aside, *adv.* Beiseite.
Ask, *v.* Fragen, bitten, fordern.
Asleep, *adv.* Schlafend.

**Asparagus, ** *n.* Spargel (*m*).
**Aspect, ** *n.* Aussehen (*n*), ansehen (*n*).
**Ass, ** *n.* Esel (*m*).
**Assail, ** *v.* Angreifen.
**Assassin, ** *n.* Meuchelmörder (*m*).
**Assault, ** *n.* Angriff (*m*): *v.* Angreifen.
**Assemble, ** *v.* Versammeln.
**Assent, ** *n.* Beifall (*m*): *v.* Zustimmen.
**Assert, ** *v.* Verfechten, behaupten.
**Assign, ** *v.* Anweisen, abtreten.
**Assist, ** *v.* Helfen.
**Assistance, ** *n.* Beistand (*m*), Hilfe (*f*).
**Assistant, ** *n.* Gehilfe (*m*), Helfer (*m*).
**Associate, ** *v.* Genosse (*m*): *v.* Gesellen.
**Association, ** *n.* Vereinigung (*f*).
**Assortment, ** *n.* Sortiment (*n*).
**Assume, ** *v.* Annehmen.
**Assurance, ** *n.* Versicherung (*f*), Vertrauen (*n*).
**Assure, ** *v.* Versichern.
**Asthma, ** *n.* Asthma (*n*).
**Astonish, ** *v.* In Erstaunen setzen.
**Astonishment, ** *n.* Erstaunen (*n*).
**Asylum, ** *n.* Zufluchtsort (*m*); lunatic asylum, Irrenhaus (*n*).
**At, ** *prep.* An, auf, bei, gegen, in, zu.
  **At first, ** zuerst.
  **At home, ** Empfangstag (*m*).
  **At last, ** endlich.
  **At least, ** wenigstens.
  **At length, ** schliesslich.
  **At once, ** sofort.
  **At times, ** zuweilen.
  **Not at all, ** durchaus nicht.
**Athlete, ** *n.* Athlet (*m*), Wettkämpfer (*m*).
**Atlas, ** *n.* Landkartensammlung (*f*), Atlas (*m*).
**Atrocity, ** *n.* Abscheulichkeit (*f*).
**Attach, ** *v.* Anheften, befestigen.
**Attack, ** *n.* Angriff (*m*): *v.* Angreifen.
**Attempt, ** *n.* Versuch (*m*): *v.* Versuchen.
**Attend, ** *v.* Aufmerken, begleiten, bedienen.

**Attendance, ** *n.* Bedienung (*f*).
**Attendant, ** *n.* Diener (*m*), Aufwärter (*m*).
**Attention, ** *n.* Aufmerksamkeit (*f*).
**Attic, ** *n.* Dachstube (*f*), Dachkammer (*f*).
**Attitude, ** *n.* Haltung (*f*), Stellung (*f*).
**Attract, ** *v.* Anziehen.
**Attribute, ** *v.* Beimessen.
**Auction, ** *n.* Versteigerung (*f*).
**Auctioneer, ** *n.* Auktionator (*m*).
**Audience, ** *n.* Audienz (*f*), Gehör (*n*).
**Aunt, ** *n.* Tante (*f*).
**Author, ** *n.* Verfasser (*m*), Verfasserin (*f*).
**Authority, ** *n.* Ansehen (*n*), Autorität (*f*).
**Authorize, ** *v.* Ermächtigen.
**Automatic, ** *adj.* Automatisch.
**Autumn, ** *n.* Herbst (*m*).
**Avail, ** *v.* Nützen, helfen.
**Avalanche, ** *n.* Lawine (*f*).
**Avenge, ** *v.* Rächen.
**Avenue, ** *n.* Allee (*f*), Anfahrt (*f*), Zugang (*m*).
**Average, ** *n.* Durchschnitt (*m*).
**Aviary, ** *n.* Vogelhaus (*n*), Vogelhecke (*f*).
**Aviation, ** *n.* Fliegen (*n*).
**Aviator, ** *n.* Flieger (*m*).
**Avoid, ** *v.* Vermeiden.
**Await, ** *v.* Erwarten.
**Awake, ** *v.* Aufwecken, aufwachen.
**Aware, ** *adj.* Gewahr.
**Away, ** *adv.* Weg, fort.
**Awful, ** *adj.* Entsetzlich, furchterregend.
**Awkward, ** *adj.* Ungeschickt.
**Axe, ** *n.* Axt (*f*).
**Axle, ** *n.* Achse (*f*).
**Azure, ** *adj.* Himmelblau.

B

**Baboon, ** *n.* Pavian (*m*).
**Baby, ** *n.* Kleinkind (*n*).
**Bachelor, ** *n.* Junggeselle (*m*).
**Back, ** *n.* Rücken (*m*), *adv.* Hinterwärts, zurück.
**Backbone, ** *n.* Rückgrat (*n*).
**Background, ** *n.* Hintergrund (*m*).
**Backward, ** *adj.* Langsam: *adv.* Zurück.

Bacon, *n.* Speck (*m*).
Bad, *adj.* Schlecht, böse.
Badness, *n.* Schlechtigkeit (*f*), Bosheit (*f*).
Baffle, *v.* Verwirren.
Bag, *n.* Beutel (*m*), Sack (*m*), Tasche (*f*).
Bailiff, *n.* Gutsverwalter (*m*).
Bait, *n.* Köder (*m*): *v.* Ködern.
Bake, *v.* Backen.
Baker, *n.* Bäcker (*m*).
Bakery, *n.* Bäckerei (*f*).
Balcony, *n.* Balkon (*m*).
Bald, *adj.* Kahl.
Bale, *v.* Ausschöpfen.
Ball, *n.* Ball (*m*), Kugel (*f*), Tanzfest (*n*).
Balloon, *n.* Luftballon (*m*).
Bamboo, *n.* Bambus (*m*).
Ban, *n.* Bann (*m*), Acht (*f*): *v.* Verbieten.
Banana, *n.* Banane (*f*).
Band, *n.* Band (*n*), Binde (*f*), Musikkapelle (*f*).
Bandmaster, *n.* Kapellmeister (*m*).
Bandsman, *n.* Militärmusiker (*m*).
Baneful, *adj.* Verderblich.
Bang, *n.* Knall (*m*), Schlag (*m*): *v.* Knallen.
Banish, *v.* Verbannen.
Banister, *n.* Treppengeländer (*n*).
Bank, *n.* Bank (for money) (*f*), Ufer (of river) (*n*): *v.* Eindämmen, Deponieren.
Bank Holiday, *n.* Bankfeiertag (*m*).
Banknote, *n.* Banknote (*f*).
Bankrupt, *adj.* Bankrott.
Banner, *n.* Banner (*n*).
Baptism, *n.* Taufe (*f*).
Bar, *n.* Bar (for refreshment) (*f*), Reck (*n*), Stange (crow-bar) (*f*), Taktstrich (in music) (*m*): *v.* Versperren.
Barb, *n.* Widerhaken (*m*).
Barber, *n.* Barbier (*m*).
Bare, *v.* Entblössen: *adj.* Bloss, nackt.
Barely, *adv.* Kaum.
Bargain, *n.* Handel (*m*): *v.* Handeln.
Bark, *n.* Rinde (of tree) (*f*): *v.* Bellen.
Barmaid, *n.* Schenkmädchen (*n*).
Barn, *n.* Scheune (*f*).

Barometer, *n.* Wetterglas (*n*), Barometer (*n*).
Baron, *n.* Baron (*m*), Freiherr (*m*).
Barrack, *n.* Hütte (*f*), Kaserne (*f*).
Barrage, *n.* Damm (*m*), Wehr (*n*), Sperrfeuer (military) (*n*).
Barrel, *n.* Fass (*n*).
Barrow, *n.* Bahre (*f*), Trage (*f*).
Basement, *n.* Tiefparterre (*n*), Grundmauer (*f*).
Bashfulness, *n.* Schüchternheit (*f*), Verschämtheit (*f*).
Basin, *v.* Becken (*n*), Schüssel (*f*).
Basket, *n.* Korb (*m*).
Bat, *n.* Schläger (for cricket, etc.) (*m*), Fledermaus (the animal) (*f*).
Bath, *n.* Bad (*n*).
Bathchair, *n.* Rollstuhl (*m*).
Bathe, *v.* Baden.
Bathroom, *n.* Badezimmer (*n*).
Battle, *n.* Schlacht (*f*); *v.* Kämpfen.
Bawl, *v.* Laut schreien.
Bay, *n.* Bucht (sheet of water) (*f*), Lorbeerbaum (tree) (*m*); *v.* Bellen, jagen.
Bayonet, *n.* Bajonett.
Be, *v.* Sein, existieren, werden.
Beach, *n.* Gestade (*n*), Strand (*m*).
Beacon, *n.* Leuchtfeuer (*n*).
Bead, *n.* Tropfen (*m*), Kügelchen (*n*).
Beak, *n.* Schnabel (*m*).
Beam, *n.* Balken (constructional) (*m*), Strahl (ray) (*m*).
Bean, *n.* Bohne (*f*).
 Broad bean, Saubohne (*f*).
 French bean, Grüne Bohne (*f*).
 Haricot bean, Stangenbhone (*f*).
Bear, *n.* Bär (*m*).
Beard, *n.* Bart (*m*).
Beast, *n.* Vieh (*n*), Tier (*n*).
Beastliness, *n.* Gemeinheit (*f*).
Beastly, *adj.* Gemein, scheusslich.
Beat, *n.* Schlag (*m*), Takt (in music) (*m*), Klopfen (of the heart) (*n*): *v.* Schlagen.

**Beautiful, ** adj. Schön.
**Beautify, ** v. Verschöne.
**Beauty, ** n. Schönheit (f).
**Beaver, ** n. Biber (m).
**Because, ** conj. Weil.
**Become, ** v. Werden, geziemen.
**Bed, ** n. Bett (for sleeping) (n), Beet (for flowers) (n).
**Bedclothes, ** n. Bettzeug (n).
**Bedroom, ** n. Schlafzimmer (n).
**Bedstead, ** n. Bettstelle (f).
**Bed-time, ** n. Schlafenszeit (f).
**Bee, ** n. Biene (f).
**Beech, ** n. Buche (f).
**Beef, ** n. Rindfleisch (n).
**Beefsteak, ** n. Beefsteak (n), Rinderbraten (m).
**Beehive, ** n. Bienenstock (m).
**Beer, ** n. Bier (n).
**Beetroot, ** n. Rote Rübe (f).
**Before, ** prep. Vor: adv. Früher, vorher.
**Beg, ** v. Betteln (for charity), Bitten (ask).
**Beggar, ** n. Bettler (m).
**Begging, ** n. Betteln (for charity) (n).
**Begin, ** v. Anfangen.
**Beginner, ** n. Anfänger (m).
**Begone, ** interj. Fort, packe dich, weg.
**Begrudge, ** v. Missgönnen.
**Beguile, ** v. Betrügen, verkürzen.
**Behave, ** v. Sich betragen.
**Behaviour, ** n. Betragen (n), Benehmen (n).
**Behead, ** v. Enthaupten.
**Behest, ** n. Befehl (m).
**Behind, ** prep. Hinter: adv. Hinten.
**Behold, ** v. Erblicken: interj. Siehe da.
**Being, ** n. Dasein (n), Wesen (n).
**Belabour, ** v. Durchprügeln.
**Belated, ** adj. Verspätet.
**Belfry, ** n. Glockenturm (m).
**Belie, ** v. Lügen strafen.
**Belief, ** n. Glaube (m).
**Believe, ** v. Glauben, vertrauen.
**Bell, ** n. Glocke (f), Klingel (f), Schelle (f).
**Bellow, ** v. Brüllen.
**Bellows, ** n. Blasebalg (m).
**Belly, ** n. Bauch (m).
**Belong, ** v. Gehören, betreffen.

**Belongings, ** n. Habe (f).
**Beloved, ** adj. Geliebt.
**Below, ** adv. Unten: prep. Unter.
**Belt, ** n. Gürtel (m).
**Bench, ** n. Bank (f), Richterstand (legal) (m).
**Bend, ** v. Biegen: n. Biegung (f).
**Beneath, ** adv. Unten: prep. Unter.
**Benefice, ** n. Pfründe (f).
**Beneficial, ** adj. & adv. Dienlich, heilsam.
**Benefit, ** n. Wohltat (f), Vorteil (m): v. Vorteil bringen.
**Bent, ** adj. Gebogen.
**Benumb, ** v. Betäuben, erstarren.
**Benzene, ** n. Benzin (n).
**Bequeath, ** v. Vermachen.
**Berry, ** n. Beere (f).
**Berth, ** n. Ankerplatz (ships position) (m), Koje (sleeping place on ship) (f), Bett (on trains) (n): v. Verankern.
**Beseech, ** v. Anflehen, bitten.
**Beset, ** v. Bedrängen.
**Beside, ** prep. Neben.
**Besides, ** adv. Ausser.
**Besiege, ** v. Belagern.
**Bespeak, ** v. Bestellen.
**Best, ** adj. Best: adv. Best, ambesten: n. Beste (n).
**Bet, ** n. Wette (f): v. Wetten.
**Betroth, ** v. Verloben.
**Betrothal, ** n. Verlobung (f).
**Better, ** adj. & adv. Besser, gesünder, lieber; n. Wettende (m).
**Between, ** prep. Zwischen.
**Beverage, ** n. Getränk (n).
**Beware, ** v. Sich hüten: interj. Achtung.
**Bewilder, ** v. Verwirren, bestürzt machen.
**Bewilderment, ** n. Verwirrung (f).
**Bewitch, ** v. Behexen.
**Beyond, ** prep. Jenseits, über: adv. Darüber hinaus.
**Bib, ** n. Geiferlätzchen (n).
**Bicycle, ** n. Fahrrad (n), Zweirad (n).
**Bid, ** n. Gebot (n); v. Befehlen, bieten.
**Bide, ** v. Ertragen, abwarten, wohnen.
**Bier, ** n. Totenbahre (f), Bahre (f).

Big   Blush

Big, *adj.* Gross, stark.
Bigamy, *n.* Doppelehe (*f*).
Bilberry, *n.* Heidelbeere (*f*).
Bilious, *adj.* Gallig, gallsüchtig.
Bill, *n.* Schnabel (of bird) (*m*), Plakat (on hoarding) (*n*), Wechsel (legal) (*m*), Rechnung (*f*).
Billiards, *n.* Billard (spiel) (*n*).
Bill of Fare, *n.* Speisekarte (*f*).
Bill Poster, *n.* Zettelankleber (*m*).
Bind, *v.* Binden, verpflichten (taking a vow).
Bindweed, *n.* Winde (*f*).
Binoculars, *n.* Operngucker (*m*).
Biplane, *n.* Doppeldecker (*m*), Zweidecker (*m*).
Birch, *n.* Rute (for punishment) (*f*), Birke (tree) (*f*).
Bird, *n.* Vogel (*m*).
Birdcage, *n.* Vogelbauer (*m*).
Bird's-eye, *n.* Aus der Vogelschau gesehen (*f*).
   Bird's-eye view, Vogelperspektive (*f*).
Birth, *n.* Geburt (*f*).
Birthday, *n.* Geburtstag (*m*).
Biscuit, *n.* Biskuit (*n*), Zwieback (*m*).
Bishop, *n.* Bischof (*m*), Läufer (in chess) (*m*).
Bit, *n.* Stück (*n.*), Bissen (*m*) Gebiss (*n*).
Bite, *n.* Biss (*m*), *v.* Beissen, stechen.
Bitter, *adj.* Bitter.
Black, *adj.* Schwarz: *v.* Schwärzen.
Blackbeetle, *n.* Schabe (*f*).
Blackberry, *n.* Brombeere (*f*).
Blackbird, *n.* Amsel (*f*).
Blackcurrant, *n.* Schwarze Johannisbeere (*f*).
Blackguard, *n.* Schuft (*m*), Lump (*m*).
Blacklead, *n.* Reissblei (*n*), Graphit (*m*), Bleistift (lead pencil) (*m*).
Blacksmith, *n.* Grobschmied (*m*).
Bladder, *n.* Blase (*f*).
Blade, *n.* Blatt (*m*), Halm (*m.*), Klinge (*f*).
Blame, *n.* Tadel (*m*), *v.* Tadeln.

Blancmange, *n.* Flammeri (*m*).
Blanket, *n.* Wolldecke (*f*), Bettdecke (*f*).
Blare, *v.* Schmettern, blöken.
Blast, *n.* Windstoss (*m*); *v.* Sprengen.
Blaze, *n.* Brand (*m*), Flamme (*f*), Lichtstrahl (*m*), Weisser Fleck (*f*).
Bleach, *v.* Bleichen.
Bleak, *adj.* Rauh, kahl, öde, kalt.
Bleed, *v.* Bluten, zur Ader lassen.
Bleeding, *n.* Aderlass (*m*), Blutung (*f*).
Blemish, *n.* Schandfleck (*m*).
Blend, *v.* Vermischen.
Bless, *v.* Segnen.
Blessing, *n.* Segen (*m*).
Blight, *v.* Verderben; *n.* Meltau (*m*).
Blind, *n.* Vorhang (window) (*m*), Jalousie (Venetian) (*f*), Blind (unable to see) (*m*): *v.* Blenden: *adj.* Blind.
Blink, *v.* Vermeiden, blinzeln.
Blinker, *n.* Blinzler (*m*). Scheuklappe (horses) (*f*).
Blithe, *adj.* Fröhlich, lustig.
Blizzard, *n.* Schneesturm (*m*).
Bloater, *n.* Bücking (*f*).
Blockhead, *n.* Dummkopf (*m*).
Blood, *n.* Blut (*n*).
Bloodhound, *n.* Bluthund (*m*).
Bloodshot, *adj.* Blutunterlaufen.
Blood-vessel, *n.* Blutgefäss (*n*).
Bloom, *n.* Blüte (*f*); *v.* Blühen.
Blooming, *adj.* Blühend.
Blot, *n.* Klecks (*m*): *v.* Klecksen.
Blotting-paper, *n.* Löschpapier (*n*).
Blow, *n.* Schlag (*m*), Stoss (*m.*): *v.* Wehen (weather), putzen (the nose), aufblasen tyres).
Blue, *n.* Blau (*n*); *adj.* Blau, traurig, trübe.
Bluebell, *n.* Wilde Hyazinthe (*f*).
Blunt, *adj.* Stumpf: *v.* Abstumpfen.
Blush, *v.* Erröten: *n.* Schamröte (*f*).

Bluster   **Breathless**

Bluster, v. Grosstun; n. Ungestüm (m).
Boar, n. Eber (m).
Board, n. Brett (n), Bohle (f), Bord (seafaring) (m).
Boarding House, n. Pension (f), Kosthaus (n).
Boarding School, n. Pensionat (n).
Boast, v. Prahlen.
Boaster, n. Prahler (m).
Boat, n. Boot (m), Kahn (m), Fähre (f).
Boating, n. Bootfahren (n), Kahnfahrt (f).
Body, n. Körper (m), Leib (m), Leichnam (dead body) (m).
Boil, v. Kocher; n. Geschwür (n).
Boiler, n. Sieder (m), Kochkessel (m).
Bold, adj. Kühn, dreist, keck, mutig.
Boldness, n. Kühnheit (f).
Bolt, n. Bolzen (m), Pfeil (m); v. Verriegeln.
Bomb, n. Bombe (f).
Bond, n. Band (n), Seil (n), Schuldschein (shares) (m).
Bondage, n. Knechtschaft (f).
Bondman, n. Fröner (m), Höriger (m).
Bone, n. Gräte (f), Knochen (m).
Bonfire, n. Freudenfeuer (n).
Bonus, n. Zulage (f), Gratifikation (f).
Bony, adj. Knochig.
Book, n. Buch (n), Heft (n); v. Eintragen.
Bookbinder, n. Buchbinder (m).
Booking-office, n. Fahrkartenschalter (m), Fahrkartenausgabe (f).
Bookshop, n. Buchhandlung (f).
Boon, n. Wohltat (f).
Boot, n. Stiefel (m).
Boots, n. Stiefelputzer (m).
Border, n. Grenze (frontier) (f), Rand (m), Saum (m).
Bore, v. Bohren.
Born, adj. Geboren.
Borrow, v. Borgen, leihen.
Borrower, n. Borger (m).
Both, adj. Beide, beides.

Bother, n. Mühe (f): v. Plagen, bemühen.
Bottle, n. Flasche (f).
Bottom, n. Boden (m), Grund (m).
Bough, n. Ast (m), Zweig (m).
Bounce, v. Aufspringen.
Bounty, n. Freigebigkeit (f), Prämie (f).
Bouquet, n. Strauss (m).
Bow, n. Bogen (for arrow and violin) (m), Schleife (for necktie, etc.) (f).
Bowels, n. Eingeweide (n).
Bowl, n. Becken (n), Schüssel (f).
Box, n. Büchse (f), Schachtel (f).
Boxing, n. Boxen (n), Boxkampf (m).
Box-office, n. Kasse (f), Kartenausgabe (f).
Boy, n. Junge (m), Knabe (m).
Bracelet, n. Armband (n).
Braces, n. Hosenträger (m).
Bracket, n. Wandbrett (n), Klammer (in printing) (f).
Brain, n. Verstand (m).
Brake, v. Bremsen.
Branch, n. Ast (m), Abschnitt (m), Zweig (m).
Brandy, n. Kognac (m).
Brass, n. Messing (n), Erz (n).
Brave, adj. Tapfer.
Brawl, n. Schlägerei (f), Geschrei (n).
Bread, n. Brot (n).
Bread and butter, n. Butterbrot (n).
Breadth, n. Breite (f), Weite (f).
Break, v. Brechen, anbrechen, abgewöhnen, zureiten, mitteilen; n. Bruch (m), Lücke (f), Pause (f), Riss (m), Absatz (m).
Breakdown, n. Zusammenbruch (m).
Breakfast, n. Frühstück (n); v. Frühstücken.
Breast, n. Brust (f), Buser (m).
Breath, n. Atem (m), Hauch (m).
Breathe, v. Atmen.
Breathless, adj. Atemlos.

Breed   **By and by**

Breed, *n.* Brut (*f*), Rasse (*f*), Zucht (*f*): *v.* Züchten, zeugen, wachsen.
Brew, *n.* Bräu (*n*), Gebräu (*n*): *v.* Brauen.
Brewer, *n.* Brauer (*m*).
Brewery, *n.* Brauerei (*f*).
Brick, *n.* Backstein (*m*).
Bride, *n.* Braut (*f*).
Bridegroom, *n.* Bräutigam (*m*).
Bridesmaid, *n.* Brautjungfer (*f*).
Bridge, *n.* Brücke (*f*), Bridge (*n*).
Brief, *adj.* Bündig, kurz, knapp.
Brigand, *n.* Strassenräuber (*m*).
Bright, *adj.* Hell, erleuchtet, klar.
Brim, *n.* Rand (*m*), Krempe (hat brim) (*f*).
Bring, *v.* Bringen.
Brink, *n.* Rand (*m*).
Broad, *adj.* Breit, gross, weit.
Broadcast, *n.* Rundfunksendung (*f*).
Broken, *adj. & partic.* Gebrochen.
Broker, *n.* Makler (*m*).
Brood, *n.* Brut (*f*); *v.* Brüten.
Broom, *n.* Besen (*m*).
Brother, *n.* Bruder (*m*).
Brother-in-law, *n.* Schwager (*m*).
Brow, *n.* Augenbraue (*f*), Stirn (*f*).
Brown, *adj.* Braun.
Brownbread, *n.* Weizenschrotbrot (*n*).
Bruise, *v.* Quetschen; *n.* Quetschung (*f*).
Brush, *n.* Bürste (*f*), Pinsel (paint b.) (*m*): *v.* Bürsten.
Brussels sprouts, *n.* Rosenkohl (*m*).
Brutal, *adj.* Viehisch, brutal.
Brute, *n.* Vieh (*n*), Bestie (*f*).
Bubble, *n.* Wasserblase (*f*).
Bucket, *n.* Eimer (*m*).
Buckle, *n.* Schnalle (*f*): *v.* Schnallen.
Bud, *n.* Knospe (*f*).
Budget, *n.* Budget (*n*), Brieftasche (*f*), Haushaltsplan (*m*).
Buffalo, *n.* Büffel (*m*).
Buffer, *n.* Puffer (on trains) (*m*), Stosskissen (*n*).

Buffet, *n.* Büfett (*n*), Faustschlag (*m*).
Bug, *n.* Wanze (*f*).
Build, *v.* Bauen.
Building, *n.* Bauen (*n*), Bau (*m*), Gebäude (*n*).
Bulge, *n.* Anschwellung (*f*): *v.* Ausbauchen.
Bull, *n.* Bulle (*m*), Stier (*m*).
Bulldog, *n.* Bullenbeisser (*m*), Bulldogge (*f*).
Bullet, *n.* Kugel (*f*).
Bullock, *n.* Ochse (*m*).
Bull's eye, *n.* Ochsenauge (*n*), Volltreffer (*m*).
Bully, *n.* Flegel (*m*).
Bump, *n.* Stoss (*m*), Beule (a swelling) (*f*): *v.* Puffen, stossen.
Bunch, *n.* Bündel (*n*), Strauss (of flowers) (*m*), Weintraube (of grapes) (*f*).
Bungalow, *n.* Einstöckiges Sommerhaus (*n*).
Bunion, *n.* Schwellung am Fuss (*f*).
Buoy, *n.* Boje (*f*).
Burden, *n.* Bürde (*f*): *v.* Aufbürden, beladen.
Burglar, *n.* Einbrecher (*m*).
Burglary, *n.* Einbruch (*m*).
Burial, *n.* Begräbnis (*n*).
Burn, *v.* Brennen.
Burnish, *v.* Polieren.
Burst, *v.* Bersten, platzen.
Bury, *v.* Begraben.
Bush, *n.* Busch (*m*).
Business, *n.* Geschäft (*n*).
Bustle, *n.* Auflauf (*m*), Lärm (*m*), Rührigkeit (*f*).
Busy, *adj.* Unruhig, fleissig, beschäftigt.
But, *conj.* Aber, allein, als, dennoch, doch, sondern.
Butcher, *n.* Fleischer (*m*).
Butt, *n.* Bütte (*f*), Kolben (of rifle) (*m*).
Butter, *n.* Butter (*f*).
Buttercup, *n.* Butterblume (*f*).
Butterfly, *n.* Schmetterling (*m*).
Button, *n.* Knopf (*m*).
Buy, *v.* Kaufen.
Buyer, *n.* Käufer (*m*).
By, *adv.* Nahe, dabei, vorbei; *prep.* Auf, bei, neben, nach, von, vermittelst, zu.
By and by, *adv.* Bald, sogleich.

C

Cab, *n*. Droschke (*f*), Taxi (*f*).
Cabbage, *n*. Kohl (*m*).
Cabin, *n*. Hütte (*f*), Kabine (*f*).
Cable, *n*. Ankertau (*n*), Kabel (*n*).
Cabman, *n*. Droschkenkutscher (*m*).
Cage, *n*. Käfig (*m*).
Cake, *n*. Kuchen (*m*), Stück Seife (cake of soap) (*n*).
Calamity, *n*. Kalamität (*f*), Unglück (*n*).
Calculate, *v*. Rechnen, berechnen.
Calendar, *n*. Kalender (*m*).
Calf, *n*. Kalb (*n*), Wade (c. of leg) (*f*).
Call, *v*. Rufen, nennen, heissen, wecken.
Calm, *adj*. Ruhig, sanft.
Calve, *v*. Kalben.
Camel, *n*. Kamel (*n*).
Camera, *n*. Kamera (*f*).
Camp, *n*. Lager (*n*).
Campaign, *n*. Feldzug (*m*).
Can, *n*. Kanne (*f*).
Can (I can, ich kann).
Canal, *n*. Kanal (*m*).
Cancel, *v*. Ausstreichen.
Candle, *n*. Kerze (*f*), Licht (*n*).
Candy, *n*. Kandizucker (*m*).
Cane, *n*. Rohr (*n*), Rohrstock (*m*): *v*. Durchprügeln.
Cannibal, *n*. Menschenfresser (*m*).
Cannon, *n*. Kanone (*f*).
Canoe, *n*. Kanu (*n*), Paddelboot (*n*).
Canvas, *n*. Kanevas (*m*).
Cap, *n*. Deckel (*m*), Kappe (*f*), Mütze (*f*).
Capable, *adj*. Fähig.
Capacity, *n*. Fähigkeit (being capable) (*f*), Inhalt (containing) (*m*).
Cape, *n*. Kap (*n*), Cape (*n*), Vorgebirge (*n*).
Capital, *n*. Haupstadt (city) (*f*), grosse Buchstabe (in print) (*m*): *adj*. Haupt.
Capsize, *v*. Kentern, umwenden.
Capstan, *n*. Ankerspill (*n*), Gangspill (*n*).
Captain, *n*. Kapitän (of a ship) (*m*), Hauptman (of army, etc.) (*m*).
Captivate, *v*. Einnehmen.
Car, *n*. Auto (*n*), Wagen (*m*), Karren (*m*).
Caravan, *n*. Karawane (*f*).
Card, *n*. Karte (*f*), Spielkarte (*f*), Visitenkarte (*f*).
Care, *n*. Sorge (*f*), Sorgfalt (*f*.), Pflege (*f*), Vorsicht (taking care) (*f*): *v*. Sorgen.
Career, *n*. Laufbahn (*f*).
Careful, *adj*. Besorgt, vorsichtig.
Careless, *adj*. Sorglos, nachlässig.
Caress, *n*. Liebkosung (*f*): *v*. Liebkosen.
Caretaker, *n*. Wächter (*m*).
Cargo, *n*. Ladung (*f*).
Carpet, *n*. Teppich (*m*).
Carriage, *n*. Fracht (*f*), Fuhre (*f*), Wagen (*m*).
Carry, *v*. Fahren, fortbringen.
Cart, *n*. Karren (*m*), Wagen (*m*).
Cartridge, *n*. Kartätsche (*f*).
Carve, *v*. Schnitzen, tranchieren (meat).
Case, *n*. Fall (*m*), Futteral (*n*), Etui (cigarette) (*n*), Kartentasche (pocket) (*f*).
Cash, *n*. Kasse (*f*).
Cask, *n*. Fass (*n*).
Castle, *n*. Schloss (*n*), Turm (in chess) (*m*).
Cat, *n*. Katze (*f*).
Catalogue, *n*. Katalog (*m*).
Catch, *v*. Fangen; *n*. Fang (*m*).
Cathedral, *n*. Dom (*m*), Kathedrale (*f*).
Cattle, *n*. Vieh (*n*).
Cauliflower, *n*. Blumenkohl (*m*).
Cause, *n*. Ursache (*f*); *v*. Verursachen.
Caution, *n*. Warnung (*f*), Vorsicht (*f*).
Cave, *n*. Höhle (*f*).
Cease, *v*. Aufhören.
Celery, *n*. Stangensellerie (*m*. or *f*).
Cellar, *n*. Keller (*m*).
Cement, *n*. Zement (*m*).
Cemetery, *n*. Friedhof (*m*).
Censor, *n*. Zensor (*m*).
Centre, *n*. Mittelpunkt (*m*).
Century, *n*. Jahrhundert (*n*).
Ceremony, *n*. Zeremonie (*f*), Gepränge (*n*).
Certain, *adj*. Gewiss.

Certificate — Christmas

Certificate, *n.* Zeugnis (*n*).
Certify, *v.* Bescheinigen.
Chafe, *v.* Enzürnen (to fret), reiben (to wear).
Chain, *n.* Kette (*f*).
Chair, *n.* Stuhl (*m*).
Chairman, *n.* Vorsitzender (*m*).
Chalk, *n.* Kreide (*f*).
Challenge, *n.* Herausforderung (*f*): *v.* Herausfordern.
Challenger, *n.* Herausforderer (*m*).
Chamber, *n.* Zimmer (*n*), Logis (*n*).
Chameleon, *n.* Chamäleon (*n*).
Chamois, *n.* Gem e (*f*).
Champion, *n.* Kämpe (*m*), Meister (*m*).
Chance, *n.* Zufall (*m*).
Chancellor, *n.* Kanzler (*m*).
Change, *n.* Veränderung (alter) (*f*), Kleingeld (money) (*n*): *v.* Ändern.
Changeable, *adj.* Veränderlich.
Channel, *n.* Kanal (*m*): *v.* Aushöhlen.
Chant, *v.* Singen: *n.* Gesang (*m*).
Chanticleer, *n.* Hahn (*m*).
Chaos, *n.* Chaos (*n*).
Chap, *n.* Riss (*m*), Kerl (*m*), Bursche (*m*).
Chaperon, *n.* Anstandsdame (*f*).
Chaplain, *n.* Kaplan (*m*).
Chapter, *n.* Kapitel (*n*).
Character, *n.* Charakter (*m*), Merkmal (*n*).
Charcoal, *n.* Holzkohle (*f*).
Charge, *n.* Last (*f*), Ladung (*f*): *v.* Beladen, angreifen.
Chariot, *n.* Kriegswagen (*m*).
Charitable, *adj.* Wohltätig.
Charity, *n.* Almosen (*n*), Wohltätigkeit (*f*).
Charm, *n.* Liebreiz (*m*), Zauber (*m*), Amulett (*n*): *v.* Bezaubern.
Charming, *adj.* Bezaubernd.
Charwoman, *n.* Scheuerfrau (*f*).
Chase, *v.* Jagen, verfolgen.
Chaste, *adj.* Keusch.
Chastise, *v.* Züchtigen.
Chat, *v.* Plaudern: *n.* Geplauder (*n*).
Chatterbox, *n.* Plappermaul (*n*).

Chauffeur, *n.* Schofför (*m*).
Cheap, *adj.* Billig.
Cheat, *n.* Betrüger (*m*); *v.* Betrügen.
Check, *n.* Kontrolle (a control) (*f*), Hemmung (when preventing) (*f*), Karo (squared pattern) (*n*), Schach (in chess) (*n*); *v.* Kontrollieren, hemmen.
Cheek, *n.* Backe (*f*), Wange (*f*), Unverschämtheit (abuse) (*f*).
Cheeky, *adj.* Frech.
Cheese, *n.* Käse (*m*).
Chemical, *n.* Chemikalien (*f*): *adj.* Chemisch.
Chemist, *n.* Apotheker (*m*), Chemiker (*m*).
Cheque, *n.* Scheck (*m*).
Cherish, *v.* Pflegen, schätzen.
Cherry, *n.* Kirsche (*f*).
Chess, *n.* Schach (*n*).
Chessman, *n.* Schachfigur (*f*).
Chest, *n.* Brust (part of body) (*f*), Kiste (box, case) (*f*).
Chestnut, *n.* Kastanie (*f*).
Chew, *v.* Kauen.
Chewing-gum, *n.* Kaugummi (*n*).
Chicken, *n.* Hühnchen (*n*).
Chicken-pox, *n.* Windpocken (*f*).
Chicory, *n.* Cichorie (*f*).
Chide, *v.* Schelten, schmälen.
Chief, *adj.* Hauptsächlich; *n* Erste (*m*), Oberhaupt (*n*).
Chilblain, *n.* Frostbeule (*f*).
Child, *n.* Kind (*n*).
Chill, *n.* Kälte (*f*), Verkühlung (*f*), Erkältung (*f*).
Chilly, *adj.* Frostig, Kalt.
Chimney, *n.* Schornstein (*m*).
Chin, *n.* Kinn (*n*).
China, *n.* Porzellan (*n*).
Chip, *v.* Schnitzeln.
Chisel, *n.* Meissel (*m*).
Chivalry, *n.* Ritterschaft (*f*).
Chocolate, *n.* Schokolade (*f*).
Choice, *n.* Wahl (*f*).
Choke, *v.* Ersticken.
Choose, *v.* Wählen.
Chop, *v.* Spalten; *n.* Kotelette (*n*).
Chopper, *n.* Hackmesser (*n*).
Chord, *n.* Akkord (*m*).
Christening, *n.* Taufe (*f*).
Christmas, *n.* Weihnachten (*n*).

Chrysanthemum — Colliery

Chrysanthemum, *n.* Chrysanthemum (*n*).
Chuck, *v.* Glucken.
Chum, *n.* Kamerad (*m*).
Church, *n.* Kirche (*f*).
Churchyard, *n.* Kirchhof (*m*).
Cider, *n.* Apfelwein (*m*).
Cigar, *n.* Zigarre (*f*).
Cigarette, *n.* Zigarette (*f*).
Cinder, *n.* Löschkohle (*f*).
Cinema, *n.* Kino (*n*).
Circle, *n.* Kreis (*m*), Zirkel (*m*).
Circus, *n.* Zirkus (*m*).
Cistern, *n.* Wasserbehälter (*m*).
Citizen, *n.* Bürger (*m*).
City, *n.* Stadt (*f*).
Civilize, *v.* Verfeinern.
Claim, *n.* Anspruch (*m*); *v.* Fordern, beanspruchen.
Clamber, *v.* Klettern.
Clamour, *n.* Geschrei (*n*).
Claret, *n.* Rotwein (*m*).
Clarify, *v.* Abklären.
Clasp, *v.* Umarmen; *n.* Umarmung (*f*).
Class, *n.* Klasse (*f*).
Classify, *v.* Klassifizieren.
Clause, *n.* Klausel (*f*).
Claw, *n.* Klaue (*f*), Schere (of shell fish) (*f*).
Clay, *n.* Ton (*m*), Lehm (*m*).
Clean, *adj.* Rein, sauber; *v.* Reinigen, bürsten (boots).
Clear, *adj.* Klar, rein, deutlich.
Cleave, *v.* Spalten.
Clematis, *n.* Waldrebe (*f*).
Clergy, *n.* Geistlichkeit (*f*).
Clerk, *n.* Schreiber (*m*), Kommis (*m*).
Clever, *adj.* Gescheit, gewandt.
Cliff, *n.* Klippe (*f*).
Climate, *n.* Klima (*n*).
Climb, *v.* Klettern.
Cling, *v.* Anklammern.
Clip, *v.* Beschneiden.
Cloak, *n.* Mantel (*m*), Umhang (*m*).
Cloak-room, *n.* Garderobe (*f*).
Clock, *n.* Uhr (*f*).
Close, *v.* Verschliessen, werden: *n.* Schluss (*m*), Einzäunung (*f*); *adj.* Dicht, knapp, drückend.
Clot, *n.* Klumpen (*m*).
Cloth, *n.* Tuch (*m*), Zeug (*m*), Stoff (*m*).
Clothe, *v.* Kleiden, bekleiden.

Clothes, *n.* Kleider (to wear) (*n*), Bettzeug (for bed) (*n*).
Cloud, *n.* Wolke (*f*).
Clover, *n.* Klee (*m*).
Clown, *n.* Hanswurst (*m*), Clown (*m*).
Club, *n.* Klub (*m*), Kreuz (*n*), Treff (playing card) (*n*).
Clue, *n.* Leitfaden (*m*).
Clumsy, *adj.* Plump, ungeschicklichkeit.
Clutch, *v.* Greifen, packen: *n.* Kupplung (machinery) (*f*).
Coach, *n.* Kutsche (*f*).
Coal, *n.* Kohle (*f*).
Coalmine, *n.* Kohlengrube (*f*).
Coarse, *adj.* Derb, grob, gemein.
Coast, *n.* Küste (*f*).
Coat, *n.* Rock (*m*), Pelz (of animals) (*m*), Anstrich (of paint) (*m*).
Coax, *v.* Schmeicheln.
Cobweb, *n.* Spinngewebe (*n*).
Cock, *n.* Hahn (*m*).
Cockle, *n.* Herzmuschel (*f*).
Cocoa, *n.* Kakao (*m*).
Cocoon, *n.* Puppe (*f*).
Coddle, *v.* Verhätscheln.
Code, *n.* Gesetzbuch (*n*).
Coerce, *v.* Zwingen.
Coffee, *n.* Kaffee (*m*).
Coffee-pot, *n.* Kaffeekanne (*f*).
Coffin, *n.* Sarg (*m*).
Cog, *n.* Zahn (*m*).
Cog-wheel, *n.* Zahnrad (*n*).
Coil, *n.* Rolle (*f*), Spule (*f*); Windung (*f*); *v.* Aufspulen.
Coin, *n.* Münze (*f*).
Coinage, *n.* Geld (*n*).
Coincide, *v.* Zusammentreffen.
Coincidence, *n.* Zusammentreffen (*n*).
Coke, *n.* Koks (*m*).
Cold, *adj.* Kalt; *n.* Erkältung (illness) (*f*).
Colic, *n.* Bauchkrampf (*m*).
Collapse, *v.* Zusammenfallen.
Collar, *n.* Kragen (*m*), Kumt (*n*).
Collect, *v.* Sammeln.
Collection, *n.* Sammlung (*f*).
Collector, *n.* Sammler (*m*).
College, *n.* Kollegium (*n*), Hochschule (*f*).
Collide, *v.* Zusammenstossen.
Collie, *n.* Schäferhund (*m*).
Colliery, *n.* Kohlenbergwerk (*n*).

Collision — Confederation

Collision, *n.* Zusammenstoss (*m*).
Colon, *n.* Doppelpunkt (*m*).
Colonel, *n.* Oberst (*m*).
Colonial, *adj.* Kolonial.
Colonize, *v.* Kolonisieren.
Colony, *n.* Kolonie (*f*).
Colour, *n.* Farbe (*f*): *v.* Färben.
Colt, *n.* Füllen (*n*).
Column, *n.* Säule (*f*), Spalte (of print) (*f*).
Comb, *n.* Kamm (*m*).
Combat, *n.* Kampf (*m*).
Combine, *v.* Verbinden.
Come, *v.* Kommen.
Comedian, *n.* Komödiant (*m*).
Comedy, *n.* Lustspiel (*n*).
Comfort, *v.* Trösten, erquicken: *n.* Trost (*m*).
Comfortable, *adj.* Tröstlich.
Comfortless, *adj.* Trostlos.
Comic, *adj.* Komisch.
Coming, *adj.* Künftig.
Comma, *n.* Komma (*n*).
Command, *v.* Befehlen: *n.* Befehl (*m*).
Commander, *n.* Befehlshaber (*m*).
Commence, *v.* Anfangen.
Commencement, *n.* Anfang (*m*).
Commend, *v.* Empfehlen.
Commerce, *n.* Handel (*m*).
Commission, *n.* Auftrag (*m*) Offizierspatent (in army) (*n*):
Commit, *v.* Anvertrauen, begehen (a wrong).
Committee, *n.* Ausschuss (*m*).
Common, *adj.* Gewöhnlich (ordinary), gemein (vulgar).
Commotion, *n.* Erschütterung (*f*), Aufruhr (*m*).
Communicate, *v.* Mitteilen.
Community, *n.* Gemeinde.
Compact, *adj.* Gedrängt, kompakt.
Companion, *n.* Gefährte (*m*).
Company, *n.* Gesellschaft (*f*).
Compare, *v.* Vergleichen.
Compartment, *n.* Abteil (*m*).
Compass, *n.* Kompass (*m*).
Pair of compasses, Zirkel (*m*).
Compel, *v.* Zwingen.
Compensate, *v.* Entschädigen.
Compensation, *n.* Ersatz (*m*), Entschädigung (*f*).
Compete, *v.* Konkurrieren.

Competitor, *n.* Wettbewerber (*m*).
Compile, *v.* Zusammenstellen.
Complain, *v.* Sich beklagen.
Complaint, *n.* Beschwerde (*f*), Klage (*f*).
Complete, *adj.* Vollendet, gänzlich.
Complexion, *n.* Gesichtsfarbe (*f*), Aussehen (*n*).
Complicate, *v.* Verwickeln.
Compliment, *n.* Kompliment (*n*); *v.* Komplimentieren.
Compose, *v.* Zusammensetzen.
Composer, *n.* Komponist (*m*), Verfasser (*m*).
Composition, *n.* Zusammensetzung (*f*).
Compound, *v.* Zusammensetzen: *n.* Gemisch (*n*).
Compulsion, *n.* Zwang (*m*).
Concave, *adj.* Konkav.
Conceal, *v.* Verhehlung, verbergen.
Conceit, *n.* Einbildung.
Concentrate, *v.* Konzentrieren.
Concern, *v.* Betreffen, angehen; *n.* Sache (*f*), Unruhe (anxiety) (*f*).
Concert, *n.* Konzert (*n*).
Concertina, *n.* Ziehharmonika (*f*).
Concise, *adj.* Kurz.
Conclude, *v.* Beenden, folgern, schliessen.
Conclusion, *n.* Schluss (*m*).
Concord, *n.* Eintracht (*f*).
Concrete, *n.* Beton (*m*); *adj.* Konkret.
Concussion, *n.* Erschütterung (*f*).
Condemn, *v.* Verdammen.
Condense, *v.* Kondensieren.
Condescend, *v.* Sich herablassen.
Condition, *n.* Zustand (*m*).
Condole, *v.* Kondolieren.
Condolence, *n.* Beileid (*n*).
Conduct, *n.* Führung (*f*): *v.* Führen.
Conductor, *n.* Führer (leader) (*m*), Schaffner (on vehicle) (*m*), Kapellmeister (of a band) (*m*).
Cone, *n.* Kegel (*m*).
Confectioner, *n.* Konditor (*m*).
Confectionery, *n.* Konditorei (*f*).
Confederation, *n.* Bund (*m*).

Conference, *n.* Konferenz (*f*).
Confess, *v.* Gestehen.
Confession, *n.* Geständnis (*n*), Beichte (*f*).
Confessor, *n.* Beichtvater (*m*).
Confide, *v.* Vertrauen.
Confident, *adj.* Vertrauend.
Confine, *v.* Begrenzen.
Conflict, *n.* Kampf (*m*).
Conform, *v.* Anpassen, gemäss.
Confuse, *v.* Verwirren.
Confusion, *n.* Verwirrung (*f*).
Congeal, *v.* Gefrieren.
Congested, *adj.* Mit Blut überfüllt.
Congratulate, *v.* Gratulieren.
Congregation, *n.* Gemeinde (*f*).
Congress, *n.* Kongress (*m*).
Conifer, *n.* Nadelholzbaum (*m*).
Conjugal, *adj.* Ehelich.
Conjugation, *n.* Konjugation (*f*).
Conjunctive, *n.* Konjunktive (*m*).
Conjurer, *n.* Zauberer (*m*).
Connect, *v.* Verbinden.
Connection, *n.* Verbindung (*f*), Zusammenhang (*m*).
Connoisseur, *n.* Kenner (*m*).
Conquer, *v.* Erobern.
Conqueror, *n.* Eroberer (*m*).
Conquest, *n.* Eroberung (*f*).
Conscience, *n.* Gewissen (*n*).
Conscientious, *adj.* Gewissenhaft.
Conscript, *n.* Wehrpflichtiger (*m*).
Consecrate, *v.* Weihen.
Consecutive, *adj.* Aufeinander folgend.
Consent, *n.* Einwilligung (*f*): *v.* Einwilligen.
Consequence, *n.* Folge (*f*).
Conservative, *adj.* Konservativ.
Conservatory, *n.* Gewächshaus (*n*).
Consider, *v.* Betrachten, überlegen.
Considerable, *adj.* Beträchtlich.
Considerate, *adj.* Bedächtig.
Consideration, *n.* Betrachtung (*f*).
Consign, *v.* Übersenden.
Consist, *v.* Bestehen.
Console, *v.* Trösten.
Consolidate, *v.* Konsolidieren.

Consort, *n.* Gemahl (*m*), Gefährte (*m*): *v.* Vereinigen.
Conspicuous, *adj.* Auffallend.
Conspirator, *n.* Verschwörer (*m*).
Conspire, *v.* Sich verschwören.
Constable, *n.* Schutzmann (*m*), Polizist (*m*).
Constant, *adj.* Entschlossen, beständig, treu (loyal).
Constipation, *n.* Verstopfung (*f*).
Constitute, *v.* Ausmachen, bilden.
Constitution, *n.* Natur (human body) (*f*), Verfassung (of nations, etc.) (*f*).
Constrict, *v.* Zusammenziehen.
Construct, *v.* Bilden, Bauen, Errichten.
Construction, *n.* Bau (*m*), Deutung (*f*).
Consul, *n.* Konsul (*m*).
Consult, *v.* Befragen.
Consume, *v.* Verzehren.
Consumption, *n.* Verbrauch (when using) (*m*), Schwindsucht (disease) (*f*).
Contact, *n.* Berührung (*f*).
Contagious, *adj.* Ansteckend.
Contain, *v.* Enthalten.
Contaminate, *v.* Anstecken, besudeln.
Contemplate, *v.* Beabsichtigen.
Contemporary, *n.* Zeitgenosse (*m*).
Contempt, *n.* Verachtung (*f*).
Content, *n.* Zufriedenheit (*f*).
Contented, *adj.* Zufrieden.
Contents, *n.* Inhalt (*m*).
Contest, *n.* Streit (*m*): *v.* Streiten.
Continent, *n.* Festland (*n*).
Continual, *adj.* Fortwährend, beständig.
Continue, *v.* Fortsetzen.
Contraband, *n.* Schmuggelei (*f*), Konterbande (*f*).
Contract, *n.* Vertrag (*m*), Kontrakt (*m*): *v.* Zusammenziehen (to grow less), schliessen (of marriage).
Contractor, *n.* Lieferant (*m*).
Contradict, *v.* Widerspruch (*m*).
Contrary, *adj. & prep.* Entgegengesetzt.
Contribute, *v.* Beitragen.
Contribution, *n.* Beitrag (*m*).

Contrive, *v.* Ersinnen.
Control, *n.* Kontrolle (*f*), Beherrschung (*f*), Leitung (*f*); *v.* Kontrollieren.
Convalescence, *n.* Genesung (*f*).
Convenience, *n.* Bequemlichkeit (*f*).
Convenient, *adj.* Schicklich, bequem.
Convent, *n.* Nonnenkloster (*n*).
Converge, *v.* Zusammenlaufen.
Conversation, *n.* Unterhaltung (*f*).
Converse, *v.* Sprechen.
Convert, *v.* Verwandeln.
Convey, *v.* Transportieren, befördern, führen.
Convict, *n.* Zuchthäusler (*m*), Sträfling (*m*): *v.* Verurteilen, überführen.
Convince, *v.* Überzeugen.
Convulsion, *n.* Krampf (*m*).
Cook, *n.* Koch (*m*), Köchin (*f*): *v.* Kochen.
Cookery, *n.* Kochkunst (*f*).
Cookery book, *n.* Kochbuch (*n*).
Cool, *adj.* Kühl: *v.* Kühlen.
Copper, *n.* Kupfer (*n*).
Copy, *n.* Abschrift (*f*), Abdruck (*m*): *v.* Kopieren.
Copyright, *n.* Verlagsrecht (*n*).
Coral, *n.* Koralle (*f*).
Cord, *n.* Schnur (*f*), Strick (*m*), Kordel (*f*): *v.* Zuschnüren.
Cork, *n.* Kork (*m*).
Corkscrew, *n.* Korkzieher (*m*).
Corn, *n.* Korn (cereal) (*n*), Hühnerauge (medical) (*n*).
Corner, *n.* Ecke (*f*), Winkel (*m*).
Cornet, *n.* Zinke (*f*).
Cornflower, *n.* Kornblume (*f*).
Coroner, *n.* Leichenbeschauer (*m*).
Corporal, *n.* Korporal (*m*).
Corporation, *n.* Körperschaft (*f*).
Corpse, *n.* Leichnam (*m*).
Corpulent, *adj.* Wohlbeleibt.
Correct, *adj.* Richtig; *v.* Verbessern, strafen.
Correspond, *v.* Korrespondieren.
Corridor, *n.* Gang (*m*), Korridor (*m*).
Corrode, *v.* Zerfressen, zernagen.
Corrugated, *adj.* Gewellt.
Corrupt, *adj.* Verfault, verderbt; *v.* Verderben.
Corset, *n.* Korsett (*n*).
Cost, *n.* Kosten (*no sing.*), Preis (*m*): *v.* Kosten.
Costly, *adj.* Kostbar.
Costume, *n.* Kostüm (*n*).
Cosy, *adj.* Behaglich, gemütlich.
Cot, *n.* Kinderbett (bed) (*n*).
Cottage, *n.* Hütte (*f*), Landhäuschen (*n*).
Cotton, *n.* Baumwolle (*f*).
Cotton thread, *n.* Nähgarn (*n*).
Couch, *n.* Lager (*n*), Sofa (*n*).
Cough, *n.* Husten (*m*); *v.* Husten.
Count, *n.* Graf (title) (*m*); *v.* Zählen, rechnen.
Counteract, *v.* Entgegenwirken.
Counterfeit, *n.* Fälschung (*f*).
Counterfoil, *n.* Abschnitt (*m*), Kontrollblatt (*n*).
Counterpane, *n.* Steppdecke (*f*).
Countess, *n.* Gräfin (*f*).
Country, *n.* Land (*n*), Vaterland (*n*).
Countryman, *n.* Landsmann (*m*), Landbewohner (*m*).
County, *n.* Grafschaft (*f*).
Couple, *n.* Paar (*n*).
Coupon, *n.* Coupon (*m*).
Courage, *n.* Mut (*m*).
Courageous, *adj.* Mutig.
Course, *n.* Kursus (of study) (*m*), Gang (menu) (*m*), Lauf (of river) (*m*), Rennbahn (for races) (*f*).
Of course, natürlich.
Court, *n.* Hof (*m*), Gericht (*n*).
Court-card, *n.* Bild in der Karte (*n*).
Courtesy, *n.* Höflichkeit (*f*).
Court-martial, *n.* Kriegsgericht (*n*).
Courtship, *n.* Werbung (*f*).
Cousin, *n.* Vetter (*m*).
Cover, *v.* Bedecken, decken; *n.* Kuvert (*n*), Deckel (*m*) Decke (*f*).
Covet, *v.* Begehren: *adj.* Begehren.
Cow, *n.* Kuh (*f*).
Coward, *n.* Feigling (*m*).
Cowslip, *n.* Schlüsselblume (*f*).
Coxcomb, *n.* Stutzer (*m*).

Crab, n. Taschenkrebs (m).
Crack, n. Riss (m), Knall (m) Sprung (m).
Cradle, n. Wiege (f).
Craft, n. Gewerbe (skilled work) (n), List (trickery) (f).
Cramp, n. Krampf (m).
Crane, n. Krahn (m), Kranich (m).
Crash, v. Abstürzen (while flying), zusammenstossen (collision), brechen (breaking); n. Krach (m).
Crawl, v. Kriechen: n. Kriechen (n).
Crazy, adj. Baufällig.
Cream, n. Rahm (m), Sahne (f).
Crease, v. Falten: n. Falte (f).
Create, v. Verursachen.
Creature, n. Geschöpf (n).
Credit, n. Glaube (m), Kredit (m).
Creep, v. Kriechen, schleichen.
Crescent, n. Halbmond (m).
Crest, n. Kamm (m), Federbusch (m), Wappen (heraldry) (n).
Crevice, n. Riss (m).
Crew, n. Mannschaft (f), Schiffsvolk (n).
Cricket, n. Cricketspiel (the game) (n), Grille (the insect) (f).
Crime, n. Verbrechen (n).
Criminal, adj. Verbrecherisch; n. Verbrecher (m).
Crimson, adj. Karmesinrot.
Cripple, n. Krüppel (m).
Crisis, n. Krise (f).
Crisp, adj. Kraus, bröckelig.
Critic, n. Kritiker (m).
Crochet, n. Häkelarbeit (f): v. Häkeln.
Crockery, n. Geschirr (n).
Crocodile, n. Krokodil (n).
Crocus, n. Krokus (m).
Crop, n. Ernte (f), Kropf (m).
Cross, n. Kreuz (n); adj. Ärgerlich (angry).
Crow, n. Krähe (f); v. Krähen.
Crowd, n. Gedränge (n), Haufen (m).
Crown, n. Krone (f).
Cruel, adj. Grausam.
Cruise, n. Seefahrt (f), Kreuzen (n): v. Seefahrt machen.
Crumb, n. Krume (f).

Crush, v. Zerquetschen: n. Stoss (m), Gedränge (n).
Crust, n. Rinde (f), Kruste (f).
Cry, v. Schreien (shout), weinen (tears): n. Schrei (m), Zuruf (m).
Crystal, n. Kristall (m).
Cub, n. Junge (n).
Cube, n. Kubus (m).
Cuckoo, n. Kuckuck (m).
Cucumber, n. Gurke (f).
Cuddle, v. Umarmen.
Cuff, n. Manschette (f), Puff (m).
Culprit, n. Schuldige (m), Missetäter (m).
Cultivate, v. Anbauen, Kultivieren.
Culture, n. Kultur (f), Anbau (m), Bildung (f).
Cunning, adj. Listig, schlau.
Cup, n. Tasse (f), Becher (m) Kelch (m).
Cupboard, n. Schrank (m).
Cur, n. Köter (m).
Curate, n. Hilfsgeistlicher (m).
Curb, n. Kinnkette, Zaum (for horses) (m).
Cure, v. Heilen, einpökeln: n. Kur (f), Arznei (f).
Curious, adj. Neugierig (anxious to know), merkwürdig (unusual).
Curl, v. Kräuseln; n. Locke (f).
Currant, n. Korinthe (f), Johannisbeere (f).
Curse, v. Verwünschen; n. Verwünschung (f).
Curtail, v. Abkürzen, stutzen.
Curtain, n. Vorhang (m).
Curtsy, n. Knicks (m), Verneigung (f).
Curve, n. Krümme (f), Kurve (f).
Cushion, n. Kissen (n).
Custody, n. Haft (f), Verwahrung (f).
Custom, n. Sitte (f), Gebrauch (m), Zoll (at frontier) (m).
Customary, adj. Gebräuchlich.
Custom House, n. Zollamt (n).
Cut, v. Schneiden; n. Schnitt (m).
Cutlet, n. Kotelett (n).
Cycle, n. Fahrrad (n), Kreis (m), Zyklus (m).
Cycling, n. Radfahren (n).

**Cylinder, **n. Zylinder (m), Walze (f).
**Czar, **n. Zar (m).

D

**Daffodil, **n. Gelbe Narzisse (f), Affodil (m).
**Dagger, **n. Dolch (m).
**Daily, **adj. Täglich.
**Daintiness, **n. Leckerhaftigkeit (f).
**Dainty, **adj. Lecker, niedlich.
**Dairy, **n. Melkerei (f).
**Daisy, **n. Gänseblaume (f).
**Dam, **n. Damm (m).
**Damage, **n. Schade (m), Verlust (m).
**Dame, **n. Dame (f), Frau (f).
**Damn, **v. Verdammen.
**Damp, **adj. Feucht, dumpfig.
**Damsel, **n. Jungfer (f), Mädchen (n).
**Damson, **n. Zwetsche (f).
**Dance, **v. Tanzen; n. Tanz (m).
**Dancer, **n. Tänzer (m), Tänzerin (f).
**Dandelion, **n. Löwenzahn (m).
**Danger, **n. Gefahr (f).
**Dangerous, **adj. Gefährlich.
**Dare, **v. Herausfordern, wagen.
**Daring, **adj. Beherzt, kühn, verwegen.
**Dark, **adj. Dunkel, trübe.
**Darkness, **n. Dunkelheit (f), Verborgenheit (f).
**Darling, **n. Liebling (m).
**Dart, **n. Wurfspiess (m), Wurfgeschoss (n).
**Dash, **v. Schlagen, schmeissen stossen.
**Date, **n. Datum (time) (n), Dattel (fruit) (f).
**Daub, **v. Beschmieren.
**Daughter, **n. Tochter (f).
**Daughter-in-law, **n. Schwiegertochter (f).
**Dawn, **n. Dämmerung (f); v. Dämmern.
**Day, **n. Tag (m), Frist (f).
**Daybreak, **n. Tagesanbruch, (m).
**Daylight, **n. Tageslicht (m).
**Daytime, **n. Tageszeit (f).
**Dazzle, **v. Blenden.
**Dead, **adj. Öde, leer, schal, todt.
**Deadly, **adj. Tödlich.
**Deaf, **adj. Dumpf, taub.
**Deafness, **n. Taubheit (f).
**Deal, **v. Handeln, austeilen, ausstreuen: n. Geschäft (commerce) (n), Menge (much) (f), Tannenholz (timber) (n).
**Dealer, **n. Händler (m).
**Dear, **adj. Lieb, theuer; n. Liebling (m).
**Dearth, **n. Mangel (m), Theuerung (f).
**Death, **n. Tod (m).
**Debate, **n. Wortwechsel (m), Debatte (f).
**Debt, **n. Schuld (f).
**Debtor, **n. Schuldner (m).
**Decade, **n. Jahrzehnt (n).
**Decanter, **n. Karaffe (f).
**Decapitate, **v. Köpfen, enthaupten.
**Decay, **n. Verfall (m), Verfaulen (n); v. Verfallen.
**Decease, **n. Tod (m), Ableben (n).
**Deceit, **n. Betrug (m), List (f).
**Deceitful, **adj. Betrügerisch, listig.
**Deceive, **v. Betrügen, anführen.
**December, **n. December (m).
**Decency, **n. Anstand (m).
**Decent, **adj. Züchtig, anständig.
**Decide, **v. Entschieden.
**Decimal, **adj. Dezimal; n. Zehntel (n).
**Decision, **n. Entscheidung (f).
**Deck, **n. Deck (n), Verdeck (n): v. Bekleiden.
**Declaration, **n. Erklärung (f).
**Declare, **v. Erklären, behaupten.
**Decompose, **v. Verwesen, zerlegen.
**Decorate, **v. Dekorieren, schmücken, verzieren.
**Decoration, **n. Dekoration (f), Schmuck (m), Verzierung (f).
**Decoy, **n. Lockung (f); v. Locken, ködern.
**Decrease, **n. Abnahme (f): v. Vermindern.
**Decree, **n. Verordnung (f), Beschluss (m): v. Verordnen, beschliessen.
**Decrepit, **adj. Abgelebt.
**Decry, **v. Tadeln, verrufen.
**Dedicate, **v. Widmen, zueignen.
**Deduct, **v. Abrechnen, abziehen.

Deed, n. Handlung (f), Tat (f) Urkunde (f).
Deep, adj. Gründlich, dunkel, geheim, tief.
Deer, n. Hirsch (m), Reh (n).
Default, n. Fehler (m): v. Unterlassen.
Defeat, n. Niederlage (f), Vernichtung (f); v. Schlagen, vereiteln.
Defect, n. Mangel (m), Fehler (m).
Defence, n. Schutz (m), Vertheidigung (f).
Defenceless, adj. Schutzlos.
Defend, v. Schützen, vertheidigen.
Defendant, n. Beklagte (m).
Defer, v. Aufschieben.
Defiance, n. Trotz (m), Herausforderung (f).
Deficient, adj. Mangelhaft.
Deficit, n. Defizit (n).
Define, v. Definieren, erklären.
Definition, n. Definition (f), Erklärung (f).
Deformed, adj. Entstellt, hasslich.
Defraud, v. Betrügen, bevortheilen.
Defray, v. Bestreiten.
Deft, adj. Gewandt.
Defunct, adj. Verstorben.
Defy, v. Trotzen.
Degenerate, adj. Entartet; v. Entarten.
Degrade, v. Degradieren, absetzen.
Degree, n. Grad (m).
Dejection, n. Niedergeschlagenheit (f).
Delay, n. Aufschub (m); v. Hindern, aufhalten.
Delete, v. Auslöschen, streichen.
Deliberate, adj. Bedachtsam, absichtlich.
Delicacy, n. Delikatesse (f), Leckerbissen (m).
Delicate, adj. Zart, köstlich, lecker.
Delicious, adj. Köstlich, angenehm.
Delight, n. Vergnügen, Wonne (f): v. Ergötzen.
Delightful, adj. Ergötzlich.
Delirious, adj. Wahnsinnig.
Deliver, v. Befreien, liefern.
Deluge, n. Uberschwemmung (f).

Demand, v. Fordern, verlangen, fragen: n. Forderung (f).
Democracy, n. Demokratie (f).
Democratic, adj. Demokratisch.
Demolish, v. Abreissen, zerstören.
Demon, n. Dämon (m), Teufel (m).
Demonstrate, v. Demonstrieren, beweisen.
Demoralize, v. Verderben.
Demure, adj. Ernsthaft, spröde.
Denial, n. Verneinung (f), Leugnen (n).
Denote, v. Bezeichnen.
Dense, adj. Dicht.
Dentist, n. Zahnarzt (m).
Deny, v. Ableugnen, verneinen.
Depart, v. Abreisen.
Department, n. Abteilung (f), Bezirk (m).
Departure, n. Abreise (f), Abfahrt (f).
Depend, v. Herabhangen, abhängen.
Depict, v. Abmalen.
Deplore, v. Beweinen.
Depose, v. Bezeugen, entsetzen.
Deposit, v. Anzahlen: n. Satz (sediment) (m), Depositum (pay money in bank) (n).
Depraved, adj. Verderbt.
Depreciate, v. Herabsetzen, verringern.
Depression, n. Depression (f), Niederdrücken (n).
Deprive, v. Berauben, entziehen.
Depth, n. Tiefe (f).
Depute, v. Abordnen.
Derange, v. Verwirren, zerrütten.
Derangement, n. Unordnung (f).
Derelict, adj. Verlassen.
Derision, n. Verspottung (f).
Derive, v. Ableiten.
Descend, v. Absteigen, abstammen.
Descendant, n. Nachkomme (m).
Describe, v. Beschreiben.
Description, n. Beschreibung (f).
Desecrate, v. Entweihen.
Desert, n. Wüste (f), Einöde (f): v. Verlassen.

Deserter, *n.* Deserteur (*m*).
Deserve, *v.* Verdienen.
Design, *n.* Vorhaben (*n*), Absicht (*f*): *v.* Bestimmen, entwerfen.
Desire, *v.* Verlangen, wünschen: *n.* Verlangen (*n*), Wunsch (*m*).
Desirous, *adj.* Wünschend.
Desist, *v.* Abstehen.
Desk, *n.* Pult (*n*), Schultisch (*m*).
Desolate, *adj.* Verlassen, wüst.
Despair, *n.* Verzweiflung (*f*).
Desperate, *adj.* Verzweifelt.
Despise, *v.* Verachten.
Despoil, *v.* Plündern.
Dessert, *n.* Nachtisch (*m*).
Destination, *n.* Bestimmung (*f*).
Destitute, *adj.* Hilflos, entblösst.
Destroy, *v.* Verwüsten, zerstören.
Destruction, *n.* Zerstörung (*f*).
Detach, *v.* Absondern.
Detail, *v.* Umständlich erzählen; *n.* Einzelheit (*f*).
Detain, *v.* Zurückhalten.
Detect, *v.* Entdecken.
Detective, *n.* Geheimpolizist (*m*).
Deter, *v.* Abschrecken.
Deteriorate, *v.* Verschlechtern.
Determine, *v.* Festsetzen.
Detest, *v.* Verabscheuen.
Deuce, *n.* Zwei (playing cards) (*f*), Ausgleich (tennis) (*m*).
Devastate, *v.* Verwüsten.
Develop, *v.* Entwickeln.
Deviate, *v.* Abweichen.
Devil, *n.* Teufel (*m*).
Devise, *v.* Ersinnen, überlegen.
Devote, *v.* Widmen.
Devoted, *adj.* Ergeben.
Devour, *v.* Verschlingen.
Dew, *n.* Tau (*m*).
Diabetes, *n.* Zuckerkrankheit (*f*).
Diagonal, *n.* Diagonale (*f*).
Diagram, *n.* Diagramm (*n*), Figur (*f*), Riss (in geometry) (*m*).
Dial, *n.* Sonnenuhr (*f*), Zifferblatt (*n*); *v.* Wahlen (telephone).
Diameter, *n.* Durchmesser (*m*).

Diamond, *n.* Diamant (*m*), Karo (playing cards) (*n*).
Diarrhœa, *n.* Durchfall (*m*).
Diary, *n.* Tagebuch (*n*).
Dice, *n.* Würfel (*m*).
Dictate, *v.* Vorsagen, diktieren.
Dictation, *n.* Diktat (*n*).
Dictator, *n.* Diktator (*m*).
Dictionary, *n.* Wörterbuch (*n*).
Diet, *n.* Diät (*f*).
Differ, *v.* Verschieden sein.
Difference, *n.* Unterschied (*m*).
Different, *adj.* Verschieden
Difficult, *adj.* Schwierig.
Difficulty, *n.* Schwierigkeit (*f*).
Dig, *v.* Graben, bohren.
Digest, *v.* Verdauen.
Digestion, *n.* Verdauung (*f*).
Digger, *n.* Gräber (*m*).
Digging, *n.* Graben (*n*).
Dignified, *adj.* Würdevoll.
Dignity, *n.* Würde (*f*).
Dike, *n.* Damm (*m*), Deich (*m*), Graben (*m*).
Dilapidated, *adj.* Verfallen.
Dilate, *v.* Ausdehnen.
Dilemma, *n.* Dilemma (*n*).
Diligence, *n.* Fleiss (*m*), Sorgfalt (*f*).
Diligent, *adj.* Fleissig, emsig.
Dilute, *v.* Verdünnen, mildern.
Dim, *adj.* Dunkel, trübe; *v.* Trüben.
Dimension, *n.* Mass (*n*), Ausdehnung (*f*).
Diminish, *v.* Vermindern.
Dimple, *n.* Grübchen.
Din, *n.* Geklirr (*n*), Getöse (*n*).
Dine, *v.* Essen, speisen.
Dingy, *adj.* Dunkelbraun, schmutzig.
Dining-room, *n.* Speisezimmer (*n*).
Dinner, *n.* Diner (*n*), Mittagsmahl (*n*).
Dip, *v.* Eintauchen, senken.
Diphtheria, *n.* Diptheritis (*f*).
Diploma, *n.* Diplom (*n*).
Direct, *v.* Weisen, richten: *adj.* Direkt.
Direction, *n.* Richtung (*f*).
Directly, *adv.* Sogleich, sofort.
Directory, *n.* Adressbuch (*n*).
Dirt, *n.* Schmutz (*m*), Koth (*m*), Dreck (*m*).
Disable, *v.* Herabsetzen, unfähig machen.
Disadvantage, *n.* Nachteil (*m*).

Disagree, v. Nicht übereinstimmen.
Disagreeable, adj. Unangenehm.
Disappear, v. Verschwinden.
Disappearance, n. Verschwinden (n).
Disappoint, v. Enttäuschen, vereiteln.
Disappointment, n. Enttäuschung.
Disapprove, v. Missbilligen.
Disarm, v. Entwaffnen.
Disarrange, v. Verwirren.
Disaster, n. Unglück (n), Unfall (m), Katastrophe (f).
Disastrous, adj. Unglücklich.
Discard, v. Entfernen.
Discharge, n. Abfeuern (firearms) (n), Entlassung (give notice) (f), Ausfluss (empty out) (m): v. Entlassen.
Disclose, v. Enthüllen.
Discolour, v. Verfärben.
Discomfort, n. Unbehaglichkeit (f).
Disconnect, v. Abstellen, trennen.
Discontent, n. Unzufriedenheit (f).
Discontinue, v. Aufhören, aufschieben, unterbrechen.
Discount, v. Diskontieren: n. Skonto (m), Rabatt (m).
Discourage, v. Entmutigen.
Discover, v. Aufdecken, entdecken.
Discovery, n. Entdeckung (f).
Discredit, v. Bezweifeln.
Discreet, adj. Vorsichtig.
Discriminate, v. Unterscheiden.
Discuss, v. Erörtern.
Discussion, n. Erörterung (f).
Disdain, v. Verschmähen; n. Verachtung (f).
Disease, n. Krankheit (f), Leiden (n).
Disembark, v. Landen.
Disengaged, adj. Frei.
Disfigure, v. Entstellen.
Disgrace, n. Schande (f), Ungnade (f).
Disgraceful, adj. Schimpflich.
Disguise, v. Verkleiden, tarnen; n. Verkleidung (f).
Disgust, n. Ekel (m).
Disgusting, adj. Ekelhaft.

Dish, n. Schüssel (f), Gericht (n); v. Anrichten (to dish up).
Dishonest, adj. Unehrlich.
Dishonour, n. Schande (f).
Dishonourable, adj. Ehrlos, schändlich.
Disinfect, v. Desinfizieren.
Disinfectant, n. Desinfizierungsmittel (n).
Disinherit, v. Enterben.
Dislike, v. Missbilligen, **nicht** mögen.
Dislocate, v. Verrenken.
Dislodge, v. Vertreiben.
Disloyal, adj. Treulos, ungetreu.
Dismal, adj. Traurig, schrecklich.
Dismay, n. Bestürzung (f); v. Erschrecken.
Dismiss, v. Entlassen.
Dismissal, n. Entlassung.
Disobey, v. Nicht gehorchen.
Disorder, n. Störung (f), Unordnung (f).
Disparage, v. Verringern.
Dispensary, n. Apotheke (f).
Dispense, v. Austeilen.
Displace, v. Absetzen, wegsetzen.
Display, n. Auslage (f), Pomp (m), Darstellung (f): v. Auslegen, entfalten.
Dispose, v. Anordnen.
Disprove, v. Widerlegen.
Dispute, n. Streit (m), Disputation (f): v. Streiten.
Disqualify, v. Unfähig erklären, beunruhigen.
Disregard, n. Nichtachtung (f).
Disreputable, adj. Verrufen.
Disrespect, n. Missachtung (f), Geringschätzung (f).
Disrobe, v. Entkleiden.
Dissatisfaction, n. Unzufriedenheit (f).
Dissatisfy, v. Unzufrieden machen, nicht befriedigen.
Dissect, v. Zergliedern.
Dissipate, v. Verschwenden, zerstreuen.
Dissociate, v. Trennen.
Dissolve, v. Auflösen.
Dissuade, v. Abraten.
Distance, n. Entfernung (f), Abstand (m), Weite (f).
Distant, adj. Entfernt, weit.
Distaste, n. Ekel (m), Verdruss (m).

Distemper, *n.* Tünche (decorator's) (*f*), Staupe (complaint) (*f*), Wasserfarbe (*f*).
Distil, *v.* Destillieren.
Distinct, *adj.* Deutlich, unterschieden.
Distinguish, *v.* Unterschieden, auszeichnen.
Distort, *v.* Verzerren.
Distract, *v.* Ablenken.
Distraint, *n.* Beschlagnahme (*f*).
Distress, *n.* Not (*f*), Elend (*n*).
Distribute, *v.* Austeilen, verteilen.
District, *n.* Bezirk (*m*).
Distrust, *v.* Misstrauen.
Disturb, *v.* Stören.
Disturbance, *n.* Störung.
Ditch, *n.* Graben (*m*).
Dive, *v.* Tauchen, eindringen.
Diver, *n.* Taucher (*m*).
Diversion, *n.* Ablenkung (*f*).
Divert, *v.* Ablenken.
Divide, *v.* Teilen, trennen, entzweien.
Divine, *adj.* Gottlich: *n.* Geistliche (*m*).
Division, *n.* Teilung (*f*), Teil (*m*), Division (*f*).
Divorce, *v.* Verstossen, scheiden.
Divulge, *v.* Aussprengen, enthüllen.
Dizzy, *adj.* Schwindlig.
Docile, *adj.* Gelehrig, lenksam.
Dock, *n.* Dock (water) (*n*), Anklagebank (legal) (*f*): *v.* Docken.
Doctor, *n.* Doktor (*m*), Artz (*m*).
Document, *n.* Dokument (*n*).
Dodge, *v.* Ausweichen; *n.* Kniff (*m*), Schlich (*m*).
Dog, *m.* Hund (*m*), Gestell (*n*).
Dogged, *adj.* Halsstarrig.
Dog-rose, *n.* Wilde Rose (*f*), Heckenrose (*f*).
Dole, *n.* Spende (*f*), Teil (*m*).
Doleful, *adj.* Kummervoll.
Doll, *n.* Puppe (*f*).
Dolphin, *n.* Delphin (*m*).
Dome, *n.* Kuppel (*f*).
Domestic, *adj.* Häuslich.
Domicile, *n.* Wohnort (*m*), Wohnsitz (*m*).
Donation, *n.* Schenkung (*f*).
Donkey, *n.* Esel (*m*).
Donor, *n.* Geber (*m*), Geberin (*f*), Geschenkgeber (*m*).

Door, *n.* Tür (*f*).
Door-mat, *n.* Türmatte (*f*).
Dose, *n.* Dosis (*f*), Anteil (*m*).
Double, *adj.* Doppelt; *v.* Verdoppeln.
Doubt, *n.* Zweifel (*m*): *v.* Zweifeln.
Dove, *n.* Taube (*f*).
Down, *adv. & prep.* Hinunter, herunter, nieder, hinab: *n.* Flaum (of birds) (*m*).
Downhill, *adj.* Bergab, abschüssig.
Downpour, *n.* Regenguss (*m*).
Downstairs, *adv.* Treppab.
Dowry, *n.* Mitgift (*f*).
Doze, *v.* Schläfrig sein.
Dozen, *n.* Dutzend (*n*).
Draft, *n.* Tratte (*f*).
Drag, *v.* Schleppen, ziehen.
Dragon, *n.* Drache (*m*).
Drain, *n.* Abflussrohr (*n*), Abzugsgraben (*m*); *v.* Ablassen.
Drama, *n.* Drama (*n*).
Draper, *n.* Tuchhändler (*m*).
Draught, *n.* Zug (wind) (*m*), Schluck (medicine) (*m*).
Draw, *v.* Schleppen (to drag), zeichnen (pictorial), abheben (money from bank), abziehen (water, etc.).
Dread, *n.* Furcht (*f*).
Dreadful, *adj.* Fürchterlich.
Dream, *n.* Traum (*m*): *v.* Träumen.
Drench, *v.* Durchnässen, tränken.
Dress, *n.* Anzug (*m*), Kleid (*n*): *v.* Ankleiden.
Drift, *n.* Trieb (*m*).
Drill, *n.* Exerzieren (gymnastics) (*n*), Bohrer (tool) (*m*); *v.* Exerzieren.
Drink, *v.* Trinken; *n.* Getränk.
Drip, *n.* Tröpfeln.
Drive, *v.* Wegtreiben, betreiben: *n.* Treiben.
Driver, *n.* Treiber (*m*), Kutscher (*m*), Führer (*m*).
Droll, *adj.* Possierlich, drollig.
Drop, *v.* Fallen, tropfen, sinken; *n.* Fall (*m*), Tropfen (of water, etc.) (*m*).
Dropsy, *n.* Wassersucht (*f*).
Drought, *n.* Dürre (*f*), Trockenheit (*f*).
Drown, *v.* Entrinken, überschwemmen.

Drug — **Eject**

Drug, *n.* Droge (*f*), Apothekerware (*f*).
Druggist, *n.* Drogist (*m*).
Drum, *n.* Trommel (*f*), Mühlbottich (*m*).
Drunk, *adj.* Betrunken.
Drunkard, *n.* Trunkenbold (*m*).
Drunkenness, *n.* Trunkenheit (*f*).
Dry, *adj.* Dürr, Durstig, Trocken; *v.* Trocknen.
Duck, *n.* Ente (*f*), Püppchen (*n*).
Due, *adj.* Schuldig, fällig; *n.* Anteil (*m*), Recht. (*n*).
Duke, *n.* Herzog (*m*).
Dull, *adj.* Einfältig, dumm, matt, plump, träge, trübe.
Dumb, *adj.* Stumm.
Dump, *n.* Kurze (*n*), Abladestelle (*f*), Abladeplatz (*m*).
Dung, *n.* Mist (*m*).
Dungeon, *n.* Verliess (*n*), Kerker (*m*).
Duplicate, *n.* Duplikat; *v.* Verdoppeln.
During, *prep.* Während.
Dusk, *n.* Dämmerung (*f*), Dunkelheit (*f*).
Dust, *n.* Staub (*m*): *v.* Bestäuben, abstäuben.
Duster, *n.* Wischlappen (*m*).
Dutiful, *adj.* Pflichtgetreu.
Duty, *n.* Pflicht (*f*), Zoll (tax) (*m*).
Dwarf, *n.* Zwerg (*m*).
Dwell, *v.* Wohnen, verweilen.
Dwelling, *n.* Wohnort (*m*).
Dwindle, *v.* Schwinden, abnehmen.
Dye, *n.* Farbe (*f*), Farbstoff (*m*): *v.* Färben.
Dying, *adj.* Sterbend.
Dynamo, *n.* Dynamomaschine (*f*).
Dysentry, *n.* Ruhr (*f*).

E

Each, *adj.* & *pron.* Jeder, jede, jedes.
   Each other, einander.
Eager, *adj.* Eifrig, begierig, erpicht.
Eagerness, *n.* Eifer (*m*), Begierde (*f*).
Eagle, *n.* Adler (*m*).
Ear, *n.* Ohr (*n*), Gehör (*n*), Ähre (cereal) (*f*).
Earache, *n.* Ohrenschmerz (*m*).
Early, *adj.* & *adv.* Früh, zeitig.
Earn, *v.* Verdienen, gewinnen.
Earnest, *adj.* Ernstlich: *n.* Ernst (*m*).
Ear-ring, *n.* Ohrring (*m*).
Earth, *n.* Erde (*f*): *v.* Erden (radio).
Earthenware, *n.* Steingut (*n*).
Earthquake, *n.* Erdbeben (*n*).
Earwig, *n.* Ohrwurm (*m*).
Ease, *v.* Erleichtern, lindern, beruhigen: *n.* Erleichterung (*f*), Bequemlichkeit (*f*).
Easel, *n.* Staffelei (*f*).
East, *n.* Osten (*m*).
Easter, *n.* Ostern (*f*).
Eastern, *adj.* Östlich.
Easy, *adj.* Bequem, frei, leicht, willig.
Eat, *v.* Essen (people), fressen (animals), zerfressen (eat into).
Ebb, *n.* Ebbe (*f*).
Ebony, *n.* Ebenholz (*n*).
Echo, *n.* Echo (*n*), Wiederhall (*m*): *v.* Wiederhallen.
Eclipse, *n.* Finsternis (*f*).
Economise, *v.* Haushälterisch.
Economy, *n.* Sparsamkeit (*f*).
Eczema, *n.* Hautausschlag (*m*).
Edge, *n.* Schneide (cutting) (*f*), Rand (brink) (*m*).
Edible, *adj.* Essbar.
Edifice, *n.* Gebäude (*n*).
Edit, *v.* Herausgeben.
Editor, *n.* Herausgeber (*m*), Redakteur (*m*).
Educate, *v.* Erziehen.
Education, *n.* Erziehung (*f*).
Eel, *n.* Aal (*m*).
Effect, *n.* Erfolg (*m*), Wirkung (*f*): *v.* Bewirken.
Effeminate, *adj.* Weichlich, weibisch.
Effervesce, *v.* Aufbrausen.
Efficiency, *n.* Kraft (*f*).
Effort, *n.* Anstrengung (*f*), Mühe (*f*).
Egg, *n.* Ei (*n*).
Egg-cup, *n.* Eierbecher (*m*).
Eight, *adj.* Acht.
Eighteen, *adj.* Achtzehn.
Eighth, *adj.* Achte.
Eighty, *adj.* Achtzig.
Either, *pron.* Einer (*m*), Eine (*f*), Eines (*n*).
Eject, *v.* Ausstossen.

Elapse, *v.* Verfliessen.
Elastic, *adj.* Elastisch: ***n.*** Gummiband (*n*).
Elate, *v.* Aufblähen.
Elbow, *n.* Ellbogen (*m*).
Elder, *adj.* Älter: ***n.*** Holunder (*m*).
Eldest, *adj.* Älteste.
Elect, *v.* Erwählt.
Election, *n.* Wahl (*f*).
Electricity, *n.* Elektrizität (*f*).
Electrify, *v.* Elektrisieren.
Elegance, *n.* Eleganz (*f*), Zierlichkeit (*f*).
Elementary, *adj.* Elementarisch.
Elephant, *n.* Elefant (*m*).
Elevate, *v.* Erheben, erhöhen.
Eleven, *adj.* Elf.
Eleventh, *adj.* Elfte.
Eligible, *adj.* Wählbar.
Ellipse, *n.* Ellipse (*f*).
Elm, *n.* Ulme (*f*).
Elocution, *n.* Vortag (*m*).
Elope, *v.* Durchgehen, entlaufen.
Elopement, *n.* Entlaufen (*n*).
Eloquence, *n.* Beredsamkeit (*f*).
Else, *adj.* Ander; *adv.* Anders.
Elsewhere, *adv.* Anderswo.
Elude, *v.* Ausweichen.
Emaciate, *v.* Ausmergeln, abzehren.
Emaciation, *n.* Abmagerung (*f*).
Embalm, *v.* Einbalsamiren.
Embankment, *n.* Uferwerk (*n*), Eindämmung (*f*).
Embark, *v.* Einschiffen.
Embarrass, *v.* Verwirren.
Embassy, *n.* Gesandtschaft (*f*), Botschaft (*f*).
Embellish, *v.* Verschönern.
Embezzle, *v.* Veruntreuen.
Embezzlement, *n.* Veruntreuung (*f*).
Embrace, *v.* Umarmen.
Embrocation, *n.* Einreibung (*f*), Einreibemittel (*n*).
Embroidery, *n.* Stickerei (*f*).
Emerald, *n.* Smaragd (*m*).
Emerge, *v.* Auftauchen.
Emergency, *n.* Notfall (*m*).
Emetic, *n.* Brechmittel (*n*).
Emigrant, *n.* Auswanderer (*m*).
Emigrate, *v.* Auswandern.
Emit, *v.* Auswerfen.
Emotion, *n.* Rührung (*f*).
Emperor, *n.* Kaiser (*m*).

Emphasis, *n.* Nachdruck (*m*).
Emphatic, *adj.* Nachdrücklich.
Empire, *n.* Reich (*n*).
Employ, *v.* Beschäftigen, anwenden: ***n.*** Stellung (*f*), Amt (*n*), Gebrauch (*m*), Dienst (*m*).
Employer, *n.* Dienstherr (*m*).
Employment, *n.* Amt (*n*).
Empress, *n.* Kaiserine (*f*).
Empty, *adj.* Leer, nichtig, ledig: *v.* Ausleeren.
Emulate, *v.* Wetteifern.
Enable, *v.* Befähigen.
Enact, *v.* Verfügen.
Enamel, *n.* Emaille (*f*).
Enclose, *v.* Einschliessen.
Enclosure, *n.* Einhegung (*f*).
Encore, *n.* Zugabe (*f*): *interj.* Dakapo.
Encounter, *v.* Treffen, stossen auf: ***n.*** Gefrecht (*n*), Zweikampf (*m*).
Encourage, *v.* Ermutigen.
End, *n.* Ende (*n*), Schluss (*m*), Tod (*m*): *v.* Beendigen, endigen.
Endanger, *v.* Gefährden.
Endear, *v.* Lieb machen, wert machen.
Endeavour, *n.* Bestreben (*n*): *v.* Sich bestreben.
Endive, *n.* Endivie (*f*).
Endless, *adj.* Endlos, unendlich.
Endorse, *v.* Indossieren.
Endow, *v.* Begaben, dotieren.
Endure, *v.* Aushalten.
Enema, *n.* Einlauf (*m*), Klistier (*n*).
Enemy, *n.* Feind (*m*), Gegner (*m*).
Energetic, *adj.* Kräftig, energisch.
Enforce, *v.* Erzwingen.
Engage, *v.* Verpflichten, angreifen, anstellen.
Engaged, *adj.* Verlobt (to be married,) besetzt (reserved), beschäftigt (busy).
Engine, *n.* Maschine (*f*), Lokomotive (*f*).
Engineer, *n.* Ingenieur (*m*), Techniker (*m*).
English, *adj.* Englisch.
Engrave, *v.* Stechen, gravieren.
Engraving, *n.* Steindruck (*m*).
Enjoy, *v.* Geniessen, mögen.
Enjoyable, *adj.* Genussreich.

Enlarge — Excite

Enlarge, v. Erweitern, vergrossern.
Enlighten, v. Aufklären.
Enlist, v. Anwerben.
Enliven, v. Beleben.
Enormous, adj. Ungeheuer.
Enough, adj. Genug, ganz.
Enquire, v. Untersuchen.
Enrol, v. Einschreiben.
Enslave, v. Unterjochen.
Ensnare, v. Verstricken, fangen.
Entangle, v. Verwickeln.
Enter, v. Eintreten, eindringen.
Enterprise, n. Unternehmen (n).
Entertain, v. Unterhalten, bewirten.
Entertainment, n. Unterhaltung (f).
Enthusiasm, n. Begeisterung (f).
Entire, adj. Ganz.
Entitle, v. Betiteln.
Entrance, n. Eingang (m).
Entrust, v. Anvertrauen.
Entry, n. Eintritt (m), Meldung (f), Einfuhr (f).
Enumerate, v. Aufzählen.
Envelop, v. Einhüllen.
Envelope, n. Brief umschlag (m), Kuvert (n).
Envious, adj. Neidisch.
Environs, n. Umgebung (f).
Envoy, n. Gesandter (m).
Envy, n. Neid (m); v. Beneiden.
Epoch, n. Epoche (f).
Epsom salts, n. Bittersalz (n).
Equal, adj. Gleich.
Equator, n. Aquator (m).
Equip, v. Ausrüsten.
Equipment, n. Ausrüstung (f).
Equivalent, adj. Gleichwertig.
Era, n. Zeitrechnung (f).
Erase, v. Ausstreichen.
Ere, conj. & pr. Ehe, eher.
Err, v. Abweichen, sich verirren.
Errand-boy, n. Laufbursche (m).
Erratic, adj. Erratisch.
Error, n. Irrtum (m).
Escalator, n. Rolltreppe (f).
Escape, n. Entkommen; Entrinnen.
Escort, n. Geleit (n); v. Geleiten.
Essay, n. Aufsatz (m), Versuch (m): v. Versuchen.

Essence, n. Essenz (f).
Establish, v. Einsetzen, errichten, establieren.
Estate, n. Gut (n), Stand (m), Rang (m).
Esteem, v. Achten; n. Achtung (f).
Estimate, v. Veranschlagen n. Schätzung (f).
Estimation, n. Schätzung (f).
Estuary, n. Mündung (f).
Etching, n. Radierung (f).
Eternity, n. Ewigkeit (f).
Ether, n. Äther (m).
Etiquette, n. Etikette (f).
Evacuate, v. Räumen (military), abführen (medical).
Evade, v. Umgehen.
Evaporate, v. Verdunsten, verdampfen.
Evasion, n. Ausflucht (f).
Even, adj. Eben, gerade, glatt, gleich.
Evening, n. Abend (m).
Event, n. Begebenheit (f).
Ever, adv. Immer, jemals.
Every, adj. Jeder, jede, jedes.
Everybody, jedermann.
Everyone, jedermann.
Everything, alles.
Everywhere, allenthalben überall.
Evict, v. Gerichtliche wegnehem, vertreiben.
Evidence, n. Beweis (m), Zeuge (m), Zeugnis (n).
Evil, adj. Schlecht, böse, übel; n. Übel (n).
Evoke, v. Hervorrufen.
Evolve, v. Herausarbeiten, entwickeln.
Ewe, n. Mutterschaf (n).
Ewer, n. Wasserkanne (f).
Exact, adj. Genau; v. Fordern, erpressen.
Exaggerate, v. Übertreiben.
Examination, n. Prüfung (f).
Examine, v. Prüfen.
Example, n. Beispiel (n), Muster (n).
Exceed, v. Überschreiten.
Except, prep. Ausser, ausgenommen; v. ausnehmen.
Excessive, adj. Übermässig.
Exchange, v. Tauschen, wechseln; n. Tausch (m), Fernsprechamt (telephone exch:) (n), Kurs (rate of exch:). (m).
Excite, v. Aufregen.

**Exclaim, ** v. Ausrufen.
**Exclude, ** v. Ausschliesslich.
**Excursion, ** n. Abschweifung (f).
**Excuse, ** n. Entschuldigung (f); v. Entschuldigen.
**Executor, ** n. Testamentsvollstrecker (m).
**Exempt, ** adj. Frei:: v. Ausnehmen.
**Exercise, ** n. Übung (f), Aufgabe (f): v. Üben.
**Exert, ** v. Ausüben, sich anstrengen.
**Exhaust, ** v. Erschöpfen: n. Auspuff (machinery) m.
**Exhibit, ** v. Ausstellen, darstellen: n. Ausstellungsstück.
**Exhibition, ** n. Ausstellung (f), Darstellung (f).
**Exile, ** n. Verbannung (f), Verbannte (m-f).
**Exit, ** n. Ausgang (m).
**Expand, ** v. Ausspannen.
**Expect, ** v. Vermuten, denken, erwarten.
**Expel, ** v. Ausstossen.
**Expenditure, ** n. Ausgabe (f).
**Expensive, ** adj. Tuer.
**Experience, ** n. Erfahrung (f), Erlebnis (n): v. Erfahren.
**Experiment, ** v. Experimentieren; n. Experiment (n).
**Expert, ** adj. Erfahren: n. Fachmann (m).
**Expiate, ** v. Sühnen.
**Explain, ** v. Erklären.
**Explode, ** v. Sprengen, ausbrechen.
**Explore, ** v. Erforschen.
**Export, ** n. Ausfuhr (f): v. Ausführen.
**Exposure, ** n. Belichtung (photography) (f).
**Express, ** n. Schnellzug (m).
**Exquisite, ** adj. Auserlesen.
**Extend, ** v. Verlängern, erweisen.
**Extensive, ** adj. Ausgedehnt.
**Exterior, ** n. Äussere (n): adj. Äusserlich.
**Extinct, ** adj. Ausgestorben.
**Extinguish, ** v. Auslöschen.
**Extra, ** adj. Use the prefix, Extra — , Neben — or Sonder—.
**Extract, ** n. Auszug (m): v. Ausziehen.
**Extraction, ** n. Ausziehen (n).

**Extravagant, ** adj. Verschwenderich.
**Extreme, ** adj. Äussert, höchst. (f).
**Eye, ** n. Auge (n).
**Eyeball, ** n. Augapfel (m).
**Eyebrow, ** n. Augenbraue (f).
**Eyeglasses, ** n. Augengläser (n).
**Eyesight, ** n. Augenlicht (n), Sehkraft (f).

F

**Fabric, ** n. Gewebe (n), Gebäude (n).
**Fabricate, ** v. Erbauen, verfertigen.
**Face, ** n. Gesicht (n), Zifferblatt (of clock) (n).
**Facility, ** n. Leichtigkeit (f).
**Fact, ** n. Tatsache (f), Tat (f).
**Factory, ** n. Geschäftsführer (m), Fabrik (f).
**Fad, ** n. Liebhaberei (f).
**Fade, ** v. Verwelken, verschiessen.
**Faggot, ** n. Reisigbündel (n).
**Fail, ** v. Unterlassen, mangeln, versiegen, durchfallen (at exam.), Konkurs machen (bankrupt).
**Faint, ** v. Vergehen, ohnmächtig werden.
**Faintly, ** adj. Schwach. zaghaft.
**Faintness, ** n. Schwäche (f).
**Fair, ** adj. Fair, blond, rein, heiter: n. Messe (f), Schöne (f) Jahrmarkt (m.)
**Fairy, ** n. Fee (f).
**Faith, ** n. Glaube (m), Vertrauen (n): adj. Treu.
**Faithless, ** adj. Treulos, ungläubig.
**Fall, ** n. Sturz (m), Fall (m), Senkung (f): v. Fallen, abnehmen, stürzen.
**False, ** adj. Falsch, unecht.
**Falsehood, ** n. Lüge (f), Unwahrheit (f).
**Fame, ** n. Ruf (m), Ruhm (m).
**Familiar, ** adj. Vertraut, intim, häufig.
**Family, ** n. Famillie (f).
**Famine, ** n. Hungersnot (f).
**Famous, ** adj. Berühmt.
**Fan, ** n. Fächer (m); v. Fächeln.
**Fanatic, ** n. Fanatiker (m).
**Fanciful, ** adj. Phantastisch.

**Fancy, ** n. Phantasie (f), Einbildung (f), Neigung (f), v. Sich einbilden.
Fancy-dress, n. Maskenkostüm (n).
Far, adv. Fern, weit.
Farce, n. Posse (f), Schwank (m).
Fare, n. Fahrgeld (n), Fargast (m), Fahrpreis (m), Kost (f).
Farewell, n. Abschied (m): interj. Lebe wohl.
Farm, n. Landgut (n), Bauernhof (m).
Farmer, n. Landwirt (m).
Farrier, n. Hufschmied (m).
Farther, adv. Ferner, weiter.
Farthest, adv. Am weitesten.
Fascinate, v. Bezaubern.
Fashion, n. Form (f), Mode (f), Gestalt (f).
Fashionable, adj. Modisch, modern.
Fast, adj. Fest, stark, sehr, schnell: v. Fasten.
Fasten, v. Befestigen.
Fastener, n. Verschluss (m).
Fastidious, adj. Ekel, wählerisch.
Fat, adj. Fett, plump, dick: n. Fett (n)
Fatal, adj. Tödlich.
Fatality, n. Verhängnis (n), Unglücksfall (m).
Fate, n. Verhangnis (n), Schicksal (n).
Father, n. Vater (m).
Father-in-law, n. Schwiegervater, m.
Fatherly, adj. Väterlich.
Fatigue, n. Ermündung (f), Müdigkeit (f): v. Ermünden.
Fatness, n. Fettigkeit (f).
Fault, n. Fehler (not correct) (m), Schuld (scolding) (f), Mangel (m).
Faultless, adj. Fehlerfrei.
Faulty, adj. Fehlerhaft.
Favour, n. Gunst (f), Gefälligkeit (f): v. Begünstigen.
Favourite, n. Günstling (m): adj. Lieblings.
Fear, n. Furcht (f), Scheu (f): v. Fürchten.
Fearful, adj. Fürchterlich, schrecklich.
Fearless, adj. Furchtlos.
Feat, n. Tat (f).
Feather, n. Feder (f).

February, n. Februar (m).
Fear, n. Lohn (m), Gebühr (f),
February, n. Februar (m).
Fee, n. Lohn (m), Gebühr (f), Honorar (n).
Feeble, adj. Schwach.
Feed, v. Füttern.
Feel, v. Sich fühlen; n. Gefühl (n).
Feeling, adj. Fühlend.
Feline, adj. Katzenartig.
Fell, v. Fällen.
Felony, n. Schweres Verbrechen (n).
Felt, n. Filz (material) (m).
Female, adj. Weiblich: n. Weibliche Person (f).
Feminine, adj. Weiblich.
Fence, n. Zaun (m), Schutzwehr (f).
Fencer, n. Fechter (m).
Fencing, n. Fechtkunst (f).
Fender, n. Kaminvorsetzer (m).
Fern, n. Farnkraut (n).
Ferocious, adj. Wild, grimmig.
Ferret, n. Frettchen (n).
Ferry, n. Fähre (f).
Fertile, adj. Fruchtbar.
Festival, adj. Festlich.
Fetch, v. Bringen, holen.
Feud, n. Felde (f).
Fever, n. Fieber (n).
Few, adj. Wenig.
Fibre, n. Fiber (f), Faser (f).
Fickle, adj. Unbeständig, veränderlich.
Fiction, n. Dichtung (f), Erdichtung (f), Roman (m).
Fictitious, adj. Erdichtet.
Fidget, v. Zappeln, unruhig sein; n. Zappelhans (m).
Fidgety, adj. Unruhig.
Field, n. Feld (n).
Fiend, n. Teufel (m), böse Geist (m).
Fierce, adj. Wild, grimmig.
Fiery, adj. Feurig, jähzornig, hitzig (tempered).
Fifteen, adj. Fünfzehn.
Fifteenth, adj. Fünfzehnte.
Fifth, adj. Fünfte.
Fiftieth, adj. Fünfzigste.
Fifty, adj. Fünfzig.
Fig, n. Feige (f), Putz (m).
Fight, n. Kampf (m), Gefecht (n); v. Kämpfen.
Figure, n. Figur (m), Gestalt (f), Ziffer (f).

File   120   **Footstep**

File, n. Feile (implement) (f), Ordner (as letter file) (m), Reihe (gymnastics) (f).
Fill, n. Füllen.
Film, n. Film (m), Häutchen (thin layer) (n).
Filter, n. Filter (m).
Filth, n. Kot (m), Schmutz (m).
Fin, n. Flosse (f).
Final, adj. Endlich, endgültig.
Finance, n. Finanz; v. Finanzieren.
Find, v. Antreffen, bemerken, finden: n. Fund (m).
Fine, adj. Schon, fein, zart: n. Geldbusse (f), Geldstrafe (f).
Finger, n. Finger (m).
Finish, v. Ausbilden, endigen, vollenden, beenden: n. Ende (n), Schluss (m).
Fir, n. Tanne (f), Kiefer (f).
Fire, n. Feuer (n), Brand (m): v.Feuern.
Fire alarm, n. Feuermelder (n).
Fireproof, adj. Feuerfest.
Firewood, n. Brennholz (n).
Fireworks, n. Feuerwerk (n).
Firm, adj. Derb, fest.
First, adj. Erst: adv. Zuerst.
Fish, n. Fisch (m), Kauz (m): v. Fischen, angeln.
Fishmonger, n. Angelhaken (m), Fischhändler (m).
Fist, n. Faust (j).
Fit, n. Anfall (complaint) (m). v. Anpassen, passen: adj: Passend.
Five, adj. Fünf.
Fix, v. Befestigen; n. Klemme (f).
Flag, n. Flagge (f), Fahne (f), Schwertlilie (plant) (f).
Flagon, n. Flasche (f).
Flake, n. Blättchen (n).
Flame, n. Flamme (f).
Flannel, n. Flansche (f).
Flap, n. Klappe (f), **Lappen** (m): v. Klapsen, flattern.
Flare, n. Geflacker (n), Lohe (f).
Flash, n. Aufblitzen (n).
Flask, n. Flasche (f), Flakon (n).
Flat, adj. Platt, flach: n. Mietwohnung (house) (f).
Flatter, v. Schmeicheln.
Flavour, n. Geschmack (m): v. Würzen.

Flaw, n. Fehler (m), Spalt (m).
Flax, n. Flachs (m).
Flea, n. Floh (m).
Flee, v. Fliehen.
Fleet, n. Flotte (f): adj. Flüchtig, schnell.
Flesh, n. Fleisch (m), Körper (л).
Flexible, adj. Biegsam.
Flight, n. Flucht (f).
Flinch, v. Zurückweichen.
Fling, v. Werfen, schiessen, springen.
Flirt, n. **Kokette** (f): v. Schnellen.
Float, v. Schwimmen, dahintreiben, flossen: n. Floss (f).
Flock, n. Flug (m), Herde (f).
Flood, n. Fluth (f), Flut (f): v. Überschwemmen.
Floor, n. Fussboden (m).
Florist, n. Blumenhändler (m).
Flour, n. Feine Mehl (n).
Flourish, v. Blühen, schnörkeln, schwingen.
Flow, v. Fliessen, strömen.
Flower, n. Blume (f), Blüte (f); v. Blühen.
Flue, n. Rauchfang (m).
Fluent, adj. Geläufig, flüssig.
Fluid, n. Flüssigkeit (f): adj. Flüssig.
Flush, v. Ausspülen, erröten.
Fly, n. Fliege (f), Flügel (m): v. Fliegen, fliehen.
Foal, n. Füllen.
Foam, n. Schaum.
Fodder, n. Viehfutter (n).
Foe, n. Feind (m).
Fog, n. Grumt (n), dicke **Nebel** (m).
Foggy, adj. Nebelig.
Fold, v. Falten, pferchen: n. Falte (f).
Foliage, n. Laubwerk (n).
Follow, v. Verfolgen, folgen.
Follower, n. Nachfolger (m).
Folly, n. Torheit (f).
Fond, adj. Liebevoll, vernarrt, zärtlich.
Food, n. Speise (f), Essen (n).
Fool, n. Narr (m), Tor (m).
Foolery, n. Narrheit (f).
Foolish, adj. Närrisch.
Foot, n. Fuss (m), Tritt (m), Fussvolk (n).
Footpath, n. Fussweg (m).
Footstep, n. Fusstritt (m).

**For, ** *pr. & conj.* Für, mit, nach, wegen, aus, an, auf, zu.
**Forbid, ** *v.* Verbieten.
**Force, ** *n.* Kraft (*f*), Gewalt (*f*), Stärke (*f*): *v.* Zwingen, erstürmen.
**Forefathers, ** *n.* Vorfahren (*m*).
**Forefinger, ** *n.* Zeigefinger (*m*).
**Forego, ** *v.* Verzichten, aufgeben.
**Forehead, ** *n.* Stirn (*f*).
**Foreign, ** *adj.* Ausländisch.
**Foreigner, ** *n.* Fremde (*m*), Ausländer (*m*).
**Foremost, ** *adj.* Vorderst, erst, vornehmste.
**Forest, ** *n.* Forst (*m*), Wald (*m*).
**Forestall, ** *v.* Zuvorkommen.
**Forfeit, ** *v.* Verwirken, verlieren: *n.* Pfand (at games) (*n*).
**Forge, ** *v.* Schmieden (to make in metal), fälschen (to imitate).
**Forgery, ** *n.* Verfälschung (*f*).
**Forget, ** *v.* Vergessen.
**Forget-me-not, ** *n.* Vergissmeinnich (*n*).
**Forgive, ** *n.* Vergeben.
**Forgiveness, ** *n.* Vergebung.
**Fork, ** *n.* Gabel (*f*).
**Forlorn, ** *adj.* Verlassen, einsam.
**Form, ** *n.* Form (shape) (*f*), Formular (document) (*n*), Klasse (class) (*f*).
**Former, ** *adj.* Ehemals, früher, vorig.
**Formula, ** *n.* Formel (*f*).
**Forsake, ** *v.* Verlassen, entsagen.
**Fort, ** *n.* Fort (*n*), Festungswerk (*n*), Schanze (*f*).
**Fortieth, ** *adj.* Vierzigste.
**Fortification, ** *n.* Befestigung (*f*).
**Fortify, ** *v.* Stärken, befestigen.
**Fortnight, ** *n.* Vierzehn Tage (*m*).
**Fortress, ** *n.* Festung (*f*).
**Fortunate, ** *adj.* Glücklich.
**Fortune, ** *n.* Glück (*n*), Schicksal (*n*), Vermögen (*n*).
**Forty, ** *adj.* Vierzig.
**Forward, ** *adv.* Vorwärts: *v.* Senden.
**Foul, ** *adj.* Schmutzig, garstig.
**Found, ** *v.* Giessen (in metal), gründen.
**Foundry, ** *v.* Giesserei (*f*).
**Fountain, ** *n.* Springbrunnen (*m*).
**Four, ** *adj.* Vier.

**Fourteen, ** *adj.* Vierzehn.
**Fourteenth, ** *adj.* Vierzehnte.
**Fourth, ** *adj.* Vierte.
**Fowl, ** *n.* Geflügel (*n*).
**Fox, ** *n.* Fuchs (*m*).
**Foxglove, ** *n.* Fingerhut (*m*).
**Fraction, ** *n.* Bruch (*m*).
**Fracture, ** *n.* (Knochen) Bruch (*m*).
**Fragile, ** *adj.* Zerbrechlich.
**Fragrance, ** *n.* Duft (*m*).
**Frail, ** *adj.* Zart, zerbrechlich.
**Frame, ** *n.* Rahmen (*m*).
**Frantic, ** *adj.* Wahnsinnig.
**Fraternal, ** *adj.* Brüderlich.
**Fraud, ** *n.* Betrug (*m*), Schwindel (*m*).
**Fraudulent, ** *adj.* Betrügerisch.
**Fray, ** *n.* Gefecht (*n*), Tumult (*m*).
**Freak, ** *n.* Grille (*f*), Einfall (*m*), Missgeburt (*f*).
**Freckle, ** *n.* Sommersprosse (*f*).
**Free, ** *adj.* Frei, *v.* Befreien.
**Freedom, ** *n.* Freiheit (*f*).
**Freehold, ** *n.* Freigut (*n*).
**Freeze, ** *v.* Frieren.
**Freezing, ** *adj.* Eisig.
**Freight, ** *n.* Fracht (*f*).
**French, ** *adj.* Französisch.
**Frenzy, ** *n.* Raserei (*f*).
**Frequent, ** *adj.* Häufig: *v.* Verkehren.
**Fresh, ** *adj.* Frisch.
**Friday, ** *n.* Freitag (*m*).
**Friend, ** *n.* Freund (*m*).
**Friendly, ** *adj.* Freundschaftlich.
**Frieze, ** *n.* Fries (*n*).
**Fright, ** *n.* Entsetzen (*n*).
**Frighten, ** *v.* Erschrecken.
**Frigid, ** *adj.* Eisig.
**Frill, ** *n.* Krause (*f*).
**Fringe, ** *n.* Franse (*f*).
**Frivolous, ** *adj.* Leichtsinnig, frivol, leichtfertig.
**Frog, ** *n.* Frosch (*m*).
**From, ** *prep.* Aus, nach, von, vor, wegen.
**Front, ** *n.* Vorderseite (*f*), Vorderteil (*n*).
**Frontier, ** *n.* Grenze (*f*).
**Frost, ** *n.* Frost (*m*).
**Froth, ** *n.* Schaum (*m*).
**Frown, ** *v.* Die Stirn runzeln: *n.* Stirnrunzeln (*n*).
**Fruit, ** *n.* Frucht (*f*).
**Fruiterer, ** *n.* Obsthändler (*m*).

Frustrate, v. Vernichten, vereiteln.
Fry, v. Braten, rösten.
Fuchsia, n. Fuchsie (*f*).
Fuel, n. Brennstoff (*m*), Feuerung (*f*).
Fulfil, v. Erfüllen.
Full, adj. Voll, gänzlich: *adv.* Völlig, genau, recht.
Fun, n. Scherz (*m*), Spass (*m*).
Fund, n. Fonds (*m*), Kapital (*n*).
Funeral, n. Begräbnis (*n*).
Funnel, n. Trichter (for pouring liquids) *m*, Schlot (part of engine) (*m*).
Fur, n. Pelz (*m*), Belag (*m*).
Furious, adj. Rasend, wütend.
Furnace, n. Ofen (*m*).
Furnish, v. Möblieren, versehen.
Furniture, n. Möbel (*n*).
Further, adj. Ferner, überdies, weiter.
Fury, n. Wut (*f*).
Fuss, n. Wesen (*n*).
Future, n. Zukunft (*f*): *adj.* Künftig.

G

Gain, n. Gewinn; *v.* Gewinnen.
Gale, n. Sturm (*m*), frische Wind (*m*).
Gallant, adj. Tapfer.
Gallery, n. Galerie (*f*).
Gallop, n. Galopp (*m*): *v.* Galoppieren.
Gallows, n. Galgen (*m*).
Gamble, n. Glücksspiel (*n*): *v.* Spielen.
Game, n. Spiel (*n*), Wildbret (*n*).
Gang, n. Bande (*f*), Trupp (*m*).
Gangway, n. Durchgang (*m*).
Gaol, n. Gefängnis (*n*).
Gap, n. Bresche (*f*), Riss (*m*).
Garage, n. Garage (*f*).
Garden, n. Garten (*m*).
Gardener, n. Gartner (*m*).
Gargle, v. Gurgeln; *n.* Gurgelwasser (*n*).
Garlic, n. Knoblauch (*m*).
Garment, n. Gewand (*n*).
Garrison, n. Garnison (*f*).
Garter, n. Strumpfband (*n*).
Gas, n. Gas (*n*).
Gash, n. Hieb (*m*).
Gasp, v. Keuchen.
Gate, n. Tor (*n*), Pforte (*f*).
Gather, v. Sammeln, erntenpflücken.
Gay, adj. Heiter.
Gazette, n. Zeitung (*f*), Amtsblatt (*n*).
Gear, n. Kleidung (*f*).
Gem, n. Edelstein (*n*).
Gender, n. Gattung (*f*), Gerschlecht (grammar) (*n*).
General, n. General (*m*): *adj.* Allgemein.
Generally, adv. Im allgemeinen.
Generate, v. Erzeugen.
Generation, n. Erzeugung (*f*), Geschlecht (*n*).
Generosity, n. Edelmut (*m*), Freigebigkeit (*f*).
Genius, n. Genie (*n*).
Genteel, adj. Fein, elegant, vornehm.
Gentile, n. Heide (*m*).
Gentle, adj. Artig, fein, gütig.
Gentleman, n. Herr (*m*), Gentleman (*m*).
Genuine, adj. Echt.
Geography, n. Geographie (*f*).
Geology, n. Geologie (*f*).
Geometry, n. Geometrie (*f*).
Geranium, n. Geranium (*n*).
Germ, n. Keim (*m*).
Get, v. Bekommen (to have), bringen (to bring), verdienen (to earn), werden (to grow).
To get above, übertreffen.
To get back, zuruckbekommen.
To get down, hinuntergehen.
To get from, abnehmen.
To get off, aussteigen.
To get on (make progress), weiterkommen.
To get on (mount on), anziehen.
To get out, herausbringen.
To get up (from bed), aufstehen.
Ghost, n. Geist (*m*).
Giant, n. Riese (*m*).
Giddiness, n. Schwindel (*m*), Schwindelanfall (*m*).
Gift, n. Gabe (*f*), Geschenk (*n*).
Gigantic, adj. Riesenhaft.
Gild, v. Vergolden.
Gimlet, n. Bohrer (*m*).
Gin, n. Schlinge (*f*), Wacholderbranntwein (*m*).
Ginger, n. Ingwer (*m*).

Gingerbread, *n.* Pfefferkuchen (*m*).
Gipsy, *n.* Zigeuner (*m*).
Girl, *n.* Mädchen (*n*).
Give, *v.* Geben, erteilen, aufgeben, schenken.
Glad, *adj.* Erfreut, froh.
Glade, *n.* Lichtung (*f*).
Glance, *n.* Blitz.
Glare, *n.* Blendende Glanz (*m*).
Glass, *n.* Glas (*n*).
Glazier, *n.* Glaser (*m*).
Glee, *n.* Freude (*f*), Heiterkeit (*f*).
Glen, *n.* Tal (*n*).
Glide, *v.* Gleiten (*n*): *v.* Gleiten.
Glimpse, *n.* Schimmer (*m*).
Globe, *n.* Kugel (*f*), Globus (*m*).
Gloom, *n.* Dunkelheit (*f*).
Gloomy, *adj.* Dunkel.
Glorify, *v.* Verherrlichen.
Glove, *n.* Handschuh (*m*).
Glow, *v.* Glühen.
Glue, *n.* Leim (*m*): *v.* Leimen.
Glutton, *n.* Fresser (*m*), Vielfrass (*m*).
Gnat, *n.* Mücke (*f*).
Gnaw, *v.* Nagen.
Go, *v.* Gehen.
Go ahead, vorwärtsgehen.
Go away, abreisen.
Go back, zurückgehen.
Go by, vorbeigehen.
Go off (depart), abgehen.
Go with, mitgehen.
Go without, entbehen.
Goal, *n.* Ziel (ambition) (*n*), Tor (football) (*n*).
Goat, *n.* Ziege (*f*).
He goat, Ziegenbrock (*m*).
God, *n.* Gott (*m*).
Godfather, *n.* Pate (*m*).
Godmother, *n.* Patin (*f*).
Gold, *n.* Gold (*n*).
Golden, *adj.* Golden.
Gong, *n.* Gong (*m. & n*).
Good, *adj.* Gut; *n.* Gute (*n*), Wohl (*n*), Habe (*f*).
Good bye, *interj.* Leben Sie wohl.
Goodness, *n.* Güte (*f*), Gütigkeit (*f*).
Goose, *n.* Gans (*f*).
Gooseberry, *n.* Stachelbeere (*f*).
Gossip, *n.* Klatschbase (*f*), Gerede (*n*), Gevatter (*m*).
Gout, *n.* Gicht (*f*).

Govern, *v.* Regieren.
Government, *n.* Regierungsform (*f*).
Governor, *n.* Befehlshaber (*m*), Prinzipal (*m*), Statthalter (*m*).
Gown, *n.* Talar (*m*), Kleid (*n*), Frauenkleid (*n*).
Grab, *v.* Greifen.
Grace, *n.* Gnade (*f*), Anmut (*f*), Gunst (*f*).
Graceful, *adj.* Anmutig.
Gracious, *adj.* Gnädig, anmutig.
Gradient, *n.* Steigung (upwards) (*f*), Neigung (downwards) (*f*).
Gradual, *adj.* Allmählich, stufenweise.
Grain, *n.* Korn (*n*), Getreide (*n*), Gran (*m. & n*), Längsfaser (of wood) (*f*).
Grammar, *n.* Grammatik (*f*).
Granary, *n.* Kornboden (*m*).
Grand, *adj.* Gross, erhaben.
Grandchild, *n.* Enkel (*m*), Enkelin (*f*).
Grandfather, *n.* Grossvater (*m*).
Grandmother, *n.* Grossmutter (*f*).
Grant, *v.* Bewilligen; *n.* Bewilligung (*f*).
Grape, *n.* Traube (*f*), Weintraube (*f*).
Grape-fruit, *n.* Pampelmuse (*f*).
Grasp, *v.* Greifen.
Grass, *n.* Gras (*n*).
Grate, *n.* Gitter (*n*), Rost (*m*): *v.* Rasseln, knirschen.
Grateful, *adj.* Dankbar.
Gratify, *v.* Befriedigen.
Gratitude, *n.* Dankbarkeit (*f*).
Gratuity, *n.* Geschenk (*n*).
Grave, *n.* Grab (*n*): *adj.* Ernst, feierlich.
Gravel, *n.* Gries (*m*), Kies (*m*).
Gravy, *n.* Saft des Fleisches (*m*), Sauce (*f*).
Gray, *adj.* Grau, dämmerig.
Grease, *n.* Fett (*n*); *v.* Schmieren.
Greasy, *adj.* Schmierig.
Great, *adj.* Grosse (size) berühmt (important).
Greed, *n.* Gier (*f*), Geiz (*m*).
Green, *n.* Grün (*n*): *adj.* Grün.
Greengage, *n.* Reineclaude (*f*).

Greengrocer 124 **Hard**

Greengrocer, *n.* Gemüsehändler (*m*).
Greenhouse, *n.* Gewächshaus (*n*).
Greet, *v.* Grüssen.
Grey, *adj.* Grau, dämmerig.
Greyhound, *n.* Windspiel (*n*).
Grief, *n.* Kummer (*m*), Gram (*m*).
Grievance, *n.* Beschwerde (*f*).
Grieve, *v.* Kränken, ärgern.
Grill, *n.* Bratrost (*m*): *v.* Rösten.
Grim, *adj.* Grimmig.
Grime, *n.* Schmutz (*m*).
Grin, *v.* Grinsen: *n.* Grinsen (*n*).
Grind, *v.* Mahlen, schleifen.
Grip, *n.* Griff (*m*).
Grit, *n.* Griess (*m*), Grütze (*f*), Festigkeit (tenacity) (*f*).
Groan, *v.* Seufzen; *n.* Seuzer (*m*).
Grocer *n.* Kolonialwarenhändler (*m*), Materialwarenhändler (*m*).
Grocery, *n.* Kolonialwaren (*f*).
Groin, *n.* Leisten (body) (*f*), Grat (architecture) (*m*).
Groove, *n.* Furche (*f*), Nut (*f*), Rinne (*f*).
Gross, *adj.* Grob (coarse); *n.* Gros (144) (*n*).
Ground, *n.* Grund (*m*), Boden (*m*).
Group, *n.* Gruppe (*f*).
Grow, *v.* Wachsen, werden.
Growl, *v.* Brummen.
Growth, *n.* Wachstum (*n*).
Grudge, *n.* Groll (*m*), Neid (*m*).
Gruesome, *adj.* Grausig.
Grumble, *v.* Brummen, murren.
Grunt, *v.* Grunzen.
Guard, *n.* Wache (*f*), Schaffner (on trains) (*m*): *v.* Schützen, Bewachen.
Guess, *v.* Raten, mutmassen; *n.* Vermutung (*f*).
Guest, *n.* Gast (*m*).
Guide, *v.* Führen (*m*).
Guide-book, *n.* Reiseführer (*m*).
Guilt, *n.* Schuld (*f*), Verbrechen (*n*).
Guinea-pig, *n.* Meerschweinchen (*n*).
Gulf, *n.* Golf (*m*), Meerbusen (*m*), Abgrund (*m*).

Gum, *n.* Gummi (*n*), *v.* Gummieren.
Gums, *n.* Zahnfleisch (*n*).
Gun, *n.* Gewehr (*n*), Geschütz (*n*).
Gunpowder, *n.* Schiesspulver (*n*).
Gurgle, *v.* Gurgeln.
Gust (of wind), *n.* Windstoss (*m*).
Gusty, *adj.* Stürmisch.
Gut, *n.* Darm (*m*).
Gutter, *n.* Gosse (*f*), Rinne (*f*).

H

Haberdasher, *n.* Bandhändler (*m*).
Habit, *n.* Anzug (*m*), Zustand (*m*), Gewohnheit (*f*).
Habitable, *adj.* Bewohnbar.
Hail, *v.* Hageln, anrufen; *n.* Hagel (*m*).
Hair, *n.* Haar (*n*).
Hairbrush, *n.* Haarbürste (*f*).
Hairdresser, *n.* Haarkünstler (*m*), Friseur (*m*).
Hairpin, *n.* Haarnadel (*f*).
Hale, *adj.* Frisch, gesund, hell.
Half, *adj.* Halb (*f*), Hälfte (*f*).
Hall, *n.* Halle (public hall) (*f*), Saal (*m*), Flur (entry to house) (*m*).
Halt, *v.* Halt machen, anhalten.
Halve, *v.* Halbieren.
Ham, *n.* Schenkel (*m*), Schinken (*m*).
Hammer, *n.* Hammer (*m*).
Hammock, *n.* Hängematte (*f*).
Hamper, *n.* Packkorb (*m*).
Hand, *n.* Hand (*f*).
Handful, *n.* Handvoll (*f*).
Handkerchief, *n.* Taschentuch (*n*), Halstuch (*n*).
Handle, (*n*) Griff (*n*), Kurbel (*f*), Stiel (*m*): *v.* Handhaben, angreifen.
Handsome, *adj.* Hübsch, zierlich.
Handy, *adj.* Geschickt.
Hang, *v.* Hängen.
Happen, *v.* Sich ereignen.
Happiness, *n.* Glück (*n*).
Happy, *adj.* Glücklich.
Harass, *v.* Quälen, plagen.
Harbour, *n.* Hafen (*m*), Zufluchtsort (*m*).
Hard, *adj.* Hart, **streng, mühsam.**

Harden — Hero

Harden, v. Härten.
Hardly, adv. Kaum.
Hardship, n. Beschwerde (f).
Hardware, n. Eisenwaaren (f).
Hardy, adj. Hart, fest, kühn, stark.
Hare, n. Hase (m).
Harm, n. Schade (m), Leid (n).
Harmful, adj. Schädlich.
Harmless, adj. Harmlos.
Harness, n. Geschirr (n).
Harp, n. Harfe (f).
Harsh, adj. Streng, barsch.
Harvest, n. Ernte (f).
Haste, n. Eile (f), Hast (f).
Hasty, adj. Eilig, hastig.
Hat, n. Hut (m).
Hatch, v. Ausbrüten, brüten.
Hatchet, n. Axt (f), Beil (n).
Hate, n. Hass (m); v. Hassen.
Hateful, adj. Verhasst, gehässig.
Haughty, adj. Stolz, hochmütig.
Haul, n. Fang (a catch) (m); v. Ziehen, schleppen.
Haunt, n. Aufenthaltsort (m); v. Beschweren.
Have, v. Haben, halten, handeln.
Haversack, n. Rucksack (m).
Havoc, n. Zerstörung (f).
Hawk, n. Falke (m), Habicht (m).
Hawker, n. Hausierer (m).
Hawthorn, n. Hagedorn (m).
Hay, n. Heu (n).
Hay-rick, n. Heufeime (f).
Hazard, v. Wagen; n. Gefahr (f), Ungefähr (n).
Haze, n. Dunst (m), leichte Nebel (m).
Hazel, n. Haselstaude (f).
Hazy, adj. Dunstig, nebelig.
He, pron. Er.
Head, n. Haupt (n), Kopf (m), Gipfel (m).
Headache, n. Kopfweh (n).
Headlamp, n. Scheinwerfer (m).
Headmaster, n. Schuldirektor (m).
Head-waiter, n. Oberkellner (m).
Head-wind, n. Gegenwind (m).
Heal, v. Heilen.
Health, n. Gesundheit (f).
Healthy, adj. Gesund.

Heap, n. Menge (f), Haufen (m).
Hear, v. Hören, anhören, verhören.
Hearing, n. Hören (n), Gehör (n).
Heart, n. Herz (n).
Hearth, n. Boden (m).
Hearth-rug, n. Kaminvorleger (m).
Heartless, adj. Grausam, herzlos.
Heat, n. Hitze (f); v. Heizen.
Heave, v. Heben.
Heaven, n. Himmel (m).
Heavy, adj. Schwer, träge, stürmisch.
Hedge, n. Hecke (f).
Hedgehog, n. Igel (m).
Heed, v. Beachten, aufmerken.
Heedless, adj. Unachtsam, achtlos.
Heel, n. Ferse (f), Absatz (m), Huf (m).
Heifer, n. Junge Kuh (f).
Height, n. Gipfel (m), Höhe (f), Grosse (f).
Heinous, adj. Abscheulich.
Heir, n. Erbe (m).
Heiress, n. Erbin (f).
Heliotrope, n. Sonnenwend (the plant) (f), Heliotropfarbe (f).
Hell, n. Hölle (f).
Helmet, n. Helm (m).
Help, v. Helfen, verhelfen; n. Hilfe.
Helper, n. Helfer.
Helpful, adj. Hilfreich.
Helpless, adj. Hilflos.
Hem, n. Saum (m); v. Säumen.
Hemorrhage, n. Blutung (f), Blutsturz (m).
Hen, n. Henne (f).
Hence, adv. Von hier, hinfort, daher.
Her, pron. Sie, ihre, ihr.
Herb, n. Kraut (n), Gras (n).
Herbalist, n. Kräuterhandler (m).
Herd, n. Herde (f).
Here, adv. Hier, hiesigen.
Hereafter, adv. Hernach; n. Jenseits (n).
Hereby, adv. Hierdurch.
Herewith, adv. Hiermit.
Heritage, n. Erbgut (n).
Hermit, n. Einsiedler (m).
Hero, n. Held (m).

Heroine, *n.* Heldin (*f*).
Heroism, *n.* Heldenmuth (*m*).
Heron, *n.* Reiper (*m*).
Herring, *n.* Hering (*m*).
Hers, *pron.* Ihrer (*m*), ihre (*f*), ihrs, ihres (*n*).
Hesitate, *v.* Zögern.
Hesitation, *n.* Zögern (*n*), Unschlüssigkeit (*f*).
Hibernate, *v.* Überwintern.
Hiccup, *n.* Schlucken.
Hide, *n.* Haut (*f*); *v.* Verbergen.
Hideous, *adj.* Schensslich.
High, *adj.* Erhaben, hoch, stolz.
Highway, *n.* Landstrasse (*f*).
Highwayman, *n.* Strassenräuber (*m*).
Hill, *n.* Hügel (*m*), Berg (*m*).
Hilly, *adj.* Hügelig.
Him, *pron.* Ihn, ihm.
Himself, *pron.* Selbst.
Hinge, *n.* Haspe (*f*), Hauptsache (*f*).
Hint, *v.* Andeuten; *n.* Wink (*m*).
Hip, *n.* Hagebutte (*f*).
Hippopotamus, *n.* Nilpferd (*n*).
Hire, *v.* Vermieten: *n.* Miete (*f*).
His, *pron.* Sein (*m. & n. sing*), seine (*f. & all pl.*).
Hiss, *v.* Zischen.
History, *n.* Geschichte (*f*).
Hit, *v.* Schlagen: *n.* Schlag.
Hitch, *v.* Festmachen: *n.* Ruck (*m*), Störung (*f*).
Hither, *adv.* Hierher.
Hitherto, *adv.* Bisher.
Hive, *n.* Bienenstock (*m*), Schwarm (*m*).
Hoard, *v.* Hamstern; *n.* Hort (*m*).
Hoarding, *n.* Bauzaun (*m*).
Hoar-frost, *n.* Reif (*m*).
Hoarse, *adj.* Heiser.
Hoax, *n.* Streich (*m*), Fopperei (*f*), Schwank (*m*): *v.* Anführen, foppen.
Hobble, *v.* Humpeln.
Hobby, *n.* Steckenpferd (*n*).
Hock, *n.* Hachse (leg) (*f*), Rheinwein (wine) (*m*).
Hockey, *n.* Hockey (*n*).
Hoe, *n.* Hacke (*f*): *v.* Hacken.
Hold, *v.* Halten; *n.* Halt (*m*), Macht (*f*).
Hold back, zurückhalten.
Hold forth, darstellen.
Hold good, gültig sein, gelten.
Hold on, festhalten.
Hold out, ausstrecken.
Hold over, reservieren.
Hole, *n.* Loch (*n*).
Holiday, *n.* Feiertag (*m*).
Hollow, *adj.* Hohl, falsch, dumpf (noise).
Holly, *n.* Stechpalme (*f*).
Hollyhock, *n.* Stockrose (*f*).
Holy, *adj.* Heilig.
Home, *n.* Wohnung (*f*), Heim (*f*), Heimat (*f*).
At home, zu Hause (*n*).
Homeless, *adj.* Heimatlos, obdachlos.
Homesick, *adj.* Heimweh habend.
Homicide, *n.* Mörder (*m*), Totschlag (*m*).
Honest, *adj.* Anständig, ehrlich, redlich.
Honesty, *n.* Ehrlichkeit.
Honey, *n.* Honig (*m*).
Honeymoon, *n.* Flitterwochen (*f*), Hochzeitsreise (*f*).
Honeysuckle, *n.* Geissblatt (*m*).
Honour, *n.* Ehre (*f*), Würde (*f*): *v.* Ehren.
Hood, *n.* Haube (*f*), Kapuze (*f*), Verdeck (car) (*n*).
Hoof, *n.* Huf (*m*).
Hook, *n.* Haken (*m*): *v.* Anhaken, festhaken.
Hoop, *n.* Reif (*m*).
Hooping-cough, *n.* Keuchhusten (*m*).
Hoot, *n.* Geschrei (*n*), Heulen (animal) (*n*), Hupen (car) (*n*): *v.* Heulen, hupen, tuten.
Hooter, *n.* Hupe (car) (*f*).
Hop, *v.* Hüpfen: *n.* Hopfen (plant) (*m*).
Hope, *v.* Hoffen: *n.* Hoffnung (*f*).
Hopeful, *adj.* Hoffnungsvoll.
Hopeless, *adj.* Hoffnungslos.
Horn, *n.* Horn (*n*).
Hornbeam, *n.* Hagebuche (*f*).
Horrible, *adj.* Schrecklich.
Horrid, *adj.* Schrecklich.
Horror, *n.* Schauder (*m*) Greuel (*m*).
Horse, *n.* Pferd (*n*).
Horseradish, *n.* Meerrettich (*m*).
Hosier, *n.* Woolwarenhändler (*m*).

Hospital 127 Imitate

Hospital, *n.* Krankenhaus (*n*), Hospital (*n*).
Host, *n.* Gastgeber (of party) (*m*), Hostie (church) (*f*).
Hostile, *adj.* Feindlich.
Hot, *adj.* Heftig, heiss, hitzig, scharf.
Hotel, *n.* Hotel (*n*), Gasthof (*m*).
Hour, *n.* Stunde (*f*).
House, *n.* Haus (*n*), Hauswesen (*n*).
Housebreaker, *n.* Einbrecher (*m*).
Housekeeper, *n.* Haushälterin (*f*).
Housemaid, *n.* Hausmädchen (*n*).
Housewife, *n.* Hausfrau (*f*).
How, *adv.* Wie.
However, *adv.* Indessen, dennoch: *conj.* Jedoch.
Howl, *v.* Heulen.
Hub, *n.* Nabe (*f*), Mittelpunkt (*m*).
Huddle, *n.* Verwirrung: *v.* Hudeln.
Hug, *v.* Umarmen; *n.* Umarmung (*f*).
Huge, *adj.* Ungeheuer.
Hum, *n.* Gesumme (*n*), Gebrumm (*n*), Summen (*n*): *v.* Brummen, summen.
Human, *adj.* Menschlich.
Humane, *adj.* Liebreich.
Humble, *adj.* Demütig, bescheiden.
Humid, *adj.* Nass, feucht.
Humiliate, *v.* Erniedrigen.
Humiliation, *n.* Erniedrigung (*f*).
Humorist, *n.* Grillenfänger (*m*).
Humorous, *adj.* Launisch, humoristisch.
Hundred, *adj.* Hundert.
Hundredth, *adj.* Hunderste.
Hunger, *n.* Hunger (*m*): *v.* Hungern.
Hungry, *adj.* Hungrig.
Hunt, *v.* Jagen: *n.* Jagd (*f*).
Hunter, *n.* Jäger (*m*).
Hurl, *v.* Werfen, wirbeln.
Hurry, *v.* Treiben, beschleunigen, beeilen; *n.* Eile (*f*), Unruhe (*f*).
Hurt, *v.* Verletzen; *n.* Verletzung (*f*).
Husband, *n.* Gatt (*m*), Mann, (*m*), Ehrmann (*n*).

Hush, *interj.* Still, ruhe: *v.* Stillen.
Hush up, Vertuschen.
Husky, *adj.* Hülsig.
Hustle, *v.* Stossen, drängen, fortstossen.
Hut, *n.* Hütte (*f*).
Hyacinth, *n.* Hyazinthe (*f*).
Hydrogen, *n.* Wasserstoff (*m*).
Hygiene, *n.* Gesundheitslehre (*f*), Hygiene (*f*).
Hymn, *n.* Hymne (*f*), Loblied (*n*).
Hyphen, *n.* Bindestrich (*m*).
Hypocrite, *n.* Heuchler (*m*).
Hysterics, *n.* Hysterie (*f*).

I

I, *pron.* Ich.
Ice, *n.* Eis (*n*).
Iceberg, *n.* Eisberg (*m*).
Ice cream, *n.* Gefrorenes (*n*).
Idea, *n.* Idee (*f*), Begriff (*m*).
Ideal, *adj.* Ideal, vorbildlich.
Identical, *adj.* Identisch.
Identify, *v.* Feststellen, identifizieren.
Idiot, *n.* Dummkopf (*m*), Idiot (*m*).
Idle, *adj.* Faul, müssig, träge.
Idler, *n.* Müssiggänger (*m*).
Idol, *n.* Götze (*m*), Götzenbild (*n*).
Idolize, *v.* Vergöttern.
If, *conj.* Falls, ob, wenn.
Ignition, *n.* Zündung (*f*).
Ignoramus, *n.* Unwissende (*m*).
Ignorant, *adj.* Unkundig, unwissend.
Ignore, *v.* Ignorieren, unbeachtet lassen.
Ill, *n.* Übel (*n*): *adj.* Übel, böse, unwohl.
Illegal, *adj.* Gesetzwidrig.
Illegible, *adj.* Unleserlich.
Illegitimate, *adj.* Unehelich.
Illiterate, *adj.* Ungelehrt.
Illness, *n.* Krankheit (*f*).
Illustrate, *v.* Illustrieren, erhellen.
Illustration, *n.* Illustration (*f*), Erläuterung (*f*).
Image, *n.* Bild (*m*).
Imagination, *n.* Einbildung (*f*).
Imagine, *v.* Sich einbilden.
Imitate, *v.* Imitieren, nachbilden.

Imitation, Inconspicuous

Imitation, *n.* Nachahmung (*f*).
Immediate, *adj.* Unmittelbar.
Immediately, *adv.* Sofort, sogleich.
Immense, *adj.* Unermesslich.
Immerse, *v.* Eintauchen.
Immigrate, *v.* Einwandern.
Imminent, *adj.* Bevorstehend.
Immoderate, *adj.* Unmassig.
Immodest, *adj.* Unbescheiden.
Immoral, *adj.* Unsittlich, unmoralisch.
Imp, *n.* Kobold (*m*).
Impact, *n.* Stoss (*m*).
Impart, *v.* Mitteilen.
Impassable, *adj.* Gefühllos, ungangbar.
Impatience, *n.* Ungeduld (*f*).
Impatient, *adj.* Ungeduldig.
Impel, *v.* Antreiben.
Imperative, *n.* Imperativ (*m*): *adj.* Befehlend.
Imperfect, *adj.* Unvollkommen: *n.* Imperfekt (in grammar) (*n*).
Imperial, *adj.* Kaiserlich.
Imperil, *v.* Gefährden.
Imperishable, *adj.* Unvergänglich.
Impertinence, *n.* Frechheit (*f*), Anmassung (*f*).
Impertinent, *adj.* Frech, ungehörig.
Implicate, *v.* Verwickeln.
Implore, *v.* Anflehen, flehen.
Imply, *v.* Besagen, bedeuten, andeuten.
Impolite, *adj.* Unhöflich.
Import, *v.* Einführen: *n.* Einfuhr (*f*).
Important, *adj.* Wichtig.
Importer, *n.* Einführer (*m*), Importeur (*m*).
Importune, *v.* Beschweren.
Impose, *v.* Aufbürden, einschärfen, auflegen.
Impostor, *n.* Betrüger (*m*).
Impoverish, *v.* Verarmen.
Impracticable, *adj.* Untunlich.
Impregnate, *v.* Schwängern.
Imprisonment, *n.* Haft (*f*).
Improbable, *adj.* Unwahrscheinlich.
Improper, *adj.* Unschicklich, uneigentlich.
Improve, *v.* Verbessern, besser werden.

Imprudent, *adj.* Unklug, unvorsichtig.
Impudent, *adj.* Unverschämt, frech.
Impure, *adj.* Unrein, unkeusch.
Impurity, *n.* Unreinheit (*f*).
Impute, *v.* Zurechnen.
In, *prep.* In, an, auf, bei, zu.
Inability, *n.* Unfahigkeit (*f*).
Inaccessible, *adj.* Unzugänglich.
Inaccurate, *adj.* Ungenau.
Inactive, *adj.* Unthätig.
Inadequate, *adj.* Unzulänglich.
Inadmissible, *adj.* Unzulässig.
Inanimate, *adj.* Unbeseelt.
Inapplicable, *adj.* Unanwendbar.
Inasmuch, *adv.* Insofern.
Inattention, *n.* Unaufmerksamkeit (*f*).
Inaudible, *adj.* Unhörbar.
Incalculable, *adj.* Unberechenbar.
Incandescent, *adj.* Weissglühend.
Incapable, *adj.* Untauglich, unfähig.
Incendiary, *n.* Brandstifter (*m*).
Incentive, *adj.* Anreizend.
Incessant, *adj.* Unaufhörlich.
Inch, *n.* Zoll (*m*).
Incident, *adj.* Zufällig.
Incite, *v.* Anreizen, aufstacheln.
Incivility, *n.* Unhöflichkeit (*f*).
Inclement, *adj.* Rauh.
Incline, *v.* Lenken, neigen.
Include, *v.* Einschliessen.
Incoherent, *adj.* Unzusammenhängend.
Income, *n.* Eincommen (*n*).
Income-tax, *n.* Eincommensteuer (*f*).
Incommode, *v.* Belästigen.
Incomparable, *adj.* Unvergleichlich.
Incompetence, *n.* Unbefugtheit (*f*).
Incomplete, *adj.* Unvollständig.
Inconsiderable, *adj.* Unbedeutend.
Inconsistent, *adj.* Unvereinbar.
Inconspicuous, *adj.* Unauffällig.

Inconstant — Inherit

Inconstant, *adj.* Unbeständig.
Inconvenient, *adj.* Unbequem.
Incorrect, *adj.* Fehlerhaft.
Increase, *v.* Wachsen, erhöhen: *n.* Wachstum (*n*).
Incredible, *adj.* Unglaublich.
Incriminate, *v.* Beschuldigen.
Incubate, *v.* Brüten.
Incubator, *n.* Brutapparat (*m*).
Incur, *v.* Sich laden, sich zuziehen.
Incurable, *adj.* Unheilbar.
Indebted, *adj.* Verschuldet.
Indecent, *adj.* Unanständig.
Indeed, *adv.* In der Tat.
Indelicacy, *n.* Mangel (*m*).
Indelicate, *adj.* Grob, unfein, unzart.
Indemnity, *n.* Schadloshaltung (*f*).
Independence, *n.* Unabhängigkeit (*f*).
Indestructible, *a.* Unzerstörbar.
Index, *n.* Anzeiger (*m*), Index (*m*), Inhaltsverzeichnis (*n*).
India-rubber, *n.* Gummi (*m.* or *n.*), Radiergummi (*m.* or *n.*).
Indicate, *v.* Anzeigen.
Indicative, *adj.* Anzeigend; Indikativ (in grammar) (*m*).
Indict, *v.* Anklagen, belangen.
Indifferent, *adj.* Gleichgültig, massig.
Indigestible, *adj.* Unverdaulich.
Indigestion, *n.* Verdauungsbeschwerde (*f*).
Indignant, *adj.* Unwillig.
Indirect, *adj.* Indirekt, mittelbar.
Indisposed, *adj.* Abgeneigt, unpässlich.
Indisposition, *n.* Unpässlichkeit (*f*).
Indistinct, *adj.* Undeutlich.
Individual, *adj.* Einzeln: *n.* Individuum (*n*), Person (*f*).
Indivisible, *adj.* Unteilbar.
Indolence, *n.* Trägheit (*f*).
Indoors, *adv.* Im Hause.
Induce, *v.* Veranlassen.
Indulge, *v.* Frönen, nachgeben.
Industrious, *adj.* Fleissig.
Industry, *n.* Fleiss.
Inebriate, *adj.* Betrunken.
Inefficient, *adj.* Unwirksam.
Ineligible, *adj.* Nicht wählbar.

Inequality, *n.* Unzulänglichkeit (*f*).
Inert, *adj.* Schwerfällig.
Inevitable, *adj.* Unvermeidlich.
Inexact, *adj.* Ungenau.
Inexhaustible, *adj.* Unerschöpflich.
Inexpedient, *adj.* Unratsam, unpassend.
Inexpensive, *adj.* Billig, nicht kostspielig.
Inexperience, *n.* Unerfahrenheit (*f*).
Inexplicable, *adj.* Unerklärlich.
Infamy, *n.* Schande (*f*), Unehre (*f*).
Infant, *n.* Kind (*n*).
Infantry, *n.* Infanterie (*f*).
Infatuate, *v.* Betören.
Infect, *v.* Anstecken.
Infectious, *adj.* Ansteckend.
Inference, *n.* Folgerung (*f*).
Inferior, *adj.* Gering, minderwertig.
Infest, *v.* Plagen, wimmeln, belästigen.
Infinitive, *n.* Infinitiv (in grammar) (*m*).
Infirm, *adj.* Kraftlos, gebrechlich.
Infirmary, *n.* Krankenhaus (*n*).
Infirmity, *n.* Schwäche (*f*).
Inflame, *v.* Entflammen.
Inflammation, *n.* Entzündung (*f*).
Inflate, *v.* Aufblähen.
Inflict, *v.* Auferlegen, zufügen.
Influence, *n.* Einfluss (*m*): *v.* Einwirken.
Influenza, *n.* Influenza (*f*), Grippe (*f*).
Inform, *v.* Unterrichten, benachrichtigen.
Infrequent, *adj.* Selten, ungewöhnlich.
Infringe, *v.* Übertreten, verletzen.
Infuriate, *v.* Wütend machen.
Ingenious, *adj.* Sinnreich, erfinderisch.
Inglorious, *adj.* Unrühmlich.
Ingot, *n.* Metallbarren (*m*).
Ingratitude, *n.* Undankbarkeit (*f*).
Ingredient, *n.* Bestandteil (*m*).
Inhale, *v.* Bewohnen.
Inherit, *v.* Erben.

**Inheritance, ** n. Erbe (n).
**Inhuman, ** adj. Unmenschlich.
**Iniquitous, ** adj. Frevelhaft, widerrechtlich.
**Initial, ** n. Anfangsbuchstabe (m).
**Initiate, ** v. Einweihen.
**Inject, ** v. Einspritzen.
**Injection, ** n. Einspritzung (f).
**Injudicious, ** adj. Unverständig, unbesonnen.
**Injure, ** v. Verletzen, schädigen.
**Injury, ** n. Verletzung (f), Unrecht (n).
**Injustice, ** n. Ungerechtigkeit (f).
**Ink, ** n. Tinte (f).
**Inkstand, ** n. Tintenfass (n).
**Inlaid, ** adj. Eingelegt.
**Inland, ** adj. Inländisch.
**Inmate, ** n. Insasse (m), Bewohner (m).
**Inmost, ** adj. Innerst.
**Inn, ** n. Gasthof (m).
**Inner, ** adj. Innerlich, inner, inwendig.
**Innermost, ** adj. Innerst.
**Innkeeper, ** n. Gastwirth (m).
**Innocent, ** adj. Einfältig, unschuldig.
**Innovation, ** n. Neuerung (f).
**Innumerable, ** adj. Unzählig.
**Inoffensive, ** adj. Unanstossig.
**Inquest, ** n. Nachforschung (f).
**Inquire, ** v. Untersuchen.
**Inroad, ** n. Einfall.
**Insane, ** adj. Wahnsinnig.
**Insanity, ** n. Wahnsinn (m).
**Inscribe, ** v. Einschreiben, widmen.
**Insect, ** n. Insekt (n).
**Insecure, ** adj. Unsicher.
**Insensible, ** adj. Unmerklich, gefühllos.
**Inseparable, ** adj. Unzertrennlich.
**Insight, ** n. Einsicht (f).
**Insignificant, ** adj. Unbedeutend.
**Insincere, ** adj. Aufrichtig, falsch, unecht.
**Insist upon, ** v. Bestehen auf.
**Insolent, ** adj. Frech, unverschämt.
**Inspect, ** v. Besichtigen.
**Inspection, ** n. Aufsicht (f), Besichtigung (f).
**Inspector, ** n. Aufseher (m), Inspektor (m).

**Inspire, ** v. Einflossen.
**Install, ** v. Einsetzen.
**Instalment, ** n. Teilzahlung (f), Rate (f).
**Instant, ** n. Augenblick (m).
**Instantaneous, ** adj. Augenblicklich.
**Instead, ** adv. Anstatt.
**Instep, ** n. Rist (m), Spann (m).
**Instil, ** v. Einflossen.
**Instinct, ** n. Instinkt (m), Naturtrieb (m).
**Instinctive, ** adj. Instinktmassig.
**Institute, ** n. Anstalt (f): v. Einsetzen, stiften.
**Instruct, ** v. Unterweisen.
**Instruction, ** n. Unterweisung (f).
**Instructor, ** n. Lehrer (m).
**Instrument, ** n. Urkunde (f), Werkzeug (n).
**Insufficient, ** adj. Ungenügend.
**Insult, ** v. Beleidigen: n. Beleidigung (f).
**Insurance, ** n. Versicherung (f).
**Insure, ** v. Versichern.
**Intelligent, ** adj. Intelligenz (f).
**Intend, ** v. Beabsichtigen.
**Intense, ** adj. Gespannt, stark.
**Intent, ** n. Absicht: adj. Erpicht, gespannt.
**Intention, ** n. Absicht (f).
**Inter, ** v. Beerdigen.
**Intercept, ** v. Auffangen.
**Interdict, ** v. Untersagen: n. Interdikt (n).
**Interest, ** n. Anteil (m), Zinsen (m).
**Interfere, ** v. Einschreiten, stören.
**Interim, ** n. Zwischenzeit (f).
**Interior, ** adj. Inner: n. Innert (n).
**Interjection, ** n. Interjektion (in grammar) (f).
**Interlope, ** v. Sich eindrängen.
**Interlude, ** n. Zwischenspiel (n).
**Intermediate, ** adj. Zwischen . . . .
**Intermission, ** n. Aussetzen (n), Pause (f).
**Internal, ** adj. Innerlich.
**International, ** adj. International.
**Interpose, ** v. Dazwischen treten, dazwischen stellen, vermitteln.

Interpret   **Jaw**

Interpret, v. Erklären, darstellen.
Interpreter, n. Ausleger (m), Darsteller (m), Dolmetscher (m).
Interrogate, v. Befragen.
Interrupt, v. Unterbrechen.
Interval, n. Pause (f), Zwischenraum (m).
Interview, n. Zusammenkunft (f): v. Interviewen.
Intestate, adj. Ohne Testament.
Intestine, n. Eingeweide (n), Gedärme (f).
Intimate, adj. Vertraut: v. Andeuten.
Intimation, n. Andeutung (f).
Intimidation, n. Einschüchterung (f).
Into, prep. Hinein, in.
Intolerable, adj. Unerträglich.
Intoxicate, v. Berauschen.
Intoxication, n. Berauschung (f).
Intransitive, adj. Intransitiv (in grammar).
Intrepid, adj. Unerschrocken.
Intricate, adj. Verworren, verwickelt.
Introduce, v. Einführen.
Introduction, n. Einführung (f).
Intruder, n. Eindringling (m).
Intuition, n. Intuition (f).
Invade, v. Einfallen.
Invalid, n. Invalide (m), Kranker (m).
Invaluable, adj. Unschätzbar.
Invasion, n. Angriff (m), Einfall (m).
Invent, v. Erfinden.
Invention, n. Erfindung (f).
Inventor, n. Erfinder (m).
Invert, v. Umkehren.
Invest, v. Bekleiden, Geld anlegen (money).
Investor, n. Geldgeber (m).
Invigorate, v. Stärken, kräftigen.
Invincible, adj. Unüberwindlich.
Invisible, adj. Unsichtbar.
Invitation, n. Einladung (f).
Invite, v. Einladen.
Invoice, n. Warenrechnung (f), Faktura (f).
Involve, v. Einwickeln, verwickeln.

Inwards, adv. Einwärts.
Irate, adj. Zornig.
Iris, n. Schwertlilie (flower) (f), Regenbogenhaut (of the eye) (f).
Irksome, adj. Lästig.
Iron, n. Eisen (n).
Ironmonger, n. Eisenhändler (m).
Irregular, adj. Unregelmassig.
Irreligious, adj. Ungläubig.
Irreparable, adj. Unersetzlich.
Irresistible, adj. Unwiderstehlich.
Irrespective, adj. Abgesehen.
Irresponsible, adj. Unverantwortlich.
Irrigate, v. Bewässern.
Irritate, v. Reizen.
Irritation, n. Erbitterung (f).
Island, n. Insel (f).
Isolate, v. Absondern, isolieren.
Issue, v. Herauskommen (emerge), emittieren (publish): n. Ausgabe (m), Emission (f), Erfolg (m).
Isthmus, n. Landenge (f).
It, pron. Es, das.
Italics, n. Kursivschrift (f).
Itch, n. Krätze (f), Gelüst (n); v. Jucken.
Itinerary, n. Reisebuch (n).
Its, pron. Sein, seine, seiner, ihr, ihre, ihrer.
Itself, pron. Sich, selbst.
Ivory, n. Elfenbein (n).
Ivy, n. Epheu (m).

J

Jack, n. Matrose (m), Narr (m), Gösch (f), Wagenwinde (f).
Jackal, n. Schakal (m).
Jackdaw, n. Dohle (f).
Jacket, n. Jacke (f).
Jag, n. Kerbe (f); v. Kerben.
Jagged, adj. Zackig.
Jam, n. Marmelade (f), Fruchtmus. (n).
January, n. Januar (m).
Jar, n. Knarren (n), Misston (m), Topf (m).
Jasmine, n. Jasmin (m).
Jaundice, n. Gelbsucht (f).
Jaw, n. Kiefer (m), Kinnbacken (m).

Jay, *n.* Häher (bird) (*m*).
Jealous, *adj.* Eifersüchtig.
Jeer, *v.* Höhnen, spotten.
Jelly, *n.* Gelee (*n*).
Jerk, *n.* Stoss (*m*), Ruck (*m*): *v.* Stossen, rucken.
Jest, *n.* Spass (*m*), Scherz (*m*): *v.* Spassen, scherzen.
Jet, *n.* Jett (stone) (*n*), Strahl (of liquid) (*m*).
Jetty, *n.* Mole (*f*).
Jew, *n.* Jude (*m*).
Jewel, *n.* Juwel (*n*).
Jeweller, *n.* Juwelier (*m*).
Jewelry, *n.* Schmuck (*m*).
Jewess, *n.* Jüdin (*f*).
Jilt, *v.* Versetzen.
Jingle, *v.* Klingeln.
Job, *n.* Arbeit (*f*), Geschäft (*n*).
Jockey, *n.* Jockei (*m*).
Jog, *v.* Stossen.
Join, *v.* Zusammenfügen.
Joint, *n.* Gefüge (things made to fit) (*n*), Gelenk (human) (*n*), Braten (of meat) (*m*), Knoten (*m*).
Jointly, *adv.* Gemeinsam.
Joke, *n.* Spass (*m*), Scherz (*m*): *v.* Spassen, scherzen.
Jolly, *adj.* Fröhlich, lustig, munter: *adv.* Sehr.
Jolt, *n.* Stoss (*m*), Ruck (*m*): *v.* Stossen, rucken.
Journal, *n.* Tagebuch (*n*), Zeitung (*f*).
Journey, *n.* Fahrt (*f*), Reise (*f*): *v.* Reisen.
Joy, *n.* Freude (*f*), Fröhlichkeit (*f*).
Joyful, *adj.* Fröhlich.
Judge, *n.* Richter (legal) (*m*), Kenner (expert) (*m*); *v.* Urteilen, richten.
Judgment, *n.* Urteil (*n*), Gericht (*n*).
Judicious, *adj.* Klug, verständig.
Jug, *n.* Krug (*m*).
Juice, *n.* Saft (*m*).
July, *n.* Juli (*m*).
Jump, *n.* Sprung (*m*): *v.* Springen, hüpfen.
Junction, *n.* Vereinigung (*f*), Verbindung (*f*).
June, *n.* Juni (*m*).
Jungle, *n.* Sumpfdickicht (*n*).
Junior, *n.* Junior (*m*): *adj.* Jünger.
Juror, *n.* Geschworne (*m*).
Jury, *n.* Jury (*f*), Geschworene (*m*).
Just, *adj.* Richtig, gerecht, gehörig.
Justice, *n.* Richter (a person) (*m*), Gerechtigkeit (the quality) (*f*).
Justify, *v.* Rechtfertigen.
Jut, *v.* Hervorragen.
Juvenile, *adj.* Jung, jugendlich.

K

Kale, *n.* Krauskohl (*m*).
Kangaroo, *n.* Känguruh (*n*).
Keel, *n.* Kiel (*m*).
Keen, *adj.* Eifrig, scharf, spitzig.
Keenness, *n.* Eifer (*m*), Schärfe (*f*).
Keep, *v.* Behalten, erhalten: *n.* Kost (*f*), Obhut (*f*).
Keeper, *n.* Aufseher (*m*), Wärter (*m*).
Keepsake, *n.* Andenken (*m*).
Kennel, *n.* Hundestall (*m*), Hundehütte (*f*).
Kettle, *n.* Kessel (*m*).
Key, *n.* Schlüssel (*m*), Tonart (*f*).
Keyhole, *n.* Schlüsselloch (*n*).
Kick, *v.* Treten, ausschlagen: *n.* Tritt (*m*), Fusstritt (*m*).
Kid, *n.* Zicklein (*n*), Kind (*n*).
Kidnap, *v.* Kinder entführen.
Kidney, *n.* Niere (*f*).
Kill, *v.* Töten.
Kind, *n.* Gattung (*f*), Art (*f*); *adj.* Gütig.
Kindness, *n.* Freundlichkeit (*f*), Güte (*f*).
King, *n.* König (*m*).
Kingdom, *n.* Königreich (*n*).
Kingfisher, *n.* Eisvogel (*m*).
Kipper, *n.* Räucherhering (*m*).
Kiss, *n.* Kuss (*m*); *v.* Küssen.
Kitchen, *n.* Küche (*f*).
Kite, *n.* Papierdrache (*m*).
Kitten, *n.* Kätzchen (*n*).
Knapsack, *n.* Rucksack (*m*).
Knave, *n.* Schurke (wrongdoer) (*m*), Bube (cards) (*m*).
Knead, *v.* Kneten.
Knee, *n.* Knie (*n*).
Knee-cap, *n.* Kniescheibe (*f*).
Kneel, *v.* Knieen.
Knife, *n.* Messer (*n*).
Knife-sharpener, *n.* Messerwetzer (*m*).

Knight — Learned

Knight, *n.* Ritter (*m*).
Knit, *v.* Stricken, knüpfen.
Knitting, *n.* Strickzeug (*n*).
Knob, *n.* Knopf (*m*), Griff (*m*).
Knock, *v.* Knopfen, schlagen: *n.* Schlag (*m*).
Knocker (of door), *n.* Türklopfer (*m*).
Knot, *v.* Verknüpfen, verwirren: *n.* knoten (*m*).
Know, *v.* Wissen, erkennen, kennen, verstehen.
Knowledge, *n.* Wissen (*n*).
Knuckle, *n.* Knöchel (*m*).

L

Label, *n.* Zettel (*m*), Etikett (*n*).
Labour, *n.* Arbeit (*f*), Mühe (*f*): *v.* Arbeiten.
Labourer, *n.* Arbeiter (*m*).
Laburnum, *n.* Goldregen (*m*).
Lace, *n.* Spitze (*f*), Schnürsenkel (for shoes) (*m*): *v.* Zuschnüren.
Lack, *v.* Bedürfen.
Lad, *n.* Knabe (*m*), Junge (*m*), Bursche (*m*).
Ladder, *n.* Leiter (*f*).
Ladle, *n.* Schöpflöffel (*m*).
Lady, *n.* Dame (*f*).
Ladybird, *n.* Marienkäfer (*m*).
Ladylike, *adj.* Damenhaft.
Lag, *v.* Zaudern, zögern.
Lake, *n.* See (*m*), Lack (*m*).
Lamb, *n.* Lamm (*n*): *v.* Lammen.
Lame, *adj.* Lahm.
Lament, *v.* Jammern, klagen, wehklagen.
Lamentable, *adj.* Kläglich.
Lamp, *n.* Lampe (*f*).
Lance, *n.* Lanze (*f*); *v.* Aufstechen.
Land, *n.* Land (*n*): *v.* Landen.
Landing, *n.* Landung (*f*).
Landlady, *n.* Hauswirtin (*f*), Gutsbesitzerin (*f*).
Landlord, *n.* Hauswirt (*m*), Gutsbesitzer (*m*).
Landscape, *n.* Landschaft (*f*).
Lane, *n.* Gasse (*f*).
Language, *n.* Sprache (*f*).
Lap, *n.* Schloss (*m*), Runde (*f*), Vorstoss (*m*).
Lapse, *v.* Fallen, verfallen; *n.* Verlauf (*m*), Gleiten (*n*).
Larceny, *n.* Diebstahl (*m*).
Lard, *n.* Schweinefett (*n*).

Larder, *n.* Speisekammer (*f*).
Large, *adj.* Gross, breit, weit.
Lark, *n.* Lerche (bird) (*f*), Scherz (fun) (*m*).
Lash, *n.* Schmitze (*f*), Hieb (*m*): *v.* Peitschen.
Last, *adj.* Letzt, vorig; *v.* Währen, dauern; *n.* Leisten (*m*).
Late, *adj.* Spät, verspätet (dead).
Lately, *adv.* Kürzlich.
Lath, *n.* Latte (*f*).
Lather, *n.* Seifenschaum (*m*); *v.* Schäumen.
Latin, *n.* Latein (*n*); *adj.* Lateinisch.
Latitude, *n.* Breite (*f*), Breitengrad (*m*).
Latter, *adj.* Letztere.
Laudable, *adj.* Lobenswert.
Laugh, *v.* Lachen; *n.* Gelächter (*n*).
Launch, *n.* Pinasse (boat) (*f*).
Laundress, *n.* Wäscherin (*f*).
Laundry, *n.* Waschanstalt (*f*).
Laurel, *n.* Lorbeer (*m*).
Lavatory, *n.* Abort (*m*), Toilette (*f*).
Lavender, *n.* Lavendel (*m*).
Lavish, *adj.* Freigebig, verschwenderisch.
Law, *n.* Gesetz (*n*), Recht (*n*).
Law-court, *n.* Gerichtshof (*m*).
Lawful, *adj.* Rechtmässig.
Lawless, *adj.* Gesetzlos.
Lawn, *n.* Rosenplatz (*m*).
Lawn-tennis, *n.* Tennis (*n*).
Lawsuit, *n.* Prozess (*m*).
Lawyer, *n.* Anwalt (*m*), Advokat (*m*).
Lax, *adj.* Schlaff.
Laxative, *n.* Abführmittel (*n*).
Lay, *v.* Legen.
Laziness, *n.* Faulheit (*f*).
Lazy, *adj.* Faul, träge.
Lead, *v.* Verbleien, verleiten, führen; *n.* Blei (*n*).
Leaf, *n.* Blatt (*n*).
League, *n.* Bund (*m*).
Leak, *v.* Lecken; *n.* Leck (*n*).
Lean, *v.* Sich lehnen, sich verlassen, anlehnen: *adj.* Mager, nicht Meile (lean meat) (*f*).
Leap, *v.* Springen, hüpfen.
Leap-year, *n.* Schaltjahr (*n*).
Learn, *v.* Lernen.
Learned, *adj.* Erfahren.

Learner 134 **Limpid**

Learner, n. Lehrling (m).
Lease, n. Pacht (f): v. Verpachten.
Least, adj. Kleinste; adv. Am wenigsten.
Leather, n. Leder (n).
Leave, v. Lassen, verlassen, fortgehen: n. Urlaub.
Lecture, n. Lesen (n), Vortag (m): v. Vortragen.
Ledge, n. Leiste (f), Rand (m).
Ledger, n. Hauptbuch (n).
Leech, n. Blutegel (m).
Leek, n. Lauch (m).
Leer, v. Schielen.
Left, adj. Link, linkisch.
Leg, n. Bein (n).
Legacy, n. Vermächtnis (n).
Legal, adj. Gesetzmässig, gesetzlich.
Legation, n. Gesandtschaft (f).
Legible, adj. Leserlich.
Legion, n. Legion (f).
Legislate, v. Gesetze machen.
Legislation, n. Gesetzgebung (f).
Legitimate, adj. Legitim, gesetzmässig.
Leisure, n. Musse (f).
Lemon, n. Zitrone (f).
Lemonade, n. Limonade (f).
Lemon-squash, n. Lemon-squash (m), Zitronentrank (m).
Lend, v. Leihen.
Length, n. Länge (f), Dauer (f).
Lengthen, v. Verlängern.
Lengthy, adj. Weitschweifig.
Lenient, adj. Gelind.
Lens, n. Linse (f), Linsenglas (n).
Lent, s. Fastenzeit (calendar) (f).
Lentil, n. Linse (f).
Leopard, n. Leopard (m).
Leprosy, n. Aussatz (m).
Less, adv. Weniger, kleiner.
Lesson, n. Stunde (f), Aufgabe (f), Lektion (f).
Let, v. Lassen, vermieten (houses), gestatten (permit).
Letter, n. Brief (document) (m), Buchstabe (of the alphabet) (m).
Letter box, n. Briefkasten (m).
Lettuce, n. Salat (m), Lattich (m), Kopfsalat (m).
Level, n. Höhe (f); v. Ebnen: adj. Eben.

Lever, n. Hebel (m).
Levy, v. Heben, erbeben: n. Hebung (f), Erhebung (f), Aufgebot (military) (n).
Liability, n. Verbindlichkeit (f).
Liable, adj. Unterworfen.
Liar, n. Lügner (m), Lügnerin (f).
Libel, n. Verleumdung (f): v. Verleumden.
Liberal, adj. Freigebig.
Liberty, n. Freiheit (f).
Library, n. Bibliothek (f), Bücherei (f).
Licence, n. Lizenz (f), Freiheit (f), Führerschein (motor car) (m).
Lick, v. Lecken.
Lid, n. Deckel (m), Augenlid (eyelid) (n).
Lie, n. Lüge (falsehood) (f). Lage (lie down) (f): v. Lügen (falsehood), liegen (lie down).
Life, n. Leben (n).
Life-belt, n. Rettungsgürtel (m).
Life-boat, n. Rettungsboot (n).
Lifeless, adj. Leblos.
Lift, n. Heben (n), Aufzug (m), Fahrstuhl (m): v. Heben, aufheben.
Light, n. Licht (n), Tag (m): v. Leuchten, lichten, löschen: adj. Leicht.
Lightning, n. Blitz (m).
Like, v. Mögen, gern haben, gefallen: adj. Gleich, ähnlich.
Liking, n. Belieben (n), Gefallen (n), Vorliebe (f).
Lilac, n. Flieder (m): adj. Lila (the colour).
Lily, n. Lilie (f).
Lily of the Valley, n. Maiglöckchen (n).
Limb, n. Ast (m), Glied (n).
Lime, n. Kalk (m), Leim (m), Linde (tree) (f).
Lime-juice, n. Süsser Zitronensaft (m).
Limit, n. Grenze (f); v. Beschränken.
Limp, v. Hinken.
Limpet, n. Tellermuschel (f).
Limpid, adj. Klar.

Line — Love

Line, *n.* Linie (*f*), Geleise (railway line) (*n*), Angelschnur (fishing line) (*f*), Zeile (line of printing) (*f*): *v.* Linüeren, einfassen, füttern.

Lineament, *n.* Gesichtszug (*m*).

Linen, *n.* Leinwand (material) (*f*), Wäsche (washing) (*f*).

Linen-draper, *n.* Leinwandhändler (*m*).

Liner, *n.* Linienschiff (*n*), Passagierboot (*n*).

Linger, *v.* Zögern.

Liniment, *n.* Salbe (*f*).

Lining, *n.* Futter (*n*).

Link, *n.* Glied (*n*); *v.* Verketten.
Cuff Links, Manschettenknöpfe (*m*).
Golf Links, Golfspielplatz (*m*).

Linnet, *n.* Hänfling (*m*).

Linseed, *n.* Leinsamen (*n*).

Linseed-oil, *n.* Leinöl (*n*).

Lint, *n.* Scharpie (*f*).

Lion, *n.* Löwe (*m*).

Lioness, *n.* Löwin (*f*).

Lip, *n.* Lippe (*f*), Rand (*m*).

Lipstick, *n.* Lippenstift (*m*).

Liqueur, *n.* Likör (*m*).

Liquid, *n.* Flüssigkeit (*f*): *adj.* Flüssig.

Liquidation, *n.* Liquidation (*f*), abwicklung (*f*).

Lisp, *v.* Lispeln.

List, *n.* Liste (*f*), Schlagseite (of a ship) (*f*).

Listen, *v.* Horchen, zuhören, hören (wireless).

Listener, *n.* Zuhörer (usual) (*m*), Horcher (wireless) (*m*).

Literary, *adj.* Literarisch.

Literature, *n.* Literatur (*f*).

Lithe, *adj.* Biegsam.

Litigation, *n.* Rechtsstreit (*m*).

Litter, *n.* Unordnung (disorder) (*f*), Tragbahre (stretcher) (*f*), Wurf (of young) (*m*).

Little, *adj.* Klein (not big), kurz (time), wenig (not many), gering.

Live, *v.* Leben (not dead), wohnen (dwell).

Lively, *adj.* Lebhaft.

Liver, *n.* Leber (*f*).

Lizard, *n.* Eidechse (*f*).

Load, *n.* Ladung (*f*), Last (*f*): *v.* Laden.

Loaf, *n.* Brot (*n*), Laib (*m*).

Loam, *n.* Lehm (*m*).

Loan, *n.* Darlehen (*n*), Anleihe (*f*): *v.* Leihen.

Loathe, *v.* Verabscheuen.

Loathsome, *adj.* Ekelhaft.

Lobster, *n.* Hummer (*m*).

Local, *adj.* Örtlich, hiesig.

Lock, *v.* Zuschliessen; *n.* Schloss (*n*), Locke (of hair) (*f*), Schleuse (on river) (*f*).

Locomotive, *n.* Lokomotive (*f*).

Lodge, *n.* Häuschen (*n*), Loge (*f*), *v.* Einkehren, wohnen.

Lodgings, *n.* Wohnung (*f*).

Loft, *n.* Dachboden (*m*).

Log, *n.* Klotz (of wood) (*m*), Log (navigation) (*n*), Logbuch (logbook) (*n*).

Loin, *n.* Lenderbraten (*m*).

Loiter, *v.* Bummeln, trödeln.

Loll, *v.* Lehnen, heraustrecken, heraushangen.

Lonely, *adj.* Einsam.

Long, *adj.* Lang, lange.

Longevity, *n.* Langlebigkeit (*f*).

Look, *v.* Sehen: *n.* Blick (*m*), Aussehen (*n*).

Looking-glass, *n.* Spiegel (*m*).

Loom, *n.* Webstuhl (*m*).

Loop, *n.* Schlinge (*f*).

Loose, *adj.* Lose (not tight) liederlich (immoral).

Loosen, *v.* Lösen.

Loot, *n.* Beute (*f*).

Lop, *v.* Ausästen, zustutzen.

Lord, *n.* Lord (*m*), Gott (*m*), Herr (*m*).

Lorry, *n.* Lori (*f*), Lore (*f*), Lastauto (motor) (*n*).

Lose, *v.* Verlieren, vergeuden.
Lose one's way, irregehen.
Lose a train, versäumen.
Watch loses, nachgehen.

Loss, *n.* Verlust (*m*).

Lot, *n.* Los (*n*), Anteil (*m*), Menge (*f*), Steuer (*f*).

Lotion, *n.* Waschmittel (*n*), Abwaschung (*f*).

Lottery, *n.* Lotterie (*f*).

Loud, *adj.* Laut, grell, lärmend.

Loud speaker, *n.* Lautsprecher (*m*).

Lounge, *n.* Halle (*f*), Diele (*f*): *v.* Faulenzen.

Louse, *n.* Laus (*f*).

Lout, *n.* Lümmel (*m*).

Lovable, *adj.* Liebenswert.

Love, *v.* Lieben, mögen: *n.* Liebe (*f*), Gruss (*m*).

Lovely, *adj.* Liebenswürdig.
Lover, *n.* Liebhaber (*m*).
Low, *adj.* Niedrig, leise, tief: *v.* Muhen.
Lower, *adj.* Niedriger.
Loyal, *adj.* Treu.
Lozenge, *n.* Pastille (*f*), Raute (*f*).
Lubricant, *n.* Schmierstoff (*m*).
Lubricate, *v.* Schmieren.
Lucid, *adj.* Klar, licht, durchsichtig.
Luck, *n.* Glück (*n*), Zufall (*m*).
Lucky, *adj.* Glücklich.
Lucrative, *adj.* Einträglich.
Ludicrous, *adj.* Lächerlich.
Luggage, *n.* Gepäck (*n*).
Lull, *v.* Einlullen.
Lumbago, *n.* Hexenschuss (*m*).
Lumber, *n.* Gerümpel (rubbish) (*n*), Bauholz (timber) (*n*).
Luminous, *adj.* Leuchtend.
Lump, *n.* Klumpen (*m*), Masse (*f*).
Lumpy, *adj.* Klumpig.
Lunatic, *n.* Mondsüchtig.
Lunatic asylum, *n.* Irrenhaus (*n*).
Lunch, *n.* Mittagessen (*n*), Zwischenessen (*n*).
Lung, *n.* Lunge (*f*).
Lupin, *n.* Lupine (*f*).
Lure, *v.* Locken: *n.* Lockspeise (*f*).
Lurk, *v.* Lauern, lauschen.
Luscious, *adj.* Ekelhaft.
Lust, *n.* Lust (*f*), Trieb (*m*), Wollust (*f*).
Lustful, *adj.* Wollüstig
Lustre, *n.* Glanz (*m*).
Lusty, *adj.* Munter, rüstig.
Luxuriant, *adj.* Uppig, reichlich.
Luxury, *n.* Uppigkeit (*f*).

M

Macaroni, *n.* Makkaroni (*f*).
Machine, *n.* Maschine (*f*).
Machinery, *n.* Maschinerie (*f*).
Mackerel, *n.* Makrele (*f*).
Mackintosh, *n.* Gummimantel (*m*), Regenmantel (*m*).
Mad, *adj.* Toll, verrückt, wahnsinnig.
Madam, *n.* Gnädige Frau (*f*).
Madhouse, *n.* Tollhaus (*n*).
Madman, *n.* Toll (*m*), Wahnsinnige (*m*).
Magazine, *n.* Magazin (*n*), Zeitschrift (publication) (*f*).
Maggot, *n.* Made (*f*).
Magic, *n.* Zauberkunst (*f*).
Magician, *n.* Zauberer (*m*).
Magistrate, *n.* Polizeirichter (*m*), Friedensrichter (*m*).
Magnanimous, *adj.* Grossmütig.
Magnet, *n.* Magnet (*m*).
Magneto, *n.* Magnetapparat (*m*).
Magnificent, *adj.* Prachtvoll.
Magnifier, *n.* Lobredner (*m*).
Magnify, *v.* Vergrössern.
Magpie, *n.* Elster (*f*).
Mahogany, *n.* Mahagoni (*n*).
Maid, *n.* Mädchen (*n*), Jungfer (*f*).
Maiden, *n.* Magd (*f*), Jungfer (*f*), Jungfrau (*f*).
Mail, *n.* Panzer (armour) (*m*), Briefpost (postal) (*f*).
Mail-boat, *n.* Postschiff (*n*).
Mail-train, *n.* Postzug (*m*).
Maim, *v.* Lähmen.
Main, *adj.* Hauptsächlich.
Mainland, *n.* Festland (*n*).
Main-line, *n.* Haupteisenbahnlinie (*f*).
Maintain, *v.* Behaupten, erhalten.
Maintenance, *n.* Unterhalt (*m*).
Maize, *n.* Mais (*m*).
Majestic, *adj.* Majestätisch.
Majesty, *n.* Majestät (*f*).
Major, *n.* Major (*m*), Obersatz (*m*): *adj.* Grösser.
Majority, *n.* Mehrheit (*f*).
Make, *v.* Machen, herstellen: *n.* Gestalt (*f*), Fabrikat (*n*).
Maker, *n.* Fabrikant (*m*).
Malady, *n.* Krankheit (*f*).
Male, *n.* Mann (*m*), Männchen (*n*): *adj.* Männlich.
Malevolence, *n.* Bosheit (*f*).
Malevolent, *adj.* Böswillig.
Malice, *n.* Bosheit (*f*), Groll (*m*), Hass (*m*).
Malicious, *adj.* Boshaft.
Malign, *v.* Verlästern.
Mallet, *n.* Holzhammer (*m*).
Maliow, *n.* Malve (*f*).
Malt, *n.* Malz (*n*).
Maltreat, *v.* Misshandeln.
Mammal, *n.* Säugetier (*n*).
Mammoth, *n.* Mammut.

Man   137   **Maze**

Man, *n.* Mann (individual) (*m*), Mensch (as a group) (*m*): *v.* Bemannen.
Manacle, *n.* Handschelle (*f*).
Manage, *v.* Verwalten, leiten, fertig.
Manager, *n.* Leiter (*m*), Direktor (*m*), Verwalter (*m*).
Mandolin, *n.* Mandoline (*f*).
Mane, *n.* Mähne (*f*).
Manger, *n.* Krippe (*f*).
Mangle, *v.* Mangeln: *n.* Mangel (*f*).
Manhood, *n.* Mannheit (*f*).
Mania, *n.* Sucht (*f*).
Maniac, *n.* Wahnsinnige (*m*).
Manipulate, *v.* Handhaben.
Manly, *adj.* Männlich.
Manner, *n.* Lebensart (*f*), Art (*f*).
Manor, *n.* Rittergut (*n*).
Manslaughter, *n.* Totschlag (*m*).
Mantelpiece, *n.* Kaminsims (*m*).
Manual, *n.* Handbuch (*n*): *adj.* Eigenhändig.
Manufactory, *n.* Fabrik (*f*).
Manufacturer, *n.* Fabrikant (*m*).
Manure, *n.* Dünger (*m*).
Manuscript, *n.* Handschrift (*f*).
Many, *adj.* Viele.
   As many as, soviele als.
Map, *n.* Landkarte (*f*), Plan (*m*).
Maple, *n.* Ahorn (*m*).
Marble, *n.* Marmor (*m*).
March, *n.* März (*m*).
March, *n.* Marsh (*m*): *v.* Marschieren.
Mare, *n.* Stute (*f*).
Margarine, *n.* Margarine (*f*).
Margin, *n.* Rand (*m*).
Marigold, *n.* Ringelblume (*f*), Dotterblume (*f*).
Marine, *adj.* See . . . : *n.* Seesoldat (*m*).
Mariner, *n.* Seemann (*m*).
Mark, *v.* Zeichnen, markieren: *n.* Marke (*f*).
Market, *n.* Markt (*m*).
Marmalade, *n.* Apfelsinenmarmelade (*f*).
Marquee, *n.* Zeltdach (*n*).
Marriage, *n.* Heirat (*f*), Hochzeit (*f*).
Married, *adj.* Ehelich.

Marrow, *n.* Kürbis (vegetable m.) (*m*), Mark (pith, etc.) (*n*).
Marry, *v.* Heiraten, trauen.
Marsh, *n.* Marsch (*f*).
Martyr, *n.* Märtyrer (*m*).
Marvel, *n.* Wunder (*n*): *v.* Staunen.
Marvellous, *adj.* Wunderbar.
Mascot, *n.* Maskott (*m*).
Masculine, *adj.* Männlich; *n.* Maskulinum (grammar) (*n*).
Mask, *n.* Maske (*f*).
Masonic, *adj.* Freimaurerisch.
Masquerade, *v.* Sich verkleiden; *n.* Maskenball (*m*).
Mass, *n.* Menge (*f*), Messe (*f*), Masse (*f*).
Massacre, *n.* Metzelei (*f*), Gemetzel (*n*).
Massage, *n.* Massage (*f*); *v.* Massieren.
Massive, *adj.* Fest, massiv, dicht.
Mast, *n.* Mast (*m*).
Master, *n.* Meister (*m*), Herr (*m*), Lehrer (at school) (*m*): *v.* Meistern, beherrschen.
Masterful, *adj.* Herrisch.
Masticate, *v.* Kauen.
Mastiff, *n.* Bullenbeisser (*m*).
Match, *n.* Streichholz (lighter) (*n*), Wettspiel (sport) (*n*): *v.* Zusammenpassen.
Matchless, *adj.* Unvergleichlich.
Mate, *n.* Genosse (*m*), Gehilfe (*m*): *v.* Paaren.
Material, *n.* Material (*n*), Stoff (*m*).
Maternal, *adj.* Mütterlich.
Mathematics, *n.* Mathematik (*f*).
Matrimony, *n.* Ehe (*f*), Ehestand (*m*).
Matron, *n.* Matrone (motherly) (*f*), Vorsteherin (of hospital) (*f*).
Matter, *n.* Stoff (*m*), Eiter (*m*), Sache (*f*), Eiter (medical) (*m*).
Mature, *adj.* Reif, fallig.
Maul, *v.* Stampfen, schlagen, verletzen.
Mauve, *n.* Malvenfarbe (*f*): *adj.* Hellviolett.
Maxim, *n.* Grundsatz (*m*).
May, *n.* Mai (the month) (*m*): *v.* Dürfen, konnen.
Major, *n.* Bürgermeister (*m*).
Maze, *n.* Irrang (*m*).

Me, *pron.* Mich, mir.
Meadow, *n.* Wiese (*f*).
Meagre, *adj.* Mager.
Meal, *n.* Mahlzeit (*f*), Mehl (*n*).
Mean, *adj.* Gemein, geizig, niedrig: *n.* Mittel (*n*), Mitte (*f*), Vermögen (*n*): *v.* Meinen, bedeuten.
Meaning, *n.* Absicht (*f*), Meinung (*f*).
Meanness, *n.* Gemeinheit (*f*), Niedrigkeit (*f*).
Meantime, *adv.* Mittlerweile, indessen.
Measles, *n.* Masern (*f*), Röteln (German measles) (*pl.*).
Measure, *n.* Mass (*m*), Massstab (*m*): *v.* Messen.
Meat, *n.* Speise (*f*), Fleisch (*n*).
Mechanic, *n.* Handwerker (*m*).
Mechanical, *adj.* Mechanisch.
Medal, *n.* Denkmünze (*f*).
Meddle, *v.* Sich mischen.
Mediation, *n.* Vermittelung (*f*).
Medical, *adj.* Medicinisch.
Medicine, *n.* Arznei (*f*).
Medium, *n.* Mitte (*f*), Mittel (*n*).
Meek, *adj.* Sanftmut.
Meeting, *n.* Begegnen (*n*).
Melancholy, *adj.* Schwermüthig: *n.* Schwermuth (*f*).
Mellow, *adj.* Lieblich, reif, mürbe.
Melodious, *adj.* Melodisch.
Melody, *n.* Melodie (*f*), Singweise (*f*), Tonart (*f*).
Melon, *n.* Melone (*f*).
Melt, *v.* Auflösen, schmelzen, zerfliessen.
Member, *n.* Mitglied (*n*).
Memento, *n.* Erinnerung (*f*).
Memoir, *n.* Aufsatz (*m*), Denkschrift (*f*).
Memorial, *n.* Denkmal (*n*).
Memory, *n.* Andenken (*n*), Gedächtniss (*n*).
Men, *n.* Leute (*pl.*).
Menace, *v.* Drohen.
Mend, *v.* Verbessern, ausbessern, sich bessern.
Menial, *adj.* Gemein, häuslich; *n.* Diener (*m*).
Mental, *adj.* Geistig.
Mention, *v.* Erwähnen: *n.* Erwähnung (*f*).
Mercenary, *n.* Miethling (*m*): *adj.* Feil.

Merchandise, *n.* Handel (*m*), Waare (*f*).
Merchant, *n.* Kaufmann (*m*).
Merciful, *adj.* Barmherzig.
Merciless, *adj.* Unbarmherzig.
Mercury, *n.* Mercur (*m*).
Mercy *n.* Barmherzigkeit (*f*).
Mere, *adj.* Allein, bloss, lauter.
Merely, *adv.* Bloss, nur.
Merge, *v.* Eintauchen.
Merit, *n.* Verdienst (*n*): *v.* Verdienen.
Meritorious, *adj.* Verdienstlich.
Mermaid, *n.* Wassernixe (*f*), Seejungfer (*f*).
Merriment, *n.* Fröhlichkeit (*f*).
Merry, *adj.* Fröhlich lustig.
Mesh, *n.* Netz (*n*), Masche (*f*).
Mess, *n.* Schmutzerei (disorder) (*f*), Manscherei (badly done) (*f*), Back (navig.) (*f*), Offiziersksino (officers' mess) (*f*), Offizierstich (*m*), Gericht (*n*).
Message, *n.* Auftrag (*m*), Botschaft (*f*).
Messenger, *n.* Bote (*m*).
Metal, *n.* Metall (*n*).
Metalic, *adj.* Metallisch.
Method, *n.* Methode (*f*), Ordnung (*f*), Verfahren (*n*).
Methodical, *adj.* Methodisch.
Metropolis, *n.* Metropole (*f*), Hauptstadt (*f*).
Mew, *v.* Miauen.
Mica, *n.* Glimmer (*m*).
Microscope, *n.* Mikroscop (*n*).
Mid, *adj.* Mittel.
Midday, *n.* Mittag (*m*).
Middle, *adj.* Mittel; *n.* Mitte (*f*).
Midnight, *n.* Mitternacht (*f*).
Midsummer, *n.* Sommersonnenwende (*f*).
Midwife, *n.* Hebamme (*f*).
Midwinter, *n.* Wintersonnenwende (*f*).
Might, *n.* Gewalt (*f*), Macht (*f*).
Mighty, *adj.* Mächtig, sehr.
Mignonette, *n.* Reseda (*f*).
Migrate, *v.* Wandern.
Mild, *adj.* Mild, leicht, sanft.
Mildew, *n.* Meltau (*m*), Schimmel (*m*).
Mile, *n.* Meile (*f*).
Military, *adj.* Militärisch.
Milk, *n.* Milch (*f*); *v.* Melken.
Milkmaid, *n.* Milchmädchen (*n*).

Mill, Molecule

Mill, *v.* Mahlen: *n.* Mühle (*f*), Fabrik (*f*).
Miller, *n.* Müller (*m*).
Milliner, *n.* Modistin (*f*), Putzmacherin (*f*).
Millinery, *n.* Modewaren (*f*), Putzwaren (*f*).
Million, *n.* Million (*f*).
Mimic, *v.* Nachäffen, nachahmen: *adj.* mimisch.
Mimicry, *n.* Nachahmung (*f*).
Mince, *v.* Zerhacken, kleinhacken.
Mind, *n.* Geist (*m*), Sinn (*m*), Gemüt (*n*): *v.* Merken, achten, erinnern.
Mine, *n.* Grube (coal, etc.) (*f*), Mine (to explode) (*f*), Bergwerk (*n*).
Miner, *n.* Bergmann (*m*).
Mineral, *n.* Mineral (*n*).
Mineral-water, *n.* Sauerbrunnen (*m*).
Mine-sweeper, *n.* Minensucher (*m*).
Mingle, *v.* Mischen.
Miniature, *n.* Miniatur (*f*).
Minister, *n.* Minister (govt.) (*m*), Geistlicher (church) (*m*).
Mink, *n.* Nerz (*m*).
Minnow, *n.* Elritze (*f*).
Minority, *n.* Minderheit (*f*).
Minstrel, *n.* Spielmann (*m*).
Mint, *n.* Münze (coin) (*f*), Minzkraut (herb) (*n*).
Mintsauce, *n.* Minzsosse (*f*).
Minute, *adj.* Klein (small); *n.* Minute (*f*).
Miracle, *n.* Wunder (*n*).
Mirror, *n.* Spiegel (*m*).
Mirth, *n.* Freude (*f*), Fröhlichkeit (*f*), Lust (*f*).
Misadventure, *n.* Missgeschick (*n*).
Misapply, *v.* Falsche anwenden.
Misapprehension, *n.* Missverstandnis (*n*).
Misbehave, *v.* Sich schlecht aufführen.
Miscarriage, *n.* Fehlspruch (of justice) (*m*), Fehlgeburt (of birth) (*f*).
Miscellaneous, *adj.* Gemischt, vermischt.
Mischief, *n.* Unfug (*m*), Nachteil (*m*).
Misconduct, *n.* Fehltritt (*m*), Ehebruch (*m*).
Miscreant, *n.* Bösewicht (*m*), Schurke (*m*).
Misdeed, *n.* Missetat (*f*).
Miser, *n.* Geizhals (*m*).
Miserable, *adj.* Elend, geizig.
Misery, *n.* Elend (*n*).
Misfortune, *n.* Unglück (*n*).
Misgiving, *n.* Zweifel (*m*).
Mishap, *n.* Unfall (*m*).
Mislead, *v.* Verleiten.
Miss, *n.* Fräulein (*n*); *v.* Missen, vermissen.
Mission, *n.* Sendung (*f*).
Mist, *n.* Nebel (*m*).
Mistake, *v.* Verkennen, verwechsein: *n.* Irrtum (*m*), Fehler (*m*).
Mister (Mr.), *n.* Herr (*m*).
Mistletoe, *n.* Mistel (*f*).
Mistress, *n.* Herrin (of home) (*f*), Lehrein (of school) (*f*).
Mistrust, *v.* Misstrauen: *n.* Misstrauen (*n*).
Misty, *adj.* Nebelig, dunkel.
Misunderstand, *v.* Missverstehen.
Misuse, *n.* Missbrauch (*m*): *v.* Missbrauchen.
Mite, *n.* Milbe (*f*), Heller (*m*), Kleinigkeit (*f*).
Mitigate, *v.* Mildern, lindern.
Mix, *v.* Mischen, vermischen.
Mixture, *n.* Mischung (*f*).
Moan, *v.* Stöhen, wehklagen: *n.* Wehklage (*f*).
Moat, *n.* Wassergraben (*m*), Wallgraben (*m*).
Mob, *n.* Pöbel (*m*), Gesindel (*n*): *v.* Misshandeln.
Mobilize, *v.* Mobilisiren.
Mock, *v.* Verspotten; *n.* Spott (*m*): *adj.* Nachgemacht.
Mode, *n.* Mode (*f*), Sitte (*f*), Weise (*f*), Tonart (music) (*f*).
Model, *n.* Modell (*n*), Vorbild (*n*): *v.* Modellieren.
Moderate, *adj.* Mässig, mittelmässig: *v.* Mässigen.
Moderation, *n.* Mässigung (*f*).
Modern, *adj.* Modern, heutig.
Modest, *adj.* Bescheiden.
Modesty, *n.* Bescheidenheit (*f*).
Modify, *v.* Abändern, modifizieren.
Moist, *adj.* Feucht.
Moisten, *v.* Befeuchten.
Moisture, *n.* Feuchtigkeit (*f*).
Mole, *n.* Maulwurf (*m*).
Molecule, *n.* Molekül (*n*).

Molest, v. Belästigen, beschweren.
Molten, adj. Geschmolzen, gegossen.
Moment, n. Gewicht (n), Moment (m)
Monarch, n. Monarch (m).
Monarchy, n. Monarchie (f).
Monday, n. Montag (m).
Money, n. Geld (n).
Money changer, n. Geldwechsler (m).
Money lender, n. Geldverleiher (m).
Mongrel, n. Mischling (m): adj. Bastard . . . .
Monitor, n. Ermahner (m).
Monk, n. Mönch (m).
Monkey, n. Affe (m).
Monoplane, n. Eindecker (m).
Monopolize, v. Alleinhandel treiben, monopolisieren.
Monopoly, n. Monopol (n).
Monotonous, adj. Eintönig.
Monster, n. Ungeheuer (n).
Monstrous, adj. Ungeheuer, monströs.
Month, n. Monat (m).
Monthly, adj. Monatlich.
Monument, n. Denkmal (n).
Mood, n. Laune (f), Stimmung (f).
Moody, adj. Mürrisch.
Moon, n. Mond (m).
Moonlight, n. Mondschein (m).
Moor, n. Mohr (m), Ödland (n).
Mop, v. Abwischen, aufwischen: n. Wisch (m).
Moral, n. Moral (f): adj Sittlich, gut.
Morbid, adj. Krankhaft.
More, adv. Mehr.
Once more, noch einmal.
So much the more, umsomehr.
Moreover, adv. Uberdies.
Morning, n. Morgen (m).
Morrow, n. Morgende Tag (m), Morgen (m).
Morsel, n. Stückchen (n).
Mortal, adj. Sterblich: n. Sterbliche (m).
Mortar, n. Mörtel (m).
Mortuary, n. Leichenhaus (n).
Mosquito, n. Moskito (m).
Most, adj. Meist.
Mostly, adv. Meistens.
Moth, n. Motte (f).
Mother, n. Mutter (f).

Motherhood, n. Mutterschaft (f).
Mother-in-law, n. Schwiegermutter (f).
Motion, n. Bewegung (f).
Motor, n. Motor (m).
  Motor bus, Autobus (m).
  Motor car, Auto (n).
  Motor-cycle, Motorrad (n).
Mottled, adj. Gesprenkelt.
Mould, n. Form (shape) (f), Gartenerde (soil) (f), Schimmel (mildew) (m).
Moult, v. Mausern.
Mount, v. Besteigen, montieren: n. Berg (m), Hügel (m).
Mountain, n. Berg (m).
Mountain-ash, n. Eberesche (f).
Mourn, v. Trauern, klagen.
Mouse, n. Maus (f).
Mousetrap, n. Mausefalle (f).
Moustache, n. Schnurrbart (m).
Mouth, n. Mund (person's) (m), Maul (animal's) (n), Mündung (river) (f).
Move, v. Bewegen, anregen, rücken.
Movement, n. Bewegung (f).
Mow, v. Mähen.
Mower, n. Mäher (m).
Much, adv. Viel.
Mud, n. Dreck (m).
Muddy, adj. Dreckig.
Muddle, n. Wirrwarr (m), Verwirrung (f).
Mudguard, n. Kotflügel (m).
Muffler, n. Halstuch (n), Dämpfer (m).
Mug, n. Becher (m).
Mulberry, n. Maulbeere (f).
Mule, n. Maultier (n).
Multiplication, n. Multiplikation (f).
Multiply, v. Multiplizieren.
Multitude, n. Vielheit (f).
Mumble, v. Murmeln.
Mumps, n. Mumps (m), Ziegenpeter (m).
Munch, v. Kauen.
Murder, n. Mord (m): v. Ermorden.
Murderer, n. Mörder (m).
Murmur, n. Gemurmel (n): v. Murmeln.
Muscle, n. Muskel (m).
Muscular, adj. Muskelhaft.
Museum, n. Museum (n).

Mushroom   141   **Never**

Mushroom, *n.* Pilz (*m*).
Music, *n.* Musik (*f*).
Musician, *n.* Musiker (*m*).
Musk, *n.* Bisam (*m*), Moschus (*m*).
Muslin, *n.* Musselin (*m*).
Mussel, *n.* Muschel (*f*).
Must, *v.* Muss, müssen.
Mustard, *n.* Senf (*m*).
Musty, *adj.* Muffig.
Mute, *adj.* Stumm.
Mutilate, *v.* Verstümmeln.
Mutineer, *n.* Meuterer (*m*).
Mutiny, *n.* Meuterei (*f*).
Mutter, *v.* Murren, murmeln.
Mutton, *n.* Hammelfleisch (*n*).
Mutual, *adj.* Gegenseitig.
Muzzle, *n.* Maulkorb (dog's) (*m*), Mündung (rifle's) (*f*).
My, *adj. pron.* Mein, meine.
Myrtle, *n.* Myrte (*f*).
Myself, *pron.* Ich selbst, mich (*accus.*), mir (*dat.*).
Mysterious, *adj.* Mysteriös.
Mystery, *n.* Mysterie (*f*), Geheimnis (*n*).
Mystification, *n.* Fopperei (*f*).
Mystify, *v.* Foppen, mystifizieren.
Myth, *n.* Mythe (*f*).
Mythology, *n.* Mythologie (*f*).

N

Nail, *n.* Nagel (*m*), Klaue (*f*): *v.* Nageln.
Naked, *adj.* Nackt, bloss.
Name, *n.* Name (*n*), Ruf (*m*): *v.* Nennen.
  Christian name, Vorname (*m*).
  Surname, Zuname (*m*).
Namely, *adv.* Nämlich.
Namesake, *n.* Namensvetter (*m*).
Nap, *n.* Schläfchen (sleep) (*n*), Noppe (surface of cloth) (*f*).
Napkin, *n.* Serviette (*f*).
Narcissus, *n.* Narzisse (*f*).
Narrative, *n.* Erzählung (*f*).
Narrow, *adj.* Eng, schmal, engherzig.
Narrow-minded, *adj.* Engherzig.
Nasal, *adj.* Nasal.
Nasty, *adj.* Garstig, schmutzig, ungünstig.
Nation, *n.* Nation (*f*), Volk (*n*).
National, *adj.* National.

Native, *adj.* Natürlich: *n.* Eingeborne (*m. & f.*).
  Native country, Heimat (*f*).
Natural, *adj.* Natürlich.
Nature, *n.* Natur (*f*).
Naught, *n.* Nichts (*n*), Null (*f*).
Naughty, *adj.* Unartig.
Nausea, *n.* Ekel (*m*).
Nautical, *adj.* Nautisch.
Nave, *n.* Schiff (archit.) (*n*).
Navigate, *v.* Segeln, beschiffen.
Navigation, *n.* Schifffahrt (*f*).
Navy, *n.* Marine (*f*), Flotte (*f*).
Nay, *adv.* Nein, sogar.
Near, *adj.* Nahe, verwandt; *adv.* Ungefähr; *pron.* Nahe, neben; *v.* Sich nahen.
Nearly, *adv.* Beinahe, nahe.
Neat, *adj.* Zierlich, nett, ordentlich, zierlich.
Necessary, *adj.* Nöthig, nötig.
Necessity, *n.* Nothwendigkeit (*f*).
Neck, *n.* Nacken (*m*), Hals (*m*).
Neck-tie, *n.* Halsbinde (*f*).
Need, *n.* Bedarf (*m*): *v.* Brauchen, nöthig haben.
Needful, *adj.* Nötig, bedürftig.
Needle, *n.* Nadel (*f*).
Needless, *adj.* Unnötig.
Needy, *adj.* Dürftig.
Negative, *n.* Negativ (photo) (*n*).
Neglect, *v.* Vernachlässigen: *n.* Vernachlässigung (*f*).
Neglectful, *adj.* Nachlässig.
Negotiate, *v.* Handeln.
Negotiation, *n.* Handel (*m*).
Negress, *n.* Negerin (*f*).
Negro, *n.* Neger (*m*).
Neigh, *v.* Wiehern.
Neighbour, *n.* Nachbar (*m*).
Neighbourhood, *n.* Nachbarschaft (*f*).
Neither, *conj.* Weder.
Nephew, *n.* Neffe (*m*).
Nervous, *adj.* Nervig.
Nest, *n.* Nest (*n*).
Net, *n.* Netz (*n*): *v.* Fangen: *adj.* netto.
Nettle, *n.* Nessel (*f*).
Neuralgia, *n.* Nervenschmerz (*m*).
Neuter, *adj.* Sächlich (gramm.) unparteüsch.
Neutral, *adj.* Neutral, unparteüsch.
Never, *adv.* Nie, niemals.

Nevertheless — Nurse

Nevertheless, *adv.* Nichtsdestoweniger.
New, *adj.* Neu, frisch.
News, *n.* Nachricht (*f*).
Newspaper, *n.* Zeitung (*f*).
Newt, *n.* Sumpfeidechse (*f*).
New Year, *n.* Neujahr (*n*)
New Year's day, *n.* Neujahrstag (*m*).
New Year's eve, *n.* Neujahrsabend (*m*).
Next, *adj.* Nächst.
Nib, *n.* Spitze (*f*), Schnabel (*m*), Stahlfeder (*f*).
Nibble, *v.* Benagen.
Nice, *adj.* Fein, gut, hübsch, nett.
Nickel, *n.* Nickel (*n*).
Nickname, *n.* Spitzname (*m*).
Niece, *n.* Nichte (*f*).
Night, *n.* Nacht (*f*).
Nightdress, *n.* Nachtgewand (*n*).
Nightingale, *n.* Nachtigall (*f*).
Nightly, *adv.* Nächtlich.
Nightmare, *n.* Alpdrücken (*n*).
Nimble, *adj.* Flink, hurtig, gewandt.
Nine, *adj.* Neun.
Nineteen, *adj.* Neunzehn.
Nineteenth, *ad.* Neunzehnte.
Ninety, *adj.* Neunzig.
Ninth, *adj.* Neunte.
Nip, *v.* Kneifen, schneiden, zwicken.
Nipple, *n.* Brustwarze (*f*).
Nitric acid, *n.* Salpetersäure (*f*).
Nitrogen, *n.* Stickstoff (*m*).
No, *adv.* Nicht, nein.
Noble, *adj.* Adelig, edel.
Nobleman, *n.* Edelmann (*m*).
Nobody, *n.* Null (*f*).
Nod, *n.* Nicken (*n*): *v.* Nicken.
Noise, *n.* Lärm (*m*).
Noiseless, *adj.* Geräuschlos.
Noisy, *adj.* Geräuschvoll.
Nominate, *v.* Ernennen.
None, *adj.* Kein, keiner, keine, keines.
Nonsense, *n.* Unsinn (*m*).
Nook, *n.* Winkel (*m*).
Noon, *n.* Mittag (*m*).
Noose, *n.* Schlinge (*f*).
Nor, *conj.* Noch, weder.
North, *n.* Nord (*m*): *adj.* Nördlich.
Nose, *n.* Nase (*f*).

Nostril, *n.* Nasenloch (person) (*n*), Nüster (animal) (*f*).
Not, *adv.* Nicht.
Notable, *adj.* Merkwürdig.
Notch, *n.* Kerbe (*f*): *v.* Kerben.
Note, *n.* Note (*f*), Briefchen (passage of words) (*n*), Melodie (music) (*f*): *v.* Notieren, bemerken.
Noted, *adj.* Bekannt.
Nothing, *adv.* Nichts: *n.* Nichts (*n*).
Notice, *n.* Warnung (*f*), Notiz (*f*): *v.* Bemerken.
Notify, *v.* Bekannt machen, anzeigen.
Notoriety, *n.* Notorietät (*f*), Kundbarkeit (*f*).
Notorious, *adj.* Notorisch.
Notwithstanding, *conj.* Ungeachtet, obgleich.
Nought, *n.* Null (cypher) (*f*).
Noun, *n.* Nennwort (*n*), Hauptwort (*n*).
Nourish, *v.* Nähren.
Nourishment, *n.* Nahrung (*f*).
Novel, *n.* Roman (*m*), Novelle (*f*): *adj.* Neu.
Novelist, *n.* Romanschreiber (*f*), Novellenschreiber (*m*).
Novelty, *n.* Neuheit (*f*).
November, *n.* November (*m*).
Novice, *n.* Neuling (*m*), Novize (*m. & f.*).
Now, *adv.* Nun, jetzt.
Now-a-days, heutzutage.
Now and then, zuweilen.
Nowhere, *adv.* Nirgends.
Noxious, *adj.* Schädlich.
Nude, *adj.* Bloss, nackt.
Nudity, *n.* Nacktheit (*f*).
Nugget, *n.* Klumpen (*m*), Goldklumpen (*m*).
Nuisance, *n.* Plage (*f*), Verdruss (*m*).
Null, *adj.* Nichtig.
Nullify, *v.* Nichtigkeit (*f*).
Numb, *v.* Betäuben; *adj.* Starr, erstarrt.
Number, *n.* Zahl (*f*), Menge (*f*), Nummer (*f*): *v.* Zählen, numerieren.
Numerous, *adj.* Zahlreich.
Nun, *n.* Nonne (*f*).
Nunnery, *n.* Nonnenkloster (*n*).
Nurse, *n.* Krankenpflegerin (woman) (*f*), Krankenwärter (men) (*m*): *v.* Pflegen.

Nursery

Nursery, *n.* Kinderstube (for children) (*f*), Gärtnerei (for plants) (*f*).
Nurseryman, *n.* Kunstgärtner (*m*).
Nursery-rhyme, *n.* Kinderlied (*n*).
Nut, *n.* Nuss (fruit) (*f*), Schraubenmutter (metal) (*f*).
Nutcracker, *n.* Nussknacker (*m*).
Nutmeg, *n.* Muskatnuss (*f*).
Nutriment, *n.* Nahrung (*f*), Futter (*n*).
Nutritious, *adj.* Nährend.
Nutshell, *n.* Nussschale (*f*).

O

O, *interj.* O, oh, ach.
Oak, *n.* Eiche (*f*).
Oar, *n.* Erz (*n*), Ruder (*n*), Riemen (*m*).
Oath, *n.* Eid (*m*), Schwur (*m*).
Oatmeal, *n.* Hafermehl (*n*).
Oats, *n.* Hafer (*m*).
Obedience, *n.* Gehorsam (*m*).
Obedient, *adj.* Gehorsam.
Obey, *v.* Gehorchen.
Object, *n.* Zweck (*m*), Gegenstand (*m*): *v.* Vorhalten.
Objection, *n.* Einwand (*m*).
Objectionable, *adj.* Verwerflich, anstössig.
Objector, *n.* Gegner (*m*).
Oblige, *v.* Verpflichten, verbinden.
Obliging, *adj.* Verbindlich.
Obliterate, *v.* Auslöschen.
Oblong, *adj.* Länglich: *n.* Rechteck (*n*).
Obscene, *adj.* Schmutzig, unanständig.
Obscure, *adj.* Dunkel.
Observant, *adj.* Achtsam, aufmerksam.
Observation, *n.* Beobachtung (*f*).
Observe, *v.* Beobachten.
Obsolete, *adj.* Veraltet.
Obstacle, *n.* Hinderniss (*n*).
Obstinate, *adj.* Hartnäckig, halsstarrig.
Obstruct, *v.* Hindern, sperren, verstopfen.
Obstruction, *n.* Hinderniss (*n*), Verstopfung (*f*).
Obtain, *v.* Erlangen.
Obtainable, *adj.* Erlangbar.

On

Obtuse, *adj.* Dumm, stumpf.
Obviate, *v.* Begegnen.
Obvious, *adj.* Deutlich, augenscheinlich.
Occasion, *n.* Bedürfniss (*n*), Gelegenheit (*f*).
Occasionally, *adv.* Zuweilen.
Occupant, *n.* Inhaber (*m*).
Occupier, *n.* Inhaber (*m*), Bewohner (*m*).
Occupy, *v.* Besitzen, einnehmen, innehaben.
Occur, *v.* Verkommen, einfallen.
Occurrence, *n.* Verkommen (*n*), Vorfall (*m*).
Ocean, *n.* Weltmeer (*n*), Ozean (*m*).
Octagon, *n.* Achteck (*n*).
October, *n.* Oktober (*m*).
Oculist, *n.* Augenarzt (*m*).
Odd, *adj.* Einzeln (peculiar), ungerade (numbers).
Odds, *n.* Vorgabe (betting) *f*.
Odious, *adj.* Verhasst, gehässig.
Odour, *n.* Geruch (*m*), Wohlgeruch (*m*).
Of, *prep.* Von.
Off, *prep.* Ab.
Offal, *n.* Abfall (*m*).
Offence, *n.* Beleidigung (*f*).
Offend, *v.* Beleidigen, erzürnen.
Offender, *n.* Beleidiger (*m*).
Offensive, *adj.* Beleidigend.
Offer, *n.* Gebot (*n*), Versuch (*m*), Antrag (*m*): *v.* Anbieten, darbringen.
Office, *n.* Amt (*n*), Dienst (*m*), Bureau (*n*), Gebet (*n*).
Officer, *n.* Offizier (army) (*m*), Beamte (*m*).
Oft, Often, *adv.* Oft, öfters.
Oil, *n.* Öl (*n*): *v.* Einölen, ölen.
Oil-cloth, *n.* Wachstuch (*n*).
Oil-painting, *n.* Ölgemälde (*n*).
Oily, *adj.* Ölig, schmierig.
Ointment, *n.* Salbe (*f*).
Old, *adj.* Alt.
Old-fashioned, *adj.* Altmodisch.
Olive oil, *n.* Olivenöl (*n*).
Omelet, *n.* Omelett (*n*).
Omit, *v.* Auslassen.
Omnibus, *n.* Omnibus (*m*).
On, *adv. & pron.* An, auf, am, in, bei, mit, zu.

Once — **Outside**

Once, *adv.* Einmal (one time), einst (past event).
One, *adj. & pron.* Einer, eine, ein.
  Any one, irgend, jemand.
  Everyone, jederman.
  No one, niemand.
  One another, einander.
  Oneself, sich selbst.
  Someone, jemand.
Onion, *n.* Zwiebel (*f*).
Onlooker, *n.* Zuschauer (*m*).
Only, *adj.* Einzig: *adv.* Allein.
Onward, *adv.* Vorwärts.
Opal, *n.* Opal (*m*).
Open, *adj.* Frei, offen: *v.* Öffnen, eröffnen.
Opening, *n.* Öffnung (*f*), Loch (*n*).
Opera, *n.* Oper (*f*).
Opera-house, *n.* Opernhaus (*n*).
Operate, *v.* Operieren.
Operation, *n.* Operation (*f*).
Opinion, *n.* Meinung (*f*).
Opponent, *n.* Gegner (*m*).
Opportunity, *n.* Gelegenheit (*f*).
Oppose, *v.* Entgegenstellen.
Opposite, *adj.* Entgegengesetzt: *pron.* Gegenüber.
Oppress, *v.* Drücken, unterdrücken.
Optician, *n.* Optiker (*m*).
Opulence, *n.* Wohlstand (*m*).
Or, *conj.* Oder.
Or else, *conj.* Sonst.
Oracle, *n.* Orakel (*n*).
Oral, *adj.* Mündlich.
Orange, *n.* Orange (*f*), Apfelsine (*f*); *adj.* Orangegelb (colour).
Orangeade, *n.* Orangenlimonade (*f*), Orangenade (*f*).
Orator, *n.* Redner (*m*).
Orb, *n.* Kreis (*m*), Himmelskörper (*m*), Augapfel (*m*).
Orchard, *n.* Obstgarten (*m*).
Orchestra, *n.* Orchester (*n*).
Orchid, *n.* Orchidee (*f*).
Ordain, *v.* Verordnen, bestimmen (determine), ordinieren (clergy).
Ordeal, *n.* Heimsuchung (*f*).
Order, *n.* Ordnung (position) (*f*), Befehl (demand) (*m*), Bestellung (buying) (*f*), Orden (medal) (*m*): *v.* Ordnen.
  In order to, um zu.
Orderly, *adj.* Regelmässig, ordentlich.
Ordinary, *adj.* Regelmässig, gewöhnlich.
Ore, *n.* Metall (*n*), Erz (*n*).
Organ, *n.* Orgel (*f*).
Organize, *v.* Organisieren.
Oriental, *adj.* Östlich: *n.* Morgenländer (*m*).
Origin, *n.* Ursprung (*m*).
Originate, *v.* Entspringen.
Ornament, *n.* Schmuck (*m*), Putz (*m*), Verzierung (*f*): *v.* Verzieren.
Orphan, *n.* Waise (*f*).
Orphanage, *n.* Waisenhaus (*n*).
Orthography, *n.* Rechtschreibung (*f*).
Oscillate, *v.* Schwingen.
Ostrich, *n.* Strauss (*m*).
Other, *adj.* Ander.
Otherwise, *adv.* Anders, sonst.
Ought, *v.* Müsste, sollte.
Our, *pron. & adj.* Unser (*m. & n.*), unsere (*f*).
Ours, *pron.* Unserer (*m*), unsere (*f*), unseres (*n*).
Ourselves, *pron.* Wir selbst.
Out, *adv.* Aus: **but with verbs of motion use** hinaus **or** heraus.
Outbid, *v.* Überbieten.
Outbreak, *n.* Ausbruch (*m*).
Outcast, *n.* Verstossene (*m*); *adj.* Verworfen.
Outcome, *n.* Ergebnis (*n*).
Outcry, *n.* Schrei (*m*).
Outer, *adj.* Äussere.
Outfit, *n.* Ausrüstung (*f*).
Outfitter, *n.* Ausreeder (*m*).
Outgoing, *n.* Ausgang (*m*).
Outgrow, *v.* Entwachsen.
Outing, *n.* Ausflug (*m*).
Outlast, *v.* Überdauern.
Outlay, *n.* Auslage (*f*).
Outlet, *n.* Ausgang (*m*).
Outline, *n.* Abriss (*m*), Umriss (*m*).
Outlook, *n.* Aussicht (*f*), Auslug (on ships) (*m*).
Outlying, *adj.* Auswärtig.
Outpost, *n.* Vorposten (*m*).
Output, *n.* Ertrag (*m*).
Outrage, *n.* Beleidigung (*f*), Schimpf (*m*).
Outright, *adv.* Gänzlich.
Outset, *n.* Aufbruch (*m*).
Outside, *n.* Aussenseite (*f*): *adv.* Aussen, draussen.

Outspoken — Panic

Outspoken, *adj.* Freimütig.
Outstanding, *adj.* Ausstehend, unbezahlt.
Outstrip, *v.* Überholen.
Outward, *adv.* Aussen, auswärts.
Oval, *adj.* Eirund: *n.* Oval (*n*).
Oven, *n.* Backofen (*m*).
Over, *adv. & prep.* Über, vorbei.
Overalls, *n.* Überkleid (*n*).
Overbalance, *v.* Überwiegen.
Overbearing, *adj.* Stolz.
Overboard, *adv.* Über Bord.
Overburden, *v.* Überladen.
Overcast, *adj.* Bewölkt.
Overcoat, *n.* Überrock (*m*).
Overcome, *v.* Überwinden.
Overflow, *n.* Überlauf (*m*): *v.* Überfliessen.
Overgrow, *v.* Überwachsen.
Overhang, *v.* Überhängen.
Overhaul, *v.* Überholen.
Overhear, *v.* Belauschen.
Overjoy, *v.* Entzücken.
Overlap, *v.* Übergreifen.
Overload, *v.* Überladen.
Overlook, *v.* Übersehen, überblicken.
Overmantel, *n.* Kaminaufsatz (*m*).
Overpower, *v.* Überwältigen.
Overrate, *v.* Überschätzen.
Overrule, *v.* Verwerfen.
Oversea, *adj.* Überseeisch.
Overseer, *n.* Aufseher (*m*).
Overshadow, *v.* Überschatten.
Oversight, *n.* Versehen (*n*).
Overtime, *n.* Überstunden (*f*).
Overture, *n.* Vorschlag (*m*), Antrag (*m*).
Overwhelm, *v.* Überhäufen.
Overwork, *v.* Ermüden, überarbeiten.
Owe, *v.* Verdanken, schulden.
Owl, *n.* Eule (*f*).
Own, *v.* Besitzen, gestehen (own-up): *adj.* Eigen.
Owner, *n.* Eigentümer (*m*), Besitzer (*m*).
Ox, *n.* Ochs (*m*).
Oxygen, *n.* Sauerstoff (*m*).
Oyster, *n.* Auster (*f*).

P

Pace, *n.* Schritt (*m*).
Pacific, *adj.* Friedsam, friedlich.
Pacify, *v.* Besänftigen.
Pack, *n.* Pack (*m*), Meute (of hounds) (*f*), Spiel (of cards) (*n*): *v.* Packen.
Package, *n.* Gepäckstuck (*n*), Pack (*m*).
Packet, *n.* Paket (*n*).
Packet-boat, *n.* Postschiff (*n*).
Pad, *n.* Papierblock (of note paper) (*m*), Fussballen (foot of cat, etc.) (*m*): *v.* Polstern.
Padding, *n.* Wattierung (*f*).
Paddle, *n.* Ruder (*n*), Paddel (*n*): *v.* Rudern.
Paddle-steamer, *n.* Raddampfer (*m*).
Paddle-wheel, *n.* Schaufelrad (*n*).
Paddock, *n.* Wiese (*f*), Kröte (*f*), Sattelplatz (*m*).
Padlock, *n.* Vorlegeschloss (*n*).
Page, *n.* Seite (of book) (*f*), Page (boy) (*m*).
Pail, *n.* Eimer (*m*).
Pain, *n.* Sorge (*f*), Schmerz (*m*), Strafe (*m*): *v.* Schmerzen.
Painful, *adj.* Schmerzhaft.
Painless, *adj.* Schmerzlos.
Paint, *n.* Farbe (*f*), Schminke (*f*): *v.* Anstreichen, malen.
Painter, *n.* Maler (*m*), Fangleine (*f*).
Painting, *n.* Malerei (work of art) (*f*).
Pair, *n.* Paar (*n*).
Palace, *n.* Palast (*m*).
Palatable, *adj.* Schmackhaft.
Pale, *adj.* Blass, bleich.
Pale ale, *n.* Helle Bier (*n*).
Pallid, *adj.* Blass, bleich.
Palm, *n.* Palme (veget.) (*f*), Handfläche (of hand) (*f*).
Palmistry, *n.* Handwahrsagerie (*f*).
Palm Sunday, *n.* Palmsonntag (*m*).
Palpitation, *n.* Herzklopfen (*n*).
Paltry, *adj.* Armselig.
Pan, *n.* Pfanne (*f*), Kochtopf (*m*), Topf (*m*).
Frying pan, *n.* Bratpfanne (*f*).
Pancake, *n.* Pfannkuchen (*m*).
Pane, *n.* Glasscheibe (*f*).
Panel, *n.* Täfelung (*f*), Füllung (*f*), Liste (*f*).
Pang, *n.* Stich (*m*).
Panic, *n.* Panik (*f*).

Pansy, n. Stiefmütterchen (n).
Pant, v. Keuchen, lechzen.
Panther, n. Panther (m).
Pantomime, n. Pantomime (f).
Pantry, n. Speisekammer (f).
Pants, n. Unterhosen (f).
Papal, adj. Päpstlich.
Paper, n. Papier (n), Zeitung (newspaper) (f).
Parachute, n. Fallschirm (m).
Parade, n. Gepränge (n), Promenade (street) (f), Parade (lining-up) (f).
Paradise, n. Paradies (n).
Paraffin, n. Paraffin (n), Petroleum (n).
Paragraph, n. Abschnitt (m).
Parallel, adj. Parallel.
Paralyse, v. Lähmen.
Paralysis, n. Lähmung (f).
Paramour, n. Liebhaber (m), Buhle (m).
Parapet, n. Brustwehr (f).
Paraphrase, n. Umschreibung (f).
Parasite, n. Schmarotzer (m).
Parasol, n. Sonnenschirm (m).
Parcel, n. Packet (n), Stück (n).
Parch, v. Dörren, rösten.
Pardon, n. Verzeihung (f); v. Verzeihen.
Pardonable, adj. Verzeihlich.
Parentage, n. Abkunft (f).
Parents, n. Eltern (pl.).
Parish, n. Kirchspiel (n).
Park, n. Park (m), Gehänge (n).
Parking-place, n. Parkstelle (f).
Parlour, n. Wohnzimmer (n), Besuchzimmer (n).
Parlour-maid, n. Stubenmädchen (n).
Parody, n. Parodie (f).
Parrot, n. Papagei (m).
Parry, v. Parieren, ablenken.
Parse, v. Zerlegen.
Parsley, n. Petersilie (f).
Parsnip, n. Pastinake (f).
Parson, n. Pfarrer (m).
Parsonage, n. Pfarre (f).
Part, n. Teil (m), Anteil (m), Rolle (part in a play) (f); v. Teilen, sich trennen, scheiteln.
Partake, v. Geniessen.
Partial, adj. Teilweise.
Participate, v. Teilnehmen.
Participle, n. Partizip (n).
Particle, n. Teilchen (n).

Particular, adj. Besonder, genau, wählerisch.
Parting, n. Abreise (f), Abschied (m), Scheitel (the hair) (m).
Partly, adv. Teilweise.
Partner, n. Teilhaber (m), Gefährte (m), Tänzer (at dance) (m), Mitspieler (at cards) (n).
Partnership, n. Teihalberschaft (f).
Partridge, n. Rebhuhn (n).
Party, n. Partei (f), Gessellschaft (amusement) (f).
Pass, v. Vorbeigehen, vorübergehen, bestehen (at exams.); n. Pass (m), Durchgang (m).
Passage, n. Durchgang (m), Durchfahrt (f), Überfahrt (journey) (f).
Passbook, n. Bankbuch (m), Privatkontobuch (n).
Passenger, n. Reisende (m), Passagier (m).
Passer-by, n. Vorübergehende (m).
Passing, adj. Vorübergehend.
Passion, n. Leidenschaft (f).
Passionate, adj. Leidenschaftlich.
Passport, n. Reisepass (m).
Past, adj. Vergangen: n. Vergangenheit (f): prep. Vorbei, vorüber.
Paste, n. Kleister (m), Teig (m).
Pastime, n. Zeitvertreib (m).
Pastor, n. Pastor (m).
Pastries, n. Törtchen (plu.).
Pastry, n. Backwerk (n).
Pastry-cook, n. Konditor (m).
Pasture, n. Weide (f).
Pat, v. Streicheln, patschen: n. Patsch (m), Schlag (m).
Patch, n. Flicken (m); v. Flicken, ausbessern.
Patent, n. Patent (n).
Patent-leather, n. Lackleder (n).
Paternal, adj. Väterlich.
Path, n. Weg (m), Pfad (m).
Pathetic, adj. Pathetisch.
Patience, n. Geduld (f).
Patient, adj. Geduldig: n. Patient (m), Kranke (m).
Patriot, n. Patriot (m).
Patriotic, adj. Patriotisch.

Patriotism   147   **Perilous**

Patriotism, *n.* Vaterlandsliebe (*f*).
Patrol, *v.* Patrouillieren; *n.* Patrouille (*f*).
Patronize, *v.* Begünstigen, beschützen.
Pattern, *n.* Muster (*n*).
Pauper, *n.* Arme (*m*).
Pause, *v.* Pausieren: *n.* Pause (*f*).
Pavement, *n.* Pflaster (*m*).
Pavilion, *n.* Pavilion (*n*).
Paw, *n.* Tatze (*f*), Pfote (*f*): *v.* Scharren, streicheln.
Pawn, *v.* Versetzen: *n.* Pfand (pawnbr:), Bauer (chess) (*m*).
Pawnbroker, *n.* Pfandleiher (*m*).
Pawnshop, *n.* Pfandhaus (*n*).
Pay, *v.* Zahlen, bezahlen, büssen.
Pay attention, achtgeben.
Payment, *n.* Bezahlung (*f*).
Pea, *n.* Erbse (*f*).
Sweet Pea, *n.* Edelwicke (*f*).
Peace, *n.* Friede (*m*).
Peaceful, *adj.* Friedlich.
Peach, *n.* Pfirsich (*m*).
Peacock, *n.* Pfau (*m*).
Peahen, *n.* Pfauhenne (*f*).
Peak, *n.* Gipfel (*m*), Mützenschirm (*m*).
Peal, *n.* Schlag (*m*), Geläute (*n*), Gekrach (*n*): *v.* Krachen, schallen, ertönen (thunder).
Peanut, *n.* Erdnuss (*f*).
Pear, *n.* Birne (*f*).
Pearl, *n.* Perle (*f*).
Peartree, *n.* Birnbaum (*m*).
Pearant, *n.* Bauer (*m*).
Peat, *n.* Torf (*m*).
Pebble, *n.* Kiesel (*m*), Kieselstein (*m*).
Peck, *v.* Picken, hacken: *n.* Viertelscheffel (measure) (*m*), Menge (*f*).
Peculiar, *adj.* Eigen, sonderbar.
Peculiarly, *adv.* Besonders.
Pedal, *n.* Pedal (*n*), Trittbrett (*n*): *v.* Treten.
Pedestrian, *n.* Fussgänger (*m*): *adj.* Zu Fuss.
Pedlar, *n.* Hausierer (*m*).
Peel, *n.* Rinde (*f*), Schale (*f*): *v.* Schälen.
Peep, *v.* Piepen: *n.* Gucken (*n*).
Peer, *n.* Lord (*m*), Pair (*m*), Gefährte (*m*): *v.* Gucken.

Peevish, *adj.* Verdriesslich.
Peg, *n.* Wirbel (*m*), Pflock (*m*), Klammer (*f*), Kleiderhanken (*m*): *v.* Festpflöcken.
Pelican, *n.* Pelikan (*m*).
Pelt, *n.* Haut (*f*), Fell (*n*), Pelz (*m*): *v.* Bewerfen.
Pen, *n.* Schreibfeder (writing), Hürde (for cattle) (*f*).
Penalty, *n.* Busse (*f*), Strafe (*f*).
Penance, *n.* Busse (*f*).
Pencil, Stift (*m*), Bleistift (*m*).
Pendant, *n.* Gehänge (*n*), Anhänger (*m*).
Pending, *adj.* Schwebend: *pron.* Während.
Pendulum, *n.* Pendel (*m*).
Penetrate, *v.* Durchdringen.
Penguin, *n.* Pinguin (*m*).
Penholder, *n.* Federhalter (*m*).
Peninsula, *n.* Halbinsel (*f*).
Penitent, *adj.* Reuig, bussfertig.
Pension, *n.* Kostgeld (*n*), Pension (*f*).
Pensioner, *n.* Pensionierte (*m*).
Pensive, *adj.* Gedankenvoll.
Peony, *n.* Päonie (*f*).
People, *n.* Volk (*n*), Leute (*pl.*).
Pepper, *n.* Pfeffer (*m*).
Peppermint, *n.* Pfefferminze (*f*).
Perambulator, *n.* Kinderwagen (*m*).
Perceive, *v.* Empfinden.
Percentage, *n.* Prozentsatz (*m*).
Perception, *n.* Empfindung (*f*).
Perch, *n.* Sitzstange (for birds, etc.), Barsch (the fish) (*m*): *v.* Aufsitzen.
Perfect, *adj.* Vollkommen: *v.* Vervollkommen.
Perfection, *n.* Vollkommenheit (*f*).
Perforate, *v.* Durchlochen, durchbohren.
Perforation, *n.* Durchlochung (*f*), Durchbohrung (*f*).
Perform, *v.* Erfüllen, verrichten, aufführen, ausführen.
Performance, *n.* Vorstellung (*f*), Verrichtung (*f*).
Perfume, *n.* Wohlgeruch (*m*), Parfüm (*m*).
Perhaps, *adv.* Vielleicht.
Peril, *n.* Gefahr (*f*).
Perilous, *adj.* Gefährlich, gewagt.

Period 148 **Pious**

Period, n. Periode (f), Zeitraum (m).
Periodical, n. Zeitschrift (f): adj. Periodisch.
Periscope, n. Periskop (n).
Perish, v. Verderben, umkommen.
Perishable, adj. Leicht verderblich.
Perjury, n. Meineid (m).
Perky, adj. Keck.
Permanent, adj. Beständig.
Permission, n. Erlaubnis (f).
Permit, n. Erlaubnisschein (m).
Pernicious, adj. Verderblich, verrucht.
Perpetual, adj. Immerwährend.
Perplex, v. Verwirren, verwickeln.
Perplexed, adj. Verwirrt.
Persecute, v. Verfolgen.
Persecution, n. Verfolgung (f).
Persecutor, n. Verfolger (m).
Persevere, v. Beharren.
Person, n. Person (f), Mensch (m).
Personate, v. Vorstellen.
Perspective, n. Perspektive (f).
Perspiration, n. Schweiss (m).
Perspire, v. Schwitzen.
Persuade, v. Überreden.
Persuasion, n. Überredung (f).
Perturb, v. Verwirren.
Perusal, n. Durchlesen (n).
Pervade, v. Durchdringen.
Pest, n. Pest (f), Plage (f)
Pestilent, adj. Lästig.
Pet, n. Liebling (m), Ärger (m): v. Liebkosen, hätscheln.
Petal, n. Blumenblatt (n).
Petition, n. Bittschrift (f), Gesuch (n): v. Bitten.
Petrify, v. Versteinern.
Petrol, n. Benzin (n).
Petroleum, n. Petroleum (n).
Petticoat, n. Unterrock (m).
Petty, adj. Kleinlich, klein.
Pew, n. Kirchenstuhl (m).
Pewter, n. Hartzinn (n).
Phantom, n. Phantom (n), Trugbild (n).
Pheasant, n. Fasan (m).
Phenomenon, n. Phänomen (n).
Philosopher, n. Philosoph (m).
Phlegm, n. Phlegma (n), Schleim (m).

Phosphorus, n. Phosphor (m).
Photograph, n. Photographie (f).
Phrase, n. Phrase (f), Tonsatz (m), Satz (m).
Physic, n. Arznei (f), Heilkunst (f), Physik (f).
Physician, n. Doktor (m), Arzt (m).
Pianist, n. Klavierspieler (m).
Piano, n. Klavier (n), Flügel (grand) (m), Pianino (n).
Pick, v. Picken, pflücken: n. Picke (f).
Pickle, v. Pökeln.
Pickles, n. Pickles (pl.).
Pickpocket, n. Taschendieb (m).
Picnic, n. Picknick (n).
Pictorial, adj. Illustriert.
Picture, n. Bild (n), Gemälde (n).
Pie, n. Elster (f), Pastete (f).
Piece, n. Stück (n), Flinte (f).
Piecemeal, adv. Stückweise.
Pier, n. Seesteig (m), Pfeiler (m).
Piety, n. Frömmigkeit (f).
Pig, n. Schwein (n), Ferkel (n).
Pigeon, n. Taube (f).
Pigeon-hole, Fach (n), Regal (n).
Pigsty, n. Schweinestall (m).
Pile, n. Pfahl (m), Stoss (m): v. Aufhäufen.
Pilfer, v. Mausen.
Pilgrim, n. Pilger (m).
Pilgrimage, n. Pilgerfahrt (f).
Pill, n. Pille (f).
Pillage, n. Plünderung (f).
Pillar, n. Pfeiler (m).
Pillow, n. Kopfkissen (n).
Pilot, n. Lotse (sea) (m), Pilot (air) (m): v. Lotsen.
Pimple, n. Pickel (m), Finne (f), Bläschen (n).
Pimpled, adj. Finnig.
Pin, n. Stecknadel (f): v. Anstecken.
Pinafore, n. Schürzchen (n).
Pincers, n. Kneifzange (f).
Pinch, v. Kneifen: n. Zwick (m).
Pineapple, n. Ananas (f).
Pine-tree, n. Kiefer (f).
Pink, adj. Blassrot: n. Nelke (plant) (f).
Pioneer, n. Bahnbrecher (m).
Pious, adj. Zärtlich.

Pipe, n. Röhre (f), Pfeife (smoker's) (f).
Pirate, n. Seeräuber (m); v. Rauben.
Pistol, n. Pistole (f).
Piston, n. Kolben (m).
Pit, n. Grube (f), Graben (m), Parterre (theatre) (n).
Pitch, n. Pech (black material) (n), Wurf (m), Tonhöhe (in music) (f): v. Werfen (throw), stampfen (and toss).
Pitcher, n. Krug (m).
Pitchfork, n. Heugabel (f), Mistgabel (f).
Piteous, adj. Kläglich.
Pitfall, n. Fallgrube (f).
Pith, n. Kern (m), Kraft (f), Mark (n).
Pitiful, adj. Elend, mitleidig, erbärmlich.
Pitiless, adj. Grausam, unbarmherzig.
Pity, n. Mitleid (n): v. Bemitleiden.
Pivot, n. Drehpunkt (m).
Placard, n. Plakat (n), Anschlag (m).
Place, n. Platz (m), Wohnort (m), Stand (m): v. Stellen, legen, setzen.
Placid, adj. Sanft.
Plague, n. Plage (f), Seuche (f): v. Plagen.
Plaice, n. Scholle (f).
Plain, adj. Einfach, klar unansehnlich (features): n. Ebene (f).
Plainly, adv. Vernehmlich.
Plaint, n. Beschwerde (f), Klage (f).
Plaintiff, n. Kläger (m).
Plait, v. Falten, flechten n. Flechte (f).
Plan, n. Plan (m), Grundriss (m): v. Entwerfen.
Plane, n. Hobel (m), Fläche (f).
Planet, n. Planet (m).
Plank, n. Planke (f), Bohle (f).
Plant, n. Pflanze (f), Maschinen (pl.): v. Pflanzen.
Plantation, n. Pflanzung (f).
Plaster, n. Mörtel (m), Pflaster (n): v. Bepflastern.
Plaster of Paris, n. Gypsmörtel (m).
Plate, n. Teller (m), Platte (f), Kupferstich (m): v. Plattieren.
Plate-glass, n. Tafelglas (n).
Plate-layer, n. Streckenarbeiter (m).
Platform, n. Plattform (f), Bahnsteig (train) (m).
Platinum, n. Platin (n).
Platonic, adj. Platonisch.
Plausible, adj. Scheinbar, einnehmend.
Play, n. Spiel (games) (n), Stück (acting) (n): v. Spielen, vorstellen.
Player, n. Spieler (m), Schauspieler (m).
Playful, adj. Spielend.
Plea, n. Entschuldigung (f).
Plead, v. Processiren, plädieren.
Plead guilty, sich schuldig bekennen.
Pleasant, adj. Angenehm, lustig.
Please, v. Gefallen, belieben. **If you please,** bitte. **Please . . . ,** bitte.
Pleasing, adj. Angenehm, lustig.
Pleasure, n. Vergnügen (n).
Pledge, n. Pfand (n), Gelübde (n): v. Verpfänden (pawn), verpflichten.
Plenitude, n. Fülle (f).
Plentiful, adj. Reichlich, ergiebig, überflüssig.
Plenty, n. Fülle (f).
Pliable, adj. Geschmeidig.
Pliers, n. Zange (f).
Plight, n. Pfand (m), Zustand (m): v. Verpfänden.
Plod, v. Sich anstrengen.
Plot, v. Sich verschwören, anzetteln: n. Intrigue (f), Knoten (of a tale) (m), Grundstück (of ground) (n).
Plough, n. Pflug (m): v. Pflügen.
Ploughman, n. Pfluger (m).
Pluck, n. Pflock (m), Stöpsel: v. Pflücken.
Plug, n. Stöpsel (m): v. Verstopfen.
Plum, n. Pflaume (f), Rosine (f).
Plumage, n. Gefieder (n).
Plumbago, n. Graphit (m).
Plumber, n. Bleigiesser (m).
Plume, n. Feder (f).
Plump, adj. Fett, dick, derb, fleischig.
Plumpness, n. Beleibtheit (f).

Plunder   150   **Postmaster**

Plunder, *n.* Beute (*f*), Raub (*m*): *v.* Plündern.
Plunderer, *n.* Räuber (*m*), Plünderer (*m*).
Plunge, *v.* Tauchen.
Plural, *n.* Mehrzahl (*f*).
Plush, *n.* Plüsch (*m*).
Poach, *v.* Stossen, wildern.
   Poached eggs, *n.* Verlorene Eier (*pl.*).
Poacher, *n.* Wilddieb (*m*).
Pocket, *n.* Tasche (*f*).
Pocket-book, *n.* Taschenbuch (*n*).
Pod, *n.* Schäle (*f*), Hülse (*f*).
Poem, *n.* Gedicht (*n*).
Poet, *n.* Dichter (*m*).
Poetry, *n.* Dichtkunst (*f*), Gedicht (*n*).
Point, *n.* Punkt (*m*), Zweck (*m*), Spitze (*f*): *v.* Zuspitzen.
Pointed, *adj.* Spitz, punktiert, beissend.
Poison, *n.* Gift (*n*): *v.* Vergiften.
Poisonous, *adj.* Giftig.
Poker, *n.* Schüreisen (*n*).
Pole, *n.* Pol (*m*), Pfahl (*m*).
Police, *n.* Polizei (*f*).
Polish, *v.* Poliren, glätten; *n.* Politur (*f*), Glanz (*m*).
Polite, *adj.* Artig, fein, höflich.
Politeness, *n.* Artigkeit (*f*).
Political, *adj.* Politisch.
Politician, *n.* Politiker (*m*).
Politics, *n.* Politik (*f*).
Pollute, *v.* Entweihen, beflecken.
Pomade, *n.* Salbe (*f*), Pomade (*f*).
Pomegranate, *n.* Granatapfel (*m*).
Pomp, *n.* Prunk (*m*), Gepränge (*n*).
Pomposity, *n.* Prunk (*m*).
Pond, *n.* Teich (*m*).
Ponderous, *adj.* Schwer.
Poniard, *n.* Dolch (*m*).
Pontoon, *n.* Brückenkahn (*m*).
Pony, *n.* Pony (*m. & n.*).
Poodle, *n.* Pudel (*m*).
Pool, *n.* Pfuhl (*m*), Teich (*m*).
Poor, *adj.* Arm, dürftig: *n.* Armen (*pl*).
Poorness, *n.* Armut (*f*).
Pop, *v.* Knallen, paffen.
Pope, *n.* Papst (*m*).
Poplar tree, *n.* Pappel (*f*).
Poppy, *n.* Mohn (*m*).

Popular, *adj.* Volkstümlich, volksmassig.
Popularise, *v.* Volkstümlich machen.
Populate, *v.* Bevölkern.
Population, *n.* Bevölkerung (*f*).
Porcelain, *n.* Porzellan (*n*).
Porch, *n.* Vorhalle (*f*), Portal (*n*).
Porcupine, *n.* Stachelschwein (*n*).
Pore, *n.* Pore (*f*).
Pork, *n.* Schweinefleisch (*n*).
Porous, *adj.* Porös.
Porpoise, *n.* Tümmler (*m*), Meerschwein (*n*).
Porridge, *n.* Haferschleim (*m*), Haferbrei (*m*).
Port, *n.* Hafen (*m*), Pforte (*f*), Pfortluke (*f*).
Portcullis, *n.* Fallgatter (*n*).
Porter, *n.* Portier (at door) (*m*), Träger (for luggage) (*m*).
Portfolio, *n.* Mappe (*f*).
Portion, *n.* Anteil (*n*), Portion (*f*), Teil (*m*), Gebühr (*f*).
Portmanteau, *n.* Reisekoffer (*m*), Handkoffer (*m*).
Portrait, *n.* Porträt (*n*), Bildnis (*n*).
Portray, *v.* Abmalen, schildern.
Port-wine, *n.* Portwein (*m*).
Pose, *n.* Pose (*f*), Haltung (*f*): *v.* Posiern.
Position, *n.* Lage (*f*), Stand (*m*), Stellung (occupation) (*f*).
Positive, *adj.* Ausdrücklich.
Possess, *v.* Besitzen.
Possession, *n.* Besitz (*m*).
Possessor, *n.* Besitzer (*m*).
Possible, *adj.* Möglich.
Post, *n.* Post (*f*), Pfosten (upright support) (*m*), Stelle (occupation) (*f*): *v.* Anschlagen, einstecken (a letter).
Postage, *n.* Porto (*n*).
Postage stamp, *n.* Briefmarke (*f*).
Post card, *n.* Postkarte (*f*).
Poster, *n.* Plakat (*n*), Anschlagzettel (*m*).
Posterior, *n.* Hintere (*m*), Hinterteil (*n*).
Posterity, *n.* Nachwelt (*f*).
Postman, *n.* Briefträger (*m*).
Postmaster, *n.* Postdirektor (*m*).

**Post-mortem, **n. Leichenschau (f).
**Post-office, **n. Postamt (n).
**Postpone, **v. Aufschieben.
**Postscript, **n. Nachschrift (f).
**Posture, **n. Stellung (f), Positur (f), Lage (f).
**Pot, **n. Topf (m), Krug (m), Kanne (f).
**Potato, **n. Kartoffel (f).
**Pottery, **n. Töpferei (f), Töpferwaren (f).
**Pouch, **n. Sack (m), Tasche (f), Beutel (m).
**Poulterer, **n. Geflügelhändler (m).
**Poultice, **n. Umschlag (m), Breiumschlag (m).
**Poultry, **n. Geflügel (n).
**Pour, **v. Giessen, schütten, strömen.
**Poverty, **n. Armut (f), Mangel (m).
**Powder, **n. Pulver (n), Puder (face) (m), Staub (m): v. Pudern, pulverisieren.
**Powder-puff, **n. Puderquaste (f).
**Power, **n. Macht (f), Kraft (f), Gewalt (f).
**Powerful, **adj. Mächtig, kräftig, stark.
**Powerless, **adj. Machtlos, kraftlos.
**Practicable, **adj. Tunlich.
**Practical, **adj. Praktisch.
**Practice, **n. Gebrauch (usual custom) (m), Übung (exercising) (f).
**Practise, **v. Üben, anwenden.
Practitioner (medical) n. Praktische Arzt (m).
**Praise, **n. Lob (n), Preis (m): v. Loben, preisen.
**Praiseworthy, **adj. Lobenswert, lobenswürdig.
**Prance, **v. Bäumen, herumhüpfen.
**Prank, **n. Streich (m), Possen (m).
**Prawn, **n. Garnele (f).
**Pray, **v. Beten, bitten.
   **Pray, tell me, **Bitte, sagen Sie mir.
**Prayer, **n. Gebet (n).
   **The Lord's Prayer, **Das Vaterunser (n).
**Prayer-book, **n. Gebetbuch (n).

**Preach, **v. Predigen.
**Preacher, **n. Prediger (m).
**Precarious, **adj. Riskant, prekär, unsicher.
**Precaution, **n. Vorsicht (f).
**Precede, **v. Vorangehen.
**Precious, **adj. Recht, kostbar.
**Precipice, **n. Abgrund (m).
**Precipitate, **v. Stürzen, übereilen, fällen: n. Niederschlag (chemical) (m).
**Precise, **adj. Genau, ängstlich, steif.
**Precision, **n. Präzision (f).
**Preclude, **v. Ausschliessen, vorbeugen.
**Predecessor, **n. Vorgänger (m).
**Predicament, **n. Verlegenheit (f), Aussage (f).
**Predicate, **n. Prädikat (n).
**Predict, **v. Prophezeien.
**Preface, **n. Vorwort (n).
**Prefect, **n. Präfekt (m), Aufseher (m).
**Prefer, **v. Vorziehen, vortragen.
**Preferable, **adj. Vorzuziehen.
**Preference, **n. Vorzug (m).
**Preference share, **n. Vorzugsaktie (m).
**Prefix, **n. Vorsilbe (f).
**Pregnant, **adj. Schwanger (human), trächtig (animal).
**Prejudice, **n. Vorurteil (n), Nachteil (m): v. Benachteiligen.
**Preliminary, **adj. Vorläufig, einleitend.
**Prelude, **n. Vorspiel (n).
**Premature, **adj. Vorzeitig, frühreif.
**Premeditate, **v. Vorbedenken, vorher überlegen.
**Premier, **n. Premierminister (m): adj. Erst.
**Premises, **n. Haus (n), Lokal (n), Gebäude (n).
**Premium, **n. Aufgeld (n), Prämie (f).
**Preparation, **n. Vorbereitung (f).
**Prepare, **v. Vorbereiten, herrichten, zubereiten.
**Prepay, **v. Frankieren, vorausbezahlen.
**Preposterous, **adj. Albern, widersinnig.
**Prescribe, **v. Vorschreiben.

Prescription, n. Rezept (n), Vorschrift (f).
Present, adj. Bereit, gegenwärtig: v. Präsentieren, darstellen: n. Geschenk (n), Präsens (gram:) (n).
Presentation, n. Vorstellung (f).
Presently, adv. Bald, gleich, sogleich.
Preservation, n. Erhaltung (f).
Preservative, n. Schutzmittel (n).
Preserve, v. Einmachen (jam), behüten (guard over).
Preserves, n. Konserven (f).
Preside, v. Präsidieren.
President, n. Präsident (national) (m), Vorsitzende (at meetings) (m).
Press, n. Presse (f), Drang (m): v. Drücken, bügeln.
Pressing, adj. Dringend.
Pressure, n. Druck (m).
Presume, v. Vermuten, mutmassen.
Presumption, n. Mutmassung (f).
Pretend, v. Vorgeben, erheucheln.
Preterite, n. Präteritum (grammar) (n).
Pretext, n. Vorwand (m).
Pretty, adj. Niedlich, hübsch, nett.
Prevail, v. Vorherrschen, allgemein.
Prevent, v. Vorbeugen, verhindern.
Previous, adj. Früher, vorig.
Prey, n. Beute (f), Raub (m): v. Rauben.
Price, n. Preis (m).
Priceless, adj. Unschätzbar.
Prick, v. Stechen, spornen: n. Stich (m), Spitze (f).
Prickle, n. Stachel (m).
Pride, n. Stolz (m), Pracht (f).
Priest, n. Priester (m).
Prig, n. Eingebildete Laffe (m), Pedant (m).
Prim, adj. Geziert, zimperlich.
Prime, adj. Erst, prima; n. Beste (n), Kern (m).
Primitive, adj. Unsprünglich.
Primrose, n. Primel (f).
Prince, n. Prinz (m).
Princess, n. Prinzessin (f).

Principal, n. Prinzipal (m), Chef (m).
Principle, n. Prinzip (n).
Print, n. Druck (type) (m), Abzug (photographic) (m); v. Drucken.
Printer, n. Drucker (m).
Prior, adj. Früher: adv. Vor.
Prison, n. Gefängnis (n).
Prisoner, n. Gefangene (m).
Private, adj. Privat, geheim.
Privet, n. Liguster (m).
Privilege, n. Vorrecht (n).
Prize, n. Preis (m), Prise (f): v. Schätzen.
Probable, adj. Wohl, wahrscheinlich.
Probate, n. Testamentsbestätigung (f).
Probe, v. Sondieren.
Problem, n. Aufgabe (f), Problem (m).
Proceed, v. Hurrühren, fortfahren.
Proceeds, n. Gewinn (m), Ertrag (m).
Procession, n. Prozession (f).
Proclaim, v. Ausrufen, bekanntmachen.
Proclamation, v. Ausruf (m).
Procure, v. Besorgen, verschaffen.
Prod, n. Stich (m): v. Stechen.
Prodigal, adj. Verschwenderisch: n. Vergeuder (m).
Produce, v. Erzeugen: n. Erzeugnis (n).
Producer, n. Erzeuger (m).
Product, n. Produkt (n).
Profane, adj. Profan, ungeweiht.
Profess, v. Bekennen.
Profession, n. Beruf (m), Bekenntris (n).
Professor, n. Bekenner (m), Professor (m).
Proficient, adj. Tüchtig.
Profit, n. Gewinn (m), Vorteil (m): v. Nutzen, gewinnen.
Profuse, adj. Überfluss, reichlich.
Programme, n. Programm (n), Spielplan (m).
Prohibit, v. Verhindern.
Project, n. Projekt (n): v. Hervorstehen.
Prolong, v. Verlängern.
Promenade, n. Spazierweg (m): v. Spazieren.

**Prominent, *adj.* Hervorragend.
Promise, *v.* Versprechen: *n.* Versprechen (*n*).
Promote, *v.* Gründen, befördern.
Prompt, *adj.* Bereit, bar, fertig: *v.* Vorsagen.
Pronoun, *n.* Fürwort (*n*).
Pronounce, *v.* Aussprechen.
Pronunciation, *n.* Aussprache (*f*).
Proof, *n.* Versuch (*m*), Beweis (*m*), Probe (*f*), Abzug (printing) (*m*).
Prop, *v.* Stützen: *n.* Stütze.
Propagate, *v.* Ausbreiten.
Propel, *v.* Vorwärtstreiben.
Propeller, *n.* Propeller (*m*), Schraube (*f*).
Proper, *adj.* Eigen, passend, anständig.
Property, *n.* Eigentum (*n*), Vermögen (*n*).
Prophesy, *v.* Prophezeien.
Prophet, *n.* Prophet (*m*).
Proportion, *n.* Verhältnis (*n*), Ebenmass (*n*).
Proposal, *n.* Antrag (*m*), Vorschlag (*m*), Heiratsantrag (of marriage) (*m*).
Propose, *v.* Vorschlagen, willens sein.
Proposition, *n.* Vorschlag (*m*).
Proprietor, *n.* Eigentümer (*m*), Besitzer (*m*).
Prose, *n.* Prosa (*f*).
Prosecute, *v.* Anklagen, verklagen, verfolgen.
Prosecutor, *n.* Kläger (*m*), Ankläger (*m*).
Prospect, *n.* Aussicht (*f*), Ansicht (*f*): *v.* Schürfen.
Prospectus, *n.* Prospekt (*m*), Prospect (*m*).
Prosper, *v.* Gedeihen, segnen.
Prosperity, *n.* Wohlstand (*m*).
Prosperous, *adj.* Günstig, gedeihlich.
Prostitute, *n.* Dirne (*f*).
Prostrate, *v.* Niederwerfen, niederfallen; *adj.* Fussfälig.
Protect, *v.* Beschützen, bewahren.
Protection, *n.* Schutz (*m*).
Protector, *n.* Beschützer (*m*).
Protest, *v.* Protestieren, beteuern: *n.* Einspruch (*m*).
Protestant, *n.* Protestant (*m*): *adj.* Protestantisch.

Protrude, *v.* Hervorragen.
Proud, *adj.* Stolz, kühn, prächtig.
Proverb, *n.* Sprichwort (*n*).
Provide, *v.* Versorgen, versehen.
Providence, *n.* Vorsehung (*f*), Vorsorge (*f*).
Provider, *n.* Lieferant (*m*).
Provision, *n.* Vorrat (*m*), Vorkehrung (*f*).
Provisions, *n.* Lebensmittel (*n*).
Provoke, *v.* Herausforderung (*f*).
Prowess, *n.* Tapferkeit (*f*).
Prude, *n.* Spröde (*f*), Prüde (*f*).
Prune, *n.* Backpflaume (*f*).
Prussic acid, *n.* Blausäure (*f*).
Pry, *v.* Spähen.
Prying, *adj.* Neugierig.
Puberty, *n.* Mannbarkeit (*f*).
Public, *adj.* Öffentlich: *n.* Publikum (*n*).
Public house, *n.* Wirtshaus (*n*).
Publish, *v.* Herausgeben (books), verlegen.
Publisher, *n.* Herausgeber (books) (*m*), Verleger (*m*).
Pudding, *n.* Pudding (*m*).
Puddle, *n.* Pfütze (*f*), Lache (*f*), Lemschlag (*m*).
Puerile, *adj.* Kindisch.
Puff, *n.* Windstoss (wind) (*m*), Hauch (breath) (*m*), Prahlerei (*f*): *v.* Blasen, aufschwellen.
Pug dog, *n.* Mops (*m*).
Pugilist, *n.* Boxer (*m*).
Pull, *v.* Ziehen, reissen, rudern: *n.* Zug (*m*), Stoss (*m*).
Pullet, *n.* Hühnchen (*n*).
Pulley, *n.* Rolle (*f*), Flaschenzug (*m*).
Pulp, *n.* Brei (*m*), Pülpe (*f*).
Pulpit, *n.* Kanzel (*f*).
Pulse, *n.* Puls (*m*).
Pulverize, *v.* Pulverisieren.
Pump, *n.* Pumpe (*f*): *v.* Pumpen.
Pumpkin, *n.* Kürbis (*m*).
Pun, *n.* Wortspiel (*n*): *v.* Witzeln.
Punch, *n.* Schlag (*m*), Stoss (*m*), Locheisen (*n*), Punsch (*m*): *v.* Schlagen, lochen.
Punctual, *adj.* Pünktlich.
Punctuate, *v.* Interpunktieren.

**Punctuation, **n. Interpunktion (f).
**Puncture, **n. Stich (m), Punktur (f): v. Stechen.
**Pungent, **adj. Scharf, stechend.
**Punish, **v. Strafen.
**Punishment, **n. Strafe.
**Punt, **n. Schauke (f).
**Puny, **adj. Winzig.
**Pupil, **n. Schüler (school) (m), Schülerin (school) (f), Pupille (eye) (f).
**Puppy, **n. Hündchen (n).
**Purchase, **v. Einkaufen, kaufen: n. Kauf (m).
**Purchaser, **n. Käufer (m).
**Pure, **adj. Rein, echt, keusch (morals).
**Purgative, **n. Abführmittel (n).
**Purge, **v. Abführen, reinigen.
**Purify, **v. Reinigen.
**Purple, **n. Purpur (m).
**Purpose, **n. Vorhaben (n), Inhalt (m).
**Purposely, **adv. Vorsätzlich.
**Purr, **v. Schnurren.
**Purse, **n. Börse (f), Geldtäschchen (n).
**Pursue, **v. Verfolgen, nachstreben.
**Pursuit, **n. Verfolgung (f).
**Purveyor, **n. Lieferant (m).
**Pus, **n. Eiter (m).
**Push, **v. Schieben, stossen, treiben: n. Stoss (m).
**Put, **v. Anvertrauen, anwenden, bringen, legen, setzen, stecken, stellen, veranlassen.
  **Put by, **beiseitelegen.
  **Put in, **in den Hafen einlaufen.
  **Put off, **aufschieben.
  **Put on, **anziehen.
  **Put out, **auslöchen.
  **Put up, **aufsetzen.
**Putrefy, **v. Verfaulen.
**Putrid, **adj. Faul.
**Putty, **n. Glaserkitt (m), Kitt (m).
**Puzzle, **n. Rätsel (n), Geduldspiel (n): v. Verwirren, irremachen.
  **Crossword Puzzle, **Kreuzworträtsel (n).
**Pyjamas, **d. Schlafanzug (m).
**Pyramid, **n. Pyramide (f).
**Python, **n. Python (m).

Q

**Quadruped, **n. Vierfusser (m).
**Quagmire, **n. Moorboden (m), Sumpfboden (m).
**Quail, **n. Wachtel (f).
**Quaint, **adj. Seltsam, wunderlich.
**Quaintness, **n. Seltsamkeit (f).
**Quake, **v. Beben, zittern.
**Qualification, **n. Qualifikation (f), Eigenschaft (f).
**Qualify, **v. Berechtigen, einschränken.
**Quality, **n. Qualität (f).
**Quantity, **n. Quantität (f).
**Quarantine, **n. Quarantäne (f), Liegezeit (f).
**Quarrel, **n. Streit (m), Zank (m): v. Streiten.
**Quarrelsome, **adj. Streitsüchtig, zänkisch.
**Quarry, **n. Steinbruch (m).
**Quart, **n. Viertelmass (n).
**Quarter, **n. Viertel (n), Pardon (escape) (m), Vierteljahr (quarter of year) (n): v. Vierteilen.
**Quarter-day, **n. Quartalstag (m).
**Quarterly, **adj. Vierteljährlich.
**Quash, **v. Unterdrücken.
**Quaver, **n. Achtelnote (music) (f).
**Quay, **n. Kai (m).
**Queen, **n. Königin (f).
**Queer, **adj. Unwohl (illness), sonderbar (unusual).
**Quell, **v. Unterdrücken.
**Quench, **v. Dämpfen, löschen, stillen.
**Querulous, **adj. Streitsüchtig, zänkisch.
**Quest, **n. Suche (f).
**Question, **n. Frange (f), Untersuchung (f): v. Bezweifeln.
**Questionable, **adj. Fraglich.
**Queue, **n. Reihe (f), Schlange (f).
**Quibble, **v. Ausweichen: n. Ausflucht (f).
**Quick, **adj. Schnell.
**Quiet, **adj. Ruhig.
**Quill, **n. Federkiel (m).
**Quilt, **n. Steppdecke (f).
**Quinine, **n. Chinin (n).
**Quinsy, **n. Bräune (f).
**Quit, **v. Verlassen.
**Quiver, **v. Zittern, beben: n. Köcher (m).

Quotation — Ravine

Quotation, *n.* Zitat (*n*), Preisangabe (*f*).
Quotient, *n.* Teilzähler (*m*).

R

Rabbit, *n.* Kaninchen (*n*).
Race, *n.* Wettrennen (run) (*n*), Rasse (breed) (*f*): *v.* Rennen, laufen, wettrennen.
Race-course, *n.* Rennbahn (*f*).
Rack, *n.* Reck (*n*), Gepäcknetz (for luggage) (*n*), Folter (torture) (*f*).
Racquet, *n.* Tennisschläger (*m*).
Radiance, *n.* Glanz (*m*).
Radiate, *v.* Ausstrahlen.
Radiator, *n.* Heizkörper (*m*), Heizapparat (*m*), Kühler (of car) (*m*).
Radio, *n.* Radio (*n*).
Radio set, *n.* Radioapparat (*m*).
Radish, *n.* Radieschen (*n*).
Horse radish, *n.* Meerrettich (*m*).
Radium, *n.* Radium (*m*).
Radius, *n.* Radius (*m*).
Raffle, *n.* Lotterie (*f*), Auslosung (*f*): *v.* Auslosen.
Raft, *n.* Floss (*n*).
Rag, *n.* Lumpen (*m*), Budenulk (*m*).
Rage, *n.* Wut (*f*), Entzückung (*f*): *v.* Rasen.
Ragged, *adj.* Zerlumpt.
Rag-picker, *n.* Lumpensammler (*m*).
Rag-time, *n.* Negerrhythmus (*m*).
Raid, *n.* Überfall (*m*).
Air raid, *n.* Luftangriff (*m*).
Rail, *n.* Schiene (*f*), Geländer (*n*).
Railing, *n.* Geländer (*n*).
Railroad, *n.* Eisenbahn (*f*).
Railway guard, *n.* Schaffner (*m*).
Railway time-table, *n.* Kursbuch (*m*).
Rain, *n.* Regen (*m*): *v.* Regnen.
Rainbow, *n.* Regenbogen (*m*).
Rainy, *adj.* Regnerisch.
Raise, *v.* Heben, aufheben, erheben, erhöhen, ziehen, errichten.
Raisin, *n.* Rosine (*f*).
Rake, *n.* Rechen (*m*): *v.* Rechen, harken, schüren.
Rally, *v.* Sammeln.

Ram, *n.* Ramme (sea) (*f*), Widder (sheep) (*m*): *v.* Ausflug (*m*).
Ramble, *n.* Fusstour (*f*), Ausflug (*m*): *v.* Wandern.
Rancid, *adj.* Ranzig.
Rancour, *n.* Groll (*m*).
Random, *adj.* Zufällig.
At random, aufs Geradewohl.
Range, *n.* Umfang (limits) (*m*), Kochherd (cooking) (*m*), Schussweite (firing) (*f*), Gebirgskette (of mountains) (*f*).
Rank, *n.* Rang (*m*), Reihe (*f*), Linie (*f*): *adj.* Stark, ranzig.
Rank and file, Rang und Glied.
Ransack, *v.* Plündern, durchsuchen.
Ransom, *n.* Lösegeld: *v.* Loskaufen.
Rap, *n.* Deut (*m*), Heller (*m*), Klopfen (*n*): *v.* Klopfen.
Rapacious, *adj.* Raubgierig.
Rapacity, *n.* Raubgier (*f*)
Rape, *n.* Notzucht (*f*), Raub (*m*): *v.* Rauben.
Rapid, *adj.* Reissend, schnell.
Rapidity, *n.* Schneligkeit (*f*).
Rapier, *n.* Rapier (*n*), Stossdegen (*m*).
Rapture, *n.* Entzücken (*n*).
Rare, *adj.* Selten, kostbar.
Rascal, *n.* Schurke (*m*), Schelm (*m*).
Rash, *adj.* Unbesonnen: *n.* Hautausschlag (skin) (*m*).
Rasher, *n.* Schnitte (*f*).
Raspberry, *n.* Himbeere (*f*).
Rat, *n.* Ratte (*f*).
Rate, *n.* Geschwindigkeit (how fast) (*f*), Kurs (of exchange) (*m*), Preis (cost) (*m*): *v.* Taxieren.
Rather, *adv.* Lieber, ziemlich, vielmehr.
Ratify, *v.* Ratifizieren.
Ration, *n.* Ration (*f*).
Rattle, *n.* Geklapper (*n*), Röcheln (*n*), Klirren (*n*): *v.* Klappern, rasseln.
Rattlesnake, *n.* Klapperschlange (*f*).
Ravage, *v.* Verwüsten.
Rave, *v.* Rasen, wüten.
Raven, *n.* Rabe (*m*).
Ravenous, *adj.* Gierig.
Ravine, *n.* Schlucht (*f*).

Raw, *adj.* Roh.
Ray, *n.* Strahl (*m*).
Raze, *v.* Schleifen.
Razor, *n.* Rasiermesser (*n*).
Safety razor, Rasierapparat (*m*).
Reach, *v.* Reichen, erreichen, erlangen, überreichen.
Read, *v.* Lesen, vorlesen.
Readable, *adj.* Lesbar.
Reader, *n.* Leser (*m*).
Reading-room, *n.* Lesezimmer (*n*).
Ready, *adj.* Bereit, fertig, baar.
Real, *adj.* Echt, sächlich.
Realize, *v.* Ausführen, verwirklichen,.
Really, *adv.* Wirklich.
Realm, *n.* Reich (*n*).
Reap, *v.* Einernten, schneiden.
Reaper, *n.* Schnitter (*m*).
Rear, *n.* Nachtrab (*m*), Hintergründ (*m*): *v.* Aufrichten.
Reason, *n.* Ursache (*f*), Vernunft (*f*): *v.* Erörtern.
Reasonable, *adj.* Vernünftig.
Rebel, *n.* Rebell (*m*).
Rebellion, *n.* Empörung (*f*).
Rebuke, *v.* Tadeln; *n.* Tadel (*m*).
Recede, *v.* Zurückweichen.
Receipt, *n.* Empfang (*m*), Quittung (*f*).
Receive, *v.* Empfangen.
Recent, *adj.* Neu, frisch.
Recently, *adv.* Neulich.
Recipe, *n.* Recept (*n*), Rezept (*n*).
Recital, *n.* Aufzählung (*f*).
Recite, *v.* Erzählen, hersagen, vortragen.
Reckless, *adj.* Tollkühn.
Reckon, *v.* Rechnen.
Reckoning, *n.* Rechnen (*n*).
Reclaim, *v.* Bekehren.
Recline, *v.* Sich lehnen.
Recognise, *v.* Wiedererkennen.
Recognition, *n.* Wiedererkennung (*f*).
Recoil, *v.* Zurückprallen.
Recollect, *v.* Wieder sammeln, sich erinnern.
Recollection, *n.* Erinnerung (*f*).
Recommence, *v.* Wiederanfangen.
Recommend, *v.* Empfehlen.
Recompense, *v.* Entschädigen.
Reconcile, *v.* Versöhnen.

Record, *n.* Rekord (outstanding feat) (*m*), Schallplatte (gramophone) (*f*), Bericht (*m*), Protokoll (*n*): *v.* Registrieren.
Recount, *v.* Erzählen.
Recover, *v.* Wiederbekommen.
Recovery, *n.* Wiederherstellung (*f*).
Recreation, *n.* Erhdung (*f*).
Recruit, *n.* Rekrut (*m*).
Rectangle, *n.* Rechteck (*n*).
Rectify, *v.* Berichtigen.
Rector, *n.* Rektor (*m*), Pfarrer (*m*), Vorsteher (*m*).
Recuperate, *v.* Sich erholen, wiederherstellen.
Recur, *v.* Zurückkommen.
Red, *adj.* Rot.
Redbreast, *n.* Rotkehlchen (*n*).
Red-currant, *n.* Rote Johannisbeere (*f*).
Redeem, *v.* Bussen, erfüllen, einlösen.
Red-lead, *n.* Mennig (*m*).
Redress, *n.* Abhilfe (*f*), Ersatz (*m*).
Reduce, *v.* Verkleinern, verwandeln.
Reduction, *n.* Rabatt (*m*), Zurückführung (*f*).
Reed, *n.* Flöte (*f*), Schilfrohr (*n*).
Reef, *n.* Reff (*n*), Riff (*n*).
Reek, *v.* Rauchen.
Reel, *n.* Haspel (*m*), Rolle *f*), Tanz (*m*): *v.* Haspeln.
Refer, *v.* Beziehen, sich berufen.
Referee, *n.* Schiedsrichter (*m*).
Reference, *n.* Bezugnahme (*f*), Beziehung (*f*).
Refine, *v.* Raffinieren.
Reflect, *v.* Zurückwerfen.
Reflection, *n.* Zurückstrahlung (*f*).
Reflector, *n.* Reflektor (*m*).
Reform, *v.* Umbilden, umändern: *n.* Reform (*f*).
Reformatory, *n.* Besserungsanstalt (*f*).
Refrain, *v.* Zügeln, sich enthalten: *n.* Refrain (*m*).
Refresh, *v.* Erfrischen, auffrischen.
Refreshment, *n.* Erfrischung (*f*).
Refrigerate, *v.* Kühlen.
Refrigerator, *n.* Eisschrank (*m*), Kühlgefäss (*n*).
Refuge, *n.* Rettungsinsel (*f*).

Refugee, n. Flüchtling (m).
Refund, v. Zurückzahlen.
Refusal, n. Verweigerung (f), Vorkaufsrecht (n).
Refuse, v. Verweigern, verwerfen.
Regal, adj. Königlich.
Regard, n. Blick (m), Achtung (f), Ansicht (f): v. Achten, betrachten, ansehen.
  Kind regards, Herzliche Grüsse.
Regardless, adj. Unachtsam, ungeachtet.
Regenerate, v. Neu beleben.
Regeneration, n. Neubildung (f).
Regiment, n. Regiment (n), Schar (f).
Region, n. Gegend (f).
Register, n. Register (n), Verzeichnis (n).
Registration, n. Eintragung (f).
Registry-office, n. Standesamt (n).
Regret, v. Bedauern; n. Bedauern (n), Kummer (m).
Regular, adj. Regelmassig.
Regulate, v. Ordnen, regulieren.
Regulation, n. Vorschrift (f), Anordnung (f).
Rehearsal, n. Aufsagen (n), Probe (f).
Rehearse, v. Proben, probieren.
Reign, v. Regieren; n. Regierung (f).
Rein, n. Zügel (m).
Reindeer, n. Renntier (n).
Reject, v. Verwerfen.
Rejoice, v. Sich freuen.
Rejoicing, n. Frohlocken (n).
Rejuvenate, v. Verjüngen.
Relapse, v. Zurückfallen: n. Rückfall (m).
Relate, v. Erzählen.
Relation, n. Bericht (m).
Relax, v. Erschlaffen, nachlassen, lockern.
Relay, v. Übertragen (wireless).
Release, v. Freilassen.
Reliable, adj. Zuverlässig, verlässlich.
Reliance, n. Vertrauen (n).
Relic, n. Überbleibsel (n).
Relief, n. Erleichterung (f).
Relieve, v. Erleichtern.
Religion, n. Religion (f).

Religious, adj. Religiös.
Relinquish, v. Aufgeben.
Relish, v. Schmecken, gefallen: n. Geschmack (m).
Reluctant, adj. Unwillig.
Rely, v. Vertrauen, sich verlassen.
Remain, v. Bleiben.
Remainder, n. Rest (m).
Remand, v. Zurückstellen.
Remark, n. Bemerkung (f) v. Bemerken.
Remarkable, adj. Bemerkenswert.
Remedy, n. Heilmittel (n): v. Heilen, abhelfen.
Remember, v. Sich erinnern.
Remembrance, n. Erinnerung (f).
Remind, v. Erinnern, mahnen.
Reminder, n. Mahnung (f).
Remit, v. Remittieren, vermindern, nachlassen.
Remittance, n. Rimesse (f), Überweisung (f).
Remnant, n. Überrest (m).
Remonstrate, v. Einwendungen machen, vorstellungen machen.
Remorse, n. Gewissensbiss (m), Reue (f).
Remote, adj. Entfernt, entlegen.
Removal, n. Umzug (m). Absetzung (f), Ausziehen (n).
Remove, v. Umziehen, absetzen, ausziehen.
Remunerate, v. Belohnen.
Remuneration, n. Belohnung (f).
Rend, v. Zerreissen.
Render, v. Leisten, übersetzen, erweisen.
Renewal, n. Erneuerung (f).
Renounce, v. Abschwören, entsagen, verzichten.
Renovate, v. Renovieren, erneuern.
Renown, n. Ruhm (m), Ruf (m).
Renowned, adj. Berühmt.
Rent, n. Riss (torn) (m), Rente (f): v. Mieten, pachten.
Rental, n. Mietertrag (m).
Reorganize, v. Reorganisieren, neugestalten.
Repair, v. Ersetzen, repaieren: n. Reparatur (f).
Repeal, v. Aufheben.
Repeat, v. Wiederholen.

Repel, v. Zurückschlagen, zurückstossen.
Repent, v. Bereuen.
Repentance, n. Russe (f).
Repetition, n. Hersagen (n), Wiederholung (f).
Replace, v. Ersetzen.
Replenish, v. Wieder anfüllen.
Reply, v. Erwidern: n. Antwort (f), Erwiderung (f).
Report, n. Gerücht (n), Bericht (m), Nachricht (f), Ruf (m): v. Berichten, verbreiten, melden.
Repose, n. Ruhe (f); v. Ruhen.
Represent, v. Darstllen, schildern.
Representative, n. Vertreter (m).
Reprieve, v. Begnadigen, frist geben: n. Begnadigung (f).
Reprisal, n. Repressalie (f).
Reproach, v. Vorwerfen: n. Vorwurf (m).
Reproduce, v. Reproduzieren, nachbilden.
Reproduction, n. Reproduktion (f), Nachbildung (f).
Reprove, v. Tadeln.
Reptile, n. Kriechtier (n), Reptil (n).
Republic, n. Republik (f).
Repudiate, v. Verstossen, ableugnen.
Repugnant, adj. Zuwider, widerspenstig.
Repulse, v. Zurückschlagen.
Reputation, n. Ruf (m), gute Name (m).
Repute, v. Achten, halten fur: n. Ruf (m).
Request, n. Bitte (f), Nachfrage (f): v. Bitten.
Require, v. Verlangen, brauchen, fordern.
Requirement, n. Forderung (f).
Requisite, adj. Erforderlich: n. Erforderniss (n).
Requite, v. Vergelten, belohnen.
Rescind, v. Aufheben.
Rescue, v. Befreien, retten: n. Befreiung (f), Retung (f).
Resemblance, n. Ebenbild (n).
Resemble, v. Vergleichen.
Resent, v. Ahnden, übelnehmen.
Resentful, adj. Empfindlich.

Reservation, n. Vorbehalt (m).
Reserve, v. Zurückhalten.
Reserved, adj. Zurückhaltend.
Reservoir, n. Behälter (m).
Reside, v. Wohnen.
Residence, n. Wohnsitz (m).
Resign, v. Entsagen, abtreten.
Resignation, n. Abtretung (f), Ergebung (f).
Resist, v. Widerstehen.
Resistance, n. Widerstand (m).
Resolute, adj. Entschlossen.
Resolution, n. Auflösung (f).
Resolve, v. Beschliessen: (n), Beschluss (m).
Resort, n. Zusammenkunftsort (m), Kurort (health) (m).
Resource, n. Hilfsmittel (n).
Respect, n. Achtung (f), Rücksicht (f): v. Achten.
Respectability, n. Achtbarkeit (f).
Respectable, adj. Achtbar.
Respiration, n. Atmen (f).
Respire, v. Atmen.
Respite, n. Frist (f); v. Verschieben.
Respond, v. Entsprechen, antworten.
Response, n. Antwort (f).
Responsibility, n. Verantwortung (f).
Rest, n. Ruhe (quiet) (f), Schlaf (sleep) (m), Rest (the part left) (m), Rast (f): v. Ruhen, rasten.
Restaurant, n. Restaurant (n).
Restless, adj. Schlaflos.
Restore, v. Wiedergeben.
Restrain, v. Einschränken.
Restrict, v. Einschränken.
Restriction, n. Einschränkung (f).
Result, n. Resultat (n), Ergebnis (n), Folge (f): v. Erfolgen.
Resume, v. Zurücknehmen.
Resurrection, n. Auferstehung (f).
Retail, n. Detail (m), Kleinhandel (m): v. Im Kleinhandel verkaufen.
Retailer, n. Kleinhändler (m).
Retain, v. Behalten, bestellen.
Retard, v. Verzögern.
Reticent, adj. Schweigsam.
Retire, v. Sich zurückziehen.
Retirement, n. Zurückgezogenheit (f).
Retract, v. Widerrufen.

**Retreat, ** v. Sich zurückziehen: n. Rückzug (m).
**Retrieve, ** v. Wieder ersetzen.
**Retriever, ** n. Stöberhund (m).
**Return, ** v. Wiederkommen, zurückkommen, zurückgehen, zurückgeben: n. Rückkehr (f), Rückfall (m).
**Return ticket, ** n. Rückfahrkarte (f).
**Reveal, ** v. Enthüllen, offenbaren.
**Revel, ** v. Schwärmen: n. Schwärmen (n).
**Revelation, ** n. Offenbarung (f).
**Revenge, ** n. Rache (f); v. Rächen.
**Revenue, ** n. Ertrag (m), Einkünfte (f).
**Reverence, ** n. Ehrerbietung (f).
**Reverse, ** v. Umkehren, umstossen, umsteuern.
**Revert, ** v. Zurückwerfen.
**Review, ** v. Mustern (military, etc.), betrachten (think over), rezensieren (literary criticism): n. Übersicht (f), Revue (theatrical) (f), Heerschau (military, etc.) (f).
**Revise, ** v. Durchsehen.
**Revive, ** v. Wieder beleben, wieder aufleben.
**Reviver, ** n. Beleber (m).
**Revoke, ** v. Nicht bekennen (at cards), widerrufen.
**Revolt, ** n. Abfall (m): v. Sich empören.
**Revolution, ** n. Umlauf (m), Umdrehung (f).
**Revolve, ** v. Sich drehen.
**Revolver, ** n. Revolver (m).
**Reward, ** n. Belohnung (f); v. Belohnen.
**Rheumatism, ** n. Rheumatismus (m).
**Rhinoceros, ** n. Nashorn (n).
**Rhododendron, ** n. Rhododendron (n), Alpenrose (f).
**Rhubarb, ** n. Rhabarber (m).
**Rhyme, ** n. Reim (m), Vers (m): v. Reimen.
**Rib, ** n. Rippe (f), Inholz (n).
**Ribbon, ** n. Band (n).
**Rice, ** n. Reis (m).
**Rich, ** adj. Reich, nahrhaft, fett.
**Riches, ** n. Reichtum (m).
**Rick, ** n. Schober (m).
**Rickets, ** n. Englische Krankheit (f).

**Rid, ** v. Befreien, wegschaffen.
 **To get rid of, ** Loswerden.
**Riddle, ** n. Rätsel (n): v. Sieben, durchsieben.
**Ride, ** v. Reiten, fahren: n. Reiter (m), Fahrt (f).
**Rider, ** n. Reiter (m).
**Ridge, ** n. Grat (m), Kamm (m).
**Ridicule, ** v. Lächerlich machen.
**Ridiculous, ** adj. Lächerlich.
**Rifle, ** n. Büchse (f), Gewehr (n): v. Berauben, plündern.
**Rig, ** n. Takelung (f), Streich (m), Putz (m): v. Takeln.
**Right, ** adj. Gerade, recht: n. Recht (n).
 **All right, ** Ganz gut, schön.
 **On the right, ** Rechts.
 **To be right, ** Recht haben.
**Rigid, ** adj. Fest, starr, steif, streng.
**Rigorous, ** adj. Genau, streng.
**Rigour, ** n. Strenge (f).
**Rill, ** n. Bach (m).
**Rim, ** n. Rand (m).
**Rind, ** n. Rinde (f).
**Ring, ** n. Ring (m), Kreis (m): v. Klingeln.
**Ringworm, ** n. Ringelflechte (f).
**Rinse, ** v. Spülen.
**Riot, ** n. Schwelgerei (f).
**Rip, ** v. Aufschlitzen, auftrennen.
**Ripe, ** adj. Reif.
**Ripen, ** v. Reifen.
**Ripple, ** n. Kräuseln (n).
**Rise, ** n. Steigung (f), Zulage (in money) (f), Aufgehen (sun) (f): v. Steigen, sich erheben (revolution), aufstehen (get up).
**Risk, ** n. Risiko (n); v. Riskieren.
**Rival, ** n. Rivale (m), Konkurrent (m).
**River, ** n. Fluss (m), Strom (m).
**Roach, ** n. Rotauge (n).
**Road, ** n. Strasse (f), Landstrasse (f).
**Roam, ** v. Durchwandern, umherwandern.
**Roar, ** v. Brüllen, brausen, larmen: n. Gebrüll.
**Roast, ** v. Braten, rösten; adj. Gebraten.
**Roast beef, ** n. Roastbeef (n), Rinderbraten (m).
**Rob, ** v. Berauben, bestehlen.
**Robber, ** n. Räuber (m).

Robbery, n. Diebstahl (m), Räuberei (f).
Robe, n. Kleid (n), lange Rock (m), Talar (m).
Robin, n. Rotkehlchen (n).
Robust, adj. Rüstig, kräftig.
Rock, n. Felsen (m), Klippe (f): v. Schaukeln.
Rocking-chair, n. Schaukelstuhl (m).
Rod, n. Stange (m), Rute (f).
Roe, n. Fischrogen (fish) (m), Reh (deer) (n).
Rogue, n. Schurke (m).
Roll, v. Rollen, strecken, einwickeln: n. Rolle (as on a boat) (f), Brötchen (of bread) (f), Schnecke (tube) (f).
Romance, n. Romanze (f).
Romp, v. Ausgelassen sein: n. Wildfang (m).
Roof, n. Dach (n).
Rook, n. Saatkrähe (f).
Room, n. Zimmer (n), Stelle (f), Raum (m).
Roost, v. Schlafen, aufsitzen: n. Hühnerstange (f).
Root, n. Wurzel (f), Ursprung (m): v. Wühlen.
Rope, n. Seil (n), Tau (n): v. Anseilen.
Rose, n. Ros (f).
Rot, v. Faulen, vermoden: n. Fäulnis (f).
Rotate, v. Rotieren.
Rotten, adj. Faul, verfault, übel.
Rough, adj. Rauh, grob, roh.
Roughness, n. Roheit (f), Grobheit (f).
Round, adj. Rund: n. Runde (f).
Rouse, v. Erzürnen (make bad tempered), aufwecken (wake up).
Rout, v. In die Flucht schlagen.
Route, n. Route (f), Weg (m).
Row, v. Rudern.
Row, n. Lärm (noise) (m).
Royal, adj. Königlich.
Royalty, n. Königshaus (n).
Rub, v. Reiben, abwischen.
Rubber, n. Radiergummi (india rubber) (m), Kautschuk (m), Reibzeug (n).
Rubbish, n. Unsinn (m), Schutt (m).
Rudder, n. Ruder (n).

Rude, adj. Unhöflich (impolite), grob (coarse).
Ruffle, v. Kräuseln, verwirren.
Rug, n. Vorleger (m), Brucke (f).
Rugged, adj. Rauh.
Ruin, n. Ruine (f); v. Ruinieren.
Rule, n. Regel (f), Ordnung (f): v. Regeln, herrschen.
Ruler, n. Herrscher (m), Lineal (n).
Rum, n. Rum (m).
Rumble, v. Rumpeln.
Rumour, n. Gerücht (n): v. Aussprengen.
Rumpsteak, n. Rumpsteak (n).
Run, v. Laufen, rennen, fliessen, fliehen: n. Lauf (m).
Runner, n. Läufer (m), Kufe (f).
Running, adj. Laufend, strömend, fliessend.
Rupture, n. Bruch (m): v. Brechen.
Rural, adj. Ländlich.
Rush, v. Stürzen: n. Andrang (m), Gedränge (of people) (n), Rauschen (of water) (n), Binse (plant) (f).
Rust, n. Rost (m): v. Rosten.
Rustle, v. Rauschen.
Rusty, adj. Rostig.
Rut, n. Brunst (f), Furche (f), Geleise (n).
Rye, n. Roggen (m).

S

Sack, n. Sack (bag) (m), Plünderung (by soldiers) (f) v. Plündern.
Sacred, adj. Helig.
Sacrifice, n. Opfer (m): v. Opfern.
Sad, adj. Traurig.
Saddle, n. Sattel (m).
Sadness, n. Traurigkeit (f).
Safe, adj. Sicher: n. Geldschrank (m), Tresor (m).
Safety, n. Sicherheit (f).
Safety pin, n. Sicherheitsnadel (f).
Safety-razor, n. Rasierapparat (m).
Sag, v. Sacken.
Sagacious, adj. Scharfsichtig, scharfsinnig.
Sage, adj. Klug, weise: n. Weise (clever) (m), Salbei (plant) (f).

Sail   161   **Scent**

Sail, *n.* Segel (*n*), Schiff (*n*): *v.* Segeln, befahren.
Sailor, *n.* Matrose (*m*).
Saint, *n.* Heilige (*m. or f.*).
Salad, *n.* Salat (*m*).
Salary, *n.* Besoldung (*f*), Gehalt (*n*).
Sale, *n.* Verkauf (*m*), Absatz (*m*), Ausverkauf (*m*).
Saliva, *n.* Speichel (*m*).
Sallow, *adj.* Blass: *n.* Salweide (*f*).
Salmon, *n.* Lachs (*m*), Salm (*m*).
Saloon, *n.* Salon (*m*), erste Klasse (*f*).
Dining Saloon, Speisesaal (*m*).
Salt, *n.* Salz (*n*).
Salt-cellar, *n.* Salzfass (*n*).
Salutation, *n.* Grüssen (*n*).
Salute, *v.* Grüssen: *n.* Gruss (*m*), Salut (*m*).
Salvage, *n.* Bergung (*f*).
Salvation, *n.* Seligkeit (*f*), Rettung (*f*).
Salvation Army, *n.* Heilsarmee (*f*).
Same, *adj.* Derselbe, dieselbe, dasselbe, gleich, nämliche.
Sample, *n.* Probe (*f*), Muster (*n*): *v.* Probe nehmen.
Sanctify, *v.* Heiligen.
Sanction, *v.* Bestätigen: *n.* Bestätigung (*f*).
Sanctuary, *n.* Heligthum (*n*).
Sand, *n.* Sand (*m*).
Sanguine, *adj.* Blutreich, sanguinisch.
Sanitation, *n.* Schaffung (*f*), Hygiene (*f*).
Sanity, *n.* Gesundheit (*f*).
Sap, *n.* Saft (*m*).
Sapper, *n.* Sappeur (*m*).
Sapphire, *n.* Saphir (*m*).
Sarcasm, *n.* Bittere Spott (*m*).
Sarcastic, *adj.* Beissend, sarcastisch.
Sardine, *n.* Sardine (*f*).
Sash, *n.* Schärpe (belt) (*f*), Schiebefenster (window) (*n*).
Satchel, *n.* Tasche (*f*).
Satin, *n.* Atlas (*m*).
Satisfaction, *n.* Befriedigung (*f*).
Satisfactory, *adj.* Befriedigend.
Satisfied, *adj.* Befriedigt.
Satisfy, *v.* Befriedigen.

Saturate, *v.* Sättigen.
Saturday, *n.* Samstag (*m*).
Sauce, *n.* Sauce (*f*), Brühe (*f*).
Saucepan, *n.* Kochtopf (*m*).
Saucer, *n.* Untertasse (*f*).
Saucy, *adj.* Unverschämt.
Saunter, *v.* Schlendern.
Sausage, *n.* Wurst (*f*).
Savage, *adj.* Wilde, grausam: *n.* Wilde (*m*).
Save, *v.* Bergen, retten, ersparen, sparen.
Saving, *adj.* Sparsam: *n.* Rettung (*f*).
Savings, *n.* Ersparnisse (*f. pl.*).
Savings-bank, *n.* Sparkasse (*f*).
Saviour, *n.* Heiland (*m*).
Savoy cabbage, *n.* Wirsingkohl (*m*).
Saw, *n.* Säge (*f*), Spruch (*m*): *v.* Sägen.
Say, *v.* Sagen.
Scab, *n.* Krätze (*f*).
Scaffold, *n.* Gerüst (building erection) (*n*), Schaffot (for executions) (*n*).
Scald, *v.* Verbrühen.
Scale, *n.* Masstab (weighing) (*m*), Schuppe (on fish) (*f*), Tonleiter (musical) (*f*); *v.* Besteigen, abblättern.
Scallop, *n.* Kammmuschel (sea) (*f*).
Scalp, *n.* Kopfhaut (*f*).
Scandal, *n.* Skandal (*m*), Lästerung (*f*).
Scanty, *adj.* Knapp, sparsam, karg.
Scar, *n.* Narbe (*f*).
Scarce, *adj.* Spärlich, rar, selten.
Scarcely, *adv.* Kaum.
Scare, *n.* Panik (*f*): *v.* Erschrecken.
Scarf, *n.* Binde (*f*), Halsbinde (*f*), Halstuch (*n*).
Scarlet, *adj.* Scharlachrot.
Scarlet-fever, *n.* Scharlachfieber (*n*).
Scatter, *v.* Zerstreuen.
Scavenger, *n.* Strassenkehrer (*m*).
Scene, *n.* Szene (*f*), Bühne (*f*), Auftritt (*m*).
Scenery, *n.* Landschaft (*f*).
Scent, *n.* Geruch (the smell) (*m*), Parfüm (perfume) (*n*): *v.* Durchduften, parfümieren.

L

Scheme — Seed

Scheme, *n.* Plan (*m*), Schema (*m*): *v.* Planen.
Scholar, *n.* Schüler (*m*), Gelehrte (*m*).
School, *n.* Schule (*f*).
Schoolmaster, *n.* Schullehrer (*m*), Lehrer (*m*).
Schoolmistress, *n.* Lehrerin (*f*).
Schooner, *n.* Schoner (*m*).
Sciatica, *n.* Ischias (*f*).
Science, *n.* Wissenschaft (*f*).
Scissors, *n.* Schere (*f*).
Scoff, *v.* Spotten, verspotten.
Scold, *v.* Schelten, zanken.
Scoop, *n.* Schüppe (*f*), Schaufel (*f*).
Scorch, *v.* Sengen, brennen, ausdorren.
Score, *n.* Kerbe (*f*), Kerbholz (*n*), Partitur (*f*): *v.* Kerben (to make marks on), aufzeichnen (reckoning).
Scorn, *n.* Spott (*m*): *v.* Verachten.
Scornful, *adj.* Verächtlich.
Scoundrel, *n.* Schurke (*m*).
Scour, *v.* Scheuern.
Scourge, *n.* Geissel (*f*), Plage (*f*), Strafe (*f*).
Scout, *n.* Späher (*m*). Boy Scout, Pfadfinder (*m*).
Scowl, *v.* Finster blicken, finster aussehen.
Scramble, *n.* Gereisse (*n*), Raffen (*n*): *v.* Klettern. Scrambled eggs, Rühreier (*n. pl.*).
Scrap, *n.* Stück (*n*), Stückchen (*n*); *v.* Abschaffen.
Scrape, *v.* Kratzen, schaben, scharren.
Scratch, *v.* Kratzen, streichen (in games): *n.* Schramme (*f*).
Scream, *v.* Kreischen, schreien: *n.* Schrei (*m*).
Screen, *n.* Schirm (*m*), Leinwand (cinema) (*f*), Feuerschirm (fire) (*m*). Windscreen, Windschutz (*m*).
Screw, *n.* Schraube (*f*).
Screwdriver, *n.* Schraubenzieher (*m*).
Scribble, *v.* Kritzeln: *n.* Gekritzel (*n*).
Scribe, *n.* Schreiber (*m*).
Scripture, *n.* Heilige Schrift (*f*).
Scrub, *v.* Scheuern.

Scullery, *n.* Spülraum (*m*), Aufwaschraum (*m*).
Sculptor, *n.* Bildhauer (*m*).
Scum, *n.* Schaum (*m*).
Scurf, *n.* Schorf (*m*).
Scurry, *v.* Danhineilen.
Scurvy, *n.* Skorbut (*m*).
Scuttle, *n.* Kohlenkasten (*m*).
Scythe, *n.* Sense (*f*).
Sea, *n.* Meer (*n*), See (*f*).
Seagull, *n.* Möwe (*f*).
Seal, *n.* Siegel (enclose) (*n*), Seehund (animal) (*m*): *v.* Siegeln.
Sealing-wax, *n.* Siegellack (*m*).
Seam, *n.* Saum (clothes, etc.) (*m*), Lager (geology) (*n*).
Seaman, *n.* Seemann (*m*).
Seaplane, *n.* Wasserflugzeug (*n*).
Search, *v.* Suchen, prüfen: *n.* Suchen (*n*).
Searchlight, *n.* Scheinwerfer (*m*).
Seasickness, *n.* Seekrankheit (*f*).
Season, *n.* Jahreszeit (*f*), Saison (*f*): *v.* Würzen.
Season-ticket, *n.* Dauerkarte (*f*), Abonnementskarte (*f*).
Seat, *n.* Sitz (*m*), Stuhl (*m*), Sitzplatz (*m*): *v.* Setzen.
Seaweed, *n.* Alge (*f*), Tang (*m*).
Second, *n.* Sekunde (*f*); *adj.* Der zweite, die zweite, das zweite: *v.* Befürworten.
Secondhand, *adj.* Aus zweiter Hand.
Secret, *n.* Geheimnis (*n*): *adj.* Geheim.
Secretary, *n.* Sekretär (*m*), Sekretärin (*f*).
Sect, *n.* Sekte (*f*).
Section, *n.* Abschnitt (*m*), Abteilung (*f*), Strecke (*f*).
Secure, *v.* Sichern, befestigen: *adj.* Sicher.
Securities (stocks, shares, etc.), *n.* Wertpapiere (*n. pl.*).
Security, *n.* Sicherheit (*f*).
Sedate, *adj.* Ruhig, gesetzt.
Sedentary, *adj.* Sesshaft, sitzend.
Sediment, *n.* Bodensatz (*m*).
Sedition, *n.* Aufstand (*m*), Aufruhr (*m*).
See, *v.* Sehen, aufmerken, sorgen, besuchen.
Seed, *n.* Same (*m*), Saat (*f*).

Seek — Shatter

Seek, v. Suchen, begehren, trachten.
Seem, v. Scheinen.
Seethe, v. Sieden.
Seize, v. Ergreifen, einziehen.
Seizure, n. Verhaftung (f), Ergreifung (f), Anfall (illness) (m).
Seldom, adv. Selten.
Select, v. Wählen, auslesen: adj. Exklusiv.
Selection, n. Auswahl (f), Auszug (m).
Self, pn. & adj. Selbst.
Selfish, adj. Selbstsüchtig.
Self-starter, n. Anlasser (m).
Sell, v. Verkaufen, handeln.
Seller, n. Verkäufer (m. or f.).
Send, v. Senden, schicken, übersenden.
Senior, n. Aeltere (m): adj. Alter.
Sensation, n. Sensation (f), Eindruck (m), Gefühl (f).
Sense, n. Sinn (m), Gefühl (n), Verstand (m).
Senseless, adj. Sinnlos, bewusstlos.
Sensible, adj. Sinnlich, klug.
Sensitive, adj. Fuhlbar, empfindlich.
Sensual, adj. Sinnlich.
Sentence, n. Satz (grammar) m., Urteil (legal) (n).
Sentiment, n. Gefühl (n).
Sentry, n. Schildwache (f).
Separate, v. Trennen, absondern: adj. Getrennt.
Separately, adv. Besonders.
Separation, n. Trennung (f).
September, n. September (m).
Septic, adj. Septisch.
Sequel, n. Folge (f), Erfolg (m).
Serene, adj. Heiter.
Serge, n. Serge (f), Sarsche (f).
Sergeant, n. Feldwebel (m).
Serious, adj. Ernsthaft, ernstlich.
Sermon, n. Predigt (f).
Serpent, n. Schlange (f).
Servant, n. Diener (m), Dienstmädchen (n).
Serve, v. Dienen, servieren, anspielen.
Servile, adj. Niedrig, kriechend.
Servitude, n. Knechtschaft (f), Sclaverei (f).

Set, v. Setzen, stellen, legen, schärfen, geben, abziehen fassen: n. Satz (m), Reihe (f), Untergang (m).
Settle, v. Vermachen (money on), entscheiden (make up one's mind), begleichen (pay a debt).
Settlement, n. Festsetzung (f), Begleichung (f), Siedlung (of people) (f), Senken (n).
Seven, adj. Sieben.
Seventeen, adj. Siebzehn.
Seventy, adj. Siebzig.
Sever, v. Trennen.
Several, adj. Besonder, mehrere.
Severe, adj. Streng, heftig.
Severity, n. Strenge (f), Ernst (m), Härte (f).
Sew, v. Nähen, heften.
Sewer, n. Schleuse (f), Abzugskanal (m).
Sex, n. Geschlecht (n).
Sexton, n. Küster (m).
Shabby, adj. Lumpig.
Shade, n. Schatten (m): v. Beschatten.
Shadow, n. Schatten (m).
Shaft, n. Schaft (m), Helm (m), Pfeil (m).
Shake, n. Ershutterung (f).
Shallow, adj. Seicht.
Sham, v. Betrügen; adj. Falsch.
Shame, n. Scham (f).
Shameful, adj. Schändlich.
Shampoo, n. Shamponieren (n).
Shamrock, n. Klee (m).
Shape, n. Form (f): v. Formen.
Shapeless, adj. Unförmlich.
Share, v. Teilen: n. Teil (m), Aktie (f), Anteil (m).
  Ordinary share, Stammaktie (f).
  Preference share, Vorzugsaktie (f).
Shareholder, Aktionär (m).
Shark, n. Haifisch (m).
Sharp, adj. Scharf, spitzig. scharfsinnig: n. Dur (music) (n), Kreuz (music) (n).
Sharpen, v. Schärfen, erhöhen, wetzen.
Sharpness, n. Schärfe (f), Strenge (f).
Shatter, v. Zerschmettern, zerrütten.

Shave — Shudder

Shave, *v.* Rasieren, schaben, scheren.
Shaving, *n.* Rasieren (*n*).
Shaving-brush, *n.* Rasierpinsel (*m*).
Shaving-soap, *n.* Rasierseife (*f*).
Shawl, *n.* Schal (*m*).
She, *pron.* Sie.
Shed, *n.* Schuppen (*m*): *v.* Vergiessen, verlieren (moult, etc.).
Sheep, *n.* Schaf (*n*).
Sheet, *n.* Bogen (of paper) (*m*), Bettuch (on bed) (*n*), Platte (of metal) (*f*).
Shelf, *n.* Brett (*n*), Fach (*n*), Regal (*n*).
Shell, *n.* Schale (*f*), Hülse (*f*), Granate (*f*), Geschoss (guns) (*n*): *v.* Schälen.
Shell-fish, *n.* Schaltier (*n*).
Shell-proof, *adj.* Bombensicher.
Shelter, *n.* Obdach (*n*): *v.* Decken.
Shepherd, *n.* Schäfer (*m*).
Sherry, *n.* Sherry (*m*).
Shield, *n.* Schild (*m*): *v.* Bedecken.
Shift, *v.* Wechseln.
Shin, *n.* Schienbein (*n*).
Shine, *v.* Scheinen: *n.* Schein (*m*).
Shingle, *n.* Schindel (*f*), Kiesel (*m*): *v.* Kurz scheren (the hair).
Ship, *n.* Schiff (*n*): *v.* Verschiffen.
Shipment, *n.* Ladung (*f*), Verschiffung (*f*).
Shipwreck, *n.* Schiffbruch (*m*).
Shirk, *v.* Vermeiden.
Shirt, *n.* Hemd (*n*).
Shiver, *v.* Zittern, zerbrechen.
Shoal, *n.* Schwarm (*m*).
Shock, *n.* Stoss (*m*), Schreck (*m*): *v.* Anstoss geben.
Shock-absorber, *n.* Stossdämpfer (*m*).
Shocking, *adj.* Anstossig.
Shoddy, *adj.* Schlechte, geringwertig.
Shoe, *n.* Schuh (*m*), Hufeisen (horse) (*n*).
Shoe-maker, *n.* Schuhmacher (*m*).
Shoot, *v.* Schiessen, erschiessen (shoot dead): *n.* Schuss (*m*), Schössing (*m*).
Shooting, *n.* Jagd (*f*), Schiessen (*n*).
Shop, *n.* Laden (*m*).
Shop-girl, *n.* Ladenmädchen (*n*).
Shop-keeper, *n.* Ladeninhaber (*m*).
Shopping, *n.* Einkaufen (*n*), Ladenbesuch (*m*).
Shore, *n.* Gestade (*n*), Strand (*m*), Ufer (*n*).
Short, *adj.* Kurz, beschränkgt, klein, knapp.
Shortage, *n.* Mangel (*m*).
Shorthand, *n.* Kurzschrift (*f*).
Shortly, *adv.* Bald, kurz, kürzlich.
Short-sighted, *adj.* Kurzsichtig.
Shot, *n.* Schuss (*m*), Schrot (*m.* or *n.*), Kugel (*f*).
Shoulder, *n.* Achsel (*f*), Schulter (*f*): *v.* Schultern.
Shout, *v.* Schreien: *n.* Schrei (*m*).
Shovel, *n.* Schaufel (*f*): *v.* Schaufeln.
Show, *n.* Schau (*f*), Ausstellung (*f*), Vorstellung (*f*): *v.* Zeigen, beweisen.
Shower, *n.* Schauer (*m*).
Shower-bath, *n.* Dusche (*f*).
Showery, *adj.* Regnerisch.
Shred, *v.* Zerfetzen: *n.* Fetzen (*m*).
Shrew, *n.* Zänkerein (*f*), Spitzmaus (*f*).
Shrewd, *adj.* Schlau, verschmitzt.
Shriek, *v.* Schreien: *n.* Schrei (*m*).
Shrill, *adj.* Schrill.
Shrimp, *n.* Garnele (*f*), Knirps (*m*).
Shrine, *n.* Schrein (*m*).
Shrink, *v.* Schrumpfen.
Shrivel, *v.* Zusammenziehen, einschrumpfen.
Shroud, *n.* Leichentuch (*n*).
Shrove Tuesday, *n.* Fastnacht (*f*).
Shrub, *n.* Straude (*f*), Strauch (*m*).
Shrubbery, *n.* Gebüsch (*n*).
Shrug, *v.* Achseln zucken.
Shudder, *n.* Schauder (*m*): *v.* Schaudern.

Shuffle, *v.* Schlurfen (along), mischen (cards).
Shut, *v.* Schliessen, zumachen, zugehen.
  Shut up, Halt's Maul.
Shuttle, *n.* Schiffchen (*n*).
Shy, *adj.* Schüchtern: *v.* Scheuen.
Sick, *adj.* Ubel, krank, leid.
Sickle, *n.* Sichel (*f*).
Sickness, *n.* Krankheit (*f*).
Side, *n.* Seite (*f*), Ufer (*n*), Partei (*f*), Gegend (*f*).
Sideboard, *n.* Anrichte (*f*), Büffet (*n*).
Side-car, *n.* Beiwagen (*m*).
Side-slip, *n.* Seitenrutsch (*m*).
Sideways, *adv.* Seitwärts.
Siege, *n.* Belagerung (*f*).
Sieve, *n.* Sieb (*n*).
Sift, *v.* Sieben, sichten.
Sigh, *n.* Seufzer (*m*); *v.* Seufzen.
Sight, *n.* Sehkraft (*f*), Ansicht (*f*), Visier (*n*).
Sign, *n.* Zeichen (*n*): *v.* Unterzeichen.
Signature, *n.* Zeichen (*n*), Kennzeichen (*n*).
Signboard, *n.* Schild (*n*), Aushängeschild (*n*).
Signpost, *n.* Wegweiser (*m*).
Silence, *n.* Stille (*f*), Ruhe (*f*).
Silent *adj.* Stumm, schweigend.
Silk, *n.* Seide (*f*), Seidenzeug (*n*).
Silken, *adj.* Seiden.
Silkworm, *n.* Seidenraupe (*f*).
Silly, *adj.* Albern, einfältig.
Silver, *n.* Silber (*n*).
Similar, *adj.* Ähnlich, gleichartig.
Simmer, *v.* Brodeln.
Simple, *adj.* Einfach, einfältig.
Simplify, *v.* Vereinfachen.
Sin, *n.* Sünde (*f*): *v.* Sündigen.
Since, *adv.* Seitdem: *prep.* Seit.
Sincere, *adj.* Aufrichtig.
  Yours sincerely, Ihr ergebener.
Sinew, *n.* Sehne (*f*).
Sing, *v.* Singen, vorsingen.
Singe, *v.* Sengen, versengen.
Singing, *n.* Singen (*n*).
Single, *adj.* Einfach, einzeln, ledig.
Singular, *adj.* Einzigartig; *n.* Einzahl (*f*).

Sink, *v.* Sinken: *n.* Abzug (*m*), Gussstein (*m*).
Sinner, *n.* Sünder (*m*).
Sip, *v.* Nippen: *n.* Schlückchen (*n*).
Siphon, *n.* Siphon (*m*), Siphonflasche (*f*).
Sir, *n.* Herr (*m*).
Siren, *n.* Sirene (*f*).
Sirloin, *n.* Lendenbraten (*m*).
Sister, *n.* Schwester (*f*).
Sister-in-law, *n.* Schwägerin (*f*).
Sit, *v.* Sitzen, brüten (hens).
Sitting-room, *n.* Wohnzimmer (*n*).
Situation, *n.* Lage (locality) (*f*), **Stellung** (work) (*f*).
Six, *adj.* Sechs.
Sixteen, *adj.* Sechzehn.
Sixty, *adj.* Sechzig.
Size, *n.* Mass (*n*), Grösse (*f*), Format (*n*).
Skate, *n.* Glattroche (fish) (*m*), Schlittschuh (for ice) (*m*): *v.* Schlittschuh laufen.
Skein, *n.* Strähne (*f*).
Skeleton, *n.* Skelett (*n*), Gerippe (*n*).
Sketch, *n.* Skizze (*f*): *v.* Skizzieren.
Skewer, *n.* Speiler (*m*).
Skid, *v.* Hemmen, ausrutschen, schleudern (cars).
Skiff, *n.* Nachen (*m*), Kahn (*m*).
Skilful, *adj.* Geschickt.
Skill, *n.* Geschicklichkeit (*f*).
Skim, *v.* Abschäumen.
Skimmed-milk, *n.* Magermilch (*f*).
Skin, *n.* Haut (*f*), Schale (peel) (*f*), Fell (hide) (*n*), Balg (*m*), Hülse (*f*): *v.* Häuten, schälen.
Skinny, *adj* Häutig.
Skip, *v.* Hüpfen, springen, überhüpfen.
Skirmish, *n.* Scharmützel (*n*), Geplänkel (*n*): *v.* Plänkeln.
Skirt, *n.* Saum (*m*), Rock (*m*), Rockschoss (*m*).
Skittle, *n.* Kegel (*m*).
Skull, *n.* Schädel (*m*).
Skunk, *n.* Stinktier (*n*), Skunk (*m*).
Sky, *n.* Himmel (*m*).
Skylark, *n.* Feldlerche (*f*).
Skyscraper, *n.* Wolkenkratzer (*m*).

Slab 166 Snap

Slab, *n.* Steinplatte (*f*), Tafel (*f*).
Slack, *adj.* Schlaff, flau, träge.
Slacken, *v.* Lockern, löschen, verlangsamen.
Slacker, *n.* Drückeberger (*m*).
Slag, *n.* Schlacke (*f*).
Slake, *v.* Löschen, dämpfen.
Siam, *v.* Zuschmeissen, zuschlagen: *n.* Schlemm (at cards) (*m*), Klatsch (*m*), Schlag (*m*).
Slander, *n.* Verleumdung (*f*): *v.* Verleumden.
Slang, *n.* Slang (*n*).
Slant, *adj.* Schief: *n.* Schräge (*f*).
Slap, *v.* Schlagen, klapsen: *n.* Klaps (*m*).
Slash, *v.* Hauen, aufschlitzen: *n.* Schlitz (*m*).
Slate, *n.* Schiefer (*m*).
Slaughter, *n.* Metzelei (*f*): *v.* Schlachten.
Slave, *n.* Sklave (*m*), Sklavin (*f*).
Slavery, *n.* Sklaverei (*f*).
Slay, *v.* Erschlagen.
Sledge, *n.* Schlitten (*m*).
Sleek, *adj.* Glatt, weich.
Sleep, *v.* Schlafen; *n.* Schlaf (*m*).
Sleeper, *n.* Schläfer (person) (*m*), Schwelle (*f*), Schlafwagen (railway car) (*m*).
Sleeplessness, *n.* Schlaflosigkeit (*f*).
Sleepy, *adj.* Schläfrig.
Sleet, *n.* Graupeln (*n*), Schneeregen (*m*).
Sleeve, *n.* Ärmel (*m*).
Sleight, *n.* Kunststück (*n*), List (*f*).
Slender, *adj.* Schlank (body), karg (means).
Slice, *v.* In Scheiben zerschneiden: *n.* Schnitte (*f*).
Slide, *v.* Schleifen, ausgleiten: *n.* Gleiten (*n*), Rutschbahn (on ice) (*f*), Lichtbild (for lanterns) (*n*).
Sliding, *n.* Gleiten (*n*).
Slim, *adj.* Schlank.
Slime, *n.* Schlamm (*m*).
Sling, *n.* Schlinge (*f*).
Slip, *v.* Ausgleiten, ausrutschen.
Slipper, *n.* Pantoffel (*m*).
Slippery, *adj.* Schlüpfrig
Slit, *n.* Riss (*m*), Schlitz (*m*): *v.* Aufschlitzen.
Sloe, *n.* Schlehe (*f*).
Slop, *v.* Verschütten; *n.* Krankensuppe (*f*), Spülwasser (*n*).
Slope, *n.* Abhang (*m*): *v.* Abschrägen.
Slot, *n.* Spalte (*f*), Schlitz (*m*), Einwurf (*m*).
Slovenly, *adj.* Liederlich.
Slow, *adj.* Langsam, langweilig.
Slug, *n.* Klumpen (*m*).
Slum, *n.* Armenviertel (*n*), Hintergasschen (*n*).
Slump, *n.* Baisse (*f*): *v.* Stürzen, fallen.
Slush, *n.* Schlamm (*m*).
Sly, *adj.* Schlau.
Smack, *v.* Schmecken, schlagen: *n.* Schmatz (*m*), Schlag (*m*).
Small, *adj.* Klein.
Smallpox, *n.* Blattern (*f. pl.*), Pocken (*f. pl.*).
Smart, *adj.* Elegant (well-dressed), gescheit (knowing): *v.* Schmerzen (hurt).
Smash, *n.* Schmiss (*m*), Bankerott (financial) (*m*), Zusammenstoss (accident) (*m*): *v.* Zerschmettern.
Smear, *v.* Beschmieren: *n.* Fleck (*m*).
Smell, *n.* Geruch (*m*): *v.* Riechen, wittern.
Smelling-salts, *n.* Riechsalz (*m*).
Smelt, *n.* Stint (fish) (*m*).
Smile, *v.* Lächeln: *n.* Lächeln (*n*).
Smoke, *n.* Rauch (*m*): *v.* Rauchen.
Smoking compartment, Raucher (*m*), Raucherwagen (*m*).
Smoky, *adj.* Rauchig, rauchend.
Smooth, *adj.* Glatt.
Smother, *v.* Ersticken.
Smoulder, *v.* Schwelen, glimmen.
Smug, *adj.* Geputzt, schmuck.
Smuggle, *v.* Schmuggeln.
Smuggler, *n.* Schmuggler (*m*).
Smut, *n.* Russfleck (*m*), Zote (*f*).
Snack, *n.* Imbiss (*m*), Bissen (*m*).
Snail, *n.* Schnecke (*f*).
Snake, *n.* Schlange (*f*).
Snap, *n.* Knack (*m*), Schnappen (*n*), Biss (*m*): *v.* Schnappen.

Snapdragon — Spaniel

Snapdragon, *n.* Löwenmaul (*n*).
Snapshot, *n.* Momentaufnahme (*f*).
Snare, *v.* Verstricken; *n.* Schlinge (*f*).
Snarl, *v.* Knurren.
Snatch, *v.* Ergreifen, erschnappen.
Sneak, *n.* Kriecher (*m*), Schleicher (*m*).
Sneer, *v.* Hohnlächeln: *n.* Höhnische Blick.
Sneeze, *v.* Niesen: *n.* Niesen (*n*).
Sniff, *v.* Schnüffeln: *n.* Nasevoll (*f*).
Snore, *v.* Schnarchen.
Snout, *n.* Rüssel (*m*), Schnauze (*f*).
Snow, *n.* Schnee (*m*): *v.* Schneien.
Snowdrop, *n.* Schneeglöckchen (*n*).
Snub, *v.* Anfahren, schelten.
Snuff, *n.* Schnupftabak (*m*).
So, *adv. & conj.* So, daher, folglich, also.
Soak, *v.* Einsaugen, einweichen.
Soap, *n.* Seife (*f*).
Sob, *v.* Schluchzen; *n.* Schluchzen (*n*).
Sober, *adj.* Nüchtern.
Sociable, *adj.* Gesellig.
Social, *adj.* Sozial.
Society, *n.* Gesellschaft (company) (*f*), Verein (club) (*m*).
Sock, *n.* Socke (*f*).
Soda, *n.* Soda (*f*).
Sodawater, *n.* Mineralwasser (*n*), Sodawasser (*m*).
Sofa, *n.* Sofa (*n*).
Soft, *adj.* Weich, gelind, sanft.
Soften, *v.* Erweichen, aufweichen.
Softly, *adv.* Weichlich.
Soil, *n.* Boden (*m*), Erde (*f*).
Sojourn, *n.* Aufenthalt (*m*).
Solder, *n.* Lötmetall (*n*), Lot (*n*): *v.* Löten.
Soldier, *n.* Soldat (*m*).
Sole, *n.* Sohle (of foot) (*f*), Seezunge (fish) (*f*).
Solemn, *adj.* Feierlich, ernst.
Solicit, *v.* Belästigen, anhaltend bitten.
Solicitor, *n.* Notar (*m*), Rechtsanwalt (*m*), Anwalt (*m*).
Solicitude, *n.* Besorgnis (*f*).
Solid, *adj.* Massiv, fest, gediegen.
Solitary, *adj.* Einsam (lonely), einzeln (only).
Solitude, *n.* Einsamkeit (*f*).
Solution, *n.* Lösung (*f*).
Solve, *v.* Lösen, erklären, enträtseln.
Sombre, *adj.* Düster, dunkel.
Some, *adj. & pron.* Ein paar, einige, etwas, etliche.
Somebody, *pron.* Jemand.
Somehow, *adv.* Irgendwie.
Something, *pron.* Etwas.
Sometimes, *adv.* Manchmal, zuweilen.
Somewhere, *adv.* Ingendwo.
Son, *n.* Sohn (*m*).
Song, *n.* Gesang (*m*), Lied (*n*).
Son-in-law, *n.* Schwiegersohn (*m*).
Soon, *adv.* Bald, gern, früh.
As soon as, So bald wie.
Soot, *n.* Russ (*m*).
Soothe, *v.* Besänftigen.
Sordid, *adj.* Schmutzig, filzig, gemein.
Sore, *n.* Wund Stelle (*f*), Geschwür (*n*): *adj.* Schmerzhaft.
Sorrow, *n.* Kummer (*m*), Leid (*n*).
Sorry, *adj.* Betrübt, traurig.
Sort, *n.* Sorte (*f*), Gattung (*f*): *v.* Sortieren.
Soul, *n.* Seele (*f*).
Sound, *n.* Klang (*m*), Sonde (*f*), Ton (*m*): *v.* Ertönen, klingen, lauten: *adj.* Gesund, gründlich, derb, fest.
Soup, *n.* Suppe (*f*).
Sour, *adj.* Sauer, mürrisch, bitter.
Source, *n.* Quelle (*f*), Ursprung (*m*).
South, *n.* Süden (*m*): *adj.* Südlich.
Souvenir, *n.* Andenken (*n*).
Sovereign, *n.* Herrscher (*m*), Oberherr (*m*), Pfund-Sterling (*n*).
Sow (animal), *n.* Sau (*f*).
Sow (seeds), *v.* Säen.
Space, *n.* Raum (area) (*m*), Zeitraum (time) (*m*).
Spade, *n.* Spaten (digging) (*m*), Pik (cards) (*n*).
Spaniel, *n.* Wachtelhund (*m*).

Spanner 168 **Sprinkle**

Spanner, *n.* Schraubenschlüssel (*m*).
Spare, *v.* Entbehren (do without), ver schonen (save): *adj.* Dürr (lean), übrig (left over), karg.
Spark, *n.* Funke (*m*).
Sparking-plug, *n.* Zundkerze (*f*).
Sparkle, *v.* Funkeln: *n.* Funke (*m*).
Sparrow, *n.* Sperling (*m*).
Speak, *v.* Sprechen.
Speaker, *n.* Redner (*m*).
Spear, *n.* Speer (*m*).
Special, *adj.* Besonder, eigen, extra.
Specimen, *n.* Muster (*n*), Probe (*f*).
Speck, *n.* Fleck (*m*).
Spectacle, *n.* Schauspiel (*n*), Anblick (*m*).
Spectacles, *n.* Brille (*f*).
Spectator, *n.* Zuschauer (*m*).
Speculate, *v.* Spekulieren, grübeln.
Speech, *n.* Sprache (*f*), Rede (*f*).
Speechless, *adj.* Sprachloss.
Speed, *n.* Geschwindigkeit (*f*), Fortgang (*m*): *v.* Eilen.
Speedometer, *n.* Geschwindigkeitsanzeiger (*m*).
Speedy, *adj.* Schnell.
Spell, *v.* Buchstabieren, richtig schreiben: *n.* Zauber (*m*).
Spend, *v.* Ausgeben, verwenden.
Spendthrift, *n.* Verschwender (*m*).
Sphere, *n.* Kugel (*f*), Erdkugel (earth) (*f*), Sphäre (*f*).
Spice, *n.* Gewürz (*n*).
Spider, *n.* Spinne (*f*).
Spike, *n.* Spieker (*m*), Spitze (*f*).
Spill, *v.* Vergiessen, verschütten.
Spin, *v.* Spinnen, wirbeln.
Spinach, *n.* Spinat (*m*).
Spine, *n.* Rückgrat (*n*).
Spinster, *n.* Jungfer (*f*).
Spiral, *n.* Spirale (*f*); *adj.* Spiralförmig.
Spire, *n.* Spitzsäule (*f*), Turmspitze (*f*).
Spirit, *n.* Geist (*m*), Gespenst (*n*), Lebhaftigkeit (life) (*f*), Spiritus (alcohol) (*m*).
In high spirits, Munter.
In low spirits, Verstimmt.
Spirited, *adj.* Lebhaft, mutig, feurig, geistreich.
Spirit-level, *n.* Nievellierwage (*f*).
Spit, *v.* Spucken: *n.* Spuck (*m*).
Spite, *n.* Groll (*m*), Verdruss (*m*): *v.* kränken, ärgern.
Spiteful, *adj.* Boshaft.
In spite of, Trotz.
Splash, *v.* Bespritzen: *n.* Spritzfleck (*m*).
Splendid, *adj.* Glänzend, prächtig, prachtvoll.
Splendour, *n.* Glanz (*m*), Pracht (*f*).
Splinter, *n.* Splitter (*m*).
Split, *v.* Spalten, bersten: *n.* Spalt (*m*).
Spoil, *v.* Verderben, plündern, rauben.
Spoke, *n.* Speiche (*f*), Sprosse (*f*).
Sponge, *n.* Schwamm (*m*), Wischer (*m*).
Spontaneous, *adj.* Freiwillig, freitätig.
Spool, *n.* Spule (*f*).
Spoon, *n.* Löffel (*m*).
Spoonful, *n.* Löffelvoll (*m*).
Sport, *n.* Sport (*m*), Spiel (*n*): *v.* Spielen.
Sportsman, *n.* Sportsmann (*m*).
Spot, *n.* Fleck (mark) (*m*), Ort (position) (*m*).
Spotless, *adj.* Fleckenlos.
Spout, *n.* Schnabel (*m*), Ausguss (*m*), Tulle (*f*): *v.* Sprudeln.
Sprain, *n.* Verrenkung (*f*), Verstauchung (*f*): *v.* Verrenken.
Spratt, *n.* Sprotte (*f*).
Sprawl, *v.* Sich spreizen.
Spray, *n.* Zweig (of flowers) (*m*), Sprühregen (of water) (*m*): *v.* Sprühen.
Spread, *v.* Ausbreiten, bestreichen, verbreiten: *n.* Umfang (*m*), Verbreitung (*f*).
Sprig, *n.* Spross (*m*).
Spring, *n.* Frühling (season) (*m*), Quelle (water) (*f*), Sprung (jump) (*m*), Feder (coil) (*f*): *v.* Springen.
Sprinkle, *v.* Sprengen.

Sprout 169 **Step-mother**

Sprout, *v.* Sprossen.
　Brussels sprouts, Rosenkohl (*m*).
Spur, *n.* Sporn (*m*), Antrieb (*m*): *v.* Anspornen.
Spurn, *v.* Verschmähen, verächtlich.
Spy, *n.* Späher (*m*): *v.* Spionieren.
Squabble, *v.* Zanken, streiten: *n.* Zank (*m*).
Squalid, *adj.* Schmutzig, ärmlich.
Squall, *v.* Schreien (noise): *n.* Bö (weather) (*f*).
Squalor, *n.* Schmutz (*m*).
Squander, *v.* Verschwenden.
Square, *n.* Viereck (geometry) (*n*), Platz (locality) (*m*).
Squash, *v.* Zerquetschen.
　Lemonsquash, Selterswasser mit Zitrone.
Squeak, *v.* Quieken: *n.* Gequiek (*n*).
Squeal, *v.* Schreien.
Squeeze, *v.* Drücken, pressen.
Squint, *v.* Schielen.
Squirrel, *n.* Eichhörnchen (*n*).
Squirt, *n.* Spritze (*f*): *v.* Spritzen.
Stab, *v.* Stechen: *n.* Stoss (*m*), Wunde (*f*).
Stable, *n.* Stall (*m*).
Staff, *n.* Stab (*m*), Sprosse (*f*), Personal (of workers) (*n*).
Stag, *n.* Hirsch (*m*).
Stage, *n.* Bühne (for acting) (*f*).
Stagger, *v.* Taumeln.
Stain, *v.* Beflecken, färben: *n.* Flecken (*m*), Beize (*f*).
Stainless, *adj.* Rostfrei.
Stair, *n.* Stufe (*f*).
Stairs, *n.* Treppe (*f*).
Stake, *n.* Pfahl (post) (*m*), Einsatz (bet) (*m*): *v.* Setzen.
Stale, *adj.* Altbacken, schal, geistlos.
Stalk, *n.* Stengel (*m*).
Stall, *n.* Stand (*m*), Sperrsitz (in theatre) (*m*).
Stammer, *v.* Stottern.
Stamp, *n.* Stempel (mark) (*m*), Briefmarke (postage) (*f*): *v.* Stempel (to mark), frankieren (pay postage), stampfen (with feet).
Stampede, *n.* Wilde Flucht (*f*).

Stand, *v.* Stehen, stellen (put), ertragen (allow): *n.* Stand (*m*), Ständer (*m*), Stillstand (*m*).
Standard, *n.* Fahne (*f*).
Star, *n.* Stern (*m*).
Starboard, *n.* Steuerbord (*n*).
Starch, *n.* Stärke (*f*): *v.* Stärken.
Stare, *v.* Anstarren.
Starling, *n.* Star (*m*).
Start, *v.* Anfangen, zurückfahren, abgehen, beginnen; *n.* Anfang (*m*), Schreck (surprise) (*m*).
Startle, *v.* Erschrecken.
Starve, *v.* Verhungern, aushungern.
State, *n.* Zustand (*m*), Rang (*m*), Vermögen (*n*), Prunk (ceremony) (*m*): *v.* Erklären, angeben.
Statement, *n.* Erklärung (*f*).
Statesman, *n.* Staatsmann (*m*).
Station, *n.* Bahnhof (railway) (*m*), Rang (in society) (*m*): *v.* Stellen.
Stationary, *adj.* Stillstehend.
Stationer, *n.* Schreibwarenhändler (*m*).
Statue, *n.* Statue (*n*), Bildsäule (*f*).
Staunch, *adj.* Treu, zuverlässig, fest.
Stay, *v.* Bleiben: *n.* Aufenthalt (*m*).
Steady, *adj.* Fest, beständig, standhaft.
Steal, *v.* Stehlen.
Steam, *n.* Dampf (*m*): *v.* Dämpfen.
Steamboat, *n.* Dampfschiff (*n*).
Steam-engine, *n.* Dampfmaschine (*f*).
Steel, *n.* Stahl (*m*).
Steep, *adj.* Steil, jah: *v.* Einweichen.
Steeple, *n.* Kirchturm (*m*).
Steer, *v.* Steuern: *n.* Junge Stier (*m*).
Steerage, *n.* Zwischendeck (*n*).
Stem, *n.* Stiel (*m*), Stamm (*m*): *v.* Stemmen.
Stench, *n.* Gestank (*m*).
Stencil, *n.* Schablone (*f*).
Step, *v.* Schreiten, treten: *n.* Schritt (*m*), Stufe (*f*).
Step-father, *n.* Stiefvater (*m*).
Step-mother, *n.* Stiefmutter (*f*).

Sterile 170 Stubborn

Sterile, *adj.* Unfruchtbar.
Stern, *adj,* Ernst, streng : *n.* Spiegel (of boat) (*m*).
Stevedore, *n.* Stauer (*m*).
Stew, *n.* Ragout (*n*), geschmorte Fleisch (*n*): *v.* Schmoren.
Steward, *n.* Steward (of boat) (*m*), Verwalter (of land) (*m*).
Stick, *n.* Stock (*m*), Stecken (*m*): *v.* Stecken, ankleben.
Sticky, *adj.* Klebrig.
Stiff, *adj.* Steif, starr, teuer.
Stifle, *adj.* Ersticken.
Still, *adj.* Still, ruhig: *adj.* Immer noch: *v.* Stillen, destillieren.
Stimulate, *v.* Anreizen, anregen, ansporen.
Sting, *v.* Stechen: *n.* Stich (*m*).
Stingy, *adj.* Filzig, geizig, karg.
Stink, *v.* Stinken: *n.* Gestank (*m*).
Stint, *v.* Einschränken.
Stipulate, *v.* Bedingen, festsetzen.
Stir, *v.* Rühren, regen, bewegen: *n.* Regung (*f*).
Stitch, *n.* Stich (*m*), Masche (*f*): *v.* Stechen, heften.
Stoat, *n.* Wiesel (*n*).
Stock, *n.* Levkoje (plant) (*f*), Warenbestand (goods in store (*m*), Kolben (gun) (*m*).
Stock Exchange, *n.* Börse (*f*).
Stocking, *n.* Strumpf (*m*).
Stoke, *v.* Heizen.
Stomach, *n.* Magen (*m*).
Stomach-ache, *n.* Bauchweh (*n*), Magenschmerzen (*m*).
Stone, *n.* Stein (*m*), kern (*m*), Gewicht (*n*): *v.* Steinern, steinigen.
Stool, *n.* Schemel (*m*).
Stoop, *v.* Sich bücken.
Stop, *n.* Stillstand (*m*), Halt (*m*), Punkt (in writing) (*m*): *v.* Verstopfen, anhalten, haiten, sich aufhalten (stay with), plombieren (dental).
Store, *n.* Warenhaus (*n*): *v.* Lagern.
Stork, *n.* Storch (*m*).
Storm, *n.* Sturm (*m*), Aufruhr (*m*).
Stormy, *adj.* Stürmisch.
Story, *n.* Stock (of house) (*m*), Geschichte (tale) (*f*), Lüge (lie) (*f*).

Stout, *adj.* Stark, wacker, tapfer: *n.* Dunkle Bier (*n*).
Stove, *n.* Ofen (*m*).
Stow, *v.* Stauen.
Stowaway, *n.* Blinde Reisende (*m*).
Straight, *adj.* Gerade, sogleich.
Straightforward, *adj.* Redlich, bieder.
Strain, *v.* Spannen, strecken, quetschen: *n.* Anstrengung (*f*), Spannung (*f*).
Tea strainer, Teesieb (*n*).
Strand, *n.* Strand (place) (*m*), Strähne (of hair) (*f*).
Strange, *adj.* Fremd, seltsam.
Stranger, *n.* Fremde (*m*).
Strangle, *v.* Erdrosseln, erwürgen.
Strap, *n.* Riemen (*m*), Gurt (*m*).
Straw, *n.* Stroh (*n*).
Strawberry, *n.* Erdbeere (*f*).
Stray, *v.* Irregehen: *adj.* Veirrt.
Streak, *n.* Streifen (*m*), Strich (*m*).
Stream, *n.* Bach (*m*), Lauf (*m*), Strom (*m*).
Street, *n.* Strasse (*f*).
Strength, *n.* Stärke (*f*), Kraft (*f*).
Strengthen, *v.* Stärken.
Stretch, *n.* Strecke (*f*): *v.* Strecken.
Stretcher, *n.* Tragbahre (*f*).
Strew, *v.* Streuen.
Strict, *adj.* Streng.
Strife, *n.* Streit (*m*).
Strike, *v.* Streiken (blow), anstreichen (matches), einschlagen (by lightning): *n.* Streik (*m*).
Striker, *n.* Streiker (at work) (*m*).
String, *n.* Schnur (*f*).
Strip, *n.* Streifen (*m*) : *v.* Abstreifen, entkleiden.
Strive, *v.* Streben, streiten.
Stroke, *v.* Streicheln: *n.* Schlag (*m*), Zug (*m*).
Strong, *adj.* Fest, stark, grell.
Strop, *v.* Abziehen: *n.* Streichriemen (*m*).
Struggle, *n.* Kampf (*m*): *v.* Kämpfen.
Stubborn, *adj.* Standhaft, hartnäckig.

**Stud, **n. Kragenknopf (collar) (m), Gestüt (horses, etc.), (n).
**Student, **n. Student (m), Schüler (m).
**Studio, **n. Atelier (n).
**Studious, **adj. Lernbegierig.
**Study, **n. Studium (n): v. Studieren.
**Stumble, **v. Stolpern.
**Stump, **n. Stumpf (m), Wischer (m), Stab (cricket) (m).
**Stun, **v. Betäuben.
**Stupefy, **v. Betäuben.
**Stupendous, **adj. Kolossal, erstaunlich.
**Stupid, **adj. Albern, dumm, langweilig.
**Sturdy, **adj. Derb, dreist, stark.
**Sturgeon, **n. Stör (m).
**Stutter, **v. Stottern.
**Suave, **adj. Verbindlich, sanft.
**Subdue, **v. Unterwerfen, dämpfen.
**Subject, **v. Unterwerfen, aussetzen.
**Subjunctive, **n. Konjunktiv (m).
**Submarine, **n. Unterseeboot (n).
**Submerge, **v. Untertauchen.
**Submit, **v. Unterwerfen, sich fügen.
**Subscribe, **v. Abonnieren, unterschreiben.
**Subscriber, **n. Abonnent, unterschreiber.
**Subscription, **n. Abonnement (n), Unterschrift (f).
**Subsequent, **adj. Nachfolgend: adv. Nachher.
**Subside, **v. Abnehmen, sinken.
**Subsidy, **n. Beisteuer (f).
**Substitute, **v. Unterschieben: n. Stellvertreter (m).
**Subterfuge, **n. Ausflucht (f).
**Subterranean, **adj. Unterirdisch.
**Subtle, **adj. Fein, schlau, scharfsinnig.
**Subtract, **v. Abziehen.
**Subtraction, **n. Abziehen (n), Subtraktion (f).
**Suburb, **n. Vorstadt (f).
**Subway, **n. Unterführung (f).
**Succeed, **v. Nachfolgen (accomplish), erben (inherit).
**Success, **n. Erfolg (m).

**Successful, **adj. Erfolgreich, glücklich.
**Successive, **adj. Folgend.
**Succulent, **adj. Nahrhaft, saftig.
**Succumb, **v. Unterliegen.
**Such, **pron. Solcher, solche, solches, so.
**Suck, **v. Saugen.
**Suckle, **v. Säugen.
**Sudden, **adj. Unerwartet, plötzlich.
**Sue, **v. Verklagen, ersuchen.
**Suet, **n. Nierenfett (n).
**Suffer, **v. Leiden, gestatten, dulden.
**Sufferer, **n. Leidende (m).
**Suffering, **n. Leiden (n).
**Sufficient, **adj. Hinlänglich.
**Suffocate, **v. Ersticken.
**Suffocation, **n. Erstickung (f).
**Sugar, **n. Zucker (m).
**Suggest, **v. Eingeben, vorschlagen.
**Suggestion, **n. Eingebung (f), Vorschlag (m).
**Suicide, **n. Selbstmord (m).
**Suit, **n. Anzug (m), Prozess (legal) (m): v. Passen.
**Suitable, **adj. Passend.
**Suitor, **n. Kläger (m), Bittsteller (m).
**Sulky, **adj. Mürrisch.
**Sullen, **adj. Düster, halsstarrig.
**Sulphur, **n. Schwefel (m).
**Sulphuric-acid, **n. Schwefelsäure (f).
**Summer, **n. Sommer (m).
**Summit, **n. Spitze (f), Gipfel (m).
**Summon, **v. Vorladen, auffordern.
**Summons, **n. Vorladung (f), Aufforderung (f).
**Sun, **n. Sonne (f).
**Sunday, **n. Sonntag (m).
**Sunny, **adj. Sonnig, sonnenhell.
**Sunrise, **n. Sonnenaufgang (m).
**Sunset, **n. Sonnenuntergang (m).
**Sunshine, **n. Sonnenschein (m).
**Sup, **v. Schlürfen.
**Superb, **adj. Prächtig, herrlich.
**Superfluous, **adj. Reichlich, überflüssig.
**Superintend, **v. Die Aufsicht führen.

Superior, *adj.* Höher: *n.* Obere (*m*).
Superiority, *n.* Überlegenheit (*f*), Vorrecht (*n*).
Supersede, *v.* Verdrängen.
Superstitious, *adj.* Abergläubisch.
Supervise, *v.* Beaufsichtigen.
Supervisor, *n.* Aufseher (*m*).
Supper, *n.* Abendessen (*n*).
Supple, *adj.* Nachgiebig, geschmeidig.
Supplement, *n.* Zusatz (*m*), Ergänzung (*f*). *v.* Ergänzen.
Supplier, *n.* Versorger (*m*).
Supply, *n.* Zuschuss (*m*), Angebot(*n*),Vorrat(*m*): *v.*Versehen.
Support, *v.* Unterstützen, ertragen: *n.* Stütze (*f*).
Suppose, *v.* Annehmen, voraussetzen.
Suppress, *v.* Unterdrücken, zurückhalten.
Supremacy, *n.* Obergewalt (*f*).
Supreme, *adj.* Oberst, höchst.
Surcharge, *v.* Überladen: *n*, Überforderung (*f*).
Sure, *adj.* Sicher, gewiss.
Surely, *adv.* Sicherlich.
Surf, *n.* Brandung (*f*).
Surface, *n.* Oberfläche (*f*).
Surfeit, *n.* Überladung (*f*), Ekel (*m*).
Surgeon, *n.* Chirurg (*m*).
Surgery, *n.* Chirurgie (*f*).
Surly, *adj.* Mürrisch, grob finster.
Surname, *n.* Zuname (*m*), Familienname (*m*).
Surpass, *v.* Übertreffen.
Surplus, *n.* Überschuss (*m*).
Surprise, *v.* Überraschen, erstaunen.
Surrender, *v.* Übergeben, abtreten.
Surround, *v.* Umgeben, umringen.
Survey, *v.* Überblicken: *n.* Überblick (*m*).
Survivor, *n.* Überlebende (*m*).
Suspect, *v.* Argwöhnen.
Suspected, *adj.* Verdächtig.
Suspend, *v.* Einstellen, verschieben.
Suspenders, *n.* Strumpfhalter (*m. pl.*).
Suspense, *n.* Ungewissheit (*f*).
Suspicion, *n.* Verdacht (*m*), Argwohn (*m*).

Suspicious, *adj.* Argwöhnisch, misstrauisch.
Swagger, *v.* Grosstun: *n.* Grosstuerei (*f*).
Swallow, *v.* Schlucken, verschlingen: *n.* Schwalbe (bird)(*f*).
Swamp, *v.* Versenken, überfüllen: *n.* Sumpf (*m*).
Swan, *n.* Schwan (*m*).
Swarm, *v.* Schwärmen: *n.* Schwarm (*m*).
Sway, *v.* Schwingen: *n.* Einfluss (*m*), Herrschaft (*f*).
Swear, *v.* Schwören (take oath), fluchen (curse).
Sweat, *n.* Schweiss: *v.* Schwitzen.
Sweep, *v.* Fegen, kehren, dahinfahren.
Sweeper, *n.* Feger (*m*).
Sweet, *adj.* Süss, lieblich, freundlich: *n.* Bonbon (*m*).
Sweetheart, *n.* Geliebte[r] (*m. or f.*), Liebchen (*n*).
Sweet-pea, *n.* Wohlriechende Wicke (*f*).
Swell, *v.* Aufschwellen, zunehmen: *n.* Dünung (*f*).
Swelling, *n.* Geschwulst (*f*).
Swerve, *v.* Ausbiegen.
Swift, *adj.* Schnell, rasch.
Swim, *v.* Schwimmen.
Swindle, *v.* Beschwindeln; *n.* Schwindel (*m*).
Swine, *n.* Schwein (*n*).
Swing, *v.* Schwingen: *n.* Schwung (*m*), Schaukel (*f*).
Switch (electric), *n.* Schalter (*m*).
To switch off, Ausschalten, abdrehen.
To switch on, Einschalten, andrehen.
Swoon, *v.* In Ohnmacht fallen: *n.* Ohnmacht (*f*).
Swoop, *v.* Herabstossen : *n.* Stoss (*m*).
Sword, *n.* Schwert (*n*).
Sycamore, *n.* Sykomore (*f*).
Syllable, *n.* Silbe (*f*).
Syllabus, *n'* Lehrplan (*m*), Auszug (*m*), Prospekt (*m*).
Symmetry, *n.* Ebenmass (*n*).
Sympathetic, *adj.* Sympathisch, mitfühlend.
Sympathy, *n.* Sympathie (*f*).
Symptom, *n.* Symptom (*n*).
Syphon, *n.* Siphon (*m*).

Syringe 173 **Tenant**

Syringe, n. Spritze (f): v. Einspritzen.
System, n. System (n).

T

Tab, n. Lasche (f), Aufhänger (m).
Table, n. Tafel (f), Tisch (m), Tabelle (tabulation) (f).
Tablecloth, n. Tischtuch (n).
Tablespoon, n. Eslöffel (m).
Tablet, n. Tafel (f), Tablette (f).
Tack, v. Anschlagen, anheften: n. Stift (tin) (m).
Tackle, n. Gerät (fishing) (n); v. Anpacken (to go for).
Tadpole, n. Kaulquappe (f).
Tail, n. Schwanz (m).
Taint, n. Makel (m), Fiecken (m).
Take, v. Nehmen, empfangen, überfallen, annehmen.
Tale, n. Erzählung (f).
Talent, n. Talent (n), Begabung (f).
Talk, v. Sprechen: n. Gespräch (n).
Talkative, adj. Gesprächig.
Tall, adj. Hoch, lang, gross.
Tallow, n. Talg (m).
Tame, adj. Zahm: v. Zähmen.
Tamper, v. Fälschen.
Tan, v. Lohen, gerben.
Tangle, n. Knoten (m): v. Verwickeln.
Tank, n. Zisterne (f), Wasserbehälter (m), Tankwagen (warfare) (m).
Tankard, n. Zinnkrug (m), Krug (m).
Tantalise, v. Quälen.
Tap, n. Hahn (m), Zapfen (m): v. Klopfen, anzapfen.
Tape, n. Band (n), Zwirnband (n).
Tape-measure, n. Bandmass (n).
Taper, n. Wachskerze (f): v. Spitz zulaufen.
Tapestry, n. Gobelin (m).
Tapeworm, m. Bandwurm (m).
Tapioca, n. Tapioka (f).
Tar, n. Teer (m).
Target, n. Scheibe (f).
Tariff, n. Tarif (f).
Tarnish, v. Trube machen.

Tarpaulin, n. Teertuch (n), Persenning (f).
Tart, n. Torte (f); adj. Sauer, herb.
Tassel, n. Quaste (f).
Taste, v. Schmecken, versuchen, kosten: n. Geschmack (m).
Tasteless, adj. Geschmacklos.
Tasty, adj. Schmackhaft.
Taunt, n. Hohn (m): v. Höhnen, schmähen.
Taut, adj. Steif.
Tavern, n. Schenke (f).
Tawdry, adj. Flitterhaft.
Tax, n. Steuer (f): v. Besteuern.
Taxation, n. Besteuerung (f).
Taxicab, n. Taxi (n), Taxameter (m).
Tea, n. Tee (m).
Teach, v. Lehren, unterrichten.
Team, n. Gespann (n), Mannschaft (f).
Tear (split), n. Riss (m): v. Reissen.
Tear (crying), n. Träne (f): v. Weinen.
Tease, v. Necken.
Teat, n. Zitze (f), Lutscher (artificial) (m).
Technical, adj. Technisch.
Tedious, adj. Langweilig, ermüdend.
Teething, n. Zahnen (n).
Teetotaller, n. Abstinenzler (m).
Telegram, n. Telegramm (n).
Telephone, n. Telephon (n), Fernsprecher (m).
Telescope, n. Fernrohr (n).
Tell, v. Sagen, anzeigen, erzählen.
Tell-tale, n. Ohrenbläser (m).
Temper, n. Laune (people) (f), Härte (metal) (f).
Temperance, n. Massigkeit (f).
Temperate, adj. Gemässigt, mässig, ruhig.
Temperature, n. Temperatur (f).
Tempest, n. Sturm (m).
Temple, n. Tempel (m).
Temporary, adj. Zeitweilig.
Tempt, v. Verlocken, verleiten.
Ten, adj. Zehn.
Tenancy, n. Miete (f), Pacht (f).
Tenant, n. Mieter (m), Pächter (f).

Tennis, *n.* Tennis (*n*).
Tenor, *n.* Verlauf (*m*), Richtung (*f*), Inahlt (*m*).
Tense, *n.* Zeitform (grammar) (*f*); *adj.* Gespannt.
Tent, *n.* Zelt (*n*), Tintowein (*m*).
Tenth, *adj.* Zehnte: *n.* Zehntel (*f*).
Tenure, *n.* Besitz (*m*).
Tepid, *adj.* Lauwarm.
Term, *n.* Zeitraum (*m*), Ausdruck (*m*), Grenze (*f*).
Terminate, *v.* Endigen.
Terminus, *n.* Endstation (*f*).
Terrace, *n.* Terrasse (*f*).
Terrible, *adj.* Schrecklich, fürchterlich.
Terrify, *v.* Erschrecken.
Territory, *n.* Gebiet (*n*).
Terror, *n.* Schrecken (*m*).
Test, *n.* Probe (*f*), Prüfung (*f*), Reagens (*n*): *v.* Prüfen.
Testimonial, *n.* Zeugnis (*n*).
Texture, *n.* Textur (*f*), Gewebe (*n*).
Than, *conj.* Als.
Thank, *v.* Danken.
Thankful, *adj.* Dankbar.
Thankless, *adj.* Undankbar.
Thanks, *n.* Dank (*m. pl.*).
Thank you, *interj.* Danke.
That, *pron.* Der, die, das, jener, jene, jenes, welcher, welche, welches: *conj.* Das, damit, weil.
Thaw, *v.* Tauen: *n.* Tauwetter.
The, *art.* Der, die, das.
Theatre, *n.* Theater (*n*).
Thee, *pron.* Dir, dich.
Theft, *n.* Diebstahl (*m*).
Their, *pron.* Ihr, ihre.
Theirs, *pron.* Der ihrige, die ihrige, das ihrige, ihrer, ihre, ihres.
Them, *pron.* Sie, ihnen.
Themselves, *pron.* Sie selbst, sich selbst.
Then, *adv.* Dann, damals, alsdann.
There, *adv.* Dort.
Thereafter, *adv.* Darnach.
Thereby, *adv.* Damit, dadurch.
Therefore, *adv.* Deswegen: *conj.* Also.
Therefrom, *adv.* Davon.
Therein, *adv.* Darin.
Thereof, *adv.* Davon.

Thermometer, *n.* Thermometer (*m*).
These, *pron.* Diese.
They, *pron.* Sic.
Thick, *adj.* Dick, dicht, häufig.
Thief, *n.* Räuber (*m*), Dieb (*m*).
Thigh, *n.* Schenkel (*m*).
Thimble, *n.* Fingerhut (*m*).
Thin, *adj.* Dünn, mager, spärlich.
Thine, *pron.* Dein, der, die, das deinige.
Thing, *n.* Sache (*f*), Ding (*m*)
Think, *v.* Denken, glauben.
Thinking, *adj.* Denkend.
Thinness, *n.* Dünnheit (*f*).
Third, *adj.* Dritte: *n.* Drittel (*n*).
Thirst, *v.* Dürsten: *n.* Durst (*m*).
Thirsty, *adj.* Durstig.
Thirteen, *adj.* Dreizehn.
Thirty, *adj.* Dreissig.
This, *pron.* Dieser, diese, dieses, dies.
Thistle, *n.* Distel (*f*).
Thong, *n.* Riemen (*m*).
Thorn, *n.* Dorn (*m*).
Thorough, *adj.* Gänzlich, vollständig.
Thoroughfare, *n.* Durchgang (*m*).
No thoroughfare, Gesperrt.
Those, *pron.* Jene, diejenigen.
Thou, *pron.* Du.
Though, *conj.* Obgleich, obwohl, zwar, dennoch.
Thought, *n.* Gedanke (*m*).
Thoughtful, *adj.* Gedankenvoll.
Thoughtless, *adj.* Gedankenlos.
Thousand, *adj.* Tausend: *n.* Tausend (*n*).
Thrash, *v.* Prügeln, dreschen.
Thread, *n.* Zwirn (*m*), Faden (*m*): *v.* Einfädeln.
Threat, *n.* Drohung (*f*).
Three, *adj.* Drei.
Threshold, *n.* Schwelle (*f*).
Thrift, *n.* Sparsamkeit (*f*).
Thrill, *n.* Schauer (*m*): *v.* Durchschauern.
Thrilling, *adj.* Erschütternd.
Thrive, *v.* Gedeihen.
Throat, *n.* Kehle (*f*), Schlund (*m*), Hals (*m*).
Throb, *v.* Pochen, schlagen.
Throne, *n.* Thron (*m*).

Throttle — Towel

Throttle, *v.* Drosseln, erdrosseln.
Through, *prep.* Durch, aus: *adv.* Durch und durch.
Throughout, *adv.* Durchaus, ganz durch.
Throw, *v.* Werfen.
Thrush, *n.* Drossel (*f*).
Thud, *n.* Dumfe Schlag (*m*).
Thumb, *n.* Daumen (*m*).
Thump, *n.* Stoss (*m*), Schlag (*m*): *v.* Plumpsen.
Thunder, *n.* Donner (*m*): *v.* Donnern.
Thunder-storm, *n.* Gewitter (*n*).
Thursday, *n.* Donnerstag (*m*).
Thus, *adv.* So, daher, also.
Thy, *pron.* Dein, deine.
Tick, *v.* Ticken (clock), anhaken (mark): *n.* Schafhaus (*f*).
Ticket, *n.* Karte (*f*), Eintrittskarte (admission) (*f*), Fahrkarte (rail) (*f*), Zettel (*m*).
Tickle, *v.* Kitzeln.
Tide, *n.* Flut (high tide) (*f*), Ebbe (low tide) (*f*).
Tidy, *adj.* Sauber, ordentlich.
Tie, *v.* Binden; *n.* Schleife (*f*), Halsbinde (neck) (*f*).
Tiger, *n.* Tiger (*m*).
Tight, *adj.* Fest, dicht, eng. Air-tight, Luftdicht.
Tile, *n.* Ziegel (roof) (*m*), Fliescn (ground) (*f*), Kachel (glazed) (*f*).
Till, *v.* Ackern, pflügen, bestellen: *prep. & conj.* Bis zu: *n.* Ladenkasse (*f*).
Tilt, *v.* Kippen, stossen, überdecken: *n.* Neigung (*f*).
Timber, *n.* Bauholz (*n*).
Time, *v.* Kontrollieren: *n.* Uhr (*f*), Zeit (*f*), Zeitmass (*n*).
Timetable, *n.* Fahrplan (*m*).
Timid, *adj.* Furchtsam.
Timorous, *adj.* Furchtsam.
Tin, *n.* Zinn (*n*).
Tincture, *n.* Anstrich (*m*), Tinktur (*f*).
Tinfoil, *n.* Stanniol (*n*).
Tingle, *v.* Klingen, prickeln.
Tiny, *adj.* Winzig.
Tip, *n.* Spitze (point) (*f*), Wink (advice) (*m*), Trinkgeld (gratuity) (*n*): *v.* Bespitzen, Trinkgeld geben.
Tire, *v.* Ermüden.
Tiresome, *adj.* Ermüdend.

Tissue-paper, *n.* Seidenpapier (*n*).
Title, *n.* Titel (*m*).
To, *prep.* Zu, an, fur, bis, nach, gegen.
Toad, *n.* Kröte (*f*).
Toast, *n.* Geröstete Brotschnitte (bread) (*f*), Trinkspruch (drinking health) (*m*).
Tobacco, *n.* Tabak (*m*).
Tobacco-pouch, *n.* Tabaksbeutel (*m*).
Toboggan, *n.* Rodelschlitten (*m*).
To-day, *adv.* Heute.
Toe, *n.* Zeh (*m*).
Together, *adv.* Zusammen.
Toilet, *n.* Toilette (*f*).
Tolerable, *adj.* Leidlich, erträglich.
Tolerant, *adj.* Duldsam.
Tolerate, *v.* Dulden, leiden.
Toll, *n.* Zoll (*m*): *v.* Lauten.
Tomb, *n.* Gruft (*f*).
Tombstone, *n.* Grabstein (*m*).
To-morrow, *adv.* Morgen.
Tongs, *n.* Zange (*f*).
Tongue, *n.* Zunge (*f*), Sprache (language) (*f*).
Tonic, *n.* Stärkungsmittel (*n*).
To-night, *adv.* Heute Abend.
Too, *adv.* Zu, allzu.
Tool, *n.* Werkzeug (*n*), Gerath (*n*).
Tooth, *n.* Zahn (*m*).
Toothache, *n.* Zahnschmerz (*m*).
Top, *n.* Kreisel (toy) (*m*), First (house-top) (*m*), Wipfel (tree-top) (*m*), Gipfel (hill-top) (*m*).
Torch, *n.* Fackel (*f*).
Torment, *v.* Peinigen.
Tormentor, *n.* Peiniger (*m*).
Torrent, *n.* Strom (*m*), Giessbach (*m*).
Tortoise, *n.* Schildkröte (*f*).
Torture, *n.* Folter (*f*): *v.* Foltern.
Toss, *v.* Werfen, losen, speissen.
Total, *adj.* Gänzlich, völlig.
Touch, *v.* Befühlen, spielen: *n.* Berührung.
Tough, *adj.* Zähe, hart, steif.
Tour, *n.* Rundreise (*f*).
Tournament, *n.* Turnier (*n*).
Tow, *v.* Bugsiren, schleppen.
Towards, *prep.* Gegen, nach, zu, bis an.
Towel, *n.* Handtuch (*n*).

Tower, *n.* Thurm (*m*).
Town, *n.* Stadt (*f*).
Town hall, *n.* Rathhaus (*n*).
Toy, *n.* Spielzeug (*n*), Tand (*m*).
Track, *n.* Bahn (*f*), Gleis (*n*), Spur (*f*).
Traction-engine, *n.* Lokomobile (*f*).
Trade, *n.* Handel (*m*).
Trade-mark, *n.* Schutzmarke (*f*).
Traffic, *n.* Verkehr (*m*).
Tragedy, *n.* Tragödie (*f*), Trauerspiel (*n*).
Tragic, *adj.* Tragisch.
Trail, *n.* Fährte (*f*), Spur (*f*), Schleppe (*f*).
Train, *n.* Zug (railway) (*m*), Schleppe (of dress) (*f*): *v.* Trainieren (for sport), dressieren (teaching).
Traitor, *n.* Verräter (*m*).
Tramp, *n.* Landstreicher (vagrant) (*m*), Fusstour (walk) (*f*).
Trample, *v.* Niedertreten, trampeln.
Trance, *n.* Entzückung (*f*), Hypnose (*f*).
Tranquil, *adj.* Still, gelassen, ruhrig.
Transact, *v.* Verrichten, verhandeln.
Transaction, *n.* Geschäft (*n*).
Transfer, *v.* Übertragen, verlegen, versetzen: *n.* Übertragung (*f*), Übertrag (*m*).
Transform, *v.* Umgestalten.
Transit, *n.* Durchgang (*m*), Transit (*m*).
Translate, *v.* Übersetzen.
Translation, *n.* Übersetzung (*f*).
Transmit, *v.* Übersenden.
Transparent, *adj.* Durchsichtig.
Transplant, *v.* Verpflanzen.
Transport, *n.* Transport (*m*), Versendung (*f*), Überfahrt (*f*): *v.* Transportieren, überfahren.
Trap, *n.* Falle (*f*); *v.* Fangen.
Travel, *n.* Reise (*f*); *v.* Reisen.
Traveller, *n.* Reisende (*m*).
Tray, *n.* Speisenbrett (*n*), Tablett (*n*).
Ashtray, **Aschbecher (*m*).**

Treacherous, *adj.* Verräterisch.
Treachery, *n.* Verrat (*m*), Falschheit (*f*).
Treacle, *n.* Theriak (*m*), Syrup (*m*).
Tread, *v.* Treten: *n.* Tritt (*m*).
Treason, *n.* Verrath (*m*).
Treasure, *n.* Schatz (*m*): *v.* Schätzen.
Treasurer, *n.* Schatzmeister (*m*).
Treasury, *n.* Schatzamt (*n*).
Treat, *n.* Schmaus (*m*), Genuss (*m*), Bewirtung (*f*), Ausflug (excursion) (*m*): *v.* Behandeln, verhandeln.
Treatment, *n.* Behandlung (*f*).
Treaty, *n.* Vertrag (*m*).
Tree, *n.* Baum (*m*).
Family tree, Stammbaum (*m*).
Tremble, *v.* Zittern, beben.
Tremendous, *adj.* Schrecklich, furchtbar, ungeheuer.
Trench, *n.* Graben (*m*), Einschnitt (*m*), Schützengraben (war) (*m*).
Trespass, *v.* Übertreten, sich vergehen, unbefugt betreten.
Trespasser, *n.* Übertreter (*m*).
Trial, *n.* Probe (*f*), Prüfung (*f*), Versuch (*m*).
Triangle, *n.* Dreieck (*n*).
Tribe, *n.* Stamm (*m*).
Tributary, *n.* Nebenfluss (*m*).
Tribute, *n.* Tribut (*m*), Beisteuer (*f*).
Trick, *n.* Trug (cheating) (*m*), Kunststück (conjuring) (*n*), Stitch (made at cards) (*m*), Kniff (*m*), List (*f*).
Trickle, *v.* Tröpfeln.
Trifle, *n.* Kleinigkeit (*f*): *v.* Tändeln, spielen.
Trigger, *n.* Drücker (*m*).
Trim, *v.* Putzen, besetzen, stutzen (cut hair).
Trip, *n.* Reise (journey) (*f*); *v.* Stolpern (trip up).
Tripe, *n.* Kaldaunen (*f. pl.*).
Triple, *adj.* Dreifach.
Triplets, *n.* Drillinge (*m. pl.*).
Tripod, *n.* Dreifuss (*m*), Stativ (camera) (*n*).
Tripper, *n.* Ausflügler (*m*).
Triumph, *n.* Triumph (*m*).
Trivial, *adj.* Gemein, **platt,** alltäglich.

Trolley, n. Handwagen (m), Karren (m), Rolle (f).
Troop, n. Trupp (m).
Trophy, n. Siegeszeichen (n).
Tropical, adj. Tropisch
Tropics, n. Tropen (f. pl.).
Trot, v. Traben.
Trouble, n. Kummer (m), Sorge (worries) (f), Unruhe (unrest) (f), Schwierigkeit (difficulties) (f), Mühe (f), Verdruss (m): v. Sich sorgen, sich bemühen, belästigen.
Troublesome, adj. Lästig, verdriesslich.
Trough, n. Trog (m).
Trousers, n. Hosen (f. pl.).
Trout, n. Forelle (f).
Trowel, n. Kelle (f), Maurerkelle (f).
Truant, n. Schulschwänzer (m).
Truce, n. Ruhe (f), Waffenstillstand (m).
Truck, n. Lore (rail) (f.,), Rollwagen (m).
True, adj. Wahr, echt, treu.
Truly, adv. Wirklich.
Yours truly, Ihr ergebener.
Trump, v. Trumpfen.
Trumpet, n. Trompete (f).
Trunk, n. Reisekoffer (travel) (m), Stamm (tree) (m), Rüssel (elephant) (m), Rumpf (of body) (m).
Trunk-call, n. Fernruf (telephone) (m).
Trunk-line, n. Fernleitung (telephone) (f), Hauptlinie (railway) (f).
Truss, v. Packen, verschnüren, zäumen (chickens): n. Bruchband (body) (n), Bündel (hay) (n).
Trust, n. Vertrauen (faith) (f), Trust (company) (n): v. Trauen.
Trustee, n. Treuhändler (m), Kurator (m).
Trustworthy, adj. Vertrauenswürdig.
Truth, n. Wahrheit (f).
Try, v. Versuchen, quälen, verhören (legal).
Trying, adj. Misslich, schwierig.
Tub, n. Kübel (m), Zuber (m), Badewanne (f).

Tube, n. Rohr (n), Röhre (f), Untergrundbahn (tube railway) (f).
Tuck, v. Falten, einschlagen: n. Falte (f).
Tuesday, n. Dienstag (m).
Tug, v. Zerren, ziehen, schleppen: n. Schlepper (boat) (m).
Tug of war, n. Tauziehen (n).
Tulip, n. Tulpe (f).
Tumble, v. Umfallen, purzeln, stürzen.
Tumbler, n. Wasserglas (n), Trinkglas (n).
Tumour, n. Geschwulst (f).
Tumult, n. Tumult (m), Aufruhr (f).
Tune, n. Melodie (f), Tonstück (n).
Tunic, n. Tunika (f), Waffenrock (m).
Tunnel, n. Tunnel (m).
Turbine, n. Turbine (f).
Turbot, n. Steinbutt (m).
Turbulent, adj. Stürmisch, aufrührerisch.
Turf, n. Rennbahn (racing) (f), Torf (grass) (m).
Turkey, n. Truthahn (bird) (m).
Turmoil, n. Unruhe (f).
Turn, v. Drehen, abwenden, übersetzen.
Turn-aside, v. Abwenden.
Turn-back, v. Zurückkehren.
Turning, n. Seitenstrasse (road) (f).
Turn-off, v. Ablenken.
Turn-on, v. Andrehen.
Turn-out, v. Ausdrehen, ausfallen, weigjagen (expel).
Turn-round, v. Sich herumdrehen.
Turpentine, n. Terpentin (m).
Turtle, n. Schildkröte (f), Seeschildkröte (f).
Turtle-dove, n. Turteltaube (f).
Tutor, n. Hauslehrer (m).
Tweezers, n. Pinzette (f).
Twelve, adj. Zwölf.
Twenty, adj. Zwanzig.
Twice, adv. Zweimal, zweifach, doppelt.
Twig, n. Zweig (m), Rute (f).
Twilight, n. Zwielicht (n).
Twin, n. Zwilling (m): adj. Doppelt.

Twine, *n.* Bindfaden (*m*), Schnur (*f*).
Twinge, *n.* Stich (*m*), Stechen (*n*): *v.* Stechen.
Twinkle, *v.* Blinken, flimmern, funkeln.
Twist, *v.* Drehen, verdrehen.
Twitch, *v.* Zucken.
Two, *adj.* Zwei.
Type, *n.* Schrift (for print) (*f*), Art (kind) (*f*), Vorbild (model) (*n*): *v.* Mit der Schreibmaschine schreiben (type-write).
Typewriter, *n.* Schreibmaschine (*f*).
Typhoid, *n.* Typhus (*m*): *adj.* Typhusartig.
Typical, *adj.* Vorbildlich, typisch.
Typist, *n.* Maschinenschreiber [in] (*m.* or *f.*).
Tyrant, *n.* Tyrann (*m*).
Tyre, *n.* Reifen (*m*).

U

Ugliness, *n.* Hässlichkeit (*f*).
Ugly, *adj.* Hässlich.
Ulcer, *n.* Geschwür (*n*).
Umbrella, *n.* Regenschirm (*m*).
Umpire, *n.* Schiedsrichter (*m*).
Unable, *adj.* Unfähig.
Unanimity, *n.* Einmütigkeit (*f*).
Unanimous, *adj.* Einstimmig.
Unawares, *adv.* Unversehens.
Unburden, *v.* Entbürden, entlasten.
Unbutton, *v.* Aufknöpfen.
Uncanny, *adj.* Unheimlich.
Uncivil, *adj.* Unhöflich.
Unclaimed, *adj.* Unverlangt.
Uncle, *n.* Onkel (*m*).
Unconcern, *n.* Gleichgültigkeit (*f*).
Unconscious, *adj.* Bewusstlos.
Unconventional, *adj.* Zwanglos.
Uncork, *v.* Entkorken.
Uncover, *v.* Aufdecken, entblössen.
Undeceive, *v.* Aufklären.
Under, *prep. & adv.* Unter, unten, weniger, geringer.
Under-done, *adj.* Ungar, blutig.
Underhand, *adj.* Hinterlistig.
Underneath, *prep.* Unter, unterwärts.
Understand, *v.* Verstehen, wissen, hören.
Understudy, *n.* Stellvertreter (*m*).
Undertaker, *n.* Leichenbestatter (*m*).
Underwriter, *n.* Assekurant (*m*).
Undignified, *adj.* Würdelos, unedel.
Undo, *v.* Aufmachen, auflösen, zerstören.
Undoing (downfall), *n.* Verderben (*n*).
Undoubted, *adj.* Unzweifelhaft.
Undress, *v.* Auskleiden.
Unduly, *adv.* Ungebührlich.
Unearth, *v.* Ausgraben.
Uneasy, *adj.* Ängstlich, unruhig.
Unemployed, *adj.* Arbeitslos.
Unequal, *adj.* Ungleich.
Uneven, *adj.* Uneben.
Unfold, *v.* Entfalten.
Unforeseen, *adj.* Unvorhergesehen.
Unfounded, *adj.* Grundlos.
Unfurnished, *adj.* Unmöbliert, entblösst.
Ungrateful, *adj.* Undankbar.
Uniform, *n.* Uniform (*f*).
Unimaginable, *adj.* Undenkbar.
Unintelligible, *adj.* Unverständlich.
Unpack, *v.* Auspacken.
Unprovided, *adj.* Unversorgt.
Unravel, *v.* Aufwickeln.
Unreasonable, *adj.* Unvernünftig.
Unrest, *n.* Unruhe (*f*).
Unroll, *v.* Abwickeln.
Unscrew, *v.* Losschrauben.
Unseen, *adj.* Ungesehen.
Unsettled, *adj.* Ungeordnet, unbeständig.
Unsightly, *adj.* Hässlich.
Unskilled, *adj.* Ungelernt.
Unsolved, *adj.* Ungelöst.
Unsuccessful, *adj.* Erfolglos.
Untidy, *adj.* Unordentlich.
Until, *conj.* Bis: *prep.* Bis, bis zu.
Untrue, *adj.* Untreu, unwahr.
Unveil, *v.* Entschleiern.
Unwell, *adj.* Unwohl.
Unwise, *adj.* Unklug.
Unwrap, *v.* Loswickeln.

| Up | 179 | Vibration |

Up, *adv. & prep.* Auf, aufwärts, hinauf, oben, empor.
Upheaval, *n.* Erhebung (*f*), Umwälzung (*f*).
Uphill, *adj.* Schwierig, bergan, bergauf.
Uphold, *v.* Stützen, aufrechterhalten.
Upholsterer, *n.* Möbelhändler (*m*).
Upkeep, *n.* Instandhaltung (*f*).
Upon, *prep.* An, auf, bei, nach, wegen, zufolge.
Upper, *adj.* Ober, höher.
Upperhand, *n.* Oberhand (*f*).
Uppermost, *adj.* Oberst, höchst.
Upright, *adj.* Aufrecht, gerade.
Uproar, *n.* Aufruhr (*m*).
Upset, *v.* Umwerfen, umstürzen.
Upside down, *adj.* Umgekehrt.
Upstairs, *adv.* Oben.
Upwards, *adv.* Aufwärts.
Urchin, *n.* Kleine Schelm (*m*), Kleiner Kerl (*m*).
Urge, *v.* Drängen, treiben.
Urgent, *adj.* Dringend.
Urine, *n.* Urin (*m*), Harn (*m*).
Us, *pron.* Uns.
Use, *n.* Gebrauch (*m*), Brauch (*m*), Genuss (*m*), Nutzen (*m*): *v.* Gebrauchen, anwenden.
Usual, *adj.* Üblich, gebräuchlich.
Utensil, *n.* Gerät (*n*).
Utility, *n.* Nützlichkeit (*f*).
Utmost, *adj.* Äusserst, höchst.
Utter, *adj.* Völlig; *v.* Äussern.
Utterly, *adv.* Äusserst.

V

Vacant, *adj.* Leer.
Vacation, *n.* Ferein (*f. pl.*), Räumung (*f*).
Vaccinate, *v.* Impfen.
Vacuum cleaner, *n.* Staubsauger (*m*).
Vagabond, *n.* Vagabund (*m*).
Vague, *adj.* Unbestimmt.
Vain, *adj.* Leer, eitel, nichtig.
Vale, *n.* Tal (*n*).
Valet, *n.* Lakai (*m*), Diener (*m*).
Valiant, *adj.* Tapfer, brav, kühn.
Valid, *adj.* Triftig, gültig.
Valley, *n.* Tal (*n*).
Valour, *n.* Tapferkeit (*f*).
Valuable, *adj.* Kostbar, wertvoll.
Value, *n.* Wert (*m*), Preis (*m*): *v.* Schätzen.
Vanilla, *n.* Vanille (*f*).
Vanish, *v.* Verschwinden.
Vanity, *n.* Nichtigkeit (*f*).
Vanquish, *v.* Besiegen.
Vapour, *n.* Dampf (*m*), Dunst (*m*).
Variation, *n.* Veränderung (*f*).
Varicose, *adj.* Krampfaderig.
Variety, *n.* Mannigfaltigkeit (*f*), Variete (*n*).
Various, *adj.* Verschieden.
Varnish, *n.* Firnis (*m*), Anstrich (*m*), Lac (*m*).
Vary, *v.* Abweichen, ändern.
Vast, *adj.* Weit, sehr gross, ungeheuer.
Vault, *n.* Gruft (*f*), Gewölbe (*n*).
Veal, *n.* Kalbfleisch (*n*).
Vegetable[s], *n.* Gemüse (*n*), Pflanze (*f*).
Vehicle, *n.* Fuhrwerk (*n*).
Vein, *n.* Ader (*f*), Blutader (*f*), Stimmung (*f*).
Velvet, *n.* Samt (*m*).
Veneer, *n.* Furnier (*n*).
Vengeance, *n.* Rache (*f*).
Venison, *n.* Wildbret (*n*).
Venomous, *adj.* Giftig.
Ventilate, *v.* Lüften, erörtern.
Ventilator, *n.* Ventilator (*m*).
Veranda, *n.* Veranda (*f*).
Verb, *n.* Verbum (*n*).
Verdict, *n.* Urteil (*n*), Spruch (*m*).
Verger, *n.* Küster (*m*).
Verify, *v.* Bestätigen, beglaubigen.
Vermilion, *n.* Scharlach (*m*).
Vermin, *n.* Ungeziefer (*n*).
Verse, *n.* Vers (*m*), Dichtung (*f*), Strophe (*f*).
Vertical, *adj.* Senkrecht.
Very, *adv.* Sehr: *adj.* **Gerade**, echt.
Vest, *n.* Unterjacke (*f*).
Vestry, *n.* Sakristei (*f*).
Veterinary-surgeon, *n.* Tierarzt (*m*).
Vex, *v.* Plagen, ärgern.
Viaduct, *n.* Viadukt (*m*).
Vibrate, *v.* Vibrieren, schwingen.
Vibration, *n.* Vibrieren (*n*), Schwingung (*f*).

Vicar — Wart

Vicar, *n.* Vikar (*m*), Pfarrer (*m*).
Vice, *n.* Laster (wrong) (*m*), Schraubstock (tool) (*m*).
Vicious, *adj.* Lasterhaft.
Victim, *n.* Opfer (*n*).
Victor, *n.* Sieger (*m*).
Victory, *n.* Sieg (*m*).
Victuals, *n.* Lebensmittel (*n. pl.*).
View, *n.* Aussicht (*f*), Ausblick (*m*).
Vigorous, *adj.* Rüstig, kräftig.
Vile, *adj.* Niedrig, niederträchtig.
Villa, *n.* Villa (*f*), Landhaus (*n*).
Village, *n.* Dorf (*n*).
Villager, *n.* Dorfbewohner (*m*).
Villain, *n.* Schurke (*m*).
Vine, *n.* Weinstock (*m*), Ranke (*f*).
Vinegar, *n.* Essig (*m*).
Viola, *n.* Bratsche (*f*).
Violate, *v.* Verletzen, übertreten, notzüchtigen.
Violence, *n.* Gewalt (*f*), Heftigkeit (*f*).
Violent, *adj.* Gewaltsam, heftig.
Violet, *n.* Veilchen (*n*).
Violin, *n.* Violine (*f*), Geige (*f*).
Viper, *n.* Viper (*f*), Natter (*f*).
Virgin, *n.* Jungfrau (*f*).
Virile, *adj.* Mannbar, männlich.
Virtue, *n.* Tugend (*f*), Keuschheit (moral) (*f*).
Visibility, *n.* Sicht (*f*), Sichtbarkeit (*f*).
Vision, *n.* Sehkraft (*f*), Phantom (*n*).
Visit, *n.* Besuch (*m*): *v.* Besuchen, besichtigen.
Visiting-card, *n.* Visitenkarte (*f*).
Vital, *adj.* Unentbehrlich, wesentlich.
Vivacious, *adj.* Lebhaft, munter.
Vixen, *n.* Füchsin (*f*).
Viz., *adv.* Nämlich.
Vocabulary, *n.* Wörterverzeichnis (*n*).
Vocal, *adj.* Vokal.
Vogue, *n.* Mode (*f*).
Voice, *n.* Stimme (*f*), Sprache (*f*).
Void, *n.* Leere (*f*); *adj.* Leer.
Volcano, *n.* Vulkan (*m*).
Voluble, *adj.* Beweglich, redselig.
Volume, *n.* Band (book) *m,* Volumen (quantity) (*n*).
Voluntary, *adj.* Freiwillig.
Vomit, *v.* Sich erbrechen.
Voracious, *adj.* Gierig, gefrässig.
Vote, *n.* Wahlstimme (*f*): *v.* Wählen.
Voter, *n.* Wähler (*m*), Wählerin (*f*).
Vow, *v.* Geloben; *n.* Gelübde (*n*).
Vowel, *v.* Vokal (*m*).
Voyage, *n.* Seereise (*f*), Reise (*f*): *v.* Reisen.
Vulgar, *adj.* Gemein, vulgär, pöbelhaft.
Vulture, *n.* Geier (*m*).

W

Wag, *v.* Schütteln: *n.* Spassvogel (*m*).
Wage, *n.* Lohn (*m*).
Wager, *n.* Wette (*f*): *v.* Wetten.
Waggon, *n.* Wagon (*m*).
Wagtail, *n.* Bachstelze (bird) (*f*).
Waif, *n.* Herrenlose Sache (*f*).
Wail, *n.* Klage (*f*): *v.* Beklagen.
Waist, *n.* Taille (*f*).
Waistcoat, *n.* Weste (*f*).
Wait, *v.* Warten, aufpassen: *n.* Lauer (*f*).
Waiter, *n.* Kellner (*m*), Aufwärter (*m*).
Waiting-room, *n.* Wartesaal (*m*).
Waitress, *n.* Kellnerin (*f*).
Wake, *v.* Aufwachen.
Wakeful, *adj.* Wachend.
Walk, *v.* Spazierengehen, gehen: *n.* Spaziergang (*m*).
Wall, *n.* Mauer (*f*), Wand (*f*).
Wallflower, *n.* Goldlack (*m*).
Wallpaper, *n.* Tapete (*f*).
Walnut, *n.* Walnuss (*f*).
Waltz, *n.* Walzer (*m*): *v.* Walzen.
Want, *v.* Nötig haben, wollen, brauchen: *n.* Mangel (*m*).
War, *n.* Kreig (*m*): *v.* Kriegen, kämpfen.
Warm, *adj.* Warm: *v.* Wärmen.
Warmth, *n.* Wärme (*f*).
Warn, *v.* Warnen.
Warning, *n.* Warnung (*f*).
Warrant, *n.* Vollmacht (*f*).
Wart, *n.* Warze (*f*).

Wash — Whip

Wash, *v.* Sich waschen: *n.* Wäsche (*f*).
Wash-basin, *n.* Waschbecken (*n*).
Washing (laundry), *n.* Wäsche (*f*).
Wash-stand, *n.* Waschtisch (*m*).
Wasp, *n.* Wespe (*f*).
Waste, *v.* Verwüsten, verschwenden: *n.* Abfall (*m*), Verschwendung (*f*).
Wasteful, *adj.* Verschwenderisch.
Wastepaper, *n.* Makulatur (*f*).
Wastepaper-basket, *n.* Papierkorb (*m*).
Watch, *n.* Uhr (*f*), Wache (at sea) (*f*), Taschenuhr (pocket watch) (*f*), Armbanduhr (wrist watch) (*f*): *v.* Bewachen, beobachten, hüten.
Watchful, *adj.* Wachsam.
Watchmaker, *n.* Uhrmacher (*m*).
Water, *n.* Wasser (*n*): *v.* Begiessen, tränken.
  Drinking water, Trinkwasser (*n*).
  Hot water bottle, Wärmflasche (*f*).
  W.C., Klosett (*n*).
Watercress, *n.* Brunnenkresse (*f*).
Waterfall, *n.* Wasserfall (*m*).
Waterproof, *n.* Regenmantel (*m*).
Wave, *n.* Welle (sea) (*f*); *v.* Winken (the hand), wellen (the hair).
Wax, *n.* Wachs (*n*).
Way, *n.* Weg (*m*), Weise (*f*), Bahn (*f*).
Way out, *n.* Ausgang (*m*).
We, *pron.* Wir.
Weak, *adj.* Schwach.
Weaken, *v.* Schwächen.
Wealth, *n.* Reichtum (*m*), Wohlstand (*m*).
Wealthy, *adj.* Wohlhabend, reich.
Wean, *v.* Entwöhnen.
Weapon, *n.* Wehr (*n*), Waffe (*f*).
Wear, *v.* Tragen, abtragen, abnutzen: *n.* Tragen (*n*).
Weary, *adj.* Müde, matt.
Weather, *n.* Wetter (*n*), Witterung (*f*): *v.* Lüften.
Weave, *v.* Weben.

Web, *n.* Gewebe (*n*).
Wed, *v.* Heiraten.
Wedding, *n.* Hochzeit (*f*).
Wedding ring, *n.* Trauring (*m*).
Wedge, *n.* Keil (*m*): *v.* Verkeilen.
Wednesday, *n.* Mittwoch (*m*).
Weed, *n.* Unkraut (*n*): *v.* Jäten.
Week, *n.* Woche (*f*).
Week-day, *n.* Werktag (*m*).
Week-end, *n.* Wochenende (*n*).
Weep, *v.* Weinen, triefen, beklagen.
Weigh, *v.* Wiegen, wägen, schätzen.
Weight, *n.* Gewicht (*n*).
Weir, *n.* Wehr (*n*).
Weird, *adj.* Unheimlich, sonderbar, seltsam.
Welcome, *v.* Willkommen: *n.* Willkommen (*m*): *adj.* Willkommen.
Weld, *v.* Schweissen.
Welfare, *n.* Wohlfahrt (*f*).
Well, *n.* Quelle (*f*), Brunnen (*m*): *v.* Quellen: *adj.* Wohl, leicht, gut, gesund.
West, *n.* Westen (*m*), Abend (*m*).
Westerly, *adj.* Westlich.
Whale, *n.* Walfisch (*m*).
Wharf, *n.* Kai (*m*), Werft (*f*. & *n*.), Landeplatz (*m*).
What, *pron.* Was, wie, welcher, welches.
Whatever, *adv.* Was auch, was auch immer, was nur.
Wheat, *n.* Weizen (*m*).
Wheel, *n.* Rad (*n*), Fahrrad (*n*).
Wheelbarrow, *n.* Schubkarren (*n*).
Whelk, *n.* Kinkhorn (*n*).
When, *adv. & conj.* Wenn, wann, als, da, wo.
Whence, *adv.* Woher.
Where, *adv.* Wo, wohin.
Whereas, *adv.* Während, da, doch.
Wherefore, *adv.* Weshalb.
Whereupon, *adv.* Worauf.
Whether, *conj.* Ob.
Which, *pron.* Welcher, **welche,** welches, der, die, das.
While, *conj.* Während.
Whine, *v.* Wimmern.
Whip, *n.* Geissel (*f*), Kutscher (*m*): *v.* Springen, geisseln.

| Whirlpool | 182 | Wren |

Whirlpool, *n.* Strudel (*m*).
Whiskers, *n.* Backenbart (*m*).
Whisky, *n.* Whisky (*m*).
Whisper, *v.* Wispern, flüstern: *n.* Geflüster (*n*).
Whist, *n.* Whist (*n*).
Whistle, *n.* Pfeife (instrument) (*f*), Pfiff (sound) (*m*).
White, *adj.* Weiss.
Whitsunday, *n.* Pfingstsonntag (*m*).
Who, *pron.* Wer, welcher, welche, welches.
Whoever, *pron.* Jeder, wer auch.
Whole, *adj.* Ganz, gesund, heil.
Wholesale, *adj.* Gross.
Whooping-cough, *n.* Keuchhusten (*m*).
Whore, *n.* Hure (*f*).
Whose, *pron.* Wessen, dessen, deren.
Why, *adv.* Warum.
Wicked, *adj.* Gottlos, verrucht, böse.
Wicket (cricket), *n.* Dreistab (*m*).
Wide, *adj.* Weit, breit, sehr.
Widow, *n.* Witwe (*f*).
Widower, *n.* Witwer (*m*).
Width, *n.* Breite (*f*), Weite (*f*).
Wife, *n.* Frau (*f*), Gattin (*f*).
Wig, *n.* Perücke (*f*).
Wild, *adj.* Wild (savage), toll (maddened), roh.
Wilful, *adj.* Eigenwillig, eigensinnig.
Will, *n.* Wille (*m*), Verlangen (*n*), Testament (*n*): *v.* Wollen, vermachen.
Willing, *adj.* Willig, gern, bereit.
Win, *v.* Gewinnen.
Winner, *n.* Gewinner (*m*).
Winning-post, *n.* Ziel (*n*).
Wind, *n.* Wind (*m*), Blähung (*f*): *v.* Winden.
Windmill, *n.* Windmühle (*f*).
Window, *n.* Fenster (*n*).
Windpipe, *n.* Luftröhre (*f*).
Wine, *n.* Wein (*m*).
Wineglass, *n.* Weinglas (*n*).
Wing, *n.* Flügel (*m*).
Wink, *v.* Winken: *n.* Blinzeln (*n*).
Winter, *n.* Winter (*m*).
Wipe, *v.* Wischen, austilgen.
Wire, *n.* Draht (*m*).
Wireless, *n.* Radio (*n*).

Wireless-operator, *n.* Funker (*m*).
Wisdom, *n.* Weisheit (*f*), Klugheit (*f*).
Wise, *adj.* Weise, klug, verständig.
Wish, *n.* Wunsch (*m*): *v.* Wünschen.
Witch, *n.* Hexe (*f*), Zauberin (*f*).
With, *prep.* Mit, bei, für, auf, durch.
Within, *adv.* Drinnen: *prep.* In, innerhalb.
Without, *prep.* Ohne, vor; *adv.* Draussen.
Witness, *n.* Zeuge (*m*), Zeugnis (*n*).
Witty, *adj.* Witzig.
Wizard, *n.* Zauberer (*m*).
Woe, *n.* Weh (*n*).
Wolf, *n.* Wolf (*m*), Wölfin (*f*).
Woman, *n.* Frau (*f*), Weib (*n*).
Womb, *n.* Gebärmutter (*f*).
Wonder, *n.* Wunder (*n*), Verwunderung (*f*): *v.* Sich wundern.
Wonderful, *adj.* Wunderbar.
Wood, *n.* Holz (material) (*n*), Wald (forest) (*m*).
Wool, *n.* Wolle (*f*).
Woollen, *adj.* Wollen.
Word, *n.* Wort (*n*), Losung (*f*), Nachricht (*f*).
Work, *n.* Arbeit (*f*), Werk (*n*): *v.* Arbeiten.
Workhouse, *n.* Armenhaus (*n*).
Workman, *n.* Arbeiter (*m*).
World, *n.* Welt (*f*), Erde (*f*).
Worm, *n.* Wurm (insect) (*m*), Gewinde (thread of screw) (*n*).
Worry, *n.* Sorge (*f*), Besorgnis (*f*): *v* Sich sorgen.
Worse, *adj.* Schlechter, schlimmer, ärger.
Worst, *adj.* Schlechteste, schlimmste; *n.* Ärgste (*n*).
Worth, *n.* Wert (*m*), Verdienst (*n*): *adj.* Wert.
Wound, *v.* Verwunden: *n.* Wunde (*f*).
Wrap, *v.* Hüllen, wickeln, einschlagen: *n.* Umhang (*m*).
Wrapper, *n.* Kreuzband (*n*), Umschlag (*m*).
Wreath, *n.* Kranz (*m*).
Wreck, *n.* Wrack (*n*), Schiffbruch (*m*): *v.* Zertrümmern.
Wren, *n.* Zaunkönig (*m*).

Wrench   183   **Zoology**

Wrench, *v.* Verrenken, entwinden, reissen: *n.* Ruck (*m*), Verrenkung (*f*).
Wrestle, *v.* Ringen, kämpfen.
Wrestler, *n.* Ringkämpfer (*m*).
Wretched, *adj.* Unglücklich.
Wring, *v.* Ringen, peinigen, bedrücken.
Wrinkle, *n.* Runzel (face) (*f*), Falte (face) (*f*): *v.* Runzeln.
Wrist, *n.* Handgelenk (*n*).
Write, *v.* Schreiben.
Writer, *n.* Schreiber (*m*), Schriftsteller (composer) (*m*).
Writing, *n.* Schrift (*f*).
Writing-Paper, *n.* Schreibpapier (*n*).
Wrong, *adj.* Unrecht, verkehrt, falsch.

Y

Yacht, *n.* Jacht (*f*).
Yard, *n.* Hof (*m*), Hofraum (*m*).
Yawn, *v.* Gähnen.
Year, *n.* Jahr (*n*).
Yell, *v.* Gellen, kreischen, schreien: *n.* Schrei (*m*).
Yellow, *adj.* Gelb.
Yes, *adv.* Ja.
Yesterday, *adv.* Gestern.
Yet, *adv.* Noch: *conj.* Aber, dennoch, doch.
Yew, *n.* Eibe (*f*).
You, *pron.* Du, dich, ihr, sie, euch, einen.
Young, *adj.* Jung.
Youngster, *n* Jüngling (*m*).
Your, *pron.* Euer, ihr, dein.
Yours, *pron.* Euer, eurig, eurige, ihr, dein.
Youth, *n.* Jugend (*f*).

Z

Zebra, *n.* Zebra (*n*).
Zero, *n.* Null (*f*), Nullpunkt (*m*).
Zest, *n.* Würze (*f*), Genuss (*m*), Eifer (*m*).
Zinc, *n.* Zink (*n*).
Zip-fastener, *n.* Reissverschluss (*m*).
Zoology, *n.* Tierkunde (*f*), Zoologie (*f*).

GEOGRAPHICAL NAMES
(GEOGRAPHISCHE NAMEN)

Africa—Afrika
America—Amerika
Antwerp—Antwerpen
Asia—Asien
Atlantic Ocean — Atlantische Meer
Athens—Athen
Australia—Australien
Bavaria—Bayern
Belgium—Belgien
Bohemia—Böhmen
Brussels—Brüssel
Bulgaria—Bulgarien
Canada—Kanada
China—China
Denmark—Dänemark
Europe—Europa
France—Frankreich
Geneva—Genf
Genoa—Genua
Germany—Deutschland
Great Britain—Grossbritannien
Greece—Griechenland
Hungary—Ungarn
Italy—Italien
Lorraine—Lothringen
Mediterranean—Mittelländische
Moscow—Moskau
Munich—München
Naples—Neapel
Netherlands—Niederlande
Norway—Norwegen
Ostend—Ostende
Persia—Persien
Poland—Polen
Prague—Prag
Prussia—Preussen
Pyrenees—Pyrenäen
Rhine—Rhein
Rome—Rom
Russia—Russland
Scotland—Schottland
Spain—Spanien
Sweden—Schweden
Switzerland—Schweiz
Turkey—Türkei
United States — Vereinigten Staaten

GERMAN VERBS

(† Conjugated with **Sein**)

Infinitive	Imperfect	Past Partic.	English
Befehlen	Befahl	Befohlen	To order
Beissen	Biss	Gebissen	to bite
Bergen	Barg	Geborgen	to hide
Biegen	Bog	Gebogen	to bend
Binden	Band	Gebunden	to bind
Bitten	Bat	Gebeten	to beg
Bleiben	Blieb	Geblieben	to stay
Brechen	Brach	Gebrochen	to break
Dringen†	Drang	Gedrungen	to press
Erschrecken	Erschrak	Erschrocken	to be frightened
Essen	Ass	Gegessen	to eat
Fahren†	Fuhr	Gefahren	to drive
Fallen†	Fiel	Gefallen	to fall
Fangen	Fing	Gefangen	to catch
Finden	Fand	Gefunden	to find
Fliegen†	Flog	Geflogen	to fly
Fliessen†	Floss	Geflossen	to flow
Geben	Gab	Gegeben	to give
Gehen†	Ging	Gegangen	to go
Gelten	Galt	Gegolten	to be worth
Geniessen	Genoss	Genossen	to enjoy
Geschehen	Geschah	Geschehen	to happen
Gewinnen	Gewann	Gewonnen	to win
Gleichen	Glich	Geglichen	to be like
Graben	Grub	Gegraben	to dig
Greifen	Griff	Gegriffen	to seize
Halten	Hielt	Gehalten	to hold
Hangen	Hing	Gehangen	to hang
Heissen	Hiess	Geheissen	to be called
Helfen	Half	Geholfen	to help
Klingen	Klang	Geklungen	to sound
Kommen†	Kam	Gekommen	to come
Laden	Lud	Geladen	to load
Lassen	Liess	Gelassen	to let (allow)
Laufen†	Lief	Gelaufen	to run
Leiden	Litt	Gelitten	to suffer
Lesen	Las	Gelesen	to read
Liegen	Lag	Gelegen	to lie
Nehmen	Nahm	Genommen	to take
Raten	Riet	Geraten	to advise
Reissen	Riss	Gerissen	to tear
Rufen	Rief	Gerufen	to call
Scheiden	Schied	Geschieden	to separate
Scheinen	Schien	Geschienen	to seem
Schieban	Schob	Geschoben	to push
Schlafen	Schlief	Geschlafen	to sleep
Schlagen	Schlug	Geschlagen	to beat
Schleifen	Schliff	Geschliffen	to sharpen
Schliessen	Schloss	Geschlossen	to shut
Schneiden	Schnitt	Geschnitten	to cut
Schreiben	Schrieb	Geschrieben	to write
Schwimmen†	Schwamm	Geschwommen	to swim
Sehen	Sah	Gesehen	to see
Singen	Sang	Gesungen	to sing
Sitzen	Sass	Gesessen	to sit
Sprechen	Sprach	Gesprochen	to speak

GERMAN VERBS—Continued

Infinitive	Imperfect	Past Partic.	English
Springen†	Sprang	Gesprungen	to jump
Stechen	Stach	Gestochen	to sting
Stehen	Stand	Gestanden	to stand
Stehlen	Stahl	Gestohlen	to steal
Tragen	Trug	Getragen	to carry
Treffen	Traf	Getroffen	to meet
Treiben	Trieb	Getrieben	to drive
Treten†	Trat	Getreten	to step
Trinken	Trank	Getrunken	to drink
Tun	Tat	Getan	to do
Vergessen	Vergass	Vergessen	to forget
Verlieren	Verlor	Verloren	to lose
Verstehen	Verstand	Verstanden	to understand
Wachsen†	Wuchs	Gewachsen	to grow
Weisen	Wies	Gewiesen	to point out
Werfen	Warf	Geworfen	to throw
Ziehen	Zog	Gezogen	to draw
Zwingen	Zwang	Gezwungen	to force

USEFUL PHRASES FOR THE TRAVELLER

Good morning : Guten Morgen.
    (Goot'-en morg'-en)
Good evening: Guten Abend.
    (Goot'-en ah'-bent)
Good night: Gute Nacht.
    (Goot'-ter nahkt)
Good bye: Leben Sie wohl.
    (Lay'-ben zee vohl)
How do you do? Wie befinden Sie sich?
    (Vee be-fin'-den zee sik)
Please: Bitte.
    (Bit'-ter)
If you please: Gefälligst Bitte.
    (Ge-fell'-ikst bit'-ter)
Have you: Haben Sie
    (Hah'-ben zee).
Give me: Geben Sie mir.
    (Gay'-ben zee meer)
Thanks: Danke.
    (Dan'-ker)
Thank you: Ich danke.
    (Ik dan'-ker)
Very well: Sehr wohl.
    (Zair vohl)
Allow me: Erlauben Sie mir.
    (Air-lowb'-en zee meer)
Pardon me: Verzeihen Sie.
    (Fair-tsy'-gen zee)
Excuse me: Entschuldigen Sie.
    (Ent-shool'-digen zee)
How much? Wie viel?
    (Vee feel)
Bring me: Bringen Sie mir.
    (Bring'-en zee meer)

USEFUL PHRASES FOR THE TRAVELLER

I want: Ich brauche.
    (Ik browk-erh)
Will you: Wollen Sie.
    (Voll'-en zee)
Do you know: Wissen Sie.
    (Viss'-en zee)
At once: So fort.
    (Soh fort)
I should like: Ich möchte.
    (Ik mowh'-h-te)
My luggage: Mein Gepäck.
    (Mine gay-peck')
A ticket: Ein Billett.
    (Eye'-n bil-yett')
I want a first, second, third class ticket: Geben Sie mir ein Billett, erster, zweiter, dritter Klasse.
    (Gayb'-en zee meer ine bill-yett', ers'-ter, tsvy'-te, dritt-ter klass'-se)
Where is the ticket office? Wo ist der Billett-Schalter?
    (Voh ist dayr bill-yett' shal-ter)
Where is the cloak room?: Wo ist die Garderobe?
    (Voh ist dee gahrd-rohb'-er)
Where is the luggage office?: Wo ist das Gepäck-Bureau?
    (Voh ist dahs gay-peck' beer-oh')
Which is the train for—?: Welches ist der Zug nach—?
    (Velk'-es ist dayr tsook nahkt—)
Non-smokers: Nichtraucher.
    (Nikt roy'-ker)
Is this seat taken?: Ist dieser Platz besetzt?
    (Ist dee'-zer platz be-zett'-st)
These are my things: Diese sind meine Sachen.
    (Dee'-zeh sindt mine'-erh sahk'-n)
What is the fare to—?: Wie viel kostet es nach—?
    (Vee feel kost'-et s nahkt)
How long do we wait here?: Wie lange halten wir hier?
    (Vee lahng'-er hahl'-ten veer heer)
I have nothing to declare: Ich habe nichts zu verzollen.
    (Ik hah'-ber nikts tsoo fair-tsol'-en)
Call a taxi: Rufen Sie ein Auto.
    (Roof'-en zee ine owe'-toe)
I am very sorry: Es tut mir sehr leid.
    (Ess toot meer zair lite)
Have you a bedroom?: Haben Sie ein Schlafzimmer?
    (Hah'-ben zee ine shlahf'-tzim-er)
Where is the—?: Wo ist der—?
    (Voh ist dayr—)
Wake me at — o'clock: Wecken Sie mich um—Uhr.
    (Veck-en zee mich oom—oohr)
What have you ready?: Was haben Sie bereit?
    (Vass hah'-ben zee be-rite')
Bring me my bill: Bringen Sie mir die Rechnung.
    (Bring'-en zee meer dee rek'-noong)
Yes, sir: Ja, mein Herr.
    (Yah, mine hair)
I cannot decide yet: Ich kann mich noch nicht entschliessen.
    (Ik kahn mich nok nikt ent-schlees'-en)
Have you seen my—?: Haben Sie mein—gesehen?
    (Hah'ben zee mine—ge-zay'-en)

USEFUL PHRASES FOR THE TRAVELLER

I do not know where it is: Ich weiss es nicht.
                (Ik veiss ess nikt)
Yes, you are right: Ja, Sie haben recht.
                (Yah, zee hah′ben rekt)
Am I not right?: Habe ich recht oder nicht?
                (Hah′-ber ik rekt oh-der′ nikt)
I have not enough money: Ich habe nicht genug Geld.
                (Ik hah′-ber nikt ge-nook′ gelt)
I shall pay: Ich werde bezahlen.
                (Ik vair-der bet-sahl′-en)

LIST OF NUMERALS
CARDINAL NUMBERS (GRUNDZAHLEN)

1. Eins
2. Zwei
3. Drei
4. Vier
5. Fünf
6. Sechs
7. Sieben
8. Acht
9. Neun
10. Zehn
11. Elf
12. Zwölf
13. Dreizehn
14. Vierzehn
15. Fünfzehn
16. Sechszehn
17. Siebenzehn
18. Achtzehn
19. Neunzehn
20. Zwanzig
21. Einundzwanzig
22. Zweiundzwanzig
23. Dreiundzwanzig
24. Vierundzwanzig
25. Fünfundzwanzig
26. Sechsundzwanzig
27. Siebenundzwanzig
28. Achtundzwanzig
29. Neunundzwanzig
30. Dreissig
31. Einunddreissig
32. Zweiunddreissig
40. Vierzig
41. Einundvierzig
42. Zweiundvierzig
50. Fünfzig
51. Einundfünfzig
52. Zweiundfünfzig
60. Sechzig
61. Einundsechzig
62. Zweiundsechzig
70. Siebzig
71. Einundsiebzig
72. Zweiundsiebzig
73. Dreiundsiebzig
74. Vierundsiebzig
75. Fünfundsiebzig
80. Achtzig
81. Einundachtzig
82. Zweiundachtzig
90. Neunzig
91. Einundneunzig
92. Zweiundneunzig
100. Hundert
101. Hunderteins (Hundert und eins)
102. Hundertzwei
110. Hundertzehn
120. Hundertzwanzig
130. Hundertdressig
140. Hundertvierzig
150. Hundertfünfzig
160. Hundertsechzig
170. Hundertsiebzig
180. Hundertachtzig
190. Hundertneunzig
200. Zweihundert
300. Dreihundert
400. Vierhundert
500. Fünfhundert
600. Sechshundert
700. Siebenhundert
800. Achthundert
900. Neunhundert
1,000. Tausend
1,001. Tausendundeins
2,000. Zweitausend
5,000. Fünftausend
1,000,000—Eine Million

ORDINAL NUMBERS (ORDNUNGSZAHLEN)

1st. Der Erste	15th. Der Fünfzehnte
2nd. Der Zweite	16th. Der Sechzehnte
3rd. Der Dritte	17th. Der Siebzehnte
4th. Der Vierte	20th. Der Zwanzigste
5th. Der Fünfte	21st. Der Ein und zwanzigste
6th. Der Sechste	30th. Der Dreissigste
7th. Der Siebente	40th. Der Vierzigste
8th. Der Achte	50th. Der Fünfzigste
9th. Der Neunte	60th. Der Sechzigste
10th. Der Zehnte	70th. Der Siebzigste
11th. Der Elfte	80th. Der Achtzigste
12th. Der Zwölfte	90th. Der Neunzigste
13th. Der Dreizehnte	100th. Der Hundertste
14th. Der Vierzehnte	1000th. Der Tausendste

FRACTIONS (BRÜCHE)

Half: Die Hälfte (Halb)	Fifth: Das Fünftel
Quarter: Das Viertel	Sixth: Das Sechstel
Third: Das Drittel	Tenth: Das Zehntel

COLLECTIVE NUMBERS (SAMMLUNGSZAHLEN)

A pair, Ein Paar	Singly, Einzig
A dozen, Ein Dutzend	The last but one, Der Vorletzte
A score, Zwanzig	The first time, Das erste Mal
The last, Der Letzte	The second time, Das zweite Mal
Once, Einmal	Double, Doppelt
Twice, Zweimal	Triple, Dreifach
Three times, Dreimal	Firstly, Erstens

THE MONTHS
(DIE MONATE IM JAHR)

January—Januar	July—Juli
February—Februar	August—August
March—März	September—September
April—April	October—Oktober
May—Mai	November—November
June—Juni	December—Dezember

DAYS OF THE WEEK
(DIE WOCHENTAGE)

Sunday—Sonntag	Thursday—Donnerstag
Monday—Montag	Friday—Freitag
Tuesday—Dienstag	Saturday—Sonnabend
Wednesday—Mittwoch	

COLOURS
(FARBEN)

Black, Schwarz	Olive, Olivenfarbig
Blue, Blau	Orange, Orange
Brown, Braun	Pink, Rosa
Carmine, Karmin	Purple, Purpur
Cream, Crème	Red, Rot
Crimson, Karmesin	Scarlet, Scharlach
Fawn, Beige	Violet, Violet
Flesh-colour, Fleischfarbig	White, Weiss
Green, Grün	Yellow, Gelb
Grey, Grau	

(Lighter = Hellere: Darker = Dunklere)

TIME
(DIE ZEIT)

A year, Ein Jahr	Spring, Der Frühling
A month, Ein Monat	Summer, Der Sommer
A fortnight, Vierzehn Tage	Autumn, Der Herbst
A week, Eine Woche	Winter, Der Winter
A day, Ein Tag	Christmas, Weihnachten
An hour, Eine Stunde	New Year's Day, Neujahrstag
Half an hour, Eine halbe Stunde	Palm Sunday, Palmsonntag
Quarter of an hour, Eine Viertelstunde	Good Friday, Karfreitag
A minute, Eine Minute	Easter, Ostern
Morning, Der Morgen	Whitsun, Pfingsten
Noon, Der Mittag	Midsummer Day, Johannistag
Afternoon, Der Nachmittag	The anniversary, Der Jahrestag
Evening, Der Abend	The birthday, Der Geburtstag
Night, Die Nacht	Leap-year, Das Schaltjahr
Midnight, Die Mitternacht	A holiday, Ein Feiertag

A GUIDE TO MENUS
BILL OF FARE (SPEISEKARTE)

Anchovy—Sardelle (f)
Apple—Apfel (m)
Apricot—Aprikose (f)
Asparagus—Spargel (m)
Bacon—Speck (m)
Banana—Banane (f)
Bean—Bohne (f)
Beef—Rindfleisch (n)
  ,, Boiled— ,, Gekocht
  ,, Salt— ,, Gesalzenes
  ,, Stewed—Suppenrindfleisch
Beefsteak—Beefsteak (n)
Beer—Bier (n)
  ,, Bottled—Flaschen Bier
Beetroot—Rote Rübe (f)
Biscuit—Biskuit (n)
Brandy—Cognac (m)
Bread—Brot (n)
  ,, Black—Schwarzbrot
  ,, White—Weissbrot
Broth—Fleischbrühe (f)
Brussels Sprouts — Rosenkohl (m)
Burgundy—Rotwein (m)
Butter—Butter (f)
Cabbage—Kohl (m)
Cake—Kuchen (m)
Carrot—Karotte (f)
Cauliflower—Blumenkohl (m)
Celery—Sellerie (m)
Cheese—Käse (m)
Cherry—Kirsche (f)
Chicken—Huhn (n)
Chocolate—Schokolade (f)
Chop—Kotlett (n)

Cider—Apfelwein (m)
Claret—Bordeauwein (m)
Cocoa—Kakao (m)
Coffee—Kaffee (m)
Coffee with Milk—Milchkaffee
Cream—Sahne (f)
Currant—Rosine (f)
Cutlet—Kotlett (n)
Cutlet of Veal—Kalbskotlett
Duck—Ente (f)
Egg—Ei (n)
  ,, Boiled—Gekochtes
  ,, Fried—Gebranteness-Ei
Fish—Fisch (m)
Fowl—Geflügel (n)
French Beans—Bohnen (f)
Fruit—Frucht (f)
Game—Wildpret (n)
Goose—Gans (f)
Gooseberry—Stachelbeere (f)
Grape—Traube (f)
Ham—Schinken (m)
Herring—Hering (m)
Ice—Eis (n)
Ice Cream—Gefrorenes (n)
Jam—Marmelade (f)
Jelly—Gelee (n)
Kidney—Niere (f)
Lamb—Lamm (n)
Lemon—Zitrone (f)
Lemonade—Limonade (f)
Liver—Leber (f)
Marmalade—Orangemarmelade (f), or Apfelsinenmus (n)
Meat—Fleisch (n)

189

A GUIDE TO MENUS—Continued

Milk—Milch (f)
Mineral Water — Mineralwasser (n)
Mushroom—Pilz (m)
Mustard—Senf (m)
Mutton—Hammelfleisch (m)
Omelet—Omlett (n)
Orange—Orange (f)
Oyster—Auster (f)
Pancake—Pfannkuchen (m)
Pastry—Torte (f)
Pea—Erbse (f)
Peach—Pfirsich (m)
Peanut—Erdnuss (f)
Pear—Birne (f)
Pepper—Pfeffer (m)
Pheasant—Fasan (m)
Pineapple—Ananas (m)
Plum—Pflaume (f)
Pork—Schweinefleisch (n)
Potato—Kartoffel (f)
Pudding—Pudding (n)
Rabbit—Kaninchen (n)
Raspberry—Himbeere (f)
Rice—Reis (m)
Rumpsteak—Rumpsteak (n)
Salad—Salat (m)
Salt—Salz (n)
Sandwich—Belegtes butterbrot (n)
Sausage—Wurst (f)
Sole—Seezunge (f)
Soup—Suppe (f)
Spinach—Spinat (m)
Spirits—Branntwein (m)
Strawberry—Erdbeere (f)
Sugar—Zucker (m)
Tart—Torte (f)
,, Apple—Äpfeltorte
,, Plum—Pflaumentorte
Tea—Tee (m)
Toast—Geröstete Brotschnitte (f)
Turbot—Zander (m)
Turkey—Truthahn (m)
Vegetables—Gemüse (n)
Vinegar—Essig (m)
Water—Wasser (n)
Wine—Wein (m)
,, Sparkling—Schaumwein

MEALS
THE MEAL TABLE (TISCHGEDECK)

Breakfast—Frühstück (n)
Lunch—Mittagessen (n)
Tea—Tee (m)
Dinner—Essen (n) Diner (n)
Supper—Abendessen (n)
Knife—Messer (n)
Fork—Gabel (f)
Spoon—Löffel (m)
Plate—Teller (m)
Cup—Tasse (f)
Saucer—Untertasse (f)
Cruet—Gewürzgefäss
Wineglass—Weinglas (n)
Tablecloth—Tischdecke (f)
Cold—Kalt
Hot—Heiss
Soup, clear—Suppe, klare (f)
,, thick—Suppe, dicke (f)
Mineral Water—Mineralwasser (n)
Teapot—Teekanne (f)
Refreshment—Erfrischung (f)
Bill of Fare—Speisekarte (f)
Waitre—Kellner (m)

MOTORING
(AUTOMOBILFAHREN)

Accelerator—Beschleuniger
Accumulator—Akkumulator
Axle—Achse
Brake—Bremse
Camshaft—Nockenwelle
Carburetter—Vergaser
Chassis—Untergestell
Commutator—Stromsammler
Crankshaft—Kurbelwelle
Cylinder—Zylinder
Dynamo—Dynamo
Electric Battery — Elektrische Batterie
Electric Bulb — Elektrische lampe
Exhaust—Auspuff
Fan—Ventilator
Gear—Getriebe
Grease Gun—Fettpresse
Horse Power—Pferdestärke
Ignition—Zündung
Jack—Wagenheber
Jet—Strahl
Layshaft—Vorgelegewelle
Lubrication—Schmierung
Magneto—Magnetapparat
Mudguard—Kotflügel
Number Plate — Nummernschild.
Oil Pump—Ölpumpe

MOTORING—Continued

Oil Tank—Ölbehälter
Overhaul—Untersuchung
Petrol Tank—Benzinbehälter
Piston—Kolben
Propeller Shaft — Schrauabenwelle
Radiator—Kühler
Self-Starter—Anlasser
Sparking Plug—Zündkerze
Speedometer — Geschwindigkeitsmesser
Spoke—Speiche
Steering—Steurung
Switch—Schalter

Tank—Behälter
Tappet—Steuerknagge
Throttle—Drosselklappe
Tyre—Reifen
Tyre Pump — Luftpumpe für pneumatik
Valve—Ventil
Water—Wasser
Wheel—Rad
Wheel (Steering)—Steuerrad
Windscreen—Windschutz
Windscreen Wiper — Windschutzwischer

RELATIONSHIPS

(VERWANDTSCHAFTSGRADE)

Man, Der Mensch, der Mann
Woman, Die Frau
A young man, Ein junger Mann
A young lady, Ein Fräulein
A young woman, Eine junge Frau
A baby, Ein Säugling
An infant, Ein kleines kind
A little boy, Ein kleiner Knabe
A little girl, Ein kleines Mädchen
Youth, Die Jugend
Manhood, Die Mannbarkeit
Age, Das Alter
Old age, Das hohe Alter
Birth, Die Geburt
Life, Das Leben
Death, Der Tod
The father, Der Vater
The mother, Die Mutter
The son, Der Sohn
The daughter, Die Tochter
The grandson, Der Enkel
The grand-daughter, Die Enkelin
The grandfather, Der Grossvater
The grandmother, Die Grossmutter
The father-in-law, Der Schwiegervater

The mother-in-law, Die Schwiegermutter
The son-in-law, Der Schwiegersohn
The daughter-in-law, Die Schwiegertochter
The uncle, Der Onkel
The aunt, Die Tante
The cousin, Der Vetter, Die Muhme
The nephew, Der Neffe
The niece, Die Nichte
The husband, Der Ehemann
The wife, Die Ehefrau
The widower, Der Witwer
The widow, Die Witwe
The family, Die Familie
The relations, Die Verwandten
The parents, Die Eltern
The children, Die Kinder
The stepfather, Der Stiefvater
The stepmother, Die Stiefmutter
The stepson, Der Stiefsohn
The stepdaughter, Die Stieftochter
The brother, Der Bruder
The sister, Die Schwester
The bride, Die Braut
The bridegroom, Der Bräutigam

WEIGHTS AND MEASURES

(GEWICHTE—MASSE)

Throughout Germany (including Austria) the Metric System is used.

WEIGHTS—AVOIRDUPOIS

1 grain	= ·0648	grammes
1 ounce	= 28·35	,,
1 pound	= 453·6	,,
1 quarter	= 12·7	kilogrammes
1 hundredweight	= 50·8	,,
1 ton	= 1016·046	,,
1 gramme	= 15·4321	grains
1 kilogramme	= 2 lbs. 3 ozs. 4 drams	

LENGTH

1 inch	= 25·4 millimetres
,,	= 2·54 centimetres (zentimeter)
1 foot	= 304·8 millimetres
,,	= 30·48 centimetres
1 yard	= 91·44 ,,
1 mile	= 1,609 metres (meter)
1 millimetre	= ·03937 inches
1 centimetre	= ·3937 inches
1 decimetre	= 3·937 inches
1 metre	= 39·37 inches
1 kilometre	= 1093·63 yards (roughly $\frac{5}{8}$ mile)

SQUARE MEASURE

1 square inch	= 6·45	square centimetres	
1 ,, foot	= 929	,,	,,
1 ,, yard	= 8,361	,,	,,
1 ,, metre	= 1·195	,,	yards

LIQUID MEASURE

1 fluid ounce	= 28·4 cubic centimetres
1 pint	= 568 c.c. or ·568 litre (liter)
1 quart	= 1,136 c.c. or 1·136 litres
1 gallon	= 4·544 litres
1 litre	= 1¾ pints

CURRENCY

100 pfennig = 1 reichsmark (RM)
At standard rate, 200 RM = £1
Then 1 RM = 1s. and 50 pf. = 6d.
and 4·20 RM = 1 dollar (U.S.A.)

TEMPERATURES

Zero centigrade	= 32 degrees F.	(Freezing point)
1 degree ,,	= 33·8 ,,	
10 degrees ,,	= 50 ,,	
37 ,, ,,	= 98·6 ,,	
50 ,, ,,	= 122 ,,	
100 ,, ,,	= 212 ,,	(Boiling point)